The Art of Making Do in Naples

The Art of Making Do
in Naples

JASON PINE

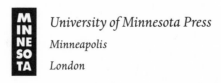

University of Minnesota Press

Minneapolis

London

All photographs were taken by the author unless otherwise indicated. The photograph in chapter 1 on page 20 and the photograph in the Epilogue on page 294 are by Giuseppe Zevola.

Copyright 2012 by the Regents of the University of Minnesota

Published by the University of Minnesota Press
111 Third Avenue South, Suite 290
Minneapolis, MN 55401-2520
http://www.upress.umn.edu

Library of Congress Cataloging-in-Publication Data
Pine, Jason.
The art of making do in Naples / Jason Pine.
Includes bibliographical references and index.
ISBN 978-0-8166-3631-0 (hardback)
ISBN 978-0-8166-7601-9 (pb)
1. Crime—Italy—Naples.   I. Title.
HV6995.N3P56 2012
364.1060945'731—dc23

2012031590

Printed in the United States of America on acid-free paper

The University of Minnesota is an equal-opportunity educator and employer.

20 19 18 17 16 15 14 13 12   10 9 8 7 6 5 4 3 2 1

for Reyn

Contents

Acknowledgments

THE WENNER-GREN FOUNDATION provided significant support for this project. I also express my appreciation to the Warner Fund at the University Seminars at Columbia University for its help in publication. Material in this book was presented to the University Seminar: Studies in Modern Italy.

There are many people to thank for help with this project. I am deeply grateful for the intellectual engagement and inspiration, as well as the friendship, I have enjoyed with Steve Caton, Jane Schneider, Peter Schneider, and Katie Stewart. Many ideas and nuances would not have emerged without Scott Webel's creative and intensive readings of the manuscript. Francesco Pepe, Reyn Rossington, and Michelle Stewart generously read several drafts, and each time I learned something important from them. I also thank many others who made their own contributions as readers, interlocutors, and friends: Ahmed Afzal, Felia Allum, Zehra Arat, Fernando Coronil, Veit Erlmann, Simona Frasca, Mark Galeotti, Rudi Gaudio, Lloyd Gilden, Gabriella Gribaudi, Chrys Ingraham, Ward Keeler, Marcella Marmo, Pietro Maturi, Shaka McGlotten, Walter Montagna, Ana Orellana, Eleonora Pasotti, Veronica Perera, Marta Petrusewicz, Joe Sciorra, Don Scott, Joel Sherzer, Giovanni Vacca, Halide Velioglu, and Agustin Zarzosa.

I am grateful to many people for their knowledge, research assistance, time, and patience, in particular Enrica Amaturo, Annalucia Bonavolta, Angela Catello, Alfonso Chiarazzo, Fabio Corbisiero, Linda D'Ancona, Daniela D'Antonio, Mimmo Dany, Pierpaolo De Iulis, Raffaela De Rosa, Salvatore Filangieri, Francesco Nappo, Mauro Nardi, Maria Nazionale, Gianfranca Ranisio, Filippo Ricci, Anna Ricci, Luigi Ricci, Walter Ricci, Amalia Signorelli, Federico Vacalebre, Valentina, and Francesca Zazzaro.

Many thanks to Maurizio De Fazio, Jay Kaplan, Francesco Pepe, Fatimah Tuggar, and Giuseppe Zevola for assistance with illustrations in the book.

Special recognition goes to Francesco Pepe for generously sharing his vast knowledge of Campanian music, film, video, and literature. I appreciate that he deeply respects the sensibilities of the people who make and enjoy these cultural forms.

I appreciate people's friendship and many forms of support that made me fall in love with Naples: Sandro Dionisio, Andrea Fiorillo, Antonio Monaco, Rosanna Montagna, Teresa Sequino, Anna Trovato, Marco Trovato, Michele Trovato, Gaetano Zazzaro, Giuseppe Zevola, and Barbara Zoleo.

My sincere thanks to University of Minnesota Press editor Jason Weidemann. His commitment to ideas and the narratives that carry them has been a great encouragement. Two anonymous readers who challenged me with provocative critiques were enormously helpful.

In many instances, the names of people, places, and other identifying details have been changed to protect the privacy and ensure the safety of individuals referenced in this book.

Detail of the Palazzo dei Telefoni, designed by Camillo Guerra and completed in 1924. The building was the location of the former state telephone company offices, and the ground floor once hosted telephone stations open to the public.

The Contact Zone
Where Organized Crime and Everyday Life Comingle

A MAN WITH A DEEP-LINED CHARCOAL TAN is leaning against the wall of a corpulent, prerationalist-style palazzo at Piazza Nolana. Once white, now covered in soot, the building's two marble caryatids (figured as Mercury the trickster, messenger of the gods, patron of commerce, and guide to the underworld) can barely hold up the second-floor balcony. Next to the man lies his filthy blanket of ceramic trinkets, rusted alarm clocks, and twisted shoes that look like the evidence of unseen violence. He is gesturing with outstretched, needle-marked arms at a man propped against a dented blue car. The other man is talking to him loudly, elongating his vowels and finishing his sentences with intonation that sounds like bellicose whining. A third man is squatting beside his own discolored blanket, which is littered with box sets of pliers, nails, shiny watches of dubious working quality, and limbless nude Barbies. He is playing with a pair of long, black-handled scissors, opening and closing them, entranced by the *slice-slice* of the blades.

Passersby pick their way through the crowded, narrow sidewalk, some choosing to step off the curb into the busy street, bypassing the motley assortment of undesirable objects for sale and the piles of ashen newspapers leftover from the street fires that warm heroin junkies at night. Their main destination is the market known as 'Ncopp' 'e Mmura (Above the walls), the magnificent fish market that begins at the crumbling fifteenth-century Aragonese city gate, Porta Nolana, one of whose towers (the Tower of Faith) bears the weight of a modern three-story apartment building that someone likely built without a permit. Through the arch and past the gate, women with large green plastic bags make their way to the wide shallow crates of mussels, clams, oysters, squid, sardines, anchovies, swordfish, grouper, cod, bass, and eel. Their sacks are stuffed with kilo-loaves of hard, crusty bread, long-stemmed artichokes, leafy lemons, and knotted bags of mozzarella balls in cloudy white water. A woman stops before a vendor who, with already bloodied hands, majestically takes hold of a live octopus, lifts it into the air and, with a long shout and a swing of his machete, massacres it. He promptly cleans it while calling out in song for the next customer.

The windows of the shops flanking the market are lined with bottles of olive oil and the sulfurous wines of the region, split bread loaves, and inverted dangling bouquets of salami with skin blotched powdery-white with age. Inside the shops are stacks and stacks of pasta—long, short, twisted, ridged, smooth, toothed, rounded, fat, and bulbous. It's lunch-time, and every other pedestrian has some kind of delicacy in hand, wrapped in yellow paper napkins, half peeking out: oily bread filled with prosciutto, provola, and tomato or mozzarella and red peppers, a square slice of pizza, or a buttery phyllo-dough treat filled with escarole and olives. Some are standing and eating while talking on cell phones, gesticu-lating with food in hand. Others are walking slowly, weaving leisurely through the kinetic fervor as they go.

A stray dog with patches of missing fur is arching its back, keeping its hind legs close together as if preparing for a graceful Olympic dive. Instead, it shits on the cobblestones, already strewn with pedestrians'

grease-stained napkins. Around a corner in a narrow *vicolo*,[1] a young man, shirtless and in shorts, is sitting on the threshold of his *basso* (ground-floor dwelling).[2] He points a bottle at his baby's mouth, and the infant gulps hungrily. The bottle slips, and with a slurp the nipple and infant separate. In an instant, the baby lets out a wide scream. It sounds in tune with the numerous other extended vowels sung at full throttle by market vendors announcing in aggressively plaintive, undulating tones *Fresh fish! Lemons of Sorrento!* The vocal performances are so extravagant and competitive that they seem just as orchestrated as that of the sexy, olive-skinned thug in tight pants who sings "The strength to decide" to a full-figured teen strutting by in an even tighter ensemble of low-cut jeans and a half-shirt. Effortlessly, she ignores him. Or it may be that his melodramatic serenade is for the young man walking behind her. "What I don't have / is the strength to decide / I'd erase you if I could / from my heart."[3]

These life-scenes might convey to visitors that Naples is flush with the sensory intensities that smolder mainly in the "lower bodily stratum."[4] Indeed, many Neapolitans say that 'Ncopp' 'e Mmura is part of the "belly of Naples," as the popular writer Matilde Serao famously described the city's poorest quarters in 1884.[5] To me, a white middle-class American man, 'Ncopp' 'e Mmura, host to both heroin packets and baby bottles, sumptuous foods and animal filth, the avid shouts of vendors and the naked songs of lovers, felt precisely like the "promiscuous public space" identified by the nineteenth-century European bourgeoisie who sought to circumscribe it.[6]

The fish market, however, is not merely a place where undisciplined passions and interests run amok.[7] Here a brutal and occulted territorial system undergirds these forces. 'Ncopp' 'e Mmura, and the *quartiere* (quarter) Mercato in which it is situated, is dominated by a crime clan that, together with several rival and allied clans that claim other parts of the city and the wider Campania region as their territories, are commonly called "the camorra." For now, the dominant clan in Mercato goes by the surname of its leaders: Mazzarella.

The heroin comes to Piazza Nolana by way of the Mazzarella clan, which shares with other clans the services of independent broker–traffickers to import the drug from the Balkans. When the broker arrives with the delivery, each clan takes its share, then cuts, packages, and sells the heroin to the *spacciatori* (drug dealers) who work the piazzas in its territories.[8] Spacciatori usually operate as independent entrepreneurs who pay *tangenti* (tributes) to the crime clan affiliates in whose territory they conduct business. Additionally, uncountable tons of the market's fish are defrosted or contaminated contraband coming from Tunisia, Turkey, Thailand, China, and Australia. They are sold by vendors in 'Ncopp' 'e Mmura who label the fish as "fresh" and "from the Gulf of Naples."[9] Moreover, some of the vendors are affiliates of the Mazzarella clan, which also owns a fishmonger's shop in the neighborhood. The clan's affiliates also run an extortion racket by paying nonaffiliated residents to demand access fees from the drivers of fish delivery trucks and parking fees from anyone else wanting to use the area's public lots.

Heroin and counterfeit fish are just two of the many illegal goods that change hands in 'Ncopp' 'e Mmura. The DVDs and CDs of Neapolitan, "Italian," English, and American videos and music that men and women lay out for sale on card tables among the fish vendors are counterfeit and pirated. In fact, the quartiere Mercato is a major hub for the mass reproduction, warehousing, citywide distribution, and sale of these recordings.[10] Since at least the time of the audiocassette, the barons of this illicit commerce even certify, whether ironically, earnestly, or arrogantly, the authenticity of their pirated products. Until the late 1990s one locally renowned mixtape "brand" label contained the "mixed message" seen in the figure opposite.

The dominant genre of these recordings is *la musica neomelodica*. Its voicy Neapolitan-language lyrics, disco-pop tones, and melodramatic (and ironic) melodies resound through 'Ncopp' 'e Mmura and many of the city's poorer quarters in its center, in the urban *periferia* (periphery), throughout Campania and other southern Italian regions, such as Sicily, Puglia, and parts of Calabria. Neomelodica music and musicians also circulate in southern Italian diasporas in northern Italy, Belgium, Germany, and other countries.[11]

Neomelodica music can be heard anywhere in Naples and its surrounding provinces, and well beyond. Adults sing along with the radio at home or in the car, and kids play songs to each other on their cell phones while at school. Singers perform neomelodica music at modest baptism celebrations and at ostentatious wedding parties, and they lip-synch their songs on local private television broadcasts and sometimes on nationally popular television talk shows. Additionally, neomelodica music is the inspiration for transnationally circulating, low-budget, Neapolitan-

A   B

| DATE · · ☐MONO Normal Bias N.R. | DATE · · ☐MONO Normal Bias N.R. |
| TIME · · ☐STEREO EQ-120µs | TIME · · ☐STEREO EQ-120µs |

10 ANNI DI SUCCESSI

MAURO CAPUTO

ATTENZIONE: Le cassette con fotocopie non sono

Mixed by Erry

LA DIMENSIONE IDEALE PER UN ASCOLTO PULITO

1) Pe' sempe	1) Favola
2) Soffro pe' te	2) E' troppo grande
3) T'aggia scurdà	3) Me sto perdenno pe' te
4) 'A storia d''o pittore	4) Sto murenno d'ammore
5) Velenosamente	5) Si v'addimanna 'e me
6) Desiderio 'e sole	6) Comme aggia fà
7) Ciente peccate	7) L'autografo
8) Chi si'	8) Si perdo a te
9) Sulo c''a fantasia	9) Te telefono stasera

N.B. PER QUALSIASI **FESTA** CON **KARAOKE** E DISCOTECA **BY ERRY** Rivolgiti al tuo rivenditore di **FIDUCIA.**

"Warning: Tapes with photocopied inserts are not mixed by Erry, the ideal dimension for clean listening. P.S. For any kind of party with karaoke and dancing, go to your TRUSTED reseller." *Pulito* (clean) in this context denotes good sound quality.

language musical films. It even dominates the soundtrack of the feature film *Gomorra* (Gomorrah), the 2008 Grand Prix winner at Cannes.

Neomelodici singers and their associates, together numbering in the hundreds, maybe even thousands, compose, record, publicize, and perform their growing repertoires within overlapping "legitimate," do-it-yourself (DIY), and clandestine fields of practice.[12] Some of the big players on the scene are powerful crime clan affiliates; they operate as talent managers and songwriters. Most of the scene's protagonists, however, are young men in their teens and twenties who have little formal education, and at best irregular employment and limited access to resources.[13]

They linger in this milieu for years, following uncertain opportunities while negotiating the risks of contact with criminal associations.

The Art of Making Do

I began research on the neomelodica scene in 1998, at the tail end of the "Neapolitan Renaissance," the hoped-for result of Mayor Antonio Bassolino's ambitious project of urban renewal. For decades Naples had been wracked by soaring unemployment, infrastructural collapse, a cholera epidemic, a calamitous earthquake, rampant illegal rebuilding, and spiking intraclan violence.[14] This turmoil was enmeshed with local and national political upheaval. In 1992 a team of magistrates in Milan launched the *Mani pulite* investigations (Operation Clean Hands) into corruption networks entangling organized crime affiliates, public administration, all ranks of political office, and business elites throughout the country. Milan, and by extension the entire Italian state, was popularly renamed Tangentopoli (Bribesville), where politicians collected "a second layer of taxes" that they systematically solicited or extorted as bribes in exchange for public works contracts, public-sector employment, and business-friendly legislation.[15] In a little over a year, the magistrates, armed with the confessions of many business leaders and urged on by a disenfranchised and indignant public, convicted nearly one-third of Parliament's deputies and toppled the ruling political elite. Although the trials demonstrated that corruption was a nationwide problem, between 1992 and 1993 twenty-six Campanian regional councils were disbanded for mafia infiltration, far more than in other regions.[16]

When Bassolino became mayor of Naples in 1993, it appeared he had a cleaner slate for urban renewal. He aimed to change the city's image within Italy and in the G7 nations.[17] His primary target was the immense and densely populated *centro storico* (historic center). He focused on Neapolitans' relationship to public space by curbing the sprawl of illegal parking, clearing away trash, and reopening architectural landmarks that had long been shuttered and ignored.[18] His intention was to replace the collapsing industrial economy with a self-sustaining tourism industry that drew on the cultural resources of Naples and Campania.

One of these local cultural resources is Neapolitan-language song. Song is an allusive and alluring language of great historical significance in Naples. The city's mythological name is Parthenope, the siren who drowned herself in despair when she failed to lure Ulysses. The earliest Neapolitan-language vocal music texts date back to the thirteenth century. In the fifteenth and sixteenth centuries, Naples was home to a proliferation of single-voice and polyphonic villanelle, ironic and lurid songs from whom "gentlemen" collectors gathered the inspiration for the comparatively formal madrigals that they diffused in cities of the north such as Florence and Venice. At the end of the eighteenth century, Naples was considered throughout Europe Italy's music capital, and Neapolitans were believed to have an "innate" capacity for artful song. At the end of the nineteenth century, Naples was the center of an international popular song industry commanded by bourgeois lyricists. For nearly half a century, they composed a massive repertoire of romantic and picturesque poems, later named *la canzone classica,* or "classic song." These songs circulated transnationally with the mass migrations of Italians from all over Italy to Europe, the Americas, and Australia.

By the 1950s the Neapolitan song culture industry had declined. Television connected the dominant pop music scenes of Italy, the United Kingdom, and the United States and inspired new musical forms, lyrical content, and types of composition in Naples. In the 1970s many new musical styles emerged from Naples, but one genre in particular has had an enduring afterlife among the popular classes: *canzoni 'e mala,* or "songs of the underworld." Although many were composed decades earlier by the very same bourgeois poets of the canzone classica, the canzoni 'e mala resonated, perhaps for some listeners too much, with the tumultuous day-to-day realities of the 1970s. In the 1980s neomelodica song, a genre described as "erotic-sentimental," emerged from this same milieu. Strikingly, these songs were composed not in the poetic language of the middle classes but in the everyday vernaculars of the popular classes. In fact, the composers, performers, producers, distributors, and the fans all, on the whole, came from the same milieu. Through the availability of private and pirate television and affordable recording technologies, the protagonists of interconnected DIY music scenes began to make themselves more audible and visible. Their audiences grew to the hundreds of thousands across southern Italy and among southern Italian "emigrants" in the north and transnationally.[19] By the mid-1990s hundreds of independent singers, songwriters, and technicians crowded into these scenes,

For years counterfeit and pirated music CD vendors have worked this spot in La Pignasecca (The Dried Pinecone), a market in the centro storico. I also have photographed them for years. On one occasion, I realized years later, I captured Ciro Petrone, who played a protagonist in *Gomorra* (2008). Ciro helps his father working as a fruit vendor in the market.

hoping to make a living or even make it big in what looks like an alternative culture industry. Today in 2012, for hundreds, maybe thousands, of people, song is a prime cultural resource for making do.

Neomelodici protagonists say that maneuvering in the scene is a precarious business that requires artfulness and artifice. For them, this means being on alert for the resources and tools that might enhance their ever-emerging plans for a better life. It means speculating on the future even as the camorra colonizes or kills it. They adapt to events and relations as they emerge, prepared to leverage multiple forms of value—publicity, favors, and varieties of social capital. Shaking off encumbrances like rigid ethical codes, they apply instrumental reason to ethical practice.[20] People in the neomelodica music scene call their creative pragmatics *l'arte di arrangiarsi,* or "the art of making do." Making do means more to them than simply "getting by." Many people in the scene want more than to merely live with chronic indeterminacy. They seek self-determination and a life that escapes precarity altogether.

In the melodramas of making do in the neomelodica scene, people's desires for self-determination crystallize in the figure of the personal sovereign.[21] The personal sovereign (in this scene typically male) makes for himself and his (actual or potential) family a life of security and a path to something even better. He transforms chronic indeterminacy into unqualified potential. He enacts a "sovereign decision" that "springs out of a normative nothingness and from a concrete disorder."[22] This figure is a fantasy that is not necessarily mimed in everyday practice, but it lures people into its shoes from where it stands, just beyond the limits of speculation. It activates "the perception of one's own vitality, one's sense of aliveness, of changeability (often signified as 'freedom')."[23] The personal sovereign fully exploits his field of potential.

Contact Zones

The neomelodica music scene is one of many instances where the so-called formal, informal, and illicit economies overlap in Campania and beyond.[24] The scene is a contact zone where the art of making do brushes up against organized crime. In a contact zone, where heterogeneous epistemologies, sensibilities, and practices comingle, it is not readily apparent who or what dominates.[25] Everyone and everything is potentially deterritorialized in this transient space of encounter.[26]

A contact zone is a field of potential where the rules of engagement are suspended. People enter the scene in search of self-determination while avoiding ensnaring debts and obligations to criminal associations. To do so, they must attune themselves to the occulted dimension of the market and to the very real possibility that things are often *more than* what they seem. For them, this surplus, rather than being the "hidden" or "real truth," is the unregulated and undocumented vitality—and the death throes—of things. Its potency is registered in volatile events and shapeless suspicions.

Attuned to the pulsions and tensions of this contact zone, people communicate, interact, and create in ways that extend its rhythms. They harness or deflect this potency with melodramatic flamboyance and seductiveness, ironic playfulness and dissimulation, suspicion and secrecy, and overdrawn hopes—the aesthetic qualities of the art of making do. These qualities resonate in musical performances and in day-to-day engagements. They form a "porous, affective scene of identification among strangers," or an "intimate public."[27]

The art of making do is a speculative performance, the staging of a better life. Enacting it requires creative tactics for seizing opportunities and negotiating risk. Excessive speculation, however, can lead to violent determinations: the ad hoc art of making do has the potential to transmogrify into organized crime. Under these conditions the figure of the self-realized sovereign incarnates as a *camorrista* (crime clan affiliate). This is because organized crime in Campania works through contact, forever roping in new associates and affiliates. While in Sicily the mafia *padrino* (godfather) is the embodiment of a single hermetic and enduring center of power, the Campanian role of *capoclan* (clan boss) shifts or is shared among members of a family generation.[28] Clans can also splinter into autonomous, even rival groups, inciting extraordinary levels of violence. In Naples dozens of clans have carved out and then parsed numerous territories of control as they forge federations, undergo scissions, and form new alliances. Organized crime in Naples is shape-shifting and volatile, rendering "organized" a tenuous attribution.

More importantly, crime clan affiliates extend association to thousands of residents in their territories in the form of flexible employment opportunities. While association with a crime clan through part-time and temporary employment does not entail the same commitments as affiliation, it constitutes an ambiguous relationship that can easily shift into deeper entanglements such as indenture. One major source of non-affiliate employment is pirated music and video sales. Another source of employment—the focus of this story—is singing neomelodica music at weddings, baptisms, and piazza festivals.

The Camorra Is Not a Thing

It is a unique challenge to write about organized crime in southern Italy because it has a potent affective allure. In Naples criminal organizations cloak themselves in mystery while engaging in spectacular acts of self-exposure. Organized crime affiliates cultivate fearful secrecy by making their faces and their uncapped potential for violence known among the residents of their territories.[29] While "captive" publics are gripped with fear, broader publics are captivated, at best, by the spectacle. Indeed, journalists, artists, scholars, and their publics contribute, unwittingly and willfully, to the affective allure of "Italian" organized crime by rendering it an object of fetishizing, even eroticizing attention.[30]

As an object of fear, fascination, and fantasy, organized crime in Naples has acquired thinglike qualities.[31] It has been depicted as a determinate organization that honors a precise code of silence and controls a circumscribable "shadow" economy through ritualized violence. It has been described as an illegitimate entity, an alternative state that attacks the nation-state like a predator or a parasite, or a cancer to be cut out of the life of the nation.[32] While some of these qualities can sometimes be attributed to crime clans in Naples, they do not capture a *thing*. Neapolitan crime clans engage in illicit economic practices and compete with the state's legitimated monopoly on violence, but they are not exactly distinguishable from the nation-state. Crime clans operate antagonistically *and* collaboratively with legitimated authorities as extortionists and as partners in the private exchange of public resources. It is difficult, if not impossible, to clearly discriminate between formal, informal, and illicit economic activities or, for that matter, between crime clans and big business. The blurriness of the borders is, in fact, the binding material of these groups' interdependence.

Another, related reason why it is challenging to write about organized crime in Italy is because, particularly among Italophiles and Italianists, it always already constitutes a discourse. Inevitably, references to "southern Italy and organized crime" conjure the criminal anthropologist Cesare Lombroso's racialized figure, the "violent criminal type."[33] They also summon the political scientist Edward Banfield's "amoral familism," distilled in the figure of the amoral Family, or the crime clan. In the master melodrama of modernization, amoral familism is supposed to be defeated by the "Western" figure of "civil society."[34]

Writing about southern Italy and organized crime also conjures the "Italian South," the original figuration that grounds all the others. In 1875, fifteen years after Italian unification, the historian Pasquale Villari (a liberal revolutionary who was exiled from Naples and settled in the northern city of Florence) and his intellectual contemporaries raised what he called the "Southern Question," the problem of the socially and economically underdeveloped south. Amid his searing depictions of poverty and ignorance in the former Kingdom of Naples, Villari argued that liberal intellectuals had shirked their national responsibility to lead southern Italians out of their backwardness and misery. In this way, he helped ground the figure of "the South" in a broader Italian nationalist program.[35] Since Villari and his contemporaries, southern Italy has been consistently impugned by northern Italians and Europeans as the exception to the laws of modernization and to the rule of law itself.[36]

In contemporary political, popular, and scholarly discourses on organized crime in Italy, the north–south distinction often surfaces more or less in its denigrating mid-nineteenth-century figuration. This "moral geography"[37] is reproduced across an array of binaries: in law (legal vs. illegal), economics (free markets vs. rackets), civics (associations vs. clans), and ethics (right vs. wrong). This binary thinking continues to affect how the South is imagined and how its people figure themselves.

Affective–Aesthetic Effects

Binary thinking cannot draw the line between the camorra and the non-camorra. A crime clan holds together through forms of social organization and has determinate material effects in its territories, but it also activates potently indeterminate relations and affects. A crime clan has an atmospheric presence. An atmosphere is an object of perception, but one that is elusive, particularly when localized, identifiable *things* are a person's primary objects of attention.[38] An atmosphere is apprehended through other forms of perception, through situatedness and sensitivity in a "qualitative, quasi-energetic and affective field of forces."[39]

In turn, a crime clan is animated by the affective–aesthetic relations it activates with its territorialized residents and their relations with one another. People "find themselves" in a state and communicate and act in highly aestheticized ways.[40] They are attuned to the occulted potency of things, and they harness it in melodramatic, ironic, and seductive performances. In doing so, they also generate and reproduce the atmosphere.

Like Mercato, the broader centro storico immediately hit me like a welter of aesthetically and affectively charged activity. Outside 'Ncopp' 'e Mmura, the market of narcotic, gustatory, olfactory, and sensual desires, a tumult of visual stimuli also becomes noticeable. Foremost is the disarray of architectural splendor and atrocity: from the unearthed ancient Greek ruins to the aboveground palazzi revealing Byzantine, Gothic, and Angevin strata; from the upward-sprawling and chipped pale-pink baroque churches, marred by black graffiti and the gray of loitering seagulls, to the crumbling Renaissance villas with faded ceiling frescoes that peek through sooty windows and decades-old scaffolding; from the cavelike medieval arcades to the illegal steel-roofed shacks, overgrown with antennae, erected atop buildings everywhere, regardless of their historical significance. Here the "Italian North" and "the camorra" continue to produce "the South" through ongoing ruination.[41]

Outside the market, the aural density and kinetic vitality of Naples also attracts attention. Foremost are the vociferously performed life-scenes that seem to overinhabit the porous spaces throughout the centro storico:[42] from the unseen singing that accompanies, or overwhelms, the latest recording of a neomelodica song to the clanking of dinner dishes and cheering-in-unison during Sunday TV soccer matches; from the long, exaggerated horn-honking of eternal traffic jams at intersecting vicoli to the whizzing and weaving of *motorini* (scooters) stacked with man, woman, and child, and sometimes only the latter, chatting at maximum volume over the roar of engines on a cell phone or with another *centauro* (half person, half motorino), whose hand she holds while riding beside her; from the hyperbolic threats and tragic or indignant wailing that accompany scuffles, slaps, stabbings, and occasional shootings to the elaborate gestural contact among pedestrians who engage in exuberant, loving reunions and disengage again in the narrow cobblestone streets and across the unseen barriers of windows, balconies, the traffic, and other people doing the same along their own vectors.

Walter Benjamin and Asja Lacis noted something similar in 1927, when they wrote of Neapolitans, "In everything they preserve the scope to become a theater of new, unforeseen constellations. The stamp of the definitive is avoided. No situation appears intended forever, no figure asserts its 'thus and not otherwise.'"[43] Although everyday life is never mere theater and *no* life, for that matter, is "definitive," I could not simply dispel my initial impressions or the stereotypes composed by the many European and American travelers who have been taken by the atmospheres of Naples. Instead I attended to some of the affective–aesthetic events that animate these impressions and stereotypes.

Take, for instance, the bullet holes that appeared on the outside walls and steel barriers of some of the neighborhood shops on New Year's Eve of 2008. Every year, San Silvestre invokes a cataclysmic celebration in Naples, where people throughout the area launch heavy fireworks, set off explosives, and fire guns. That is why residents in the area of Mercato might have interpreted the damage on some of the storefronts in the morning as the work of errant bullets—but they knew better. The bullet holes, a resident who works for a social policy initiative told reporters under the condition of anonymity, were likely warning messages issued by clan affiliates to shopowners who had resisted paying tangenti. When a bomb exploded in front of a *pescheria* on the same street two days later, the message was less ambiguous. New Year's celebrations last for days, but the police believe that clan affiliates used the continuing clamor as their cover. As is often the case, the shop owner, the person perhaps in the "best" position to interpret the explosion, knew nothing.[44]

Take, for example, how commonplace sounds and ordinary speech acts can assume added significance. For five minutes every Friday at around midnight, fireworks explode from the rooftop of an apartment building in the historic center. Some of the neighbors say clan affiliates are signaling the arrival of a drug shipment and beckoning local spacciatori to fetch their shares. Relatedly, every day and at any hour, residents call out for their kin from apartment windows and balconies. Some of them are employed by drug handlers as their lookouts. They are beckoning *Maria!* and *Pascà!* to signal the approach of intruders.[45]

Crime clans are determinate political economic forces that reproduce themselves in indeterminacy. Crime clans do not simply impose their rule on everyday political economic life; they also insinuate themselves as affective–aesthetic effects. On the one hand, they exact violence to extort from residents their personal resources while interpellating them in tyrannical systems of deprivation and reward. They seize control of the distribution of public resources and broker dependent relationships that ensnare the resourceless. On the other hand, crime clans accomplish a great deal without doing any*thing.* An important part of their work is affective and aesthetic—composed in patterns of bullet holes and names called from balconies. Ephemeral, polysemous, and unreliable gestures and performances capture affect to generate an atmosphere. The atmosphere has a particular affective register that in turn registers itself in the sensory experience of its territorialized residents.

The radial effects of clan affiliates' violence traverse residents' lives in overdetermined and unsettlingly indeterminate ways. Crime clans create the atmosphere that they dominate, territorializing residents in an affective–aesthetic world suffused with fear, seduction, and "epistemic murk."[46] In this sense, "the camorra" is not a circumscribable thing but a part of everything, the atmospheric state of things.[47] In fact, crime clan affiliates and associates do not use the term *camorra*. Instead, they refer to *sistemi* (systems).[48] People who find themselves in the atmosphere of a system are alert to its indeterminacies and unruly forces.

The Art of Making Do in the Field

When I first made contact with the neomelodica music scene, I sensed atmospheres charged with fear and seduction. This had a direct impact on how people interacted with me. Interviews were out of the question; they inspired only the shellacked performances of endearing *napoletanità*, or "Neapolitanness," that, evidently, outsiders affectionately expect when they go to Naples. Casual conversation while hanging out was rarely a straightforward communication practice. Communication was often saturated with irony, flirting, warnings, and histrionics, and often all of these at once. If speculations and affirmations were not preposterously exaggerated or categorically dismissed, as they often were, they were lodged in metaphorical, allegorical, and proverbial language that resisted most of my attempts at disambiguation. My efforts to clear things up, in fact, only solicited less subtle forms of evasion, from omissions by ellipsis to dissimulation and bald-faced lies.

If talking was problematic, so was silence. When I was silent, people regarded me with suspicion. When they were silent, even if I asked them direct questions, their refusal to answer meant that I had crossed a line. I was not an investigative reporter or an infiltrator, but I felt that I was becoming one by default. And if that was how I also appeared to the people I met, then I demonstrated laughable ineptitude.

The people I met on the neomelodica scene expected me to study classic Neapolitan songs such as "Torna a Surriento" (Come back to Sorrento) and "'O sole mio" (My sun)—or much older music forms such as the villanella, the tarantella, and the tamurriata.[49] Folklore is abundant in Naples, and self-folklorizing tactics are part of the poetic repertoire some people use to gracefully keep strangers at a distance. This is one reason why many people were vexed—and some notably unnerved—when I explained that my interest was contemporary Neapolitan music, *their* scene.

It did not help matters that I carried a video camera with me, but how could I resist? There was so much to register. But to many people, "an

American with a video camera" meant opportunity. They heaped on me their hopes that I would connect them to a better future while anxiously wondering when I would go back to the future, the America of their dreams. They puffed up and self-dramatized, both courting and evading my video camera in a singular performance. They created distracting scenes to capture my attention while they made me the medium for their clichéd and self-aggrandizing autobiopics.

I was dumbfounded by how little control I had over my lens and stunned by the hours of "colorful" and "melodious" footage it accumulated. For months I frequented recording studios and TV stations, attended festivals, weddings, and baptisms, and visited the homes of composers, songwriters, managers, singers, and their fans, but it seemed I learned virtually nothing. How was that possible? Seduced by my mere presence, people opened their homes and studios to me. At the same time they feared I might get too close. The reason was in part that I, despite my better judgment, wanted to know more about the role of the camorra in the scene. I was not interested in unveiling the dirty truth about neomelodica music, but I could not help wondering whether the scene really was dominated by crime boss–impresari. If so, what did that mean for the hundreds of people who transacted with them on a regular basis?

It was clear that no one was going to talk straight with me, so I began to instigate conversation through indirection. I made music videos and TV commercials for broadcast on pirate television. I developed a portfolio with which to launch a business. I partnered with a recording studio, and through it I met a boss–impresario. Before long, I became the boss–impresario's in-house "American music video director," stepping quite effortlessly into the ad hoc performances that awaited me. These included writing my own songs and preparing, before I was interrupted, for my debut as a neomelodico singer. Like others on the scene, I gave myself over to surges of becoming-sovereign. Like my associates, I was alert to the scene's uncertainties, duplicities, and potentialities, oscillating between the rush of affect and paranoiac entrenchment.

Between vitality and fear in the contact zone, "the camorra" resonates across multiple relations. These include ambivalent tolerance, wary forgiveness, mutual recognition, ironic playfulness, homosocial excess, erotic allure, creeping obligation, ensnaring indebtedness, burning resentment, competition, subjugation, paralyzed passivity, willful unknowing, and adamant disavowal. My participation in these relations fired up the "attentional activities" that "traverse" cognitive processes, entraining me to the neomelodica scene's atmospheres.[50]

The Melodramatic Mode of Attention

This book stages a melodrama of contact. Contact is an affective–aesthetic happening, a commotion. It is the crossing of wires and short-circuiting of "perspective." Rather than privilege sight, contact summons multiple senses, including kinesthesia, intuition, and the sympathetic sense, opening you up to being affected. It also encompasses states of inattention such as deferred knowing or unknowing.

Contact is what happens in the zone where the rules are suspended and moral uncertainty can reign—and where play, threat, seduction, and histrionics are often the only resources for acting your way through scenes of intensity.[51] In the milieu where I lingered, contact describes how people interact in an atmosphere of fear, titillation, opportunity, and risk, drawing each other into performative entanglements. It is a modality through which meaning effects are communicated, negotiations wrought from indeterminacy, and self-determination and prepotency, at least momentarily, achieved.[52] Contact happens when people reach for the figure of the personal sovereign, but instead brush up against an excessive limit: the camorrista. In the neomelodica scene, contact describes what happens during the musical performances of an intimate public that has contact with the camorra.

Contact necessarily also describes the entanglements of fieldwork and of meeting things proximally, laterally, and through indirection. It is a "contaminated critique" that unfolds in the affective–aesthetic time and space of complicity.[53] When contact happens, identifications and representations give way to the qualities and qualia of relation.[54]

In this story, I dispose myself to affective–aesthetic atmospheres. I yield to events of the senses that flare up like "profane illuminations," as Benjamin described the productive disorientations that puncture the seamless sameness of bourgeois ("formal") capitalist experience.[55] By performing these dis-positions in writing, I want to conjure a contact zone charged with seductive vitalities and uncertain threats, leaving you to make your way among camorristi, people who behave like camorristi, and people (including me) who perform the art of making do.[56]

This book is about the production, performance, and consumption of a tremendously popular Neapolitan-language music genre of the contact zone. How do neomelodica music and organized crime make contact and spark an "underground" culture industry? This question has led many people to read in the neomelodica scene a melodrama of cultural hegemony and consent, a.k.a. complicity. However, the assertion that organized criminals use neomelodica music for the amoral education of hundreds of thousands of fans presumes a clear etiology of contact. It is the denouement of the didactive melodrama that defeats ambiguity.[57] Instead, the questions I pursue in my melodrama are as follows: What modes of attention let organized crime and neomelodica music become entangled? What worlds form through these shared experiences? What economies take effect and how do they feel to inhabit? What modes of attention let crime clan affiliates, crime clan associates, and people who simply live in the same milieu share affective–aesthetic experiences?

Like any other Italophile or Italianist focusing their attentions on Italy, I came into contact with the neomelodica music scene through affective, aesthetic, and interested entanglements. In this book, I bring them into relief. I offer my understanding of crime clan affiliates, associates, and nonassociates without evacuating the ambiguities. My understanding is modulated by paranoid fear, anger, revulsion, intense curiosity, erotic allure, the desire to belong, the injury of being exploited, and the determination to carry out and "complete" my research, just as many of these forces have modulated others' understanding of me. Rather than look "'before' or 'beyond'" these modulations for "narratives of origin and telos," I struggle to train, and not without lapses, my attention on atmospheres.[58] Instead of telling sovereign truths, these stories perform truths in the transient affective–aesthetic time and space between speculation and unknowing. They invite contact with an atmosphere saturated with the intimacies, vulnerabilities, and indeterminacies of fieldwork.[59]

ONE

Where There's Money, There's the Camorra

WHERE THERE'S MONEY, THERE'S THE CAMORRA. Like a contemporary proverb, these words seem to travel across all of Naples's social and economic scenes. The camorra colonizes every entrepreneurial activity where there is profit to "tax." Like any proverb, the saying has certain poetic properties, such as repetition and structural balance, that make people feel that if it sounds good and feels good to say, it must be true.[1] It argues "traditionally"; it possesses the impersonal historical authority of folklore.[2]

On its own, the saying is a linguistic artifact and an inaccurate generalization. The camorra has been multiple things simultaneously, depending on the territories in which it operates, whether in the city, the provinces, or the urban periphery.[3] In this chapter I sketch out how the camorra has taken different forms and has engaged in diverse operations over its long, discontinuous, and disputed history. The camorra exists more as a powerfully murky historical figure than as a distinct organization with a clear genealogy. The murk that makes the camorra even overdetermines how the camorra is figured.

Of course, many Neapolitans make or come across money but never cross paths with the camorra, per se. The declaration *where there's money, there's the camorra* does not denote a fact; it incites people to notice affective facts or affective situations.[4] The statement doesn't "mean." Instead, it has the power to make people aware, to make them "pragmatically speculative" in anticipation of very real potentialities.[5] For many people, it is a speculation that comes and goes. It does not necessarily apply to their own situation, but they sense that it connotes *something* that *must* be happening to *someone, somewhere,* even to someone they know. The words evoke the camorra as not yet materialized, as virtual.[6]

Where there's money, there's the camorra circulates when someone expresses a desire for a better life. It draws attention to fleeting opportunities and surges of hope, creeping suspicions and palpable risks. It intimates and activates public feelings of uncertainty and fear. It invokes tacit understandings about the current state of things and about indefinite or dead futures.

The saying draws attention to the contact zone where some people perform l'arte di arrangiarsi, or the art of making do. Many Neapolitans use this phrase to describe the entrepreneurial tactics, social sensibilities, and the performances of personal sovereignty that people enact as they pursue possibilities for a better life for themselves and their families. Personal sovereignty is performed in the creative decisions— decisions that are never subsumed under a rule or norm—that people make in pursuit of their private interests, which include their interest in others.[7]

L'arte di arrangiarsi entails cobbling together diverse resources and personal skills, often with the resources and skills of others, to harness multiple forms of value. This can involve, for example, performing a combination of part-time work (regulated and documented or unregulated and undocumented) and small-scale entrepreneurial work, such as a woman who sews handbags in a factory two days a week and sells handmade jewelry door-to-door to a clique of neighborhood clients on weekends. L'arte di arrangiarsi might entail occasionally or regularly engaging in what are commonly defined as illicit forms of exchange, such as buying and reselling stolen gold chains and watches, in order to pay a requested bribe to a bureaucrat in exchange for a janitorial position in a public hospital. Or purchasing from an acquaintance a counterfeit high school diploma—the prerequisite for a city office job—after verifying with a cop friend that the diploma is a passable fake.

People also perform l'arte di arrangiarsi as a social sensibility that entangles affects and interests. For instance, a woman hosts weekly evening games of la tombola in her kitchen, where she enjoys the company of her guests while also demonstrating to them her generosity and synching up with their gossip.[8] Favor exchanges such as chauffeuring an acquaintance in one's car or promising him or her help from a friend—not infrequently without the latter's consent—have value, in part, as goodwill investments that can bring future returns. L'arte di arrangiarsi activates, and whenever possible expands, social support networks, including relationships that have in the past been unreliable, contentious, or morally compromising.[9] It entails relational thinking, improvisational preparedness, and moral flexibility. Practitioners of this art, rather than follow an ethical code, engage in ethical practice.[10] Practicing the art of making do forestalls definition and anticipates potentiality.

Neapolitans ordinarily associate the art of making do with people who have limited skills or wealth and structural access to power brokers, but it is not universally or exclusively applicable to such individuals. The word *arrangiarsi* (to make do) is sometimes used as a coded insult to describe any perceived unprofessional work practice and its products.[11] Unprofessional can refer to the context of the work, such as an unregistered and unregulated set of economic relations; the mode of the work, such as arrhythmic labor, a fluctuating labor supply, and an unsteady flow of resources; the mode of communication, such as sporadic accessibility and changing prices and conditions of service; or the final product of the work, as when it bears the visible seams of any of these work practices.[12]

However, people more often use the expression l'arte di arrangiarsi to positively refer to the alertness, adaptability, and celerity that are awakened by a challenge.[13] Engaging in the art of making do means enacting one's personal sovereignty. Many people feel distaste for what they consider subservient labor, such as factory work, preferring instead the perceived self-enfranchising activities of entrepreneurship.[14] Campania has suffered from chronic "official" unemployment for decades, particularly since the deindustrializing early 1990s, when tens of thousands of jobs were lost.[15] Scarcity turned employment into a privilege, inflating the power of business owners, managers, and the "informal" brokers. Ordinary employees bear the cost of this inflation in the form of low pay and little hope for advancement.[16]

In order to have anything or be anything, it is necessary to be "out there" and freely circulating. Giuseppe, an unemployed thirty-year-old neomelodica music composer with a middle school education, living with his parents in a poor quartiere on the city's north edge, once explained this to me.[17] "It's not like you go out on the street and you necessarily become someone or become friends with someone good; you can also have bad experiences in the streets. But I'm convinced that if you're in the streets for years and years and years, something good will happen to you. But if you're always shut in an office doing your job and only your job, what can that bring you in life?"

To practice the art of making do means to speculate on and in a field of potential where an encounter with a stranger might mean opportunity, risk, or neither of the two. Or it might mean both. People like Giuseppe in the neomelodica music scene recognize that new encounters are charged with high indeterminacy and potential entanglements. Like Giuseppe, they seek a better future, and they are willing to maneuver the occulted relations that might carry them there. They are willing to gamble on personal sovereignty at the risk of falling subject, through indenture or even criminal association, to a camorrista. Indeed, during my fieldwork, Giuseppe began orbiting a boss–impresario whom he thought could launch his career while dodging the boss's encroachments on his freedom.

Entrepreneurs in other milieus try to entirely avoid strange encounters or, failing that, immediately try to extricate themselves from deeper entanglements. These are commonly business owners and vendors approached by a camorrista demanding a *tangente*. A tangente refers to either a bribe extorted or a bribe paid. A tangente is duplicitous; it activates a relation between individuals, a relation that can itself be duplicitous. This is especially the case when paying an extorted bribe is beneficial to the "victim," and the relation between "extortionist" and "briber" is more like a business partnership than predatory taxation. The businesses that get entangled in such relations are typically the larger and more powerful corporations whose market success a crime clan prefers to support and enhance.

Where there's money, there's the camorra articulates how organized crime haunts all entrepreneurial types in Campania (and not only in Campania).[18] Entrepreneurs engage the camorra across a range of relations that include avoidance, fearful unknowing, exhausted resignation, silent coalescence, and, on the neomelodica music scene, inconstant flirtations. Some entrepreneurs operating at the far ends of this continuum either actively collude with or directly oppose the camorra. Overt colluders and opponents hail from all social worlds, and they are not just entrepreneurs. Anticamorra protagonists include politicians and public administrators, law enforcement, the magistrature, as well as journalists, scholars, educators, and grassroots activists whose shared objective is to diffuse a "culture of legality."[19] The success of these efforts might be measurable in improved school attendance, higher "formal" employment, lower crime rates, and an increase in arrests, but a great deal of the camorra's success is felt in its persistent affective–aesthetic effects. When people say, *where there's money, there's the camorra*, they are referring to a way of operating that is as diffuse as it is "organized"—diffuse enough to engulf them. When they say *where there's money, there's the camorra*, people refer to the very state of things, to something that is a part of everything, to an atmosphere.[20] Whether fearful, tolerant, or embracing, but most always secretive, they help generate the atmosphere.

The passages below move through the affective–aesthetic atmospheres of "the camorra" by way of proverbial truths, folklore, ethnographic events, police reports, political memoirs, journalistic accounts, cinematic expressions, and historiography. This chapter is less a history of the camorra than a story about the camorra told heterologically—that is, gesturing toward what is ineffable or inapprehensible in histories of the camorra.[21] These movements simulate how some public feelings about organized crime have circulated, conjured atmospheres, and sometimes accreted in cultural forms, institutions, and even constitutions.

Who Am I and Who Are You?

The camorra refers both to real criminal organizations and to a diffuse way of operating. Entrepreneurs must contend with potential encounters with camorristi as well as people who "behave like camorristi." They are ultimately faced with the challenge of becoming sovereign. When people seeking a better life encounter strangers, their primary concern is not necessarily identifying them as camorristi or pretenders but figuring out how to engage or disengage from them.

Rino, a middle-class, thirty-five-year-old college graduate who opened a nightclub, managed to disengage when he had a strange encounter. Rino played bass guitar in a local glam rock band. In 2002 he partnered with a friend and opened a bar where they could showcase musicians on the alternative scene, including Rino's own band.

They found what seemed to be the perfect space to lease on Spaccanapoli (Split-Naples), the long, narrow street that cuts all the way through the historic center. Spaccanapoli begins halfway up the steep hill above the bay and plummets into the busy fish, fruit, and vegetable market called La Pignasecca (The Dried Pinecone) before continuing past the imposing Carafa family villas and the baroque, Gothic, and Romanesque churches. Then it pushes through clotted stretches of over-stuffed tourist shops of mandolin-shaped bottles of *limoncello* and packages of meter-long multicolored fettuccine. From there, the street runs

under a canopy of purple wisteria, coasts along the wall of the university, passes the immaculate ecclesiastical shops displaying candelabras
and clerical robes, crosses Via Duomo (Cathedral way) to become Via
Vicaria vecchia (Ancient law-court way), where it cuts through the quartiere of Forcella (Fork), which until recently was known locally as the
"casbah" of contraband cigarettes, pirated music, and residences with
hidden escape passages built into the walls.[22] Spaccanapoli ends here, in
this half-dilapidated "kingdom" ruled for thirty years by the crime clan
boss Luigi Giuliano, a.k.a. 'O rre (The king), before he turned *pentito*
(collaborator with the "justice system") in 2002. He was succeeded by his
sister, Erminia, a.k.a. Celeste (Sky-blue, the color of her eyes), who was
sentenced to ten years in prison in 2006.

The space Rino and his partner found was located not in Forcella but
on the other side of Via Duomo, amid the tourist shops. Rino negotiated
with the broker. All was going well until, at the final stages, a stranger
approached him while he was inspecting the property with a contrac-
tor. "It was a man I have never seen before. He told me there were some
'extra' brokerage fees that we would have to pay. I don't know if he was
sent by the owners or if he came on his own," Rino recounted. "I asked
the owners who this man was but they didn't say that they sent him and
they didn't say that they *didn't* send him. They said things like, 'So, who
is this again? Are you sure it wasn't our broker?'" Rino didn't understand
whether the owners were feigning ignorance or if they really didn't
know. Maybe they wanted to profit from the confusion.

The vagaries of the stranger's insinuation presented the business partners with some unnerving questions. Who was he, what were his actual affiliations, and what danger did he really present? Was he merely a
pretender to power, taking advantage of the fact that public knowledge
about the identity, reach, and intensity of the camorra is always only
approximate? Was he merely compounding these unknowns to tap the
public fears they spawn? Was he capitalizing on the force of the camorra
or was he, in fact, the camorra incarnate?

They could take their cue and ask the stranger to name his sum and
then make arrangements to pay him. Or they could overtly refuse, asserting that in their business plan only contracts and transparent relationships
were acceptable. As first-time and middle-class entrepreneurs, they had
only the implicit knowledge that *where there's money, there's the camorra.*
Its implicitness left room for doubt, even hope, and the impulse to resist.

The scenery shifts dramatically when walking down Spaccanapoli and crossing Via Duomo and into Forcella: there is a mix of modern and older architecture, without any shops that appear to cater to tourists. Occasionally one sees a contraband cigarette or a counterfeit or pirated CD vendor; this neighborhood, more than any other in Naples, was associated with this commercial activity in the decades after World War II. Turning into the vicoli of Forcella that intersect Spaccanapoli, there is a labyrinthine reticulation of gorgeous vicoli, some only a few meters in width, others partly composed of steps. Many peculiar public events have taken place in the streets of this quartiere, from firework celebrations for the release of camorristi from prison to regal funerals for crime clan bosses, their kin, and their spouses, with six black horses pulling a carriage holding the coffin.

But instead of resisting, Rino chose to respond to the stranger with ambiguity: "OK, we'll talk about it, we'll see." This response is consistent with a tactic I have observed in multiple, albeit less volatile, situations. "Never immediately say yes or no. That way you can decide later if you have to," a fifty-year-old upper-middle-class Neapolitan male friend once explained to me. This was how Rino and his partner hoped to indefinitely, maybe even definitively, defer the decision to either refuse or capitulate to the could-be camorrista.

"It's *vulimme ffà chi song'io e chi si tu?*" Rino explained to me. He used the abbreviated form of the expression that means *Do we really have to make it clear who I am and who you are? (Or will you back down so that we don't have to perform that redundant operation?)*. When a person addresses someone else in this manner, things are about to reach a tipping point. The expression insinuates that someone is about to encroach on someone else's personal sovereignty. The words serve as a challenge, a threat. At the same time, they can very well be a bluff. The game is to see how far you can get and how much you can get without having to exert any force—or reveal who you really are. Bluffing often works because people will always wonder, what if it's *not* a bluff?

When I asked Rino if he thought the stranger was bluffing, he answered with exasperation, "How am I supposed to know who's a camorrista and who isn't?"

Instead of trying to identify the stranger, Rino treated the matter like an ordinary disagreement over a lease, which it ostensibly was, and pulled out of the deal. This entailed no outright refusal and it did not call anyone's bluff. Fortunately, the matter ended there. They had no further contact with the property owners, the broker, or anyone else claiming to be part of the deal.

Neither did they have any unsettling contact with "strangers" when they opened up their club in another space in the same neighborhood. The club had a fun two-year run before it ran out of money. "And no one ever came to us for a tangente," Rino said. "Anyone could see that there was no money in what we were doing. It was just our overgrown drugs and rock 'n' roll adolescent fantasy."

Rino felt that had they been serious entrepreneurs and hadn't themselves been bluffing, their encounter with the stranger would have gone a different way. The shoes of the stranger figure would have likely been filled by a person whose bluff they would have had a much harder time

calling. This was the case with a prominent family that owns a prestigious jewelry shop in the quartiere Pendino. An upper-middle-class friend
called Marco told me their story.

"Try and open up a business without the camorra stepping in,"
Marco began. "One day the father of my friend of twenty years, Giulia,
was approached by a man who demanded a tangente of ten million lira
(about U.S.$10,000). Giulia told me about it only when it was impossible
for her to hide her fear. What happened was her father had refused to
pay the tangente, and the following week a bomb exploded in the drive-
way of their villa, here in Posillipo." Marco gestured toward his living
room window and his panoramic view from the tranquil wooded hilltop
neighborhood overlooking the bay. The area's original Greek name is
Pausylipon, which means free of pain, or respite from worry.

As he continued his story, Marco's eyes seemed to darken. "Her father,
desperate and terrified for his family, contacted the police. And how did
they respond? They actually advised him to pay the tribute! It's unbeliev-
able! What do you do when even the police admit that they are powerless?" By *powerless* Marco meant that the police have shared their power
with crime clan affiliates, giving in to intimidation or bribery or both.
Corruption may begin with intimidation, but the extorted relationship
that results can be beneficial to both oppressor and victim, making victim-
hood an ambiguous status. This is also true when an entrepreneur becomes a prominent player on the market. Entanglements with organized
crime clans are ever more likely, and if the entrepreneur commands a large
market, these entanglements can take the form of opportunistic partner-
ships. For example, in 2000 police investigations revealed that executives
of the corporate food giants Cirio and Parmalat, by conceding the tangenti
extorted by affiliates of Casalesi crime clans, were essentially buying into a
violently enforced monopoly across several regions of Italy.[23]

Marco told me that he never learned the outcome of Giulia's family
troubles. Twice he asked them what they had decided to do, and each
time they replied with the refrain, "Everything is fine now." Their response was eerily resolute. The implicit message was that there was to be
no more discussion.

What makes this story especially remarkable is that Marco is a judge.
Moreover, he handled cases of mafia association. The magistrature (the
independent executive body that encompasses the public prosecution
and the judiciary) has had considerable success in securing convictions

of crime clan affiliates since the passage of the Rognoni–La Torre law in 1982, which introduced the crime of *associazione di stampo mafioso* or mafialike association (including camorristic association), a law distinct from one that punishes *associazione per delinquere*—when three or more persons associate to commit crimes. Rather than focus on the unjust advantages seized by a criminal organization (e.g., quasi-legal commercial activity and public works contracts), the law punishing mafia-type association addresses its methods: intimidating by threats of reprisals from the association and using the association's "system of subordination and *omertà* [silence secured by threat]" to commit crime or gain unfair economic advantages for themselves or others.[24] This law at once defines and punishes "mafioso" or "camorristic" methods.[25]

I first met the judge when friends invited me to join them for a night at the theater. Marco is young, slight in build, and soft-spoken, but he has an imperious countenance. After the evening at the theater, we met several more times for dinners, art openings, and parties, and we gradually became good friends. Although I trusted him, I did not talk to him much about my research. I was uneasy about what the ethical implications would be if he, and by extension the justice system, were to begin taking a special interest in the same milieu that interested me. I was also concerned about my safety.

The first evening I had dinner at the judge's home, I learned that my concerns were not entirely unfounded. His stories depicted the intelligence and bravery his job demanded. In a recent case he dealt a coup to eighteen members of a camorristic association. He explained that the judges' painstaking task is to establish the existence of an organizational structure, precisely the thing that crime clans invest great care and energy in obscuring. They use encrypted language when communicating information and instructions. They use *prestanomi,* or "borrowed names," such as the names of spouses and kin, on the titles to their properties and businesses. They intimidate potential witnesses to secure their silence, and they buy/extort complicity from police and even judges. Several months into one of his own anticamorra cases, Marco discovered that a police officer was providing suspects with advance updates on the investigation in exchange for small gifts that the officer claimed he was forced to accept. During another case, the father of the defendant phoned the judge at his home to ask him, matter of factly, whether he was "corrupt" and would be amenable to a tangente.

Once, while serving in the prosecution of a high-ranking camorra affiliate, Marco came home from work to find a note on his bed warning him that his life would be in danger if he issued a verdict of guilty. The security guard of his gated community had seen no intruder, and his apartment showed no signs of forced entry. Although the skillfulness of the threat had impressed on the judge the gravity of the message, he did not acquiesce. Happily, he has not faced any attempts at retribution, but violence against judges is not without precedent. In 1992 Sicilian mafiosi used a car bomb to kill the prosecuting magistrate Paolo Borsellino and several of his bodyguards. Earlier that year, mafiosi killed the prosecuting magistrate Giovanni Falcone and his wife by detonating explosives planted under the highway between Palermo and the city's airport.[26]

Despite these dangers, Marco wields a cutting sense of humor, which he often animates by dipping into a well of richly expressive Neapolitan-language figures of speech. His humor consists of a comical frisson generated by the contrast between his "Italian style" parlor mannerisms—a reflection of his unabashed high bourgeoisie attitude, which was supported by his high-status profession, his family name, his residence in Posillipo—and his mimicry of napoletano stretto. This frisson is most intense in the judge's courtroom anecdotes, especially when they concern his encounters with crime clan affiliates.

In one such encounter, a fugitive capoclan who had been captured in South America and extradited to Italy was brought before the judge in Naples. On the day of his hearing, the capoclan, dressed in a flashy white suit and a Panama hat, proudly entered the courtroom and slowly took his seat. Initially, the judge found him amusing. "But while we heard evidence from the *carabinieri* (national military police) and the witnesses, 'O capoclan repeatedly interrupted with his incessant and uninvited commentary. *Twice* I reprimanded him for speaking out of order. On the third time I warned him that another act of disobedience would get him banned from the courtroom," the judge recounted with irritation. "Do you know what this man did next?" he continued, switching from Italian to Neapolitan to report the boss's speech. "He stood up, looking baffled, and said, 'What's this? Am I supposed to play the detainee and that's it?'"

The kind of humor that frames many of the judge's courtroom tales reproduces the sociolinguistic divisions that separate the popular classes from the rest.[27] Comportment, gestures, language choice, and linguistic competence in the practice of "formal" institutional speech also mark important differences in the presentation of self and how people perceive institutional boundaries. However, although these courtroom scenes play out clashing performances of class, they cannot be reduced to class conflict. While the judge has the distinction of wealth, status, influence, and family name, the same is also true for the capoclan. From this perspective, the self-aggrandizing performances of 'O capoclan rival those of the judge. The judge sees an undereducated man indulging in the arrogant excesses of *smania di protagonismo* (the neurotic need to be the center of the action). 'O capoclan sees the judge, and by extension the magistrature, not as the adjudicator of a sovereign state but as a force that competes with his own personal sovereignty. A camorrista rarely fails to show up for a trial because he will always want to look his accusers in the face.[28] Both the camorrista and the judge see each other as pretenders to power.

The class distinction that the judge emphasizes in his anecdotes invokes a dichotomy that has endured in popular, political, and scholarly discourse in Naples, as elsewhere in the West since the eighteenth century: the educated and enlightened elite versus the "unattached" and depraved "dangerous classes."[29] According to this binary, the educated elite exercise reason, engage each other in debate, use their "superior knowledge" to develop the codes of liberal citizenship, and apply their "superior force" only against subjects who are noncompliant.[30] The dangerous classes, on the other hand, are the embodiment of noncompliance. They revel in idleness, they are driven by their passions, and, in the case of camorristi, they abuse everyone else around them with *sopraffazione* (oppressive bullying). The intellectual pursues his need for enlightenment and has the authority to regulate others with the impartial sovereignty of reason in the service of universal interest. The camorrista, in contrast, is a slave to his base wants, his private interests.

This dichotomy conceals how the authority of the judge (and by extension the state) and that of the camorrista parallel each other. In the landscape of power that the camorrista imagines, judges and camorristi are competing sovereigns with competing systems of value. The judge's status is founded on his education, family name, place of residence, wealth, and investiture by the state. The camorrista's status is entwined with his reputation. It is inscribed in him by his family name, his Family name, and his honorific nickname.[31] These names are charged with historical significance and, for residents in his territory, the power to determine, or kill, the future. His reputation, moreover, is tied to territory.

He performs it each time he taxes his territorial subjects, and his wealth constitutes its material proof.[32]

Finally, the camorrista's authority rests not on "formal" education but on his know-how. Rather than the presumed impartial sovereignty of reason, it is his "embodied intelligence" and his awareness of the possibilities for action that render him supreme.[33] The camorrista concerns himself less with ideas or "truth" or "justice" than with what Niccolò Machiavelli called the "effectual truth of things."[34]

While it is useful to underscore this difference in modalities to trace the phenomenology of power in the contact zone where so-called formal and rogue authorities clash, it is also essential to look at where the two authorities make contact and become entangled. Overemphasizing the contrast between the *logos* of the law with the *corpus* of the criminal falls in step with the discursive–institutional nexus that helped produce the dangerous classes in the first half of the nineteenth century. Indeed, one could argue that this same discursive nexus contributed to the emergence of figurations of the camorra both past and present.

Contemporary crime clans in Campania adhere to definitive forms of organization while embracing flexible associations with people of all social, political, and economic positions. "Organized" crime in the nineteenth century similarly embraced flexible associations. However, despite the wide range of relationships articulating the camorra, it has been and continues to be typically figured as the expression and masterwork of the lower classes.

La Camorra

The camorra's originary forms and practices have been the subject of wide-ranging speculation among historians, criminologists, journalists, and novelists. Some date the camorra back to fifteenth-century Spain as a criminal society called the Garduña (Brotherhood of armed robbery [or extortion]), suggesting that organized crime came to the Kingdom of Naples by way of Spanish rule.[35] In other accounts, the camorra emerged during the early nineteenth century in the Kingdom of Naples as the Bella Società Riformata (Beautiful reformed society). In still other accounts, the camorra did not definitively emerge until the U.S. occupation of Naples at the end of World War II.[36]

According to the most carefully documented history, particularly the work of Marcella Marmo, the camorra as an organization emerged in the prisons, galleys, and in the military in Campania and Sicily between 1820 and 1830. Camorristi first recruited in prisons, particularly the prison of the quartiere Vicaria, the traditional seat of the *capicamorra*, the head camorrista of Naples and the surrounding provinces. This organization consisted of "secret sects" that autonomously controlled the twelve quartieri of Naples. It was most concentrated in the quartieri of Pendino, Porto, and Mercato, the areas with the highest concentration of the city's poorest residents. Camorristi were like violent tax collectors who demanded a cut from all economic activities in their neighborhoods of control, both legal and illegal. Each camorrista established his sovereignty through the exercise of personal force. His superiority was repeatedly confirmed by the tangenti he received.[37]

The organization consisted of a three-tier hierarchy: in each quartiere a single *capintrino* (head camorrista) commanded a handful of camorristi, and together they made up the Società Maggiore (Major Society). Under their command was the Società Minore (Minor Society), composed of *piciotti di sgarro* (youths of courage), who oversaw *giovanotti onorati* (honorable youths) selected from among 'e guaglion 'e malavita (youths of the underworld) to do the grunt work of their superiors, without remuneration or the benefits of affiliation.[38] These youths endured years of servitude in hopes of being initiated as full-fledged camorristi.

Marmo's history is pieced together through court records, parliamentary reports, and the writings of policemen, criminal anthropologists, journalists, and liberal intellectuals. The most substantial of these documents are the report authored in 1861 by Naples's minister of interior, Silvio Spaventa, and a journalistic exposé by the Swiss-Florentine novelist and longtime resident of Naples, Marc Monnier.[39]

The reports of Spaventa and Monnier (and the texts of criminal anthropologists and novelists with which they resonate) conjure the familiar problems of historiography, and in this case the stakes are particularly high.[40] They were published during the culmination of the Risorgimento (the "resurgence" of unified Italy) and the founding of the modern Italian nation-state in 1861, and it is reasonable to assume that they are inflected with the dominant nationalist ideologies of that era. Spaventa's perspective as a former revolutionary, prisoner, and exile cannot but bear on his report. He experienced the demoralizing failure of the 1848 revolution in the Kingdom of Naples. According to some historians, in the event's aftermath, the Bourbon regime allied with camorristi against the liberals. Spaventa himself and his revolutionary contemporaries had been imprisoned with camorristi who, it is argued, were paid by the Bourbon police to spy on them lest they plot another revolution. When some of the incarcerated liberals solicited the aid of these same camorristi by offering to pay them to create unrest among the residents in their quartieri, the camorristi blackmailed the liberals for the money.[41] Moreover, some historians argue that the Bourbon regime, and the Napoleonic regime that ruled the kingdom from 1806 to 1815, relied on camorristi as a lower-rung police force for maintaining public order among the "plebes."

Monnier, like Spaventa, was well-known for his nationalist sentiments, evidenced by the book he published in response to the French poet Alphonse de Lamartine's infamous description of Italy as "the land of the dead."[42] Italy was not, Monnier declared, a decadent nation, inhabited only by relics and echoes of the past; instead, new life was unfolding. He likewise wrote *La camorra* in a nationalist vein and, like Spaventa, was motivated by the desire to address the "true obstacles that Italy meets in Naples."[43] He argued that the "reasons" for the camorra were to be found in the tyrannical Borbonic regime that, fearing revolution, had isolated the kingdom from all of Europe and left the "popolo . . . imprisoned in a splendid cell into which entered neither the ideas, nor the beliefs, nor the material gains" enjoyed by France and Britain.[44] The regime, Monnier argued, feared both liberal intellectuals and the camorra. However, recognizing the camorra's capacity to terrorize and potentially mobilize the poor, the regime partnered with them to persecute the revolutionaries.

However, the liberals, Monnier writes, did not give up. They smuggled newspapers and books into the kingdom. They spoke cautiously and only to trusted friends in private; otherwise, they simulated "the ignorance of the *lazzaroni* [idling poor]."[45] They were forced into "the shadow of isolation," where they became "living heroes left to their own devices in the land of the dead."[46] To Monnier, the "land of the dead" was not Italy; rather, it was the mezzogiorno (the south) and its dangerous classes.[47] *La camorra,* published after the liberals finally prevailed in 1860, is in fact much more about the future of the modern Italian nation state than the title indicates.

The history of the camorra is murky because, perhaps, it is partly figured by the discourses that helped shape the modern liberal nation-state.[48] Indeed, one can imagine that the state and the camorra are relatively independent, even as their agents codetermine and overdetermine each other. The modern liberal democratic nation-state is predicated, in part, on the existence of its perceived negation, the totalitarian Prince. In its self-figuration, the modern state exercises reason in the deliberation of universal interests through the medium of constitutional law, while the premodern sovereign embodies the rapid-fire calculativeness and personal force needed to exert his willpower over volatile situations. In the historiography of the Kingdom of Naples and the unified Italian state, the Prince figure hovers in the background as the ruler of the dangerous classes, and the Prince himself is ruled by his rapacious desires, especially his desire for power.

This speculation becomes more plausible when one considers a category of people that preceded the camorra and the dangerous classes by nearly two centuries: the "lazzaroni" or "lazzari," the idling poor against whom Monnier contrasted the enlightened Neapolitan liberal intellectuals. There is no single adequate translation in English for *lazzaro* (the singular of *lazzari*).[49] This is largely because its meaning has oscillated for two centuries between a savage, self-serving villain and a gentle creature that knows neither avarice nor malice. The most stable characteristics of this morphing figure found in the writings of intellectual and political elites such as Benedetto Croce at the turn of the nineteenth century, in the travelogues of northern European aristocrats who visited Naples as part of their Grand Tour education in the first half of the eighteenth century, and in the writings of northern European bourgeoisie visitors seeking a sentimental education in the latter half of the eighteenth century, is that the lazzaro is poor, has no vocation, and is seminude, wearing only tattered rags.[50]

The term likely comes from the Spanish word *lazarò* (wretch), which the Spanish rulers of Naples used to describe a subclass of the "plebes" who carried out a short-lived revolution in 1647–48. Both words may derive from the name of the biblical figure Lazarus. During the sixteenth and seventeenth centuries, Naples was the capital city of the Kingdom of Naples and ruled by Spanish viceroys.[51] As was the case during the centuries of foreign rule that preceded it, the Kingdom of Naples bore a crippling tax burden to finance wars in the sovereign's other territories.[52] Although a concatenation of forces generated the field of potential in which the revolts exploded—volcanic eruptions, earthquakes, famines, plagues, a rapidly increasing urban population, Spain's destruc-

1703 The Lazzaroni (Homeless Beggars), as they live in the Streets
of Naples, Italy.
COPYRIGHT 1902 BY H. C. WHITE CO.

The term *lazzaroni* appears in the caption of this photograph taken by a staff photographer of the American stereograph picture maker H. C. White of Vermont (or perhaps by White himself) in the early 1900s. Photograph from the Library of Congress.

tive economic policies, a financial crisis, and the exclusion of some forty-thousand plebes from political representation—it was a reinstated tax on fruit in 1647 that triggered an extraordinary irruption of collective action. The revolt indicates how disorder and "illegitimate" violence have been attributed to the "savage" poor.

In 1647 a young illiterate fisherman named Tommaso Aniello, or Masaniello, from the quartiere Mercato led a throng of the city's poorest residents in a ten-day rebellion against their heavy tax burdens. Although Masaniello was quickly identified as the leader by popular and historical accounts that spread throughout Europe (and continue to circulate in the historiography), this is a folkloric gloss. Rather, Masaniello acted within a web of relations that traversed the lower and middle classes and the rural and urban economies. He was guided by the priest and intellectual Don Giulio Genoino who, while mayor in 1620, had been involved in a popular revolt aimed at reforming the monarchy. Moreover, the 1647 rebellion was broadly backed by rural peasants targeting the feudal barons who jealously protected their autonomy from the monarchy. These latter were owners of inhabited fiefs who formed private armies of bandits and terrorized the countryside by seizing common lands and trying, convicting, and even killing rebellious vassals with impunity.[53]

In the city, Masaniello and somewhere between 100,000 and 150,000 people stormed the palace of the viceroy and set fire to the houses of the nobility. The protestors also hunted down and killed some thirty bandits, including one of their prominent employers, a baron of the Carafa family, who had ordered the assassination of Masaniello. Masaniello escaped the attempt on his life, but shortly after was killed by Genoino himself. A popular explanation for the assassination is that Masaniello turned megalomaniacal and worked nonstop for days without sleep or nourishment, driving himself insane. However, this characterization perhaps relies too heavily on the perspectives of his enemies.[54]

The rebellion quickly entered public imagination throughout Europe as a popular revolution, and it lives on in the same manner today.[55] Genoino, the bourgeoisie, and the rural upheavals receded into relative obscurity, and the rebellion was crystallized instead in the figure of the lazzaro: the savagely heroic, freedom-loving, plebeian revolutionary. The lazzaro's savagery was captured, for example, by the English historian James Howell, who wrote in 1650 that Spain held on to Naples "as one would do a Wolf by the ear."[56]

The lazzaro emerges once again in the historiography of the 1799 revolution. In the 1750s liberal sentiment swelled throughout the Kingdom of Naples. Elite intellectuals guardedly met in a growing number of Freemasonry lodges to discuss the new political and economic philosophies circulating in France and Britain and to develop their own proposals for the mezzogiorno.[57] One of their main goals, also articulated by the economist Antonio Genovese, was to end the economic and intellectual isolation of the feudalistic kingdom from northern European nations and, like those nations, enjoy the fruits of industrialization and progressive political reform.[58]

When in 1799 Napoléon's troops advanced toward Naples, King Ferdinand IV and Maria Carolina prepared to flee the city. According to Croce, a mob of lazzari rushed to the royal palace and called the king out to his balcony, imploring him not to leave. They asked him for arms and swore they would not let the French enter the city; they were ready to shed blood for God, the king, the Church, and their own wives and children.[59] But the monarchs abandoned Naples and took refuge in Palermo. Enraged, the lazzari began massacring anyone they suspected of republicanism. Republican sympathizers, fearing anarchy, quickly signed a treaty with France to help bring order to the city. For three days the lazzari ferociously defended the city from the invading French troops before succumbing to them.

In January 1799 the Neapolitan Republic was established. The Neapolitan philosopher Francesco Mario Pagano, who had pushed for reforms during the decades leading up to the revolution, played a significant role in drafting the constitution. When it was published, he prefaced it with an explanation of how it differed from that of the French Republic. Unlike the French declaration of the rights of man, which espoused equality as a foundational right, the Neapolitan constitution declared that it was the right to "self-preservation and improvement" from which all other rights (liberty of thought, private property, the right to resist despotism) derived. Contrary to the French, Pagano argued that equality was, in fact, not a right at all because "'the people' should not be understood to include either the ignorant and degraded plebes, or the 'gangrenous' aristocracy."[60] He explained that under the new constitution a restricted senate, rather than a representative assembly, would propose legislation and that "a college of censors, composed of men of wisdom," would administer the moral and intellectual education of "the people."[61]

However, the Neapolitan Republic lasted only until June 1799.[62] The *lazzari* continued with bursts of resistance throughout this period. Unable to suppress them, the French government sought instead to appease them. The army installed a *capolazzaro* (head lazzaro) as a colonel.[63] President Carlo Laubert made a public appeal to the rebels by explaining that the successful revolution on which the Neapolitan Republic was founded was the very same revolution Masaniello had valiantly tried, and failed, to realize in 1647.[64] The lazzari, however, continued to rebel.

At the same time, King Ferdinando's court in Palermo called on the influential Cardinal Fabrizzio Ruffo to recruit a band of counterrevolutionary fighters and reclaim Naples. Ruffo gathered seventeen thousand peasants and "bandits," who called themselves *sanfedisti* (men of the holy faith), and entered Naples. Violent and chaotic fighting broke out among the sanfedisti, the republicans, and the French army. The lazzari, with unrelenting ferocity, hunted down "giacobini" (Jacobins).[65] Once glorified in the romantic literary depictions that circulated throughout Europe, the lazzari of the counterrevolution were now painted as savage cannibals who went as far as dragging a man through the streets, reducing him to pieces of flesh that people bought and ate.[66]

After the restoration, King Ferdinando was comparably retaliatory against supporters of the republic. There were eight thousand trials in the kingdom, hundreds of life sentences, more than a thousand exiles, and in Naples alone, over a hundred executions. Harold Acton, an expatriate living in Naples, described the repression in the most gruesome terms. Nobles and others were beheaded or hanged in Piazza Mercato before a crowd of enthralled spectators to which the hangman and his assistant, the *tirapiedi* (lit. pull-feet), who clung to the prisoner's feet, pandered.[67] Pagano was among the hanged. The liberal reforms he and his contemporaries succeeded in getting passed during the monarchy and the short-lived Neapolitan Republic were repealed by Ferdinando and Maria Carolina.

In 1821, 1833, and 1848 political discontent erupted among laborers and the poor, as well as the propertied and professional middle classes. The Bourbon monarchy struggled to weather a significant agricultural and financial crisis. The regime made modifications to protectionist tariffs and sparked strikes for higher wages and better working conditions. In the city the number of angry and desperate unemployed and poor was alarming, but in the rural regions, it was even more so. A rapidly rising number of people were declared guilty of vagrancy, which became, under the Napoleonic Code, a crime. Changes in farming practices, effects on grazing patterns, tax increases that landowners shifted onto tenant farmers, the usurpation of common lands by land barons, restrictions on the use of Crown forests, and the Bourbon regime's push toward privatization, among other factors, caused many families to become indigent. Thousands of rural poor were barred from entering Naples, detained and harassed by the police, and forced into *case di lavoro* (poorhouses).[68]

Some of these indigents joined groups of bandits. Bandits were people deemed guilty and banished by a community or feudatory. They were denied the protection of the law and could be killed with impunity. They "existed in that confused and contested no-man's land where local and royal justice met."[69] When people struggled against French occupation in the early nineteenth century, the authorities began to use the term *brigand* to label the compounded offense of bandits banding together, or criminal association.[70]

Indeed, this confused and contested terrain is as much discursive as it is juridical. On the one hand, literature, oral narratives, and ballads tend to lionize illegal economic activities and illegitimated violence as the necessary means for survival and resistance to oppression. In 1959 the historian Eric Hobsbawm famously figured unlawful practices as the realm of the "social bandit," carrying out the will of the peasantry in "pre-political" form. In his study of "bandits" in southern Italy, Hobsbawm used the written texts and oral narratives of popular culture to locate the subaltern histories muffled by hegemonic discourse. Many critics, including Hobsbawm himself, note that this method may have figured a "noble bandit" by mistaking the romantic desires of middle-class literary productions and the impersonal historical authority of folklore for the world of the "other." Most significantly, however, Hobsbawm emphasized that the key qualities of "bandits" were their ambiguous social situation and the "undetermined, ambiguous and even ostensibly 'conservative'" quality of "banditry."[71]

In fact, some bandits worked as mercenaries for rich landowners bent on usurping the lands of smaller, less powerful landowners. Some bandits and brigands who lived in the forests intimidated the poor into providing them with supplies. Some of these "unattached" outlaws were violent monopolists of large-scale trade in contraband tobacco, salt, and other goods, a scale so great that "clandestine" is an untenable descriptor. They worked with the cooperation and protection of people across a range of political–economic positions, including aristocratic landowners, merchants, farmers, innkeepers, customs officials, and the military.[72] While "banditry" and "brigandage" referred to real problems, they also served as convenient alibis for the Napoleonic and Bourbon regimes to declare a state of emergency and apply oppressive measures in an attempt to usurp power from the barons whose relative autonomy had perennially posed a threat to the monarchy.[73]

The Disorder Party

In mid-nineteenth century Naples, camorristi had monopolized many segments of the market by imposing tangenti on numerous licit and illicit forms of commerce. They also had monopolized the city's unskilled labor. The laboring classes were "fragmented into a myriad of self-regulating corporate groups," and one such group, the camorra, leveraged corporatist norms and violence to control the supply of unskilled labor at the port and the city's food and meat markets.[74] During the transitional authority of which General Giuseppe Garibaldi took charge after conquering the Kingdom of Naples in 1860, these localized groups played a significant role in maintaining public order. Garibaldi famously managed to recruit his *mille uomini* (thousand men)—peasants, volunteers, and mercenaries—a rag-tag army that defeated the Bourbons in Sicily with unexpected force.[75] In haste King Francesco II moved to the fortress of Gaeta, from where he continued the defense. In Naples people looted, rioted, and killed, as liberal revolutionaries, the Bourbon army, supporters of the king, and camorristi engaged in what was likened to a civil war. The violence and disorder subsided before the arrival of Garibaldi, who was met by ecstatic crowds.[76]

In the months preceding Garibaldi's victory, Liborio Romano, a lawyer and former professor of law at the University of Naples, was appointed Naples's minister of the interior. Like Spaventa, who later replaced him in his post, Romano was a former liberal revolutionary. He had twice been imprisoned and exiled—first, to his hometown in the Puglia region, and then to France. In his memoirs, Liborio defends his decisions by explaining that he became minister in the midst of looting and violence in a city on the verge of civil war and anarchy, where enemies sought to profit from the confusion and "bury liberal institutions." Among these enemies of the liberal state were camorristi. To forestall or "paralyze" their "unhappy tendencies" and "save them from their participation in 'the disorder party,'" Romano devised a plan. He invited Salvatore De Crescenzo, a.k.a. Tore 'e Criscienzo the *capocamorra* (camorra chief), to a meeting at his home and offered to invest the camorrista and his affiliates with government authority. He explained to De Crescenzo that he was providing him and the other *capicamorra* the opportunity to "rehabilitate" themselves by serving as chiefs in a new citizens' watch. He told De Crescenzo that he believed he and his "friends" had taken up their "false position" as criminals not because of a failing in their "good plebeian character" but because of the "improvidence of the government," which had closed off all opportunity for "industriousness." He told him that unlike the Bourbon police, who were all "hired thugs and vile spies," the citizens' watch would be composed of honest men for whom he would "pull a veil over the past." He emphasized that because this new police force would perform the important service of maintaining public order, they would be well compensated with money and the respect of their fellow citizens.[77]

Romano writes that De Crescenzo was initially doubtful and diffident, but by the end of the meeting, he wanted to kiss Romano's hand. He promised Romano that he would fulfill his duties and that he would secure the obedience of "his friends." According to Romano, De Crescenzo kept his promise until the end, showing him that "men are not entirely good, nor are they entirely perverse, as long as they are not constrained to be so."[78]

With the help of the top camorristi, Romano brought order to the city and made way for the arrival of Garibaldi. Months later, the South was annexed to the Kingdom of Piedmont–Sardinia, which, in effect, had become its conqueror. Historical records indicate that in the intervening months of Garibaldi's transitional government, the camorra continued its practice of extortion-cum-taxation on economic activities in its territories of control, only now as police commissioners, inspectors, and agents, and as *garibaldini* (the citizens' watch of "Garibaldists"). This was an identity of which camorristi were proud. They wore on their caps tricolor cockades for the "nation of Italy," and on one occasion, as Monnier writes, a camorrista said of his contraband goods to a customs agent, "È roba d' o si Peppe [It's Uncle Peppe's stuff]."[79]

Camorra Associations

Romano's decision to install capicamorra in the new police force of Naples was a radical compromise of sovereignty, but it was not the only point of contact and collusion between political and intellectual elites and the camorra. When he succeeded Romano as minister in 1861, Spaventa had been awaiting the opportunity to address this institutionalized corruption head-on, and his opportunity came when the parliament in Turin, the capital of the newly unified Kingdom of Italy, requested of him the report from which historians have been able to sketch the structure and practices of the nineteenth-century camorra. The report was to focus on brigandage and *camorrismo* (camorrism) in the interest of national security. The former was defined as the work of "bandits" opposed to unification and the latter was described as a "criminal association of ferocious men using violence and intimidation against the weak in pursuit of illicit profit."[80] The new legislation demanded the "repression of brigandage and of camorristi in the infected provinces."[81] Spaventa's report provided the evidence to support passage of the Pica Law (named after its strongest proponent, Deputy Giuseppe Pica), which empowered the state to form a junta with the authority to place under immediate house arrest all suspected brigands and camorristi. Significantly, the junta also had the authority to arrest anyone suspected of aiding or "associating" with these figures.

The association laws were controversial because, as liberals in particular argued, they would impinge on political organizing. Their rapid passage and enforcement made a heavy impact. In Naples alone, the junta examined 2,000 cases, 1,285 of which were for camorrismo. The repression incited an aggressive backlash from camorristi, who intimidated judges and threatened Spaventa. It also sparked a letter-writing campaign that would leave evidence of just how wide the reach of these criminal networks had become. Members of the elite wrote letters of support for camorristi seeking lighter sentences or release from house arrest or incarceration. One letter writer was Rocco De Zerbi, an elected deputy of Naples and founder of the newspaper *Il Piccolo Corriere* (The little courier) in support of the well-known camorrista Pasquale Cafiero.[82] Quite extraordinarily, De Zerbi also published during this time an editorial on how he perceived the relationship between elites and the popular classes in Naples. He likened the former—an exclusive clique surrounded by a bourgeoisie composed of civil servants, merchants, and professionals—to an oyster. He wrote that the life of this oyster "has nothing in common with that of the rock to which it is attached," the rock being the masses of *la città bassa* (the lower city) "who have other habits, beliefs, tastes, inflections in their voices: they don't know us and we don't know them."[83]

De Zerbi's spurious declarations were definitively upended when a criminal investigation led by the northern senator and jurist Giuseppe Saredo uncovered a wide network of client–patron relations traversing the public administration of Naples and surrounding provinces. In 1884 the city endured a cholera epidemic that killed nearly seven thousand people, spotlighting the poverty and filth of Naples's popular quarters, which were devoid of a proper sewage system. When Saredo examined irregularities in the accounting of emergency funds for rehabilitating the city's infrastructure and constructing new housing for the poor, he discovered a vast exchange system of tangenti for public service contracts. These clientelistic networks partly intersected with camorristic networks (limited almost entirely to the camorra's "traditional" arenas, such as the custom office, contraband commerce, gambling, and prostitution). However, amid the scandalous convictions of a deputy, the mayor of Naples, and the editor of the newspaper *Il Mattino,* the misleading term *camorra amministrativa* (camorristic administration) emerged in the (northern) discourses denouncing Naples's perceived moral bankruptcy.[84] The term implies that the camorra had climbed the social ladder into the political arena and colonized it. On the contrary, the systemic corruption was a predominantly bourgeois product.

There were several other confluences between camorra networks and those of the upper classes, however. At auctions bourgeois buyers paid camorristi to intimidate competing buyers. Bourgeois gamblers frequented illegal casinos where camorristi collected tangenti on transactions and also acted as usurers. Additionally, camorristi were just beginning to expand their activities from extortion rackets among merchants and criminals into an altogether new market: the electorate.[85]

In the years 1906–12, a "maxitrial" (a trial with numerous defendants) contributed to the camorra's temporary demise. The case concerned the brutal murder of Gennaro Cuocolo and Maria Cutinelli, a married couple who specialized in burglaries and scoped out luxury apartments for a group of camorristi. When Cuocolo and two other men burgled an apartment in an upper-middle-class neighborhood, his accomplices were caught and he made off with the loot. After their release from jail, the affronted accomplices turned to the top camorrista, Ciccio Cappuccio, to resolve the conflict. However, while Cappuccio met with his affiliates to deliberate the matter, the thieves decided, precipitously, to murder the Cuocolos.

The trial was remarkable for several reasons. Unraveling the circumstances of the double murder, prosecutors unveiled the extent to which criminal networks traversed multiple markets and social worlds.[86] The Cuocolo case traced connivances with the camorra to people in a broad range of social positions, from thieves to priests and from pimps to wealthy merchants. Amid this motley assortment there was also the figure of the *guappo elegante,* the elegant thug with belle epoque style who moved into one of the chic quarters and consorted with the middle-high bourgeoisie as their usurer, blackmailer, and seducer.[87] What was most troubling for magistrates, intellectuals, and journalists, as well as the literate segment of the national public that followed the case closely through several competing newspapers, was that the boundaries of the camorra had blurred. The "octopus" camorra, they feared, was undergoing embourgeoisement, and the bourgeoisie was getting caught in its tentacles.[88]

This interpretation of the structure and operations of the camorra is steeped in disavowal. It claims that the bourgeoisie were corrupted by arrogant, scurrilous *arrivés,* and the magistrates deliberated the case from this point of departure. As they discussed the camorra's horrifying mutation, they formulated an analogy by asking each other, "What is this *'café-chantant'* [cabaret]? What does this vulgar belle epoque blend of *canzonette* [pop songs] and sex have to do with the great Neapolitan musical and vocal traditions?"[89]

The trial turned into an intense crackdown on organized crime in Naples. The magistrature's deliberations took on a distinctly decisionist character and enforced the criminal association laws with unprecedented severity, sentencing more than twenty people to prison despite dubious evidence. This was the first time that the court relied, and quite heavily, on the testimony of a pentito. Strikingly, when his testimony was discovered to be an invention, the case was not immediately reopened. Only when the pentito "formally" retracted his statement several years later did the falsely convicted receive remission.[90]

These repressive actions dealt a hard blow to the camorra, but they were not the primary cause of its demise in this period. The camorra was for decades already transforming from an autonomous antagonistic organization to an open-network configuration capable of articulating with the political and economic spheres of elites.[91] Police repression made traditional "open-air" extortion rackets risky, and usury and gambling within the bourgeois quarters became more favorable. Moreover, the extension of suffrage made articulations with electoral networks more enticing. Finally, these articulations enhanced the production of "notables" among the camorra, elite camorristi who commanded their own crime groups with more and more autonomy.[92] To many "real" elites this class transmogrification was the product of modernization. The promiscuous mixing, hybridization, and homogenization of plebes and elites portended an unsettling and uncertain future.[93] This inspired nostalgic figurations of the camorra's "golden age," when the "primitive rebel" or "social bandit" or guappo engaged in nothing more than "honorable" class conflict.[94]

Yesterday, Today, and Tomorrow

When organized crime reemerged at the end of World War II, a new golden age of the camorra was in the making. This time the nostalgic imaginings were almost contemporaneous with the political economic phenomena they folkloricized. When U.S. troops occupied Naples from 1943 to 1948, the city was suffering from extraordinary levels of homelessness, hunger, and illness. Although for four days Neapolitans courageously rebelled against the Germans and thwarted their plan to completely demolish the city before abandoning it, the Neapolitans celebrated the arrival of the American "heroes." The Americans brought great quantities of goods—food, cigarettes, clothes—which locals received as gifts, bought, stole, or paid the Americans to let them steal for sale on the black market. For most of the fascist period, there was no significant contraband trade in Naples, but organized crime did not disappear; instead it blended with less-organized forms of criminality.[95] During the war, black market trade blossomed, and in the postwar years, contraband trade took off.

During the war an enterprising resident of Forcella developed enduring connections with the Americans and amassed significant wealth. Gennaro Merolla, a.k.a. King Kong, a.k.a. 'O rre 'e Forcella (The king of Forcella), was virtually elected by the quartiere to lead the black market trade that so many of its inhabitants depended on. He also became its administrator of justice. With a team of eighteen men, he helped launch the camorra's resurgence. Forcella became the heartland of black market and contraband trade, and Merolla was its venerated leader. At the end of the war, he retired from the scene, and Pio Vittorio Giuliano, a.k.a. 'O patriarca (The patriarch), and his clan assumed full control over

Forcella and much of Neapolitan contraband more generally. In the 1950s and 1960s, contraband helped clans acquire the unprecedented wealth and international connections they would later apply to more diversified and globally articulated criminal activities, including cocaine and heroin trafficking.[96]

Contraband also provided work for tens of thousands of people. Many worked at the port, ferrying arriving shipments from ship to shore or unloading small boats at the dock. On the streets of Forcella, they sold contraband on small lightweight tables and overturned cardboard boxes. The widespread and visible participation of residents and the tolerance of state authority contributed to local public feelings that such work, and the presence of powerful crime clans, was quite ordinary.

Films of the time provide a sense not necessarily of how things were but how they felt. The Neapolitan director Vittorio De Sica's *Yesterday, Today, and Tomorrow* (1963) vividly depicts this sense of the ordinary. In the first of the film's three stories, written by the Neapolitan writer Eduardo De Filippo, Sophia Loren plays Adelina, a poor wife and mother who sells contraband cigarettes in Naples.[97] She holds a regular spot at the end of a long line of several other women who sell cigarettes on the steps of a graduated vicolo. Each woman sits on an empty wooden crate and presides over her wares, arranged on small makeshift wooden tables. When the Guardia di Finanza (the treasury police) come to inspect the vicolo, a resident arrives before them to warn the women, who promptly gather up their wares and disappear. Adelina remains at her spot, implacably composed. She reminds the police that she cannot be imprisoned until after her newborn has reached the age of six months. The police warn her that they will be back when her time is up.

Adelina has been playing with this legal loophole for years. She and her husband, Carmine, played by Marcello Mastroianni, have numerous children, all of whom sleep with the couple in a one-room basso. When Adelina gets pregnant yet again, just in time to go back to work, the news becomes a public celebration throughout the vicoli. We see a succession of brief shots of people relaying the news to one another: "Tene 'a panz'? Tene 'a panz'! [She's got the belly? She's got the belly!]." We see the words speed through everyday encounters between neighbors and vendors on the piazzas, by way of shouts in the neighborhood vicoli, and into the window of an apartment building and out the balcony on

In *Yesterday, Today, and Tomorrow* Sophia Loren's character, Adelina, is based on an actual person. Some contraband cigarette saleswomen sold *sigarette cu 'o sfizio* (cigarettes with a caprice), that is, cigarettes tucked into their bras that customers could pay extra to retrieve.

the other side. Finally, the words take on the form of a chant—"Tene 'a panz', tene 'a panz', tene 'a panz', cià cià cià [cha cha cha]"—that a growing throng of neighborhood children echo while marching through the vicoli and out to the open promenade along the bay. The children, some of them barefoot and draped in shredded clothes much like many folkloric depictions of the lazzari, stop and turn toward the water. They raise their chant to the register of a final exultant cheer: "Tene 'a Panz-Aaa!" A distant fisherman in small rowboat echoes them in the same spirit.

Rather than lazzari, these street urchins are referred to as *scugnizzi*. They are children orphaned by the war or the children of destitute parents. In popular and scholarly depictions, scugnizzi are more helpless than the lazzari, but not less innocent. The Roman film director Roberto Rossellini's *Paisan* (1946) provides a typical picture. In the segment set in Naples, a group of poor and mischievous children encircle an American soldier with playful greetings and gestures of excitement in order to distract him while picking his pockets. One boy takes a liking to him, and the two spend the day together. The child and the soldier do not speak each other's language, but they speak anyway, as if to themselves. At the end of the day, the two sit on a pile of rubble. The soldier, an African American, remembering that the life awaiting him in the United States is an unhappy one, mutters repeatedly, "I don't wanna go home. I don't wanna go home." He lulls himself to sleep, collapsing in a slumber on the rubble. The boy tries to awaken the soldier, warning him that if he continues to sleep he will have to steal his shoes. The boy would not be a scugnizzo if he didn't, and, moreover, the miserable conditions in Naples necessitate that he fulfill this destiny. The scene conveys the boy's poignant desire that the American soldier see his local world "neo-realistically." The boy, rather than reaffirm a coherently moralized world, gestures toward a "new form of reality . . . , dispersive, elliptical, errant or wavering."[98]

Following the chanting scugnizzi in *Yesterday, Today, and Tomorrow*, the film cuts to a shot of the very pregnant Adelina. She walks through the vicoli contentedly and purposefully with a box under her arm. She passes neighbors who greet and congratulate her, and she smiles and waves expressively in return. Everyone already knows the news, but now everyone can see it, too. Adelina reaches her destination, the wooden crate and small table, and decisively sets down her box. She unloads cartons of cigarettes and takes her place among her colleagues, ready to work.

The story expresses public feelings about how the family that makes do is the family in the making. In this scenario, the illicit activity of selling contraband is a necessary practice in reproducing families and communities. It was during this period that women began to play an important role in organized crime. The wives, sisters, and daughters of crime affiliates not only performed the "kin work" of growing and maintaining family networks but also contributed to the education and formation of crime Families, while protecting and even avenging the deaths of their male kin.[99] These are roles they have taken on more frequently in recent decades.

Significantly, this comic tale makes no reference to the broader political economy that generates this illicit work. In this narrative, the camorra is an implicit and benign force, but in other cinematic and literary representations of the era, particularly those from the 1970s and later, the camorra makes a more notable appearance. It is figured as the "old camorra," the "traditional" peacekeeping force of an imagined golden age before everyday life was transformed in the 1970s by the rapacious and violent "new camorra."[100]

La Nuova Camorra

Popular and scholarly histories of organized crime in Naples commonly depict the 1970s as the tipping point when the camorra exceeded even its own excessive art of making do and became a monstrously systematized violent corporation.[101] Accounts of this period attribute much of this transformation to the emergence of crime boss Raffaele Cutolo, a.k.a. 'O professor' (The professor), a.k.a. 'O principe (The prince). While incarcerated in 1970, Cutolo "formally" established a cartel of rural crime clans, the New Organized Camorra (NCO). He invented "old camorra" traditions by way of initiation rituals, statutes, and a book of *Poesie e pensieri* (Poems and thoughts) in which he expounded on his personal ideology of power and regionalism.[102] In the book Cutolo addresses poverty in the language of personal sovereignty: "The day when the people of Campania understand that it is better to eat a slice of bread as a free man than to eat a steak as a slave is the day that Campania will win."[103] Cutolo also directly defines personal sovereignty. It emerges in the art of making do, and it culminates in a sort of self-making combustion: "The value of a life doesn't consist of its length but in the use made of it; often people live a long time without living very much. Consider this, my friends, as long as you are on this earth everything depends on your willpower, not on the number of years you have lived."[104]

The implicit opponent against whom Cutolo urged his readers to use their "willpower" was not only the state authority, perceived as ignoring the most desperate victims of the economic crisis of the Italian south in the 1970s, but also the Sicilian mafia, which had allied with Cutolo's rivals to seize the contraband cigarette industry from the Marseille-based gangs. In the 1960s several mafiosi were sentenced to forced residence in Naples and in the provinces, particularly Caserta. Cutolo struck out at these Sicilian incursions. The conflict was figured in a proliferation of *polizieschi*, or crime drama films, such as Nello Rossatti's *Don't Touch the Children!* (1978) and Lucio Fulci's *Contraband* (1980), in which not only the Marseillaise gangs but also Cutolo and his "new camorra" are vilified as ruthless gangsters who do not respect "traditional" forms of honor-cum-restraint.

Cutolo was successful, in part, because he promised recruits full participation in a system of generalized reciprocity among all of its *compagni* (lit. those who share a condition or activity, or comrades) based on redistributing proceeds and power according to transparent and precise norms. He presented himself as a saintly boss, buying food for the poorer prisoners, taking care of their families on the outside, and promising salaries and protection to anyone who decided to join the NCO.[105] Cutolo seized enormous power with the aid of his seductive paternalism, his invocations of personal sovereignty, and the "icy-eyed" leadership of his sister, Rosetta, who managed many of his affairs outside prison while he remained, for most of his reign, incarcerated. In 1980 he had about seven thousand affiliates.[106]

Cutolo's many enemies, and eventually more than a few of his affiliates, perceived him to be prepotente. He wanted to "organize" all of Campania's malavita under a single charismatic leader: himself. He even imposed a tangente on the cigarette smuggling coordinated by rival bosses. Pentiti have expressed that Cutolo used violence indiscriminately, against not only his enemies but also his own affiliates as "punishment." Moreover, he frequently used violence as a recruitment strategy, which sometimes had the opposite effect, inspiring his victims to join his enemies.[107]

Cutolo's enemies were numerous, and they became a formidable force when they united against him. In 1977 a group of clans, some of them under the protection and influence of the Sicilian mafia, formed a temporary alliance with the express purpose of eliminating Cutolo and his gang. From 1978 to 1983 this temporary alliance, the New Family (NF), engaged the NCO in the "first camorra war." In the final three years of the war there were over seven hundred camorra-related homicides before the NF prevailed.[108]

The NCO and the clans of the NF evolved into complex criminal businesses. Through heroin, cocaine, and contraband cigarette trafficking and racketeering on agricultural products, these groups amassed unprecedented amounts of capital, which they invested in legal businesses such as cement factories and construction companies. They became violent entrepreneurs and offered fast-track criminal careers to hundreds of recruits, and less-illicit employment opportunities to thousands of others.[109] In the late 1970s tens of thousands of Neapolitans continued to live off contraband, but crime clans' widespread investment in bars

In *Il camorrista*, Raffaele Cutolo (played by Ben Gazzara) beckons to new recruits of his NCO and performs an initiation rite in which he and his initiates cut their wrists and clasp each other's forearms so that the wounds bleed into each other. This film and its soundtrack continue to be important referents among organized crime affiliates (Saviano, *Gomorra*). Cutolo is serving a life sentence, but he has enjoyed special treatment, including a private cell and private chef, during many of the years he has been imprisoned. This was not the luxury he aspired to have, evidenced by his purchase of a sixteenth-century castle, formerly owned by the Medici, in the provincial town of Ottaviano. In 2007 his wife gave birth to their daughter after artificial insemination.

and restaurants across the Campania region provided a wider array of jobs as well as the otherwise unimaginable possibility for rapid social advancement.[110]

The evolution of the NCO and the NF were due partly to the collusion of local politicians and public administrators. One important example is the misappropriation of public funds. When an earthquake hit the nearby Irpinia region in 1980, three hundred thousand people were left homeless. Millions of dollars in reconstruction funds were diverted to camorra-managed public works projects and to the private businesses of crime clan affiliates, politicians, and administrators. The relationship between politicians and Neapolitan crime affiliates was strong enough that when the terrorist group the Red Brigades kidnapped Ciro Cirillo, president of the Post-Earthquake Reconstruction and House Committee, Christian Democratic Party leaders promised to compensate Cutolo in exchange for the abductee's release. Cutolo played his part, but the politicians allegedly allied with Cutolo's enemies in destroying the NCO. In a "maxiblitz" the police arrested 854 people and later indicted more than 1,000 on the charge of "belonging to a Mafia-like organization." The NCO was hit hardest.[111]

In 1984 a war between the Bardellino and Nuvoletta clans cleaved the NF in two, effectively dissolving the alliance. Antonio Bardellino of the Caserta area allied with the boss Carmine Alfieri, a.k.a. 'O 'ntufato (The angry one) of the Nola area, and in 1984 they prevailed. The two allies shared power, but it was Alfieri who became the *capo dei capi* (chief of chiefs) of the provincial areas of Naples and parts of Lazio and Calabria. Alfieri eschewed the influence of the Sicilians, establishing a wholly autonomous territorialized Neapolitan organization.[112]

In 1992 one of Alfieri's most trusted men, Pasquale Galasso, was arrested and turned pentito, revealing more about the Campanian crime clans than any other collaborator with the justice system. His testimony secured the arrests of many affiliates and bosses, including Alfieri. Organized crime was far from eliminated, however. Four clans in Naples's northern periferia had meanwhile formed the extraordinarily lucrative Secondigliano Alliance, the Guiliano clan and Mazzarella clan (which would later war with the Secondigliano Alliance) reigned in the city's central quartieri, and the heirs of Bardellino, the Schiavone family led by Francesco Schiavone, a.k.a. Sandokan, grew immensely powerful in the Caserta area and began to exert influence far beyond its territory.[113]

That same year victims of systemic extortion on a national level collaborated with Operation Clean Hands, exposing the unfathomable extent of corruption among the ruling parties.[114] The Tangentopoli trials revealed a vast and virtually mechanized system of clientelistic exchange. Politicians awarded public contracts in exchange for tangenti, which they used to fund party activities. The five top parties established an accord in which contract recipients paid commissions to the parties and to local organized crime groups. Organized crime groups forced contract recipients to hire crime group associates and affiliates to perform the labor. Politicians also administered their own "exchange vote" systems, fulfilling favors for individual voters for their support at election time.[115] These exchanges sustained and entrenched lopsided relations. Clients quickly became dependent on their patrons' assistance in fulfilling their often urgent needs, such as invalidity checks (based on both real and falsified claims) and preferential access to subsidized housing.[116] Clients often felt they had no other option, and many had every reason to fear that these favors could be revoked if they failed to vote for them or if political power changed hands.

Berlusconi's Burlesque

In 1994, amid the wreckage of the nationwide corruption scandals of Tangentopoli and just four months after announcing his candidacy for prime minister, the Milanese media and real estate mogul Silvio Berlusconi won the national elections.[117] His fast-track electoral success, never before seen in Italian politics, is the masterwork of his postideological "antiparty" politics.[118] He named his party Forza Italia (Go Italy), tapping into the potent language of soccer fandom to capture masses of disoriented voters whose parties had been dismantled by Operation Clean Hands.[119]

Berlusconi inaugurated a new aesthetics of power, one that combined exhibitionism with secrecy. As a media mogul, he has the resources to amalgamate rumor and "truth" in a singular spectacle. Below I rely on the work of the journalist Alexander Stille, whose investigative skills both penetrate and participate in Berlusconi's burlesque.

Berlusconi entered politics to maintain and extend his business empire, which he had driven deep into debt. His infamous political patron, Bettino Craxi (prime minister and then president of the Italian Social Party), had legalized national private television broadcasts to accommodate Berlusconi's private networks, which had been operating semi-illegally for a decade. Another close friend of Berlusconi, Fedele Confalonieri, the president of Fininvest (the umbrella company of all Berlusconi's businesses), described this behavior as emblematic: "Some people think that unless something is specifically authorized, it should not be done. Others feel that everything that is not specifically forbidden is allowed. Berlusconi is among the latter."[120] In addition to Craxi and Confalonieri, Berlusconi had the support of Marcello Dell'Utri, who worked in Berlusconi's real estate firm, directed his advertising sales company Publitalia, and then became a senator, and Cesare Previti, Berlusconi's lawyer and director of communications at Fininvest, and later president of Forza Italia!, and finally minister of defense. Dell'Utri and Previti were convicted of serious crimes, both in the service of Berlusconi: Previti bribed a magistrate to reverse a case to favor Berlusconi's acquisition of the book and magazine divisions of Mondadori, Italy's largest publishing house; Dell'Utri served as a regular mediator between Berlusconi and Sicilian mafiosi and was convicted of tax evasion, extortion, and conspiracy with the Sicilian mafia in order to hide hundreds of millions of dollars of Publitalia's earnings.[121] Craxi was convicted of illegal party financing and soliciting bribes. Before fleeing to Tunisia to avoid prosecution, he famously explained that bribery was "the cost of politics."

The origins of Berlusconi's magnificent fortune (he is worth approximately $9 billion and is the richest person in Italy) are unknown. He began with real estate, but the capital required to build his Milano 2, an upper-middle-class planned community next to Milan, and its successor, Milano 3, has been traced to purely nominal proprietors in Switzerland and offshore, which, many have speculated, laundered illegally exported cash acquired by the Sicilian mafia.[122] Berlusconi also managed to acquire from an Italian bank massive loans far exceeding his creditworthiness and at low interest rates with extended repayment plans. Many of these extraordinary benefits can be traced to his membership in the Propaganda 2 secret Masonic lodge, with over eighteen hundred members, including army generals, bank directors, treasury employees, leaders of big business and media companies, magistrates, and members of parliament. Propaganda 2 conspired to infiltrate political parties and key posts in government with the goal of reducing the powers of the magistrature and preventing the Communist Party from taking over the country. While other members were prosecuted for their crimes, Berlusconi was caught for perjury after lying about his involvement. Later that same year, he was granted immunity by a new law.

When Berlusconi decided to run for office, he had only to merge remnants of the dismantled ruling parties "into the managerial structure of his business empire (beginning with his advertising companies) and the universe of small entrepreneurs and professionals, together with intellectuals, journalists, and show business stars."[123] His original intention was to form not a party but a vote-gathering machine. Through a combination of "telecratic" and "telepopulist" campaign strategies (making a "personal" connection with "the people" as the politician with the most television presence), "alliance politics" (forming a coalition with the Northern League and center-south National Alliance parties, which share little more than an interest in power), and political marketing (using public relations, advertising, pollster, and market research professionals of Fininvest and other companies to manage Forza Italia! and grow its membership), he saturated national and regional media circuits and became the longest-serving prime minister since World War II.[124]

For years Berlusconi was a hero in the milieu I frequented in Naples because people perceived him as a fantastically successful self-made entrepreneur. He used his media-savvy and extensive media influence to present himself to Italians as living proof of the ideology of personal economic success. He promised to create jobs, stimulate economic growth, and usher in the "new Italy."[125] He offered "a vision of a new, better world . . . a message of empowerment and liberation for small businesses that had been unable to break through into the big time; he offered a kind of utopian vision of infinite growth and infinite prosperity and well-being."[126]

People have also expressed admiration for him as a supreme *imbroglione* (swindler). Indeed, Berlusconi presents himself as a swaggering, self-aggrandizing leader by regularly flaunting his success. He repeatedly engages in flamboyant public displays of his political and sexual potency. He has compared himself to the pope, Jesus, and Napoléon, whose bed he purchased for his own use. He frequently refers to his sexual prowess, as in 2006, when he announced that he called sex lines to poll "breathy" young women on whether they preferred him or Romano Prodi (for premier).[127] He makes sexist, homophobic, and racist "jokes" with deliberate nonchalance as if to demonstrate the carefree humor of a "natural man who happens to be exceptionally good at being male" and who has the prerogative of luxuriating in his own supremacy.[128] For example, in 2008 when Barack Obama was elected president of the United States, Berlusconi announced that he would help relations between the United States and Russia, but that he did not foresee any problems because both Medvedev and Obama are "young, handsome, and suntanned."[129] In 2010 when the Italian press questioned him about accusations that he had hired the sexual services of an underage sex worker (Karima El Mahroug, a.k.a. Ruby), he announced that it is better to be sex-crazed for women than to be gay.[130] When the Catholic newspaper *Avvenire* questioned his morality, Berlusconi's family-owned newspaper *Il Giornale* ran a front-page story "exposing" the homosexuality of *Avvenire*'s editor.

Berlusconi's sense of personal potency also plays out in concrete political practice. He has successfully evaded convictions for his alleged crimes by a variety of maneuvers, including delaying trials beyond the statute of limitations and passing laws to secure his immunity. In the sphere of public opinion, he has developed an international reputation for bullying all opposition, including the magistrature, the church, and the press. He repeatedly accuses the press of misinforming the public, whom he advises to not read the newspapers. He intimidates editors and journalists, sometimes calling in to live TV talk shows to do so, and he has sued Italian newspapers, *La Repubblica* and *L'Unità*, the authors of books, and the European periodicals *El País, Le Nouvel Observateur,* and the *Economist* for slander. He redesigns public opinion through his capillary media reach, creating his own video truths.[131] He suppresses coverage on his networks of his opponents' criticisms, convinced, as he explained to Dell'Utri, that "if something isn't on television, it doesn't exist."[132] Additionally, he delegated the task of managing public opinion to his employees in news and media entertainment industries. In particular, his two popular TV talk show hosts, Vittorio Sgarbi (a conservative art critic who was convicted of defamation of antimafia magistrates and of filing for fraudulent sick leave while working in the ministry of culture, founded the Party of Beauty, served as mayor of the Sicilian commune of Salemi, and curated a show at the Italian Pavilion at the 2011 Venice Biennale titled "L'arte non è Cosa Nostra" [Art is not the mafia]) and Maurizio Costanzo (former member of the Propaganda 2 lodge who hosted Sgarbi on his show while the latter was on his fraudulent sick leave) repeatedly threw dirt at Berlusconi's opponents and chanted that the tycoon was the victim of an elaborate plot.[133] Indeed, the criminal careers of Berlusconi and his friends are exceedingly Machiavellian, enough so that they appear to be the fantasies of conspiracy theorists.

Although Berlusconi and his friends vociferously declare his (and their own) innocence, he continues to operate with undiminished *prepotenza* (arrogant bullying). In fact, he flouts constitutional law with increasing flamboyance. With literally incredible displays of "manhood"—as a sexual protagonist and as a personal sovereign who "justifies" his actions by dint of his audaciousness—Berlusconi instaurated a perpetual state of emergency to satisfy his insatiable personal interests. He demonstrates that camorristi (or mafiosi) and those who behave like camorristi can become ontologically and epistemologically indistinguishable. Practicing the art of making do means making creative maneuvers within the interstices of dominant state strategies in the pursuit of personal interest. In its hyperbolic form—smania di protagonismo—this art looks like the performances of both crime bosses and political bosses, who are not infrequently complicit. In fact, they are more and more often one and the same.[134]

The Criminal Democratic State

Many histories of revolution and counterrevolution, order and disorder in Naples tend to reify the lazzarone and camorrista figures as emblems of a particular milieu of the plebes: the dangerous classes. Figuring a counterrevolutionary, antimodern class of people such as the lazzari (and bandits, brigands, vagrants, and vagabonds) can, in effect, help generate it. The same is true of camorristi. In fact, it seems that as the lazzarone vanished, the camorrista took his place.[135] Monnier wrote in *La camorra* that after the revolution of 1860, when the Kingdom of Naples was annexed by the northern Kingdom of Piedmont–Sardinia, the Neapolitan popolo made "notable social progress."[136] Liberty had opened their minds, and the lazzarone ceased to exist. The term *lazzarone,* Monnier claimed, even "vanished from the dialect," except when used as an insult. The "man of the popolo" adopted the new name of *popolano.*[137]

The figurations of the lazzarone and the camorrista, some scholars have argued, can also be convenient for the dominant sovereign (the Bourbon regime, the Napoleonic regime, or the liberal Italian state) to expand its authority over its subjects.[138] This would suggest that "the camorra" referred to a diffuse way of operating that became organized in response to the disciplinary project of the modern nation-state. The goal of this project would have been to make the dangerous classes "visible," lodge them in public consciousness, and articulate them "as a problem calling for conscious design, specialised institutions, and their redeployment in the relationship between classes."[139]

However, tracing the origins of the camorra is like tumbling into infinite regress, and doing so risks making "it" vanish altogether.[140] Histories of conflict in the Naples region before and after 1861 suggest that a tangle of institutional and discursive practices—criminalization, politicization, and folkloricization—have helped support a binary imagination that figures distinctively "rogue" authorities in opposition to legitimate authorities. One might imagine, therefore, that organized crime and the state are relatively autonomous yet codetermined and overdetermined.[141] Whatever one imagines, the epistemological and ontological murk of the camorra and the mafia is, in fact, part of their potency. As indeterminate forces, they can lay claim to immeasurable authority. Meanwhile, those who behave enough or too much like camorristi manage to make themselves appear too real to be true.

EMANUELE
CAIANIELLO

TWO

Making Do with Art
Counterfeit Music, Pirate TV, and Crime Clan Weddings

"BETTER A BAD SINGER THAN A GOOD CRIMINAL," thirty-eight-year-old Antonio Fischetti, *nome d'arte* Antoine, told a journalist for the Milan-based Catholic newspaper *Avvenire* in 2005.[1] He was responding to recent publicity on connections between neomelodica music and organized crime, a theme that has surfaced repeatedly in public discourse in Italy since the mid-1990s. His proverbial statement invokes a timeless truth about l'arte di arrangiarsi: many neomelodici may be bad singers, but their "honest" entrepreneurial efforts are truly laudable.

The journalist who interviewed Fischetti notes for readers that there are definite links between the neomelodica scene and organized crime, but suggests that singing neomelodica music is an alternative to crime. She explains that crime clan affiliates play a significant role in the scene as songwriters and managers to whom numerous singers look for support. Like most writing about neomelodica music, her article replays the eruption between the Neapolitan film director Antonio Capuano and pentito camorra boss Luigi Giuliano, a.k.a. 'O rre (The king), a.k.a. Lovigino (because his American lovers would whisper to him "I love Luigino").[2] In 1996 Capuano used without attribution a song of Lovigino's composition in the soundtrack of a film he screened at the Venice Film Festival. Lovigino sent his lawyer to communicate his displeasure to Capuano, and the latter, explaining that he was unaware Lovigino was the author, promptly apologized.[3] Lovigino accepted Capuano's apology, and the dispute was immediately resolved. Despite this and other highly publicized scandals that expose neomelodica music's entanglements with organized crime, the journalist for *Avvenire* writes that the neomelodica music scene prevents young people from "falling into the network of crime clans" when unemployment is high and "criminality seems to be the only exit."[4]

While Fischetti and the journalist both defend the young protagonists on the neomelodica scene from accusations that they have criminal associations, their affirmations do not completely disavow the camorra.

According to Fischetti and the journalist who interviewed him, singing neomelodica music and associating with organized crime affiliates inhabit the same continuum or practical field. Singing neomelodica music is one of the entrepreneurial arts of making do, and affiliating with a crime clan is an act of entrepreneurial excess. Between them are multiple and varying potential relations.

Performing l'arte di arrangiarsi in the neomelodico scene encompasses such practices as operating DIY recording studios and performing at private parties for occasional, modest under-the-table earnings. These entrepreneurial arts can lead to greater things such as local fame and higher earnings, or even an offer to get signed by a "legitimate" music label and perform in the circuits of the dominant national music scenes. Many aspiring singers believe that getting closer to success, legitimate or otherwise, requires that they engage the services of the clandestine entrepreneurs who pirate TV and radio transmissions. Then there are the singers who also align themselves with crime boss–impresarios who underwrite their success with usury, extortion, drug trafficking, and territorial influence.

The so-called formal, informal, and illicit intersect in unpredictable ways. The ways that people are affected by and react to the potentials at this intersection are even more unpredictable. The neomelodica scene is a practical field cohabited by making do and entrepreneurial excess, two regions of potential that are not distinct from one another, but joined at dynamic thresholds.[5] This field is a contact zone where practices and aesthetic forms appear, from "a stable and centered sense of knowledge and reality," as "anomalous and chaotic."[6]

Accordingly, when the topic of neomelodica music has come up in blogs, in mainstream media circuits (newspapers, broadcast news, magazines, books, and cinema), and in the public declarations of politicians, the aim has been to deride or condemn its protagonists. The article from *Avvenire* is a rare and notable exception. Public surges of prurient fascination and revelatory outrage are regularly incited by "news events" such as Lovigino's demand for public recognition as a songwriter. Each surge anticipates the next, so that all things neomelodico—the music, the protagonists, the fans—are always already attached to "the camorra." These surges of public feeling have become a recursively motored autopoetic system that has sealed itself off from the contact zone where it first emerged, save for the investigative feelers it plants in crime scenes in order to sense the next news event. But the contact zone where people make do and others make do excessively is anything but systemlike. Indeterminacy, not foregone conclusions, is its organizing principle. Distinctions often remain elusive, relations implicit, and ethics situational.

In the latter half of the 1990s the neomelodica scene was only just beginning to make itself audible and visible in broader mainstream publics. At that time people were still capable of considering the scene in ways that were not automatically engulfed by ideological critique; musicologists, journalists, and music listeners paid greater critical attention to the music's aesthetic qualities. These critiques are valuable because they reveal fundamental differences between dominant aesthetic ideologies and the aesthetic experiences of participants in the neomelodica music scene, but are even more valuable when complemented with evocations of aesthetic experience itself. Attending to what aesthetics can *do,* rather than foreshortening aesthetic experience by immediately directing one's attention to finished aesthetic forms, brings into relief the ways aesthetic experience resonates across multiple dimensions of everyday life. The aesthetic forms and practices of the neomelodica scene incite bodily sensations and affective states that have an enduring social life. They conjure up broader ethico-political experiences of the contact zone, where l'arte di arrangiarsi continually pushes against its excessive limit, organized crime.

Dialectical Performances

I first heard neomelodica music in the summer of 1998. I went to Naples to study the language for a project on Neapolitan speech and gesture. Neapolitan speakers have an astoundingly wide gestural vocabulary, yet little scholarly work had focused on it. The most significant studies were by Andrea De Jorio in 1832 and Adam Kendon a century and a half later. Gesture, both scholars note, is often perceived to be a mere supplement to verbal speech. Instead, they treat it as a parallel system of signification.[7]

Gesture is integral to melodrama. It expresses the ineffable, the "needs, desires, states, occulted imperatives below the level of consciousness" that are "nonetheless operative within the sphere of human ethical relationships."[8] Gestures carry presence, immediacy, and "the full freight of emotional meaning."[9] Like faces, gestures compose a nonrepresentational language of affect.

I was interested in the relationship between the exceptional gestural vocabulary of Neapolitans and the unspeakable meanings it could render. Unexpectedly, before the summer was over, I developed a parallel project on hyperexpressive contemporary Neapolitan-language songs and the ineffable world of organized crime to which they gesture. In fact, I had begun this project well before I even realized it, during my Neapolitan lessons, which were about much more than language.

My language instructor, Barbara, was an educated, lower-middle-class woman of thirty living with her family in the periphery. She was reserved yet friendly. When we met, she explained that she had decided to take on the course I had requested of the school because she wanted to challenge herself. She wanted to use her ingenuity in developing a course that, as far as she or anyone else knew, had never been taught before.[10] She also wanted to confront her personal inhibitions in speaking in Neapolitan. "I'm going to treat it as if it were any other language, like Italian," she said.

We began our lessons in a methodical manner, but after a few days, Barbara's careful program fell apart. Although assiduously prepared, she was embarrassed to speak to me in Neapolitan. On the one hand, she felt uncomfortable using the language of the "uneducated." On the other, she was sometimes embarrassed to speak in Neapolitan for fear that she could not convincingly "perform Neapolitan." Compared with the way people spoke in the vicoli, it seemed Barbara was not always feeling the language's richly metaphorical expressions. I had heard many things about Neapolitan—its sensorial richness and "concreteness," the many proverbs it keeps alive—but this was not it. When Barbara spoke, the language unraveled into mere sounds and syntax, the stuff comprising "any other language, like Italian."

Of course, these judgments were unfair. Barbara was facing several challenges at once: building a lesson plan with no known instruction model to follow; teaching a language that did not have a stable orthography; crossing class boundaries to embody a sensibility that, through distinction, helped define her own. Moreover, she had a grueling thirty-hour-per-week one-on-one class with an American who observed her with what probably appeared to be schadenfreude. This is because I was intrigued by the struggle I was witnessing. From an anthropological perspective, it was quite thrilling.

Her performances swung between that of the "uneducated Italian" and the stiff *borghese* (bourgeois) slumming it as a *guagliune napulitana* (Neapolitan girl). Similar tensions emerged in my relationships with people in my vicolo. One afternoon I walked into the tobacco shop and, in Neapolitan, asked for a phone card. Amused, the cashier called out to the other customers and her coworkers (all family members) in Neapolitan: "Hey, listen to this—an American who speaks dialect!" Then to me in Italian: "Say again what you said to me."

Feeling I had no choice, I repeated my question to the expectant strangers. With a burst of exclamatory vowels—*Oooh!* and *Uèee!*—they showed how pleased they were with my performance, which to them was more endearing than well executed. I was crushed they didn't take me seriously. I had already noticed that when I spoke in Neapolitan to anyone, the moment I mispronounced a single word, they would immediately switch to Italian to assist me and as if to say, *Come on, let's not play this game anymore.* The people in the tobacco shop were more difficult to bear because they were kind, which to me felt like condescension.

There was one dubious moment of redemption, however, when the cashier's twenty-seven-year-old son asked me if I was learning Neapolitan for scholarly reasons. He too was interested in Neapolitan, and he offered to show me his collection of etymological dictionaries that were issued weekly in *Il Mattino*.[11] We became friends and every day had each other over for coffee and studying. He encouraged me to speak only in Neapolitan with him, happy with my slow progress and generous with his help.

But his patience vanished when we went to the café across the vicolo from his parents' shop. There he knew and chatted with everyone: the baristi, the cashier, the customers—all men. If I was hesitant or too soft-spoken when placing my order, or if he said something to me in Neapolitan and I didn't understand, he showed unrestrained irritation or even laughed. If I was silent while he talked to the other men, he said to me loudly while smiling, "What's wrong? Are you stoned?" His behavior was disorienting. Was he embarrassed to be staging before these other men my "travesty" as Pygmalion's ideal man? Maybe he imagined they thought it was a hopeless pursuit. A man who speaks Italian but, because of his socioeconomic background and his residence in a particular neighborhood, is expected by peers to speak Neapolitan can be perceived as effete. The same is true for a man who is more competent in Italian but attempts to speak in Neapolitan. My case was more like the second scenario; my aspirations to be "a man who speaks Neapolitan" seemed only to emphasize my perceived shortcomings.

There is a lot more to speaking Neapolitan than listening comprehension, grammar, and pronunciation. I had learned some of the gestures, which also helped loosen up my body when I talked with people or walked alone down the vicolo, yet none of it seemed to complete the performance. The aural and bodily space for performance is narrow and fleeting because one is expected to *make* and maintain a clearing. Interactions unfold with a tempo so precipitous that (speech) acts overlap. When things are going right, turn taking is more like turn seizing; conversations are layered and "contrapuntal" as people engage in mutual presencing, being heard and therefore being, despite and because of one another.[12] The key, it often seems, is to have an opinion, take a stand, and get involved. Frequent talk and often at a competitive volume also seem to be critical. In many instances, discussion is less about the con-

Vicoli are living spaces that are both public and private. This woman cleans fish for dinner.

tents than it is about phatic and emphatic expression whose syntax opens up zones of contact.

I gradually learned to participate in this manner by concentrating less on the field of language and more on the field of action. I realized that things happened when I addressed others with the right admixture of self-confidence and aggression. I understood shyness and self-conscious politeness to be wishy-washiness and weakness.

As my performed confidence developed, so did my capacity to speak Neapolitan. This is the case with any experience of language acquisition, but in this instance I acquired a particular being-in-the-world along with the language. For three weeks I underwent a certain "masculinization." I sensed this when my friend made, quite unexpectedly, a dramatic announcement.

"You're different than when I first met you. You now have more of a *faccia tosta* [lit. a hardened face] after spending time here in Naples," he said.

I could intuit what he meant, but I wanted to be sure. "What do you mean?" I asked.

He explained, "When you first got here, anyone could see you weren't from here."

"What could you see?" I asked, still unclear.

"You looked like you were *addurmuto* [asleep]."

"What does that mean?" I asked again, getting more and more frustrated and intrigued at the same time.

"Now you look like you know more about where you are," he answered, this time with an air of finality that meant, *if you need more clarification than that, then maybe you're still* addurmuto *after all*.

My friend was also priming me for the delirious game of question and answer that I would come to know when I returned to Naples some years later for fieldwork, the game where each answer led me farther and farther into the realm of the implicit. Someone who is addurmuto doesn't understand the implicit.

More immediately, he impressed on me the meaning of a thorough performance among men in his milieu. I may not have understood much of what that performance entails or what kind of men I was engaging, but I felt that I had to somehow be and do "as if," without letting on that I was living a conjecture. To have a faccia tosta means to be ready to improvise at any moment, to be *sveglio* (awake).

This sense of performance gradually held greater currency (quite literally) for me. I foiled a fair number of people's attempts to cheat me out of a few thousand lira (a few dollars) here and there. Once it seemed my faccia tosta convinced the ticket agent on the tram who discovered I had not paid the fare to let me go in order to avoid an argument. Each day, I encountered a conflict of some sort in my neighborhood and its surrounds—in the vicoli, at the markets, at the train station, in stores. I noticed people, and not just men, who seemed invested in publicly demonstrating that they sense someone else's effrontery. They seemed eager to demonstrate their ability to compose elaborate insults at a moment's notice. Saving face seemed to require it. The stakes are high, because to hold your own and clear your reputation in a public confrontation concerns valuable social capital. Many people won't risk such a loss because good relations can serve as a support network that provides access to resources and opportunities.

Walking down Spaccanapoli one bustling afternoon, just a few meters ahead of me, a young man in his late twenties with an especially hardened face carelessly bumped into a thin and wrinkled old woman who could have been no younger than eighty. Inexplicably, the man did not stop to apologize but continued on his way—unusual behavior in a neighborhood where most people are extraordinarily aware of anyone in their midst (and often generously attentive to their needs). The jostled woman scowled at the careless man as he walked onward. Shaking her head, she muttered something under her breath and flung a curselike gesture at the back of his head.

In an instant the man turned around and, scar-faced and mean-eyed, he bellowed at the frail-looking woman, "The stale cum of your ancestors—and you who rake shit in the sewers!"

"And the toothless blowjobs your mother gives to the sailors at the port on Sundays!!" the old woman shrieked back with equal ferocity.

The insults continued to fly, their elaborateness increasingly mind-boggling. I could decipher a scattered obscenity here and there, all the more intrigued by what I couldn't understand. A few other people paused to listen, some outraged, some smiling. Many others gave the scene a peripheral glance and continued on matter-of-factly. The two combatants never actually backed down from one another. Perhaps they sensed they had each met their match. Instead of capitulating, each disengaged while volleying a few final epithets and, almost gracefully, moved off in their separate directions.

The next day I announced to Barbara that I wanted to learn Neapolitan insults. No anthropologist going into the field could afford to lose face. Barbara paused a few seconds before responding. She looked a bit uneasy, or was it a trace of irony that flickered across her face? Did she think I was pricking her bourgeois sensibilities?

"Give me a couple of days," she said.

Two days later, I found myself before Pino, a male instructor with a gruff demeanor. "I'm here to give you a lesson in *malaparole* [swear words]," he said bluntly. "Barbara preferred I take over this lesson since I know these things better than her."

We entered the classroom and sat down. Pino pulled out a list of phrases, most of them unfamiliar, and read them to me, one by one. "Do you know the meaning of this?" he asked, pointing to the phrase and waiting for me to repeat it. Slowly and soberly, he explained to me various sexual positions my family members could assume, certain aberrations of male genitalia, the extraordinary possibilities for buttock mutilation, various categorizations of flatulence, the amazing feats of semen, and the many vocations involving feces. I sank deeper and deeper into my chair. Flushed red in embarrassment and sweating, I could feel my *faccia tosta* run like bad makeup. And I thought about that flicker of irony I had seen in Barbara's face. I had my own bourgeois sensibilities to ironize.

Microtonal Expression

While learning that tactical lability and a fortified exterior were essential to competent performances among both men *and* women "in the vicoli," I picked up what seemed to be another important dimension of speaking Neapolitan: emotional expressiveness. In the evenings, I watched television. At first, it was not easy to stay focused, as most of the programs were vapid talk shows or variety shows alternating between spurts of chatter, some choreographed dancing, "quizzes," and a lot of "tits and ass." This last was the signature aesthetic of Berlusconi's Mediaset networks, which heavily influenced the rest of Italian TV programming. Moreover, these programs would not enhance my Neapolitan, as they were all in Italian.

One evening while flipping through channels, I saw a program that immediately stood out from the rest—not for its quality but for its unfinished quality. Similar to cable access broadcasts in the United States, the program had poorly mixed sound and was framed by a camera that was either too stationary or overly mobile. A teenaged male hosted a live show. He stood in front of a mural depicting the bay of Naples (painted in a naïf style) and spoke into a handheld mic to a viewer who had called the flashing number that scrolled across the screen's bottom. The host and his caller were speaking a mix of Neapolitan and Italian pronounced with a Neapolitan cadence.

After a lengthy on-the-air conversation between viewer and singer, the latter asked her what song she wanted him to sing. She told him she wanted to dedicate "Napule mia" (My Naples) to Grandma Cristina of Ponticelli and to send her a kiss. When the singer said good-bye, another caller dedicated "Scugnizza" (Street urchin) to his girlfriend, Lucia. A third dedicated "Innamorato" (In love) to Salvatore, wishing him "a swift return home because unfortunately, *unfortunately* he is not here with us now." I later understood this to mean that Salvatore was imprisoned.

Most people who called the live TV show knew the singer from either previous on-the-air contact or "real" life. They talked and joked with him about recent events and people they knew in common. They praised him, wished him success, and sent him *un bacione grande, grande* (a great, big kiss). Both the callers and the singer appeared as comfortable in this televised environment as they would in their everyday world.

What was most intriguing about the show was the music. The songs were Neapolitan-language melodramatic pop ballads set to simple disco and rock beats. The young man, gesturing widely and expressively, sang the lyrics with a surfeit of vocal embellishments. A note seemed never to be merely a note; many were elaborated with a contracted flourish consisting of three or more "additional" and rapidly executed notes that ascended and descended again. The quick succession of notes emphasized the song's most affecting features, its minor key and semitones, the half steps between tones that intensify, through delay, the arrival of the "whole" tone.[13] These embellishments also sounded as if they included microtones. Microtones mark even smaller intervals than semitones. In Western classical music, the use of microtones was limited until the late nineteenth century. For a Western ear, microtones can be received as ambiguous, imprecise, even irrational; they are felt as pleasantly unsettling, like a descent into melancholy or an upward surge of emotion. When I first heard neomelodica music, I didn't like it—quite the opposite, in fact—but I was affected by it. Their voicy and expansive *American Idol*–style melodies didn't interest me, but the embellishments, microtones, and gestures with which they were executed caught my attention.

The TV program I came across teemed with the banalities of everyday life, an ordinariness that no one made much effort to "present." Whether they were lip-synching songs or fielding phone calls, the young singers paid minimal attention to "presentation style." On one show, the singer stopped mouthing lyrics and gesturing expressively long before the station manager faded out the digital recording of his song. On another, the singer conversed in a range of formal and informal registers with viewers and silent, invisible interlocutors standing somewhere off-camera. Twice, the arm of one such interlocutor reached into the frame to hand the singer a sheet of paper, which the singer unhurriedly accepted. On yet another transmission, the camera swept all around the small studio, sighting two middle-aged men engaged in an animated discussion, a child running up a staircase, and a sleepy woman who slumped in a rumpled armchair beside a stack of VHS copies labeled with the handwritten titles of Hollywood blockbusters.

The programs were at once undistinguished and enigmatic. They ran seamlessly into the talk, gesture, and bursts of song that animated people's homes and the vicoli.[14] Yet it seemed these TV channels acted as filters for the affective–aesthetic tumult outside, selecting from it a specific frequency to narrowcast into the homes of a very local public. The programs were not like the displays of dramatized intimacy performed among strangers on nationally broadcast reality TV shows such as *Big Brother*.[15] Instead, these programs captured an intimately dramatized social world *tout court*.

Access Channels

When Barbara learned I had decided to study this music scene, she laughed and said, "You mean the neomelodici?" She explained that the music was called neomelodica (neomelodic) and that its singers were called neomelodici (neomelodics). "Something to do with their singing style," she said, confessing her ignorance. Then she added, "You'll really learn *napoletano stretto* that way." The term *napoletano stretto* literally means "narrow Neapolitan" and refers to the contemporary urban version of the language spoken by the popular classes. Barbara, who by that point knew of my desire to learn "real" Neapolitan and, as I seemed to imply, the "real" Naples, was enthusiastic about my decision, but once again not without a trace of irony.

She introduced me to her colleague Raffaela, whose cousin, a policeman, knew one of the top neomelodici at the time. In fact, as I quickly learned, everybody seems to know somebody who knows a neomelodico. Anyone who spends any length of time in Naples gets networked. Even during a short stay, a visitor can have interactions of peculiar intensity. More than a few random interactions will double and triple in articulation and density so that you quickly find yourself welcomed into families and cliques. Eventually, like many people in Naples, you come to believe that you can and will inevitably meet anyone you wish. This is a unique mode of attention, a social sense that people share.

Raffaela was Barbara's opposite. She did not have a university education, she was loquacious, and she spoke to her friends and family in Neapolitan. Moreover, she was a neomelodica music fan. When I met with her, she was excited that I would get to meet Franco Ricciardi, whose songs she loved more than anyone's. "And with him you'll definitely get to practice your Neapolitan," she said.

With unexpected immediacy, my meeting with the singer was set for the next day. Raffaela gave me directions to Secondigliano, a densely populated quartiere in the city's northern periphery. The periphery of Naples is not suburban; it is just as citylike as Naples proper. These newer city zones are crowded with modern apartment buildings, many of them built in the 1980s after an earthquake east of the city left about three hundred thousand people homeless. New residential buildings were erected by the hundreds in zones where crime clans managed to divert reconstruction funds after securing building contracts via corrupt political alliances and intimidation.[16] Secondigliano is a grim-looking and densely populated area marred with imposing high-rises built in the 1960s and early 1970s. These buildings are in the area known locally as "167," referencing Law 167 of 1962, which allocated public lands across many quartieri of the periphery for subsidized housing development. Ricciardi grew up in 167 and sings a song about it.[17]

I found the address in Secondigliano Raffaela had given me and rang the bottom buzzer of a two-story building. A man opened the door, invited me in, and offered coffee. He called out for Franco, and a young man in his midthirties appeared and nodded to me. "Franco. A pleasure," he said. The man who had opened the door introduced himself as Gennaro Esposito, Franco's manager. The three of us sat around an office desk, where Franco took the "executive" seat facing us.

Without a moment's hesitation, the manager launched into what I at first thought was just a slightly long introduction to Franco's career, but he continued speaking in Italian for at least fifteen minutes. Franco sat and watched us quietly. Gennaro described Franco as the leading exponent of neomelodica music yet distinct from the neomelodica scene. Franco is an innovator, an artist apart. He's 100 percent Neapolitan, but he aims beyond Naples. He sees the bigger picture.

Gennaro turned to Franco and told him to pull open the desk door and take out a folder. Gennaro took the folder from him and opened it before me. Still speaking in what I suddenly realized was the register of a documentary video narrator, he leafed through a stack of photocopied newspaper articles chronicling Franco's performances in Campania, Calabria, Puglia, and Sicily over the past few years. One performance, the manager noted, took place in Kazakhstan. He pointed to another article, which described Franco's collaboration with a popular left-leaning Neapolitan hip-hop band called 99 Posse. "In this historic concert *le due Napoli* [the two Naples] came together," Gennaro waxed, "because Franco Ricciardi doesn't know what boundaries are; he's the *avanguardia* of the Neapolitan music scene. People from all levels of society listen to Franco Ricciardi—whether they come from the vicoli or Vomero. For this reason he's destined only to get bigger."

When I realized that my conversation with Franco was going to be entirely filtered by Gennaro, I felt that somehow undue pressure had been brought into the situation. Franco said very little. Even when I addressed him directly, it was Gennaro who replied in a mellifluous voice, not Franco. And what little Franco said was in Italian, contrary to Barbara's and Raffaela's promises. What had Raffaela told them about my interest in the music, anyway?

"How do you like that coffee?" Gennaro asked me enthusiastically.

"It's very good, thank you," I answered, stunned by his barrage of words.

"You know what kind that is? It's Kimbo. Do you know what Kimbo is? Kimbo is the smell and taste of Naples. When I open a can of Kimbo I smell this city here—the sun, the sea and Vesuvio. It's the only place where all the elements mix. When I smell Kimbo, I think, '*This* is *Napoli!*' Because in *Napoli* things are born through *contaminazioni* [contaminations]."

Having finished his coffee serenade, Gennaro laid his hands down on the desk as if declaring that he was quite satisfied with these improvisational remarks. Evidently, this was the final curtain. Before I had the chance to observe Franco and figure out what he thought of Gennaro's somewhat incoherent slam-poetry performance, we were all on our feet and getting into a car with Franco's cousin, Lello D'Onofrio, also a "Big"—as they say using the English word—on the scene. During the short drive to the bus stop, the three men spoke animatedly in Neapolitan, Franco included. Their speech sounded and looked as if it toggled between competitive joking, enthusiastic plans, and heated debate. Moreover, they looked and sounded sincere: they interrupted one another, repeated themselves emphatically until they felt acknowledged, and continually changed the volume, pitch, and speed of their speech. I use the words *looked* and *sounded* because I could interpret a surprisingly broad range of emotions but very little of the semantic content. Napoletano stretto, at least the way these men spoke it, sounded and looked overtly expressive, interactive, but it was incomprehensible to me. The language I had been learning in my daily lessons seemed only to vaguely resemble the language these guys were speaking. It was my inability to understand the meaning of their words, however, that brought into such sharp relief the multiple and intense affective registers of their interaction.

The Italian-language soliloquy I had endured in the office was dramatically sentimental, but it was a one-note performance. In contrast, no single intonation gave coherence to the performances of the three men in the car. If there was a unifying frame for their communication, it was the general quality of hyperbole. For me, napoletano stretto was like big emanations of meaningfulness within which, somewhere, there was a narrow passageway of "meaning." In the office, Gennaro's logorrhea, paradoxically motivated by some inexplicable guardedness, had stopped up all channels of communication. When we were in the car with Franco's cousin, the communication flowed in all directions. Either way, I was not granted access. Some years later, while watching a documentary on neomelodica music, I recognized "Gennaro" as one of the talking heads.[18] However, his name, displayed at the bottom of the screen, was different. "Gennaro Esposito," in fact, is the Italian equivalent of "John Doe."

Contamination and Tradition

"Gennaro" used the word *contamination* to describe both his favorite coffee and the meeting and mixing of musical styles in Ricciardi's music. It
also described how Ricciardi's music has the power to unite the many social worlds of Naples, crossing boundaries of quartiere, zone, social milieu, and class. In using the word *contamination,* Gennaro was rehearsing
a celebratory discourse that since at least the 1970s musicologists, music
critics, and musicians invoke to describe how in Neapolitan music tradition and modernity, art music and commercial music, and the local and
the global make contact. The discourse of these contaminations commonly
denotes an alternative to or even willful violation of the perceived purity
and authenticity of musical traditions and traditional regional–cultural
identities.[19]

Cultural contact, exchange, and *syncretism* (another term occasionally invoked) are of course inherent in historical processes. In writing
and talking about Neapolitan music, people seem to emphasize these
phenomena not because they are novel but because they provide a way
to respond to the preoccupations about preserving tradition that have
dominated intellectual, political, and public discourse on Neapolitan culture more broadly.[20]

Ricciardi's manager, however, was not merely rehearsing a counter-
hegemonic discourse; he was performing it full on. He and many other
protagonists on the neomelodica scene, despite my attempts to clarify
things, took me for a journalist. This possibly explains why he masked
his identity (although I don't know what he was hiding), but it certainly
explains why he adopted the self-representational language and performances he imagined were necessary for communicating in media circuits
beyond the intimate affective–aesthetic field of his milieu. Relationships
to the outside have produced for neomelodica music protagonists a sort
of boomeranging double consciousness. As a result, neomelodica music
and the milieu where it is produced and performed have taken on multiple discursive forms, including the language of genre, subculture, class
identity, language identity, and cultural–regional identity. For many journalists, music critics, scholars, and politicians, these discursive forms have
served as shorthand for the cultural–economic world to which they refer.
Moreover, these forms are haunted by "the camorra."[21]

In some ways, these reifications are convenient for participants of the

neomelodica music scene because they partly provide the forms singers and their music need to assume in order to circulate beyond their
local milieu. As unambiguously categorized and standardized aesthetic
objects from a "porous" culture, neomelodiche songs might find a place
in dominant music industry taxonomies. As "underground" musicians,
neomelodici might grab national airtime on popular talk shows and
made-for-TV documentaries. Neomelodici and their songs have indeed
entered these circulations, but their movement has been sporadic and restricted. This is because the neomelodico milieu has yet to achieve the
categorical thrust of a fully commodified *scene* in the dominant music industry. Rather, it is perceived to be the product and expression of a backward and illicit economic culture. Neomelodica music is underground
music, but without the scare quotes of the commodity sign; it is too
faithful to the original sense of the metaphor.

Locally in Naples, people denigrate neomelodici singers because they
believe that they are contaminating Neapolitan musical "patrimony."
For some musicologists, music critics, and many listeners across social
classes, neomelodica music is like an unauthorized revision of classic
Neapolitan song, otherwise known simply as *la canzone napoletana,* or
Neapolitan song. Classic Neapolitan songs are understood to be works
composed between 1880 and 1936 by "recognized" and legitimated poets
and interpreters who emphasize vocal melody and "sentimental intonation."[22] Additionally, they are composed in a "high poetic" register of the
Neapolitan language.[23] Finally, the mandolin dominates these songs.
Classic melodic songs are contrasted with songs whose emphasis is
rhythm or the comical and satirical registers and distinctive vocal styles
that characterize many *canzoni popularesche,* the "folk" songs of the region's rural and urban oral cultures.[24]

Neomelodica music fuses styles and features associated with these
historic Neapolitan musics and contemporary Anglo-American and Latin
American popular musics: vocals and melodies that are loosely reminiscent of both classic song and folk music; electronic keyboards, synthesizers, and guitars; decades-old synthesized rock and disco beats; and lyrics
sung in a mix of awkward Italian, Italianized Neapolitan, and contemporary everyday registers of the Neapolitan language as it is spoken among
people of the popular classes. Neomelodiche songs are in some senses
the contemporary update of classic Neapolitan song. In a 1997 essay, the
music critic Peppe Aiello coined the term *neomelodico* or *neomelodic,* which

Federico Vacalebre, a journalist for *Il Mattino,* subsequently made famous with his 1999 book, *In the Volcano: Neomelodic Stories and Other Stories from the Local Village.* Aiello described the neomelodico repertoire as songs of "liberation" from dominant sexual mores and other "customs."[25] He argued that, unlike classic songs, neomelodiche songs are candid depictions of what some Neapolitans might consider unseemly themes: sexual desire, betrayal, family fissures, crime, and imprisonment. He emphasized that despite these expressions of contemporary realism, neomelodiche songs refer to and sustain traditional values, namely, the unquestioned significance of family.

Perceptions of neomelodica music among nonparticipants developed within ideological tensions about contamination. In Naples, critics take neomelodica music for an unauthorized contamination that through unregulated circulations has inspired fears that it might surpass classic Neapolitan song's century-old transnational renown to become the new

A baptism celebration in a provincial town outside Naples. The family of the boy at far right has egged him on to stand with them next to the singer during a song about an estranged father who, on the urging of his son, reunites with his mother.

transnational Neapolitan music. Critics beyond Naples perceive neomelodiche songs to be the products of the promiscuous and untutored coupling
of traditional Neapolitan song and modern global pop. Its traditional features vaguely cite Neapolitan regional culture, particularly those reminiscent of the *vocalise* used by rural peasants and urban street vendors
to communicate at a distance, now circulating in regional and national
media circuits. Its modern features are inspired by parochial fantasies of
the modern and the global. Composers and singers earnestly privilege
passé synthetic rock and dance beats and riffs as if randomly selecting
them (i.e., not as ironic citation) from the remainders that have reached
them in the periphery. Combined, the "traditional" and "modern" sounds
produce dissonance, making the former into displaced sonotopes and the
latter into sonic anachronisms.

The "traditional" and the "modern" sounds of neomelodica music
render each other "schizophonic."[26] Rather than citations of the authentic
or the real, the traditional sounds are like accidental residues or remainders, as if they were modernity's leakage. Recontextualized in modern
pop song rhythms and motifs, these residues at once invoke melismatic,
microtonal arabesque songs of Turkey and the voicy, ostentatious ballads
of *American Idol*. Neomelodica music blends a modern (but not "progressive") "Orient" and an outdated (but not "vintage") "West," producing a
peculiar dissonance.

To critics, neomelodica music's traditional elements—the singing style
and lyrical sentiments—are like excessively expressive anachronisms.
Its modern elements—the instrumentation, arrangements, and lyrical
content—are bad copies of Italian, Anglo-American, and Latin American
pop. However, it is not the mutual contamination of tradition and modernity that troubles critics; rather, it is their incomplete fusion. They do not
congeal into the smooth, sealed sonic object that moves in dominant music
industry circuits. In neomelodica music, tradition and modernity are leaky,
preventing its "incorporation" as either "world music" (deterritorialized
musica popolare, or folk music) or "global beat" (global pop music).[27]

La Canzone Classica

The reasons that critics perceive neomelodica music as leakage are best
understood in the broader context of Neapolitan music. Classic Neapolitan
song emerged as a distinct category around the year 1880, when it be-

came the center of large-scale commercial interests. Naples is home to one of the earliest music industries with transnational articulations, and the canzone classica was at its center. This industry experienced its most significant growth between the end of the nineteenth century and the beginning of the twentieth century in the context of the Festival of Piedigrotta, originally a procession to the sanctuary of the Virgin Mary. By 1892 the festival was associated primarily with the great number of new Neapolitan-language songs that poets, most of them bourgeois, composed for the occasion with the express goal of promoting songs.[28] These songwriters—Salvatore Di Giacomo, Ernesto Murolo, Libero Bovio, E. A. Mario (of humble origins), and others—became the authors of classic Neapolitan song.

As one of the most notable festivals celebrated in one of Europe's largest cities, Piedigrotta was anticipated months in advance and attended by thousands of people of all social strata, including tourists from other regions of Italy and beyond. For many Europeans, the festival became synonymous with the competitive composition, staging, performance, distribution, and sale of Neapolitan popular vocal music. Neapolitan song was located at the center of multiple, mutually articulating cultural and business activities encompassing nearly a hundred local music-publishing houses and several cafés and theaters that hosted promotional concerts. Advertising practices included jingles, posters, print advertisements, and playbill cover art that drew inspiration and expertise from the thriving Neapolitan film industry. Moreover, promotion and advertising were fused in the numerous newspaper and journal articles that provided commentary and tracked intellectual debates about current song productions.[29]

Distribution practices included sheet music collections sold in shops in the city's central shopping district, bulk printing and street dissemination of low-cost or free *copielle* (sheet music in the form of flyers), and a surfeit of *posteggiatori,* or roaming musicians who diffused the music among the poorer classes. In the nineteenth century, posteggiatori played popular songs with the guitar, mandolin, violin, and flugelhorn for workaday Neapolitans in the streets, at cafés, and in taverns while holding out a plate to collect money. Additionally, middle-class business owners hired them to play in the city's cafés and restaurants and at beach establishments. They also played for tourists in the city's hotels, in cinemas to provide the soundtrack for silent films on opening night, and at private wedding and baptism parties. These performers served as musical mediators between the classes. On the one hand, they were the musicians with whom bourgeois artists had contact when they looked to the popolo for inspiration. On the other, for the first Neapolitan recording studios, posteggiatori were vehicles for getting songs into circulation in potential consumer markets among the popular classes.[30]

Classic Neapolitan songs circulated through preexisting sound networks in the local topography of listening in the narrow vicoli. There posteggiatori played and residents likely heard each other sing the latest songs, learning them from one another. Moreover, the Neapolitan music industry was integrated with Piedigrotta, which annually animated the city's public cultural life, drawing people to Naples and activating transnational communications.[31] Piedigrotta was a uniquely Neapolitan system for marketing and distributing Neapolitan song. Texts, recordings, and live performances circulated still more widely when non-Neapolitan music-publishing houses, such as the Milanese Casa Ricordi and the Leipziger Polyphon Musikwerke, expanded operations into Naples. Neapolitan song's worldwide diffusion is also intertwined with the great Italian migrations of the late nineteenth and early twentieth centuries.[32] Neapolitan emigrants, particularly in New York City, continued to produce, perform, and consume Neapolitan music, attracting listeners and collaborators of other immigrant, ethnic, and racial backgrounds as well as local mainstream publics.[33]

Despite their commercial success, these songs were canonized as Neapolitan cultural "patrimony."[34] At a time in Italy when the late emergence of operetta was igniting heated discussions about easy entertainment and declining quality of cultural production, Neapolitan song overcame the perceived contradictions between, on the one hand, popular diffusion and commercial success and, on the other, aesthetic value and regional and national cultural capital that dominated cultural criticism at the time.[35] At a formative moment in increasingly rapid global cultural flows, when the entertainment industries of Europe and the United States were just beginning to form, Naples was already home to a considerably developed transnational Neapolitan culture industry.[36]

La Musica Neomelodica

The importance of Piedigrotta to Neapolitan music began waning in the 1950s, with the growing popularity of television. At the beginning of the decade when Rai began broadcasting the newly established Festival of Sanremo and Festival of Naples, artists concentrated their creative efforts on producing popular Neapolitan songs to please national non-Neapolitan jury members and national media audiences.[37] According to many accounts, this market shift triggered a drop in quality for Neapolitan song.[38] Sergio Bruni, the singer whom the playwright Eduardo De Filippo famously called "the voice of Naples," stated that both festivals tired audiences with the same sounds year after year, shortening the life of Neapolitan song.[39]

Sanremo helped standardize a type of melodic *musica leggera* (pop music) quite like the ballads of *American Idol* in the United States and *The X Factor* in Britain. The Festival of Naples followed a similar course. It overshadowed Piedigrotta and became the dominant venue for Neapolitan artists to publicize their work. However, because the Festival of Naples limited the number of song entries, musicians produced fewer works, focusing all their efforts on attaining that "singular success." More and more Neapolitan artists adopted the musical clichés they imagined the "Italian" public wanted to hear when listening to Neapolitans. As a result, Neapolitan songs became, both lyrically and stylistically, increasingly detached from Neapolitan aesthetic sensibilities.[40]

In 1971 the Festival of Naples was discontinued amid alleged corruption. While Bruni celebrated its end by opening a bottle of champagne with his family, others experienced a loss.[41] The festival had been important particularly for Naples's popular classes because it gave airtime to quotidian experiences in the vernaculars with which they were most familiar. In contrast to the "high poetic" bourgeois language that dominated classic Neapolitan song lyrics, some musicians began composing songs in everyday registers of the Neapolitan language as it is spoken among the popular classes. These songs, moreover, focused on themes that engaged their sensibilities. Two singers in particular marked this shift for the younger generations of listeners. The first was Patrizio (Patrizio Esposito), still a child when he acquired fame with his song, "Papà . . . è Natale" (Daddy . . . it's Christmas), which recounts a boy's longing for his imprisoned father. Patrizio performed songs that addressed the trials of poverty, illness, and tragic decisions to commit crimes such as muggings to get by in times of difficulty. He later performed disco-influenced and "erotic-sentimental" songs, crossing boundaries of prudence that had been the norm in Neapolitan song, making him the number-one idol and sex symbol of teenaged girls.[42] His fans were fanatical; people recall that at his concerts women in the audience screamed with excitement while throwing their bras on the stage.

Patrizio's booming career ended suddenly in 1984 when he was found dead at the age of twenty-six from a heroin overdose. His untimely death (and rumors that rivals had tampered with his drugs to get rid of him), further heightened his popularity. Today framed photographs of Patrizio hang in memoriam on the walls of many recording studios, local television stations, and homes of people on the neomelodica scene.

The singer who in a sense took Patrizio's place in the 1980s was Nino D'Angelo. Like Patrizio, D'Angelo came from a poor neighborhood in Naples's periphery, Casoria. D'Angelo's class identity is intimately linked to the linguistic and aesthetic vernacular that marked his songs. In his autobiographical writing he describes an episode from his early career that emphasizes just how distinctive this identity was and still is. D'Angelo writes that he and his manager used to frequent Galleria Umberto I, the nineteenth-century art nouveau arcade that spreads its four glass-vaulted wings before the San Carlo opera house. La Galleria, as it is commonly called, was for decades the preeminent place of encounter for singers and impresari who were looking, respectively, to perform at or find performers for wedding and baptism celebrations. D'Angelo recounts the time he saw Bruni. The revered performer was lamenting to another man about the declining caliber of Neapolitan singers on the scene.

"It's one thing to feel like you're an artist and another to be one," Bruni said to his interlocutor.

D'Angelo, thinking he had stumbled on his lucky break, moved closer to Bruni and in his uncertain Italian said, "Maestro, I also would want [sic] to become an artist."

Bruni answered in Neapolitan, "First thing, learn how to speak."[43]

D'Angelo depicts his early musical career not as a class-based conflict, as the language ideology embedded in his exchange with Bruni would suggest, but as a struggle against poverty and crime. This particularly comes through in his account of his true lucky break. D'Angelo writes that as a teenager, in 1976, he recorded a song called "'A storia mia ('O scippo)" (My story [A purse snatching]). He brought the song to one of the regional radio stations and told the manager that he was raising money to pay a lawyer to represent his brother, who had been nabbed for purse snatching. Moved by D'Angelo's story, the station manager let him repeat it to the radio audience before playing them his song. D'Angelo thus repeated what was essentially his melodramatic musical theater performance at record stores throughout Naples, selling fifty thousand copies. Soon enough, a record producer approached him and said, "Look, if you sold the public fifty thousand copies with a mere purse snatching, then we'll give them an armed robbery."[44] D'Angelo writes that from there his career took off. He eventually sang more erotic-sentimental songs and, like Patrizio, reached a young public with his disco-influenced arrangements and pop idol persona.

Nino D'Angelo, "'A storia mia ('O Scippo)." In 1997 D'Angelo's music became more eclectic and experimental in style, incorporating what people in Italy have described as "ethnic" and "world." He mixes sounds and rhythms with hints of reggae and pronounced flourishes of rai, and includes the chantlike vocals of backup singers. The lyrics of his songs continue to be in Neapolitan.

Meanwhile, the generation of singers who already had large follow-ings in the 1960s—Mario Merola, Pino Mauro, Mario Da Vinci, Mario Trevi, and others—became even more popular in the 1970s. For some of them, the reason was their interpretations of *canzoni 'e mala* (songs of the underworld) and *canzoni-sceneggiate,* or songs staged for the theater and cinema.[45] The former date back to the late nineteenth century and the latter to the early twentieth century. Both narrate tales about crimes of passion and honor in which men claim personal sovereignty and pro-tect it in the face of incursions by other men, including agents of gov-ernment authority and camorristi. Sometimes the protagonists of these songs, rather than ordinary men of the vicoli, are themselves camor-risti. Mauro, Merola, and others revived these songs in the late 1960s and throughout the 1970s with orchestral arrangements influenced by the music of the spaghetti westerns, part of the "Italian B's" recently recov-ered by Quentin Tarantino and the Prada Foundation.[46]

The sceneggiata concerns the struggle between good and evil and the moral ambiguities of justice. Since its revival, it has ignited criti-cisms in Naples and throughout Italy that it endorses the "law of the vicolo" over that of the state. It is defined in Italian dictionaries as the Neapolitan melodrama *per eccellenza.* In fact, in the national public imagination, the genre often typifies "Neapolitan culture." This per-ception is recorded in Italian dictionaries as the second definition of the sceneggiata: "an exaggerated and often insincere display of sentiments and emotions," or "a fictitious situation created in order to confuse or affect."[47] Criticisms of the sceneggiata (and by extension canzoni 'e mala) as a cultural–aesthetic artifact are entwined with perceptions of the "B economy" where it is produced and consumed and the DIY justice system that is believed to dominate it.

Although Patrizio and D'Angelo performed songs that treated crimi-nal themes, much of their repertoire diverged from the types of songs as-sociated with such singers as Mauro and Merola, and others in the 1980s, such as Carmelo Zappulla.[48] D'Angelo is well-known throughout Italy and its diasporas for his own sceneggiata performances, some of them enacted alongside Merola. However, D'Angelo often played the role of a lovelorn or misguided young man who makes "mistakes" (such as purse snatching) but in the end repairs his ways. Or he played the role of a poor, uneducated young man who, when he gains celebrity and wealth, "wan-ders off" to the world of the elite. In these narratives of moral lapses, in the end his character returns to his humble origins, remembering what is truly important to him.

Indeed, D'Angelo describes his early real-life career like a melo-drama. He recalls the many hardships he faced: when he was very young his father emigrated to find work; when D'Angelo was old enough to look for work for himself, he endured long periods of unemployment; when he first attempted to seriously pursue singing, an impresario de-frauded him of his entire savings; when he at last started to become note-worthy, camorristi approached him, first with alluring offers of support and then with pressure. He describes his decision to quit singing in order to foreclose any further contact with the camorra. Although he doesn't explain why and how, D'Angelo eventually resumed singing and became a national success. He presents the beginning of his career as an epic nar-rative about the art of making do. He became an unequivocal local hero because he obtained success through honest pursuits that entailed over-coming familiar obstacles and resisting familiar temptations. Moreover, because he continues to sing in the vernacular aesthetics of the world in which he has lived, D'Angelo can call himself "a singer of Naples," rather than "a singer from Naples."[49]

When contemporary neomelodici name D'Angelo as their primary influence, they refer to both his music and the moral–political–economic dimension of his career. They praise his voice because it "comes from the heart," narrating life in the vicoli from which he exited yet contin-ues to honor. The sceneggiata performance that made "'O scippo" a suc-cess was at once affective, aesthetic, and economic—the perfect model for success in this moral political economy. He attuned himself to an affective–aesthetic community where interests and affects can be ex-pressed in a single voice through the aesthetic forms offered by the melo-dramatic mode. D'Angelo made art and the art of making do one and the same, realizing that in this affective–aesthetic atmosphere they were already intertwined.

The New Neomelodica

Patrizio and D'Angelo were fathered, in a sense, by the veteran maestri Mauro and Merola. This was the case with several singers across genera-tions.[50] The older generation was well positioned within circuits of com-posers, musicians, filmmakers, and studios, and they opened doors for younger singers and helped produce them. This happened not only in Campania but also in Puglia and Sicily.

In the 1990s these interconnected music scenes changed as the result of several factors. Although regional television stations broadcasted Neapolitan-language music videos at least since the early 1980s, it was a decade later that Campania's local private and pirated television stations hosted musical broadcasts with regularity.[51] Additionally, music making, recording, and broadcasting technologies became more accessible, and the hegemony of established production circuits gradually gave way to capillary DIY practices. The electronic keyboard replaced orchestras and ensembles, recording studios opened by the dozen, and growing numbers of enthusiastic young men (and some women) took up sound recording, videomaking, songwriting, composing, and singing. Private radio and TV stations became saturated with new Neapolitan-language pop music. Most of this music continued the erotic-sentimental vein of D'Angelo, while some of it recaptured the spirit of the canzone 'e mala.

On TV programs neomelodici lip-synched songs for viewers who called in dedications. Between performances, callers, many of them friends and relatives, chatted with singers. On many shows, calls were pay-per-minute, but by the late 1990s the surcharge scheme fell into disuse. The singers' primary objective was, and still is, self-promotion as live performers at private parties. Their cell phone numbers—singers' phones contained multiple slots for separate SIM cards with different numbers— scrolled across the screen alongside the message *x contatti* (for contact).[52]

Private television diffused neomelodica music across larger publics and helped make many singers into local celebrities and expanded the scene. Hundreds of singers from families with limited resources recorded songs and competed for gigs. More and more songwriters and composers teamed up and opened small makeshift music studios in their homes or in rented bassi and garages, competing for commissions. Private and pirate television stations multiplied, and a handful of impresari and videographers competitively promoted singers. Moreover, the fan base of neomelodica music grew exponentially. The numbers can only be estimated because audiocassette and CD sales, performance attendance, and TV viewership have been, on the whole, undocumented.[53]

In 1998 people involved in the neomelodica scene recited for me variations of the same clichéd story: *Once upon a time a kid asked his Dad for a Vespa, now he asks if he can record a CD*; *There are more recording studios in*

Naples than there are pizzerias; In Naples singers sprout up like mushrooms; There are more singers than there are unemployed people. These proverblike incantations fold the practices of music making into the broader tactics of l'arte di arrangiarsi. By describing the scene in this way, participants acknowledge its status as an ensemble of entrepreneurial opportunities. At the same time, they criticize what they see as populist artistry and shoddy professionalism. After several months of fieldwork, I began hearing another proverblike declaration, which further clarified this orientation: *To accomplish anything in Naples, you have to leave Naples.* The neomelodico milieu both enables and entraps artist–entrepreneurs.

From the late 1990s to the early 2000s, a few "new neomelodici," in fact, left Naples to sing in Italian on the national scene. These singers— Gigi Finizio, Gigi D'Alessio, and Gianni Fiorellino—all performed at Sanremo.[54] D'Alessio's successes are the most noteworthy. After his widely attended 1996 concert at Naples's San Paolo stadium, he was signed by the Milan-based BMG Ricordi. Since then, he has frequently appeared on popular national television broadcasts, sat for interviews with top magazines and newspapers, and performed in prestigious venues throughout the country and abroad, including New York City's Radio City Music Hall. D'Alessio has not been the only singer to attract the attention of dominant culture industry elite, but for years he was the only neomelodico singer, after D'Angelo, to sustain elite interest and enfranchise himself as a major international pop music artist.[55]

Many neomelodiche songs have been produced and circulated in ways ordinarily associated with the songs of an oral tradition. Unlike the "learned" composers of the canzone classica, neomelodici artists often did not publish their lyrics or scores. In 2004 many neomelodici songwriters, composers, and singers had not registered their works with the national copyright mediating agency Siae (Society of Italian Artists and Publishers). This agency provides free voluntary association, but artists of the neomelodica scene typically do not join. As a result, when in 2004 the Naples offices of Rai began collecting songs for the launch of its Sound Archive of Neapolitan Song, archivists had a hard time documenting authorship for the works of neomelodici. They discovered multiple recorded versions of a single song with the same lyrics but set to different arrangements and interpreted by different singers. In other instances, they found the same song included on different CD song collections, each time attributed to different authors.[56]

Neomelodica music is an alternative form of culture industry powered by DIY production, reproduction, and circulation techniques and technologies that leave distinctive marks on the final product. This happens in several ways. For example, producers may not have mastered the tools of cultural production and distribution, or they may use tools that are retrograde relative to dominant industry standards.[57] Distributors may rely on circuits such as word-of-mouth marketing or clandestine operations such as TV and radio piracy. Since about 2008, protagonists on the scene have used MySpace, Facebook, and YouTube, where multiple versions of the same product appear, reproduced and sometimes refashioned by fans. Cultural products that emerge and circulate in these contexts have, in comparison with dominant culture industry products, glitches in form and transmission that lend them an unfinished quality. As unsealed and malleable forms, alternative culture industry products are subordinated to the relations of the artist with his or her intimate public, rather than the inverse.[58] A neomelodica song is an atypical commodity, one that doesn't entirely possess the fetish character famously described by Karl Marx. Moreover, the audible traces of neomelodica music's bricolage bar its commodification as "world music."

This is because neomelodica music producers make few attempts to filter out the leakage of its production and reproduction. The leakage would likely not be grating to critics if it connoted a conscious aesthetic—ironic, experimental, even subversive. But instead it indexes the modalities and sensibilities of an alternative economy and, more importantly, a competitive alternative culture industry. Because this alternative economic culture is commonly equated with "the camorra," neomelodica music is heard as the sounds of a perverse, contaminated modernity.

The couplings and contradictions that generate neomelodica music merit a far more detailed analysis than space permits. Up until now, I have been tracing these dynamics on the level of aesthetic ideology, but this is only part of the story. There is much more to learn by following the aesthetic experiences of the scene's protagonists and participants.

Ornamentalism

Neomelodica music's use of microtonal embellishments recall the run-of-the-mill pop music of Sanremo. This is also true of the arrangements that combine minor chords and modulations with the ready-made beats found on keyboard synthesizers or in music production computer software such as Cubase. Minor chords and modulations complement or reinforce the vocal embellishments to heighten the music's affective charge. But beyond this support function, quite often the arrangements do little for a typical neomelodica song. The instrumentation, usually synthetically produced or digitally reproduced (but sometimes recorded live), seldom diverges from a standard configuration of piano, electric guitar, and snare and bass drums, and, less often, violins. Songs follow the ordinary pop song structure of stanza-refrain-stanza-refrain-bridge-refrain, and the arrangements are generally entirely subordinated to the lyrical melody. Songs frequently have brief and/or sparing introductions; when the introduction is longer it is often in order to give space to a recitative.

The arrangements play a secondary role in the song's overall effect. This is because arrangement composers know that singers and songwriters, like neomelodica music fans, are most invested in the vocal melody and the lyrics. When composers played their songs for me on the keyboard or played back recordings, they often pointed, quite literally, to peaks in the vocals. Looking at me intently, they trace the voice with an index finger in an upward spiral, moving in tight circles at the embellishments and raising the finger above the head and suspending it there at longer ornamental expressions. Neomelodica music protagonists call these embellishments *girate* (turns). In "standard" musical terms they are called melismas, and the briefer and more subtle musical ornaments can be differentiated into four types: acciacature, unaccented appoggiature, inverted mordents, and gruppetti.

One afternoon in a music studio I frequented in the city's periphery, three of the singers who drop in and out to chat and work engaged in a spontaneous vocal competition for my benefit. The composer played the keyboards while each took his turn beside him interpreting a song with the maximum display of "vocal baroque." When one singer was on, the other two crowded around him and followed his vocal moves with leaning bodies and craning necks, attuning themselves to him in a kind of anticipatory listening. Sometimes they joined him as he executed his greatest ornamental peaks at the beginning of the second ritornello, where he dramatically attacked the opening note, extended it with a sostenuto lasting several seconds, and then ascended and precipitated in a vertiginous melisma before gliding into the next lyrical syllables, some of which were adorned with appoggiature and inverted mordents. The competition was concentrated in moments like these, where the performing singer posed an implicit challenge to the other two by topping them with his vocal flamboyance and by losing them as they tried to follow him around unexpected vocal turns.

On another occasion I watched a young neomelodico singer perform nineteenth-century Neapolitan songs at a public performance in the *piazzetta* (little piazza) outside Galleria Umberto I with a small troupe of players dressed in costumes of late-eighteenth-century plebes. When the young singer soloed, audience members gasped, shouted, and applauded as he extended these embellishments in a manner similar to the style *à fronn' 'e limone* (like a leafy lemon frond), part of a family of unaccompanied vocal forms called *canto à distesa* (distended song).[59] These melismatic embellishments are composed of several tones, including microtones, sung melodically, with nasalization, and with varying duration at a single syllable.

Neomelodici typically perform both new and classic Neapolitan songs. Many neomelodica music protagonists, like many Neapolitans of all social classes, are intimately familiar with and enjoy a vast repertoire of songs from the Campania region from the nineteenth and early twentieth centuries. However, knowledge of the fine differences in regional vocal techniques and their social and cultural significances is not common. Musicologists and folklorists have described this repertoire according to distinctions of vocal style on the level of subgenre (e.g., *canzone ricamata,* or "embroidered song") and even according to types of canto à distesa.

By showcasing vocal ornamentalism, neomelodica music references musical forms that were pervasive in the Campania region for centuries.[60] The reference is at best elliptical because the ornaments in neomelodica music vocals share only some general resemblances to earlier techniques. They do not follow from a precise aesthetic intentionality, let alone a studied pattern. I have asked over one hundred songwriters, composers, recording studio managers, impresarios, and singers why these marked stylistics are so pervasive in neomelodiche songs, which at the time of writing number in the thousands, and the responses have all fallen into one of two complementary conceptions of musical practice. The first is that neomelodico ornamental style comes from a shared spontaneous aesthetic disposition: *It's how we sing; It's in our hearts to sing like this.* The second is that singers perform in the affective register that they believe can most effectively reach their publics: *It's what people expect when they're celebrating a wedding; That's how you move your audience;*

It's what people want to hear; When you're with family at a nice restaurant by the sea and you hear these moments in the music, you feel goose bumps.

Neomelodico ornamentalism does not signify a reified set of stylistic conventions called "tradition." Rather, ornamentalism generates a shared aesthetic and affective time and space and performs a historically grounded sense of locality. For neomelodica music participants, it is an element of style that incites affective–aesthetic contact. For participants, it is naturalized as part of what is simply true and beautifully affecting: it is "iconicity of style."[61] Rather than reference a style, ornamentalism enacts style.

Critics of neomelodica music share this interpretation of neomelodico ornamentalism, but only in part. They agree that ornamentalism is not stylistic citation, but only because they perceive ornamentalism as an aesthetic and affective surplus that overwhelms its participants.[62] Just as early romantic folklorists perceived "popular aesthetics" to be the spontaneous emanations of a naturally creative and undifferentiated collectivity, critics perceive neomelodico ornamentalism to be a style and lifestyle that neomelodica music scene participants can neither articulate nor objectify through conscious self-reflection, let alone weed out.[63] They suggest that ornamentalism is a sonic anachronism linked to an intractable premodern sensibility nurtured by persistent and pernicious localism (and by extension the sticky webs of familism, clientelism, and the camorra). Rather than hear neomelodiche songs as slapdash combinations of historically familiar regional vocal techniques with modern pop aesthetics, critics hear an intemperate or perverted modernization.

Another possible interpretation, and one that does not seem to emerge in aesthetic critiques, is that neomelodico ornamentalism enacts tactical knowledge of affective registers. If elaborate vocal turns set to contemporary mainstream beats and musical motifs are *what people want to hear* because they want to be moved, then protagonists have synchronized their performances with these desired effects. Ornamentalism is an expedient tactic that neomelodici tap to the max.

Performance Style

Performers demonstrate, through these extravagant flourishes, their vocal prowess (or at least their "heartfelt" investment in demonstrating their prowess). Audiences often expect hyperperformativity as an indicator of the singer's "star status," which heightens the event's importance and affective charge. Stars in this milieu, whether they are popular only in their quartiere or throughout Campania and beyond (or in independent but interconnected neomelodiche scenes in Puglia and Sicily), always remain accessible to their publics. Audience members regularly participate in the singer's performance, sometimes sharing the mic and sometimes dancing with the singer. Audience members will even put an arm around the singer and pose for pictures while a song is in progress. By performing songs and performing stardom in this manner, singers demonstrate their willingness to make affective contact.

In an autobiographical account, D'Angelo writes that his relatives complained that Bruni, when he performed in piazza festivals in their quartiere, argued with audiences for applauding him too much because he said he would rather be heard. "Who does he think he is?" D'Angelo's mother exclaimed, "the Eternal Father? We invited him to our festival and he treats us like this?"[64]

The dominant performance style of neomelodica music is also found in singers' intimate marketing and distribution practices on live private TV. The singers, the callers, and those who watch and listen off-camera at the studio and at home make up circuits of articulate phatic communication. Viewers call in requests for song dedications to publicly express their emotional connections to family, friends, and lovers. Callers' voices outline familial and romantic ties in publicly broadcast phone calls. The other viewers hear these disembodied voices and either literally recognize them (which is often the case) or seem to recognize them on a nonspecific affective level, hearing in them their own mothers, boyfriends, and grandmothers. Some callers praise a singer by emphasizing at length that his or her song "comes from the heart." These participatory listening practices create affective circuits that resonate across the broader milieu, from familial gatherings at restaurants and banquet halls to quartiere piazza festivals. Emotional expression in song and speech seems always to be well received in public. Moreover, intimacy is intensified, quite counterintuitively, when it is made public. Yet, from the outside, the spectacle appears simply maudlin.[65]

Neomelodica music makes persistent sentimental references to its local origins. These references can be textual (localized narrative figures and events, use of a regional language) or stylistic, such as musical arrangements and vocal techniques that mark regional cultural distinctions.

When textual or stylistic references to locality are synchronized with interactive performance aesthetics (call-in television dedications, close contact during live performances), singers and their intimate consumer publics are enfolded in a self-referential "familial" affectivity.

Critics in Italy perceive neomelodica music as an expression of irrational, morbid attachments to family and locality. The music echoes Neapolitans' so-called *campanilismo* (lit. church bell-ism or particularism), the loyalty to the neighborhood that falls within the sonic reach of the nearest church bell, that the political scientist Robert Putnam famously pitted against the "modern" democratic formation called "civic society."[66] The music also echoes Neapolitans' so-called amoral familism elaborated by the political scientist Edward Banfield to indicate a fragmentary "familial society" where allegiance to one's family interests occludes any consideration of the interests of the wider public.[67] Together, campanilismo and amoral familism produce southern Italy's perceived stalled modernization and its intransigence in the face of globalization. These perceptions link up with discourses about Italy's "Southern Question." But contrary to the aspired rationalization and impersonalization of music performance and distribution in dominant culture industry, in this scene celebrities are personally accessible to their publics, whom singers engage according to an alternative "economic rationality" that accounts for the value of goodheartedness.[68]

Lyrics

By now it should be clear that the songs' contents are located as much in their expressive form as in their lyrics. Many songs' subject matter directly depicts the quotidian experiences of the singer's milieu, focusing on themes such as romantic and familial love that are sometimes inflected with socioeconomic class loyalties. Others chronicle historical events, dramatically or comically, such as Andrea Zingoni's "Tu vuò fà 'o talebano" (You want to act like a Taliban):

> You wear your beard longer than a meter
> a little turban and a used cassock
> you appear as if possessed on Al Jazeera
> like a *guappo* in order to get yourself looked at[69]

The song is a parody of the famous song "Tu vuò fà l'americano" (You want to act American) first recorded by Renato Carosone in 1956:

> You wear trousers with a logo on the back
> and a cap with the visor raised
> you walk jingling down Via Toledo
> like a *guappo* wanting to be seen[70]

It captures Neapolitans' postwar-era emulation of the *'mericano* by fetishizing and coveting his clothes and wealth. In an autobiography, Carosone describes how people throughout the region flocked to Resina, the enormous flea market that overflowed with goods stolen from the World War II U.S. military convoys, to cobble together an "imported secondhand American Dream."[71] The song mocks the conflation of local flamboyant masculinity or *guapparia* (guappism) with nouveau riche consumerism. This "'mericano" is only another *guappo 'e cartone* (cardboard guappo). He drinks whiskey and soda but then gets an upset stomach. The song jaunts with the sounds of jazz and swing (novelties in Italian music at the time), with which Carosone countered the "hypermelodies" of Sanremo.[72]

Other neomelodiche songs (about 10 percent, according to several protagonists and fans) focus on run-ins with the law and organized crime affiliation. Their lyrics sometimes invoke the specificities of Neapolitan urban space—the tropes of the basso, vicolo, and quartiere, or even specific quartieri, as in Ricciardi's "167" and D'Alessio's "Fotomodelle un po' povere" (Somewhat poor fashion models):

> When you want me, you can reach me at low cost,
> twenty thousand to pay for that taxi
> It takes just half an hour because Vomero is near La Sanità
> You [too, in Vomero] are in Naples[73]

At times the lyrics are strikingly literal, unlike the strategic generalities typical of commercial Italian, Anglo-American, and Latin American pop music. When the lyrics focus on love or desire, as they most often do, they can be blunt, attracting criticism in mainstream corporate media and social media circuits including personal blogs and YouTube. The music video for nine-year-old Giuseppe Junior's song "Bellissima" (Very beautiful)[74] inspired talk of legal action from the former regional commissioner of the Green Party and the president of the antipedophilia association A Pact for Life.[75] In the video Giuseppe Junior is lying on a bed beside a slightly older girl, telling her to take off her miniskirt. "Let's make love," he sings, "my heart is rising in my throat."[76]

The lyrics can be strikingly awkward and rife with infelicitous turns

This very friendly stranger approached me while I was taking photographs near 'Ncopp' 'e Mmura. He carried himself like a local "personality" and spoke a mix of fragmented English and Neapolitan. He said he had just been to Florida. He shook my hand, told me to take a picture of him, gave me his card (presumably so that I could send him the picture), and then walked off. I lost his card, so I hope he will find this book.

of phrase "halfway between an impoverished form of Neapolitan and the kind of Italian used in *fotoromanzi,*" the still-photograph version of romance novels.[77] Moreover, the arrangements are sometimes mismatched with the lyrics and the tone of the story they narrate, shifting in style, tempo, or time signature, or all three at once, without any clear lyrical motivation.

But to listeners the lyrics are not interesting for their poetic structure. The lyrics across songs are restricted to a rather narrow rhetorical repertoire. What interests musicians and fans are less the microstructures of the narrative than the feelingful tale of the "quartieri popolari" filtered through the singer's sensibility.[78] The same is true for the music. Instead of the microstructures of the arrangements, or even

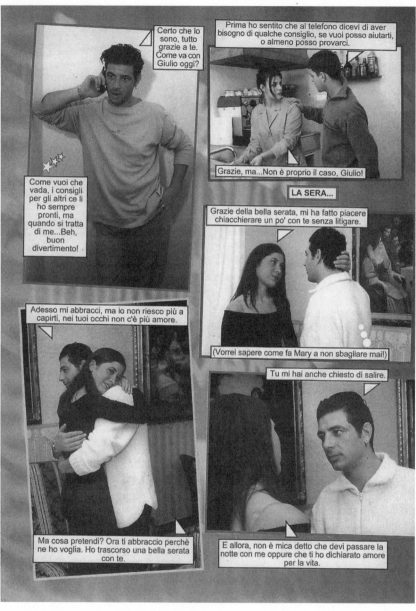

A *fotoromanzo* is a popular Italian visual text genre consisting of sequenced photo stills of movie actors acting out, in comic-strip form, a romance story. Lello D'Onofrio, the singer who appears in this fan's fantasy, was for a time a sex symbol among fans, as are many singers.

their coherence, fans (and many musicians) are entrained by the music's affective charge and its effects.

Aesthetics and Political Economy

The category neomelodica encompasses a fairly wide range of changing styles. These characterizations about its stylistics are necessarily approximate and inadequate generalizations. For example, more and more neomelodici sing in the major keys that are more familiar to mainstream Italian and Anglo-American commercial popular music. Other singers use microtonal embellishments sparingly or not at all, substituting them with the melismatic expressions made popular by soul music in the United States and have since become the *American Idol* vocal style. The group of styles represented by the category neomelodica coheres at best as a family resemblance. The family resemblance comes into relief most when tracing the political economy that generates and is generated by neomelodica music.

Singers are often young men (and a small percentage of women) who are dependent on their parents but who seek opportunities to earn an income by performing live at wedding, communion, baptism, and other family celebrations. Pursuing these opportunities requires an investment ranging from a few thousand to tens of thousands of euros. Keyboard synthesizers provide cost-effective, easily produced, and portable performances because they reproduce the sounds of several instruments, including drums. More successful singers perform live gigs with accompanists, including string players.

Aspiring singers begin their pursuit by writing their own songs or, more often, approaching the scene's songwriters and composers, most of them unschooled, for single songs or a package deal of usually five. Many songwriters and composers are as resourceless as the singers. They work out of their homes or in cramped rental spaces in neighborhood bassi and use lower-end and secondhand sound recording and mixing equipment. Writing songs, composing arrangements, and making recordings are tasks shared by as few as two individuals (e.g., the recording technician and songwriter collaborating on the arrangements) or as many as six, with three songwriters and two composers.

Many songs are poorly produced and reproduced. Vocal and instrumental tracks can sound tinny, and vocal tracks are often placed far in front, yielding a shouting effect. Fans easily overlook such flaws. In 2008 I visited a middle school in a lower-middle-class quartiere and talked to students about their favorite music, which they listened to on their cell phones like mini boomboxes. I asked them what they thought about the poor playback quality of the device or some of their idols' remarkably untuned voices. They said, matter-of-factly or with laughter, that none of that mattered. They fall in love with singers and their songs for the lyrical melody and, most of all, the lyrics.

Compared with the mainstream music industry, value in this milieu more frequently accretes in the artist's celebrity than in the artist's product. The dominant music industry shares this phenomenon, but only superficially because the phenomenon occurs within a relationship between commodities. Neomelodici break this commodity relation by cultivating celebrity status in the artist's relations with an intimate public for whom he or she can shape conventions of belonging and "provide a better experience of belonging—partly through participation in the relevant commodity culture."[79] In the neomelodico milieu more artists become celebrities, and there may be as many intimate publics as there are artists. The value of artistic achievement is not necessarily determined by the product's quality (its exchange value as commodity) and the artist's vocal abilities; more often the achievement is evaluated in terms of an artist's personal qualities and powers, such as the artist's reputation, social networks, and entrepreneurial savvy.

Critics of the neomelodica music scene perceive narcissism and self-aggrandizement where participants see a quest for personal sovereignty. When they are performing, neomelodici employ extravagant vocal and gestural expressions to stir up affect for expectant and intensely appreciative listeners. Singing with passion, even without voice training, signals a valued performance of self-production. An untrained voice can even be considered integral to a "populist aesthetic" that emphasizes the "everyman" status of the singer-cum–self-realized sovereign.[80] The hyperbolic style of singers is notable in not only their musical performances but also their performances as "professional artists." Many singers make exaggerated claims about their profits and popularity, and many express aspirations that can sound preposterously disproportionate to their abilities and circumstances. These performances are enhanced by a distinctive mode of dress, consisting of dark sunglasses, a solarium tan, elabo-

Antonio Ottiano is a "Big" in the scene. His specialty is sceneggiata performances, and he has worked with Mario Merola.

rate hair-gelled coifs, flamboyantly colorful and tight clothing, or partial nudity. CD covers, and the posters, promotional postcards, and articles in the monthly neomelodica music magazine *Sciuè* that are de rigueur for any singer who is serious about promotion, showcase the artists in affected poses. In these images they gaze sexily at the consumer as if turning to look back over their shoulder, or they look askance while lying on one side, shirtless and with puckered lips.

Luciano Caldore has an extraordinary voice, but his career successes have not reflected his talents. Caldore was massively popular in the Naples area in the early 2000s. When I attended a couple of his performances (two banquets in separate halls in the same complex in the northern periphery), the crowds were ecstatic. A throng of guests crowded around the entrance to the hall when the emcee announced his arrival. During the performances he had to ask the audience to settle down, as women were hugging and kissing him during his songs. The young males in the audience, wearing biker sunglasses, sang the lyrics in synch with Caldore to their girlfriends, as if to siphon off his sex appeal and regain their partners' attentions.

As artists performing as artists, they employ conspicuous signs and gestures that are shared by some crime clan affiliates, who enjoy making a spectacular presence and living in spectacular settings.[81] Some of these clan affiliates have gratified their desire that neomelodici reflect their aesthetic of excess. As their impresarios, they have shaped singers' images by giving them bodyguards, flashy cars (lately the Mini Cooper and the Smart Car), watches, and cash to spend during nights out on the town. They also shape market tastes by imposing their preferred singers on the circuits in their territories.

To critics, the hyperbolic performance style in neomelodica music and in the neomelodici's performances as artists is evidence of a perceived arrogant, delusional, regressive, and self-referential subculture. Music critics, journalists, and other listeners have chided neomelodici as improvised artists who do not think it is necessary to follow any of the familiar steps toward "professionalization" that structure the dominant music industry, such as musical training, acquiring standard Italian, and conducting scrupulous publicity campaigns (not including appearances on live call-in television or private performances). One singer was approached in the early 2000s by talent scouts from the label BMG Ricordi, who told him they were impressed by his performance and wanted to offer him a contract, but that he first would have to spend the year retreating to a proper distance from his public. After a year, for reasons I haven't been able to discover, the contract did not materialize.

The aesthetic qualities of neomelodica music are consonant with the political economy in which they emerge and circulate. A neomelodica song is simultaneously an artifact of the art of making do and its performance. In this milieu the songs are in themselves less meaningful than their live performance. During performances songs are less meaningful than the presence of the performer engaging their intimate public. Indeed, most of the money singers earn is not from CD sales but from their live gigs.

Making do by making music blends affects, interests, and aesthetics into a cohesive world that is in a sense self-referential and self-justifying. Neomelodica music protagonists are leaders of their own intimate public markets. Through the arts of bricolage, short-cut problem solving, improvised production, and self-display, they enact aesthetic and political economic sovereignty for themselves and their intimate publics.

Publicity

In 1995 Maurizio Costanzo, host of a popular TV talk show on Mediaset's *Canale 5*, observed a scene of delirious fanaticism at a piazza festival at Porta Capuana in Naples. Several singers, with twice as many bodyguards keeping a swelling crowd at bay, mounted the stage and sang original Neapolitan pop songs. Intrigued, Costanzo dedicated three episodes of his show to neomelodica music, inviting the singers D'Alessio, Luciano Caldore, Ciro Ricci, Stefania Lay, Ida Rendano, and Maria Nazionale. Nazionale, who later appeared on the Rai 1 show *Sottovoce* (Quietly), expressed irritation when the host, Gigi Marzullo, asked her about the "phenomenon of the neomelodici." She asked him to explain why, when a singer makes it big in Milan, a star is born, but when a singer makes it in Naples, a neomelodico is born.[82]

Costanzo's interest convinced many Neapolitan journalists who had until then snubbed the neomelodica music scene to reconsider the "phenomenon." One result was a four-episode documentary *Napoli, che passione* (Naples, what passion), broadcast on Rai 2. At the same time, derisive television skits and articles about neomelodica music began circulating in magazines such as *L'espresso* (the left-leaning periodical that Berlusconi did not manage to acquire) and newspapers such as the Milan-based center-right (but anti-Berlusconi) *Corriere della sera*. Locally, a popular Neapolitan radio show host launched an awards ceremony that he called the "postmelodic" Neapolitan Melogrammy. The intention, one of the co-organizers explained, was to pay homage and also affectionately poke fun at an emerging scene by bringing them into the limelight of the prestigious Teatro Mercadante while encouraging the neomelodici to enjoy a moment of glory without taking themselves too seriously.[83] As wider media circuits drew attention to the neomelodici, they also censured and censored them. This mediatic friction generated a resonance with a life all its own called "public opinion." Unlike the neomelodici's intimate public, whose vitality comes from contact with artists making do, this other public imagines con artists who got away with suddenly becoming "true" pop stars.

The publicity neomelodica music received, both good and bad, inflamed the ambitions of mainly young men and their families with limited wealth and education throughout Campania, and in places in Sicily, Puglia, Calabria, and even among southern Italian emigrants. As a result, neomelodica music has hundreds of thousands of fans.

Incorporation

Neomelodica music and the milieu where it is produced and performed have taken on multiple discursive forms, including the language of genre, subculture, class identity, language identity, and cultural–regional identity. For many journalists, music critics, scholars, and politicians, these discursive forms have served as shorthand for the cultural–economic world to which they refer.[84] In some ways, these reifications are convenient for participants of the neomelodica music scene because they provide partial forms singers and their music need to assume in order to circulate beyond their local milieu. As unambiguously categorized and standardized aesthetic objects, neomelodiche songs might find a place in dominant music industry taxonomies. As "underground" musicians, neomelodici might grab national airtime on popular television talk shows and documentaries. Neomelodici and their songs have indeed entered these circulations, but their movement has been sporadic and restricted.

While some mainstream media figures attempted to rehabilitate neo-melodica music by calling it the voice of a class-conscious subproletariat, others called it an expression of regional–cultural consciousness by link-ing it to "Mediterranean" and "peasant" vocal "traditions."[85] Both forms of incorporation found their aesthetic form in one song in particular. Ricciardi's "Cuore nero" (Black heart) politicizes a particular notion of Neapolitans' regional-traditional-racial identity by celebrating the "black" heritage of Neapolitans, descendants of the Saracens:[86]

> The slave markets
> Damned rhythm of chains
> We are all African
> . . . .
> we Neapolitans.

Ricciardi explained in interviews that his lyrics reference southern Italy's invaders by comparing Neapolitans to the African slaves of the Saracens, the "Arab" invaders of Africa in the Middle Ages. His song also conjures up an origin story for an authentic pan-Mediterranean iden-tity. Identifying with black Africans is a way to retool the denigrating racialized declaration, first pronounced in 1860 by chief administrator of the newly annexed Kingdom of Naples, the Piedmontese Luigi Carlo Farini, and repeated in variations even today: "This is not Italy! This is Africa: compared to these peasants, the Bedouins are the pinnacle of civilization. And what misdeeds!"[87] Ricciardi is not the first Neapolitan artist to appropriate black identity. In the 1970s the suggestive term "Naples Power" was coined to define the "musical movement" in which Neapolitan music absorbed the influences of rock, jazz, and blues from the United States and the UK and broke from Neapolitan melodic "tra-ditions." Referencing the Black Power movement in the United States, Naples Power musicians were called the "Negroes of Vesuvius." They challenged national culture industry hegemony by making music they and their milieus wanted to hear, ignoring mainstream market demands for Neapolitan mandolins and "feel-good rhetoric."[88] Eschewing romance and folklore, they produced "realist" evocations of life in a troubled city.

Blackness also resonates in the Neapolitan author Peppe Lanzetta's popular novels, whose titles sometimes make stereotypical references to poverty and crime in nonwhite (or perceived nonwhite) areas of the Americas (e.g., *Children of a Minor Bronx* and *A Neapolitan Mexico*). Lanzetta has written lyrics for Naples Power musicians James Senese (a Neapolitan with an African American father) and Pino Daniele, as well as for Ricciardi. In "Cuore nero" Ricciardi's voice blends with the repeating calls of voices such as those sampled by Moby from Alan Lomax's early African American music recordings.

Another example of politicized neomelodica music is singer Stefania Lay's "'A libertà" (Freedom), a "feminist" critique of the jealous Neapolitan macho who sequesters his wife at home:

> I want Freedom
> Fuck you, what are you hitting me for?!
> What kind of man are you?

Music journalists heavily publicized Lay's and Ricciardi's songs at the risk of making them seem representative of neomelodica music as a whole. However, the desire to politicize and thereby redeem the neomelodici was unfulfilled. In 2001 Vacalebre expressed disappointment that the neomelodici had behaved like *bacconi* (Bacchuses) by limiting their efforts to "l'arte di arrangiarsi" and squandering their opportunity to go "beyond the margins." The result, he said, was a dying scene.[89] Instead, the scene indicated that although the industry was experiencing what protagonists described as a recession, it was far from moribund. What was dead was a regional and national media blitz that had failed to incorporate the "margins" of Neapolitan cultural production. The margins turned out to be just as industrialized and enfranchised as the hypermelodic national scene at Sanremo and the industry of feel-good rhetoric at Piedigrotta, but according to a different economic logic.

The Burlesque-Grotesque

One evening at a dinner party hosted by a university student, I met a violinist of the chamber orchestra I Virtuosi di San Martino. When I asked him his opinion of neomelodica music, he said simply, *"Geniale!*

[Brilliant!]" He explained, "I have a prurient interest in the neomelodici because of the egregious errors they make—both musically and grammatically." When I asked him about musical errors, he described the arrangements of a neomelodica song in which the guitar, piano, and drums shift from a 3/4 to 6/8 time signature while a trumpet lags behind in 3/4.

I did not ask the violinist for a sample grammatical error, because I knew it would be the linguistic blunder that ironic fans universally cite when they want to capture the perceived camp spirit of neomelodica music. The error is found in the song "OK," by Valentina, who uses the conditional in place of the subjunctive smack in the middle of the refrain:

> OK / if you want me / the rendezvous is at six
> I would be crazy if I wouldn't go

This type of blunder is a notorious class marker in Italy, indicating the speaker's low education and socioeconomic level. Because Valentina is transgender, she unwittingly reproduces the camp performances of the stereotyped angry, abject *vaiassa* or *vasciaiola* (lit. basso-dweller). The vasciaiola is frequently performed in Naples on TV, in nightclubs, and in the spontaneous performances of private parties by men, often gay, as wearing a housedress and slippers while shouting obscenities with exaggeratedly elongated vowels, poised to lunge at her opponent and drag her by the hair through the vicoli.

The "duplicity" of Valentina's status as a performer operates in tandem with her (unwitting?) "metaperformance" of gender identity.[90] In her song "Me sento femmena" (I feel like a woman), Valentina sings not in falsetto, as she sometimes does, but in her natural baritone:

> A woman, I feel, a woman next to you
> . . . .
> You know everything about me
> In love you know what you're doing
> Only you are like you

At the end of the song, a chorus composed of natural mezzo-sopranos adds a marked contrast to Valentina's own deep voice.

These particularities of Valentina's performances have afforded her national notoriety. As a result, critics repeatedly single her out and have made her into an emblem of the neomelodico absurd.[91] Valentina impersonators began appearing on national television broadcasts. One impersonator, the

Valentina and I went out for a pizza one evening in the centro storico (she lives in Fuorigrotta, in the eastern part of the city). She was greeted by several people on the streets (including an illegal parking attendant) and in the pizzeria. Transgender women are rather respected in her milieu, but this is not the case for men and women who self-identify as gay. One neomelodico "Big" had a long-term relationship with a transgender woman, and transgender women have been affiliated with crime clans.

Neapolitan actress and comedian Rosalia Porcaro, came to rival Valentina's celebrity status when she appeared on the Rai transmission *Ottavo nano* (Eighth dwarf) and performed her own composition "Sesso senza amore" (Sex without love).

It was at around this time that Valentina retreated from the local music scene for nearly two years. In 2005 she returned as a comedic impersonator on *TeleGaribaldi*, a popular Neapolitan TV show on which Porcaro had appeared a few years prior. On *TeleGaribaldi* Porcaro performed her fictional character Veronica, a woman who sews handbags in an illegal factory in Naples and naively believes that her oppressive and exploitative boss, *'O mast* (master) or *donatore di lavoro* (giver of work) as she calls him, cares deeply for her well-being. Given Porcaro's previous skits on *TeleGaribaldi*, Valentina's performances acquired an ironic–burlesque intertextuality, making Valentina into a self-parody by incoherently combining the affectations of a Neapolitan parvenue with the grotesque self-sameness of her unaffected lower-class milieu.

In Naples and throughout Italy there is a public that looks at the spectacle of neomelodica music with an appreciative irony. This public simultaneously criticizes and applauds what they perceive to be the music's aesthetic failures. I have encountered several people of all social milieus in southern, central, and northern Italy who, if they have not already acquired this ironic or camp appreciation, readily adopt it once they learn of the neomelodici.

They describe themselves as awestruck by what they perceive as the full-on, unrestrained performance of a poor performance. They are taken in by the unscrupulously equal blend of trompe l'oeil, or reality-effect, and mise-en-abyme, or fiction-effect; the heartfelt performance simultaneously points to its own status as performance.[92] The reaction of these individuals approximates the reaction of "true" fans on the "inside" of neomelodico style because it recognizes that irony is intrinsic to the performance. True and camp fans alike recognize that the performer is performing performing. However, whereas camp fans derive pleasure from the disintegration the irony causes, "true" fans derive pleasure from the performer's mastery over and investment in a potent artifice.

However, Valentina performs her songs with heartfelt sincerity and conviction. She told me that she is particularly popular among young children and their mothers, who hold great affection for anyone who entertains or dotes on them. Indeed, she does precisely this when she hosts, sometimes in pigtails, her live, call-in TV transmissions.

The violinist's fascination with neomelodica music is an example of a common attitude among those who take the middle ground regarding the neomelodici. It is an ironic blend of interest and revulsion, the "base" form of seduction inflected with a "burlesque" value.[93] It is a "mode of aestheticism" that sees the world "not in terms of beauty, but in terms of the degree of artifice, of stylization," or camp.[94] This mode of reception takes place on a middle ground between dismissive exclusionary irony and mimetic empathic "over-identification."[95] It approximates the mode of attention in which neomelodici and fans engage the music, attention paid to the potency of artifice rather than its capacity to simulate veracity. In contrast, neomelodica music fans such as the violinist appreciate from an ironic distance the perceived self-sameness or naive presence of these performances.

The example of Nazionale, a singer widely recognized for her stunning vocal skills, illustrates these different responses. For audiences that include the violinist, Maria's attractiveness and strong-willed persona, combined with her highly original love song lyrics, and her dramatic autobiography, *A Difficult Life,* make her a gay icon, a tragic diva.[96] In 1997 she was awarded a Melogrammy for best up-and-coming female performer, but she and another awardee, D'Alessio, refused to participate in what they considered to be a "ghettoizing" affair.[97] Both singers have since been vindicated. D'Alessio's success (discussed below) has surpassed all expectations. When I met Maria in 2003, she had just appeared on Rai with the acclaimed performers Lucio Dalla and the Brazilian Gilberto Gil. In 2008 Simioli awarded her a second Melogrammy (figured as Naples's patron saint, San Gennaro), this time for her distinguished career, which now includes a dramatic role in the 2008 feature film *Gomorra.*

Antonio D'Addio of *Sciuè* introduced me to Maria when she was having her makeup done backstage at the annual Festival della Sanità, an important music event in the quartiere La Sanità. It had been particularly difficult to get to know female neomelodiche, not only because there were so few but also because sometimes the men in their lives—fathers, brothers, uncles—were protective. "You can't just call asking to meet with a woman like that. *Aggio fà 'na mmasciata* [I have to pass on your request for you]. Otherwise they'll wonder what you want with her. They'll think you have certain intentions," the mother of a singer once explained to me.

Maria was a widow (now remarried) in her early thirties, and the only males I encountered were her adolescent son and a middle-aged man who drove us to her gigs and spoke to the family members and organizers (always men) who invited her to perform. I accompanied her on a few of her gigs and attended a dinner party she gave at her home on her birthday. Almost all of her guests were performers of some sort. At the end of the dinner, when Maria's Ukrainian domestic worker served us limoncello, the guests took turns playing guitars and telling animated and lengthy jokes. I videotaped most of these performances, partly for their intrinsic value as verbal art and partly because videotaping gave me something to do. As a mere spectator I felt inadequate; even the few guests who did not perform performed as spectators. They knew when to call out cued responses during the ironic narratives, and they offered witty commentary when a performance ended.

During the long drive between provincial gigs, Maria told me a story about the time she performed her signature song, "Ragione e sentimento" (Sense and sensibility) at a wedding and encountered an apocalyptic response. The song consists of two vocal parts, each in Maria's own voice. One voice murmurs in low tones reasonable yet aggressive advice about the callousness and infidelities of her boyfriend. It is rapped in a regular meter in stanzas that alternate with the other voice, which sings expansively, melodically, and in a higher pitch. This other voice, that of the sentimental Maria, sings that despite everything, she cannot help loving the man all the same. The accompanying music video is composed of a split screen, with two shots of Maria seated on a sofa. Each "Maria" sings her part in alternation, and sometimes the two Marias address each other, each turning to face the other:

(voice 1) He lights you and he throws you away as if you were a cigarette
(voice 2) From head to foot, I love him
(voice 1) How many evenings have you waited for him? How many disappointments have you taken?
(voice 2) And I don't want to stop[98]

When Maria sings the song at wedding celebrations, she calls on all the women to form a circle around her in the center of the banquet hall.

When she begins the song she provokes shouts and screams from the crowd encircling her, and the young girls and women of all ages accompany Maria at the refrain with noticeable excitement. Clapping their hands and rocking to and fro, they chant, "Stupid! What are you waiting for? Dump him now. That one there, he's all infamy."

At one wedding, Maria told me, the brother of the groom approached her before her performance and asked that she please not sing "Ragione e sentimento," that it would not be appropriate. "Of course, of course," Maria answered. "Don't worry, don't worry," she added, using a common and what I found to be an infamous platitude in this milieu. Maria began her performance, and halfway through her songs she was approached by the family of the bride.

"It's OK, you can sing 'Ragione e sentimento.' It's no problem. Go ahead."

Maria immediately took up the cue and began singing. She was not even two stanzas into the song when she realized that wedding guests

The CD that includes "Sense and Sensibility" is titled *Women's Stories*. Another song on this CD is "You'll Make Me Die," about a jealous partner. At this performance at a restaurant in the provincial town Acerra, Maria invited the women to line up and sing "Sense and Sensibility" with her. This participation reflects a sort of "performance process" for becoming a Neapolitan woman.

had begun rioting on the patio at the far end of the banquet hall. Within moments the slaps and *scippi* (fistfuls of scratching fingernails smacked across the face, typically inflicted among women), kicks and punches, hurled liter bottles of water, toppled tables, and smashed chairs spread throughout the hall, surging up toward Maria, her accompanists, and the sound equipment.

Maria stood frozen for a moment in awe as she watched women holding infants in their arms battling with each other. Her manager took her by the arm and shouted, "Run!" They found their van, packed up, and drove off to the sound of gunshots. Maria explained that the groom and his family had thought the bride's family was mocking him, trying to tell him something by requesting she sing the song. "The couple had problems, and the bride was unsure about marrying him," Maria said, laughing.

"And all for the passion for music," I said to Maria, laughing too, until Maria suddenly stopped:

"*Of course* they're passionate about it," she answered with gravity.

'A Munnezz' (Trash)

Stereotypes of Neapolitans often allege that the camorra thrives in Naples because the camorra *is,* more or less, Naples. This association has been exacerbated by a highly publicized Campanian trash "crisis" entangling local politicians, business elites, and organized crime clans. For many years, a camorra trash industry monopoly has provided cut-rate dumping services for northern Italian and European businesses, resulting in egregious waste mismanagement. Piles of uncollected trash periodically line the city streets, landfills overflow, incinerators remain in perpetual disrepair, and illegal toxic waste sites proliferate. However, it was only in the mid-2000s that national and international publics began to pay serious attention to this situation. Ever since, "organized crime in Naples" has been wedded to "the trash of Naples" in mass-diffused images of garbage barricades cutting off poor quartieri and mounds of trash set ablaze by protesters and DIY waste managers.

The trash of Naples showed up in wider circuits when Naples seemed to reach a tipping point in the game *who am I and who are you?* Civil war erupted in one of the most powerful crime clan alliances, Italy's minister of justice considered military intervention, and a young journalist challenged organized crime in Campania and its atmosphere of secrecy and fear by publishing an unprecedented book-length exposé. Although the warring has abated, little else has changed. The persistent trash heaps have become emblems of exposure in an interminable refrain of evisceration without *risanamento* (reclamation).

Neomelodica music was and continues to be entangled in this ritual of exposure. But the neomelodica scene was haunted (and fueled) by trash even before the extraordinary events of 2004 to 2006. Many protagonists made continual efforts to distinguish their aesthetic and moral–economic practices from those of "the camorra." Some underscore that their goals are humble (as opposed to the hyperbolic style of protagonismo). Others, seeking to dissimulate any connection at all with the art of making do, perform "professionalism." People in the neomelodica scene, like many people outside it, aesthetically express their dilemma through uses of the word 'a munnezz', or trash.

Throughout my field research, I met many Neapolitans concerned with my choice to study neomelodica music. They hijacked my explorations by haranguing me with boisterous talk while tugging at my arms for attention and forcibly steering me toward singers of other types of Neapolitan-language music such as the jazz and blues–influenced Pino Daniele or "folk" forms such as the *tarantella*. To "do a tarantella" means, metaphorically, to make much ado about nothing. Many opponents to my research wondered why I would do such a tarantella when Neapolitan music history reaches so far back and is dense with examples of true music and artistry, whereas neomelodica music is produced by con artists. By talking fast, changing the subject, interrupting my conversations with others, and tugging on my arms or putting an arm around my shoulder to get my attention, such people would shape a group performance with the others present according to their own career interests. Often, they took my video camera from my hands and interviewed each other as experts and *virtuosi* of Neapolitan music. Interestingly, many of my hijackers were themselves participants of the neomelodica industry. When that was the case, sometimes it was clear that they felt I was moving in too closely to a territory where I didn't belong. Even longtime associates who understood that I was interested in not only the music but also the camorra behind it would suddenly lose their patience with my questions: "What do you want with all of this? Look, there's something you haven't yet understood: *Everyone* on this scene is 'a munnezz'."

For this milieu, munnezza is ultimately equated with "the camorra." The affective community in which they participate is centered in one way or another on munnezz', whether one works to distinguish oneself from it, attempts to euphemize and mask it, or takes it on wholeheartedly as a legitimate mode of expression. The camorra's influence on everyday moral, political, economic, and aesthetic life in this milieu and beyond has earned it the status of the bad copy or trashy imitation of the state, the "formal" market economy, and the aesthetics of the dominant music industry.

Some people on the scene express wariness or even militant disgust for acts of making do that bleed into what are shifting social definitions of collusion and conspiracy with the camorra. Few disapprove of l'arte di arrangiarsi if it means selling pirated CDs or contraband cigarettes, or singing at crime clan weddings and baptisms.[99] If, however, making do means joining the talent agency of a crime boss–impresario, performing on his personal wedding-gig circuit, and recording albums at studios under his purview, it ignites heavy criticism. Many critiques come, in fact, from other singers who see the pop star successes of their camorra-backed rivals as easy, bad copies of the real thing.

The Neapolitan word for trash is a particular Neapolitan insult often reserved for Neapolitans by Neapolitans, because only Neapolitans can "really" understand it. On the other hand, its Italian equivalent, immondizia, and its synonyms (spazzatura, rifiuti, sporcizia) are not used as insults. I learned this when I shot a music video for a neomelodico singer. I decided to gather B-roll footage in the streets of the poorer neighborhood called the Quartieri Spagnoli (Spanish quarters) with the accompaniment of a friend who lives in the neighborhood. My friend was acting as my ambassador. His familiar face reassured people that I had no ill intentions with my video camera, as residents of this and similar neighborhoods often react angrily when strangers point cameras at them (I have unwittingly documented many such reactions on tape). As we caught people's attention, many gestured to us by pulling down the lower eyelid of one eye with an index finger and said: "Occhio! [Eye!]." The gesture and utterance repeated throughout the quartiere with a strangely perfunctory emphasis about an unseen yet omnipresent danger. The signal seemed to bounce from each shot to the next in endless, anxious deferment. I knew from experience that this was not an indication that people were hiding some thing; rather, they were hiding from excessive entanglements.

Nothing happened during our hour-long tour with the video camera except that we came across a handwritten sign on the side of a building where lives an elderly, but not frail, camorrista who controls the parking area in the piazza opposite her basso. She sat where my ambassador told me she can always be found, day and night, with her wrinkled buzzard-like face leaning on the ledge of the low, open window as if it were a service counter for passersby. The sign on the wall just around the corner of the building hangs above a dumpster and reads in Neapolitan: "'A *munnezz'* goes here, in the container. Understand, latrine?" I included a brief shot of this sign when I edited the music video for the song titled "Siente à me" (Listen to me) for twelve-year-old singer Fulvio and his father, Pasquale, who wrote the lyrics:

> Don't listen to those others
> You're like me—you're a child of Naples
> All the mammas have just enough money to get by
> All these young guys in the street go to work

The song is a sort of rehabilitation of Naples for Neapolitans, while my ironic gesture instead pointed to what lies beneath. People laughed uncomfortably when they saw it. "It's embarrassing. You shouldn't have done it," a close associate finally told me, months later. Who knows how many others were not "taking confidence" *(piglià 'a confidenza)* from me, as people described frankness beyond some moment-by-moment, dangerously shifting standard, not saying what was really on their minds.

I had called it like it is: filth. So did someone else in a well-known pizzeria on Spaccanapoli. The pizzeria had a sign posted on the wall above the narrow counter where diners can sit on stools and eat. In a style best described as a hypercorrected linguistic baroque, the sign asks that customers throw their soda cans and disposable cups "in the container suited for such use." At the end of this sentence someone had scrawled in pen the word *munnezz'*.

Trash turned up on yet another occasion. I once conducted an experiment and began in Neapolitan a "formal," taped interview with a swaggering neomelodico star. I had gone to Carmela, a highly competitive entrepreneur on the scene who owned three record labels, a publishing house, and the primary record store with the Neapolitan name, 'A canzone 'e Napule (Neapolitan song), devoted to neomelodica music. She was also the impresaria for a number of singers and held record signings at her store. It was 1998 and the national media blitz on Naples's local music scene was beginning to die out, so Carmela was frenzied when I walked into her store. As she listened to my introduction, her listening was so active that I had the impression that she was doing all the talking. She aggressively and sloppily picked out the essentials from what I said: *America, interview, book.* She even created whatever else she needed to know: *journalist, TV, newspapers.* When she had snatched her gist of things, which took all of a few moments, she called Fabio Favola on her cell phone, the long-haired singer whose latest music video at the time was with a female porn star, his *Rondine Napoletano* (Neapolitan Swallow) who taught him things about love he hadn't known. Carmela shouted into the phone: "Fabio! Fabio! Uèee. Ciao bellissimo! You remember me? Now you'll see that I always think of you when something big happens. There's an American journalist here and he wants to interview you."

A pair of teenagers arrived at the store in a dented, rattling blue car and ushered me aboard. Carmela reassured me they were friends of Fabio's and were taking me to him. The boys and I exchanged words only when we were on the road. I spoke to them in Neapolitan, and they looked at each other, smiling. Fascinated with the American who speaks "dialect," they took turns asking me to say in Neapolitan what they said in Italian. We enjoyed this game the whole ride to Barra, one of three high-crime neighborhoods making up, at the time, *the* "triangle of death." In 2004 scientists tracking spiking cancer rates in the vicinities of illegal toxic landfills in Campania baptized Acerra-Nola-Marigliano as the new triangle of death.[100]

When we reached Fabio's parents' bar, he greeted me skillfully and expansively, as do most people in his milieu when they are interested. It was clear that he was experienced at interviews. He invited me to sit down with him at a small table in front of a large television. He was ready. "So. Talk to me," he said, waiting. I asked my first question in Neapolitan, and he began answering in Italian.

I let him finish and then told him, "You can talk to me in Neapolitan. Why don't you? I understand it."

He responded without a moment's pause, noticeably irritated, "No. That won't work. I don't do that. This is a professional situation and Neapolitan reflects the *sporcizia* (filth) of Naples." It seemed he did not use the word *munnezz'* because that would mean to answer me in Neapolitan.

Fabio's polemic was about what goes wrong when certain Neapolitans don't know when they should stop being Neapolitans. For him, it is the typical approximating, improvising, and fast-talking Neapolitan who would also give a formal interview in Neapolitan. Singing is a profession as well as an art. Many protagonists on the neomelodico scene share this view. Each often points a finger at the other as the ruin of Neapolitan music, as one of many who parade as singers, spoiling it all for the two or three true artists. As a result, neomelodica music has come to represent, from the bottom-up as well as from the top-down, a space or dimension where all that is vile about Naples surfaces. "Don't make me talk! They're dogs, they all howl like dogs," shouted Maestro Chiarazzo, a songwriter, every time the subject came up. On another afternoon, the locally renowned Ida Rendano said to me, "How can I make you *understand?*" while leaning close into my face and pointing a threatening finger: "There is only one singer here in Naples and that's *me!*" With that, she openly expressed her rage at discovering that she was not the only or the first singer from the scene I had interviewed. In her song "Canto canzoni" (I sing songs), she refers to a "thousand fans" who call out for her:

> And a tear rolls down my face
> When two roses arrive
> a card, "Ida you're great.
> Only you make us dream."[101]

On still another occasion I was introduced to a singer-songwriter during the live transmission *Kaos* at a private TV studio. The journalist who made the introduction began by saying, "I told Jason he should speak to you because you're not afraid of telling the truth."

The singer took up the cue and seemed to consciously trigger his own anger. "No, I am not afraid to tell the truth: they're all shit, everyone on this scene," he nearly shouted the words at me as his voice reached a coked-up decibel (months later, his friend told me about his drug problem, which later left his lover, another protagonist on the scene, penniless). "They are ruining Neapolitan song, that's what they're doing!" he yelled, pulling my hand and tape recorder to his mouth.

Once more, the music journalist Federico Vacalebre asks rhetorically in his book-length study of the neomelodica scene, "Why take on the challenge of sifting through trash to find in it pearls that would have otherwise been rejected by the snobbism of the dominant culture?"[102] Here the question is written in Italian, but the word used for "trash" is the English one. Trash culture in Italy generally means the *nouveau* appreciation for "bad taste" in its "conscious" and "spontaneous" forms.[103] The contributors of the popular blog Trashopolis.com demonstrate this point well. They poke fun at trash artifacts that they gather from the "mediatic underbrush" of TV in Naples while defending them against "censors" such as those who had Giuseppe Junior's music video "The Miniskirt" taken off YouTube. The blog's coeditor said that their goal is to "research, curate, and contextualize marginal cultural forms and nurture an ironic form of nostalgia."[104]

Protagonists of the neomelodica scene confound this distinction between conscious and spontaneous bad taste by maintaining a paradoxically ironically emotional involvement in their work. For example, a composer named Giuseppe repeatedly declared to me that he was disgusted by the canons of taste he is pressured to abide by. He said if he were to introduce something new like Celtic sounds, people would reject it. "I do it for the money. That's what people want, so I do it, but I hate it." One evening I found him in the studio profusely complimenting a singer on the lyrics he has brought to have arranged. "Uàaa!" Giuseppe blurted out with a nasalized ending, a common form of exclamation in his milieu. "It gives me goose bumps," he told the singer loudly, brushing his fingers slowly over his extended forearm. When I had a moment alone with Giuseppe, I asked him if he was just making a sale with all his drama. He was quick to correct me: "No. *Any* song that talks about mamma hits me here," he said, fervently touching his heart with his crooked fingers.

Similarly, Pasquale, a man in his forties who writes and arranges songs for his young son Fulvio, told me he knows the songs he writes are "silly." But at the same time, he was ready to be enthused about them if I indicated any enthusiasm myself. Our meetings always followed the same routine. He picked me up, I got in the car, and he gave me his hand to shake. Without a moment spared he would announce, "Listen to this, listen to this," while turning up the volume to excessive levels on the car stereo so that I could hear his latest composition. I feigned deep concentration on the arrangements, turning an ear toward the passenger seat speaker. Waiting for a positive sign, Pasquale looked more at me than at the nauseatingly chaotic road of interweaving Vespas, belligerent jaywalkers, and triple-parked cars. Instead of analyzing the arrangements or the lyrics, which, just as the composer Giuseppe complains, never diverge much from a rather rigid formula, I searched for something to say before the song's end. Unable to wait, Pasquale began the conversation: "It's nothing really, I know. . . . But it's pretty good, isn't it?"

Ordinarily I would feebly comfort Pasquale with a bland platitude. But for a change of pace, I decided to see his judgment and up it with, "Yeah, it's more than good." His frenzy took off, the composition getting better and better until, by the time we arrived at his home for Sunday lunch, it had become the hit of his son's career. His enthusiasm was infectious, and I ended up liking the song more than I did. It was only when Pasquale's wife, Rita, eyed me suspiciously while frying the shrimp, calamari, and *triglia* fish that I realized how big my enthusiastic artifice had become.

Finally, I asked fourteen-year-old Fabio of another musical family what he thought of the sceneggiata-style song and music video that he had become known for in Naples, "Me Manch'" (I miss her). The video begins with an extended-play recitative. A father is sitting at home on the sofa and calls Fabio to come sit with him for a talk. He explains that because mamma is now in heaven, he has to put Fabio in a Catholic school. "There they can care for you. It's not because I don't love you. I do. It's because I love you that I'm sending you there." In the next scene they're standing outside Fabio's new school, and Fabio gives his father a kiss before walking toward a welcoming nun. "Fabio!" the suddenly tormented father shouts, extending an arm in an attempt to reach his son. Fabio returns the gesture by singing to his father, "I miss mamma." A flashback follows: his mother is preparing coffee in her modest kitchen, now she is at Fabio's bedside, tucking him in. The song closes with the nun kissing Fabio on the forehead, promising that he will be happy at the school. The video is by any measure a long-winded hyperbole. When I asked Fabio about it, he told me he found it laughable. He said he preferred to sing songs that are *più pulite* (cleaner).

Exposure

When neomelodica music failed to meet middle-class expectations that it politicize or folklorize Naples's poor, it came to represent the part of Naples that is ruled by superstition, the irrationally insular relations of amoral familism, and exaggerated displays of manhood by rogue, self-proclaimed sovereigns. In public discourse in Italy in the late 2000s, neomelodica music came to refer directly to what was often only implicit in the denigrating stereotypes of disapproving listeners: the camorra. There are several contributing factors to this change.

In the late 1990s, after neomelodica music's national debut on the Costanzo show and at the height of the boom, singers could claim a combined fan base numbering in the hundreds of thousands. The publicity a handful of singers received on national television made it possible for many performers to charge more for performances, and eventually only the families with large sums of cash to spend could hire top singers. Many such big spenders are crime families. Moreover, competitively conspicuous consumption within and between families can make it an imperative to have numerous high-priced performers at important family gatherings. Until the early 2000s, it was not unusual for seven individual performers to sing in succession, interspersed with dance troupes, magicians, and comedians, at a single one-day celebration.

Neomelodiche songs, televised song dedications, and music videos occasionally gesture, both overtly and discreetly, to friends and family who are imprisoned. Singers, for example, sometimes perform songs in which a child laments the absence of his father, or the father laments his separation from his children. Additionally, fans who call in to live TV transmissions sometimes dedicate songs to their imprisoned or fugitive loved ones. These gestures toward criminal practices indicate that some of the managers of neomelodici and the most significant consumers of live neomelodica music performances are affiliates of Campanian organized crime clans.

In fact, during the neomelodico boom, when singers captured audiences throughout Campania and in other southern regions, including Puglia and Sicily (where independent yet interconnected neomelodica music circuits emerged), a handful of aspiring singers accepted the help of crime boss–impresari of Secondigliano, Tommaso Prestieri—also a painter, poet, and drug trafficker—and Luigi Ponticelli, a.k.a. Bomboletta (Spray can, because he is always armed with hairspray), brother-in-law of Luigi Giuliano, a.k.a. 'O rre (The king), a.k.a. Lovigino, crime boss and songwriter of Forcella. Prestieri and Ponticelli, in addition to drug trafficking, managed singers and produced concerts. They paid singers in advance for several gigs at a time.

Many people in the scene are used to low pay, sporadic work with no security or guarantee of regularity, and frequent bouts of "bureau-cracy" and fraud, which delay payment for as long as a year, if not indefi-nitely. Some have told me they were required to pay large bribes to get city jobs. Sometimes, they find themselves out of luck when their inside contact takes the money but never makes good on the deal. For these reasons, Prestieri and Ponticelli's cash-up-front offers appeared irresist-ible to some of the singers. According to accounts of several participants on the neomelodica music scene, the bosses gave their singers sums that were exorbitant, piecemeal, and in a variety of currencies (lira, watches, cell phones, cocaine) such that they could expect indeterminate returns. They indentured singers, requiring them to sing when and where they commanded.[105]

The money, the celebrity aura that singers were encouraged to cre-ate through conspicuous spending, their performances at high-profile crime family celebrations, and their wide exposure on regional TV and at piazza festivals organized by boss–impresari (and, it is rumored, politi-cians) turned these singers into local and regional pop stars. People on the scene said these singers earned over a thousand euros for a five-song gig and played up to twelve gigs a day during high season (May through July).

But stardom prompted many occasions to expose singers for who they "really" are, behind the mask of Pulcinella: Neapolitan parvenus complicit with "the camorra." Ironically, or perhaps not, these were sometimes occasions of self-exposure. In 1996 Giuliano drew massive public attention to himself when he clashed with the Neapolitan film di-rector Antonio Capuano. Capuano was casting the role of a young boy who could act and sing, and during the auditions many of the boys sang songs written by Ciro Ricci, a.k.a. Ciro Rigione. Intrigued, Capuano contacted Ricci and asked him to write a song for his soundtrack. Ricci happily agreed, but gave Capuano one of Lovigino's songs instead.[106]

The film recounts the true story of an anticamorra priest of the quar-tiere La Sanità. When the priest was accused of molesting a young boy and sentenced to prison, the quartiere's residents declared there was a camorra conspiracy. Rather than the film's subject matter, it was nonrec-ognition that Lovigino considered an affront. This suggests his desire for media attention, regardless of the manner and context in which he gets it.

Prestieri appears to be similarly hammy. In 2003 he went after Enrico Assante, another impresario (author of Rendano's "I sing songs") and manager of Zappulla, who was to perform a concert in the area Prestieri claimed as his territory. Prestieri wanted to murder him, but Prestieri's nephews persuaded him to content himself with having Assante *gambizzato* (kneecapped).[107]

Prestieri comanaged a lucrative heroin piazza, a veritable department in the open-air multipiazza drug supermarket called Seven Buildings. One of his two comanagers, Patrizio Grandelli, a.k.a. 'O mostro (The monster), organized Zappulla's concert, but Prestieri considered himself the leader of the territory's music industry. He owned a recording studio, talent agency, and three satellite TV channels on the Sky network—in fact, a number of crime bosses own TV and radio channels in Campania. He took Grandelli's action as an affront and went after Assante in response.[108]

Prestieri and Grandelli were significant players in Campanian organized crime because they participated in a gruesome clan war in 2004–5 in the neighborhoods of Scampia and Secondigliano. The feud, which attracted international media attention, was sparked by secessionists from the ruling Di Lauro clan alliance. Every crime family in the alliance had to choose sides, and the Grandellis and Prestieris joined the secessionists. After two hundred homicides, the secessionists secured their autonomy, but Prestieri was a sovereign in decline. His brother and two nephews turned pentiti and triggered his arrest in 2008 for his earlier crime against Assante. Because Scampia and Secondigliano had become potent sites of "organized crime in Naples" in an international imaginary, Prestieri's action acquired an added charge.

Prestieri and Giuliano performed their spectacular demands for respect by drawing on their hyperbolic, careening, narcissistic rage (or the affects and aesthetics with which they could summon rage of that intensity) to enact flamboyant, swaggering, and violent masculinity. They performed their hegemony over their territorialized publics and for broader media publics they performed, wittingly or not, their part in the sensationalization of "organized crime in Naples." After he was arrested, Prestieri donned a blue suit and a tie, and blew a kiss to a throng of photojournalists for local, regional, and national newspapers.[109]

Until now, I have considered the self-exposing acts of bosses, but there is also a case of a neomelodico singer. In 2001 D'Alessio became the focus of national attention when he was investigated for allegedly accepting 2 billion lira (about U.S. $115,000) in financial backing from the Licciardi clan, allies of the Prestieri clan, to buy up and distribute for free the tickets to his own concert in 1997 at the San Paolo Stadium in

Naples. After some months the charge was dropped, but that was not the end of the scandal that put D'Alessio and, by association, "the camorra" in the spotlight. In November 2008, just one month after Prestieri's arrest, D'Alessio talked to journalists for the Italian edition of *Vanity Fair* about his "past" associations with Neapolitan crime clan affiliates. He dismissed the scandal of 2001, in which he was investigated not only for *concorso esterno in associazione di stampo mafioso* (receiving a contribution from a mafialike association for achieving illicit ends) but also for giving his brother's identity card to a boss: "All of it absurdity."[110]

D'Alessio described how before his 1997 concert that got him signed with BMG Ricordi, he sang at the weddings and baptisms of camorristi. At one gig, the bride was late, but he had to leave for his next performance. When the father of the bride told him if his daughter did not hear D'Alessio sing, "the end of the world would have come." He stayed and waited so long that he didn't make it to his next gig. "The father of the bride 'saved me' from that other family." It was impossible to refuse the "requests" of camorristi, including requests to perform at their family functions. "Do you know how many times I received death threats?" he asked, repeating to *Vanity Fair* the camorra-style ultimatums he frequently heard: "'If you don't come to my son's wedding, I'll cut your throat'"; "'If you don't sing your stuff at my nephew's baptism lunch, I'll break your head.'"[111]

D'Alessio also elaborated on his earnings. Although he was performing at up to fifteen gigs a day for up to 1,200,000 lira (about U.S. $700) per gig, his employers often would not pay him. "Obviously, I wouldn't protest. The new camorristi don't have rules. They don't give a damn about anything or anybody. So when they asked me for the bill [at the end of my performance], I responded, 'A thank-you note with your signature is enough for me.' Their pride gratified, they even opened up their wallets."[112]

D'Alessio's choice to offer these revelations to a popular nationally distributed periodical at first appears bold, but his words are neither a denouncement nor a confession. When the journalist asked him if he "repented" (a.k.a. pentito) for having performed for several years at the weddings and baptisms of camorristi, D'Alessio responded with a resolute "No." He explained, "If you're a singer in Naples and you begin to acquire a little fame, it's inevitable that you end up in such circles. But it's one thing to do one's job and it's another to collude."[113] Making neomelodica music in Naples means practicing the art of making do. This art inevitably brings its practitioners into contact with organized crime affiliates. As long as the former continue to perform as artists, they can claim distinction from the latter.

Aesthetics of Exposure

The 2004–5 feud in Scampia and Secondigliano attracted international attention not only because of the horrific violence but also because of the publication in 2006 of an unprecedented exposé on organized crime in Naples by a young journalist named Roberto Saviano. His book *Gomorra* quickly became an international success. Although the book is composed largely from investigative reports, most of which are public record, Saviano was the first to weave them into legible narratives. He sketched identifiable characters, calling them by name, tracing their affiliations, and detailing their criminal acts. He also integrated them with his own experiences working among the Chinese at Naples's port, a hotpoint for counterfeit goods. He contrasts the physical deterioration of Scampia and Secondigliano with the agility, vitality, and choreographed precision of the multimillion-euro multinational drug trafficking enterprise it hosts. He describes an innovative flexible economy where women get pregnant by clansmen to secure pensions and where "traditional" pensioners invest in the cocaine trade. He describes how shop owners fall victim to userers, who seize both the shops and shop owners, making them the front people for the clan's newly legitimated enterprises.[114]

In the final chapter, Saviano describes how crime clans have dominated Campania's trash disposal industry, created illegal toxic landfills, and, in his home town of Casal di Principe, poured cement over the waste and built large-scale housing projects. At a public press conference in the town's central piazza, he fired his *denuncia* (denouncement) in person, addressing his enemies by name: "Schiavone, Bidognetti, Zagaria: you are worth nothing." He then urged the town's residents to oust the fugitive bosses who lurk among them.[115]

Saviano's book has been translated into several languages and has sold millions of copies, sparking public discussions, at first nationally and then internationally, about the "emergency" of Naples. Saviano appeared frequently on television and sat for interviews or published editorials in print media. In Naples an anxious atmosphere rolled in. People I talked to described a "visceral" experience of disgust, anger, and foreboding while reading or hearing Saviano's denunciations. Some noted that amid the media buzz there was an uncanny dark silence, like a sinkhole. It was not long before Saviano received death threats, and, after his many supporters outspokenly voiced their support, he received government protection.

For some, *Gomorra* marked the division between a pre- and postexposure Naples. Now that the precedent had been set, who else would speak and what would they say? There was speculation that the very practice of writing in Naples about Naples might uniformly take on a new imperative of exposure. Or would Neapolitan writers and their publics continue talking in postcards, this time replacing one set of folkloric tropes (pizza and mandolins) with another (the camorra and the Neapolitan periphery)?[116] An answer came quickly, when a proliferation of exposés on the camorra, some of them written by camorristi themselves, appeared. Some chronicled the lives of innocent victims of camorra crossfire, while others sketched the careers of camorristi. Each was an overdetermined act of camorra outing that risked contributing to a public normalization of the camorra in Naples. While Saviano's number-one Mondadori best seller continued to unsettle countless readers across Italy and throughout the world, a new sort of Neapolitan postcard began to circulate. The iconic image that contains a majestic view of the Bay of Naples and Vesuvius, with knotty pines in the foreground, became a blood-spattered panorama on the cover of *Gomorra* distributed in the U.S. market.

According to some Italian politicians, the year's events, beginning with the feud in Scampia and Secondigliano and culminating in the public outing of "the camorra," required a response. Ministers talked about "the emergency of Naples," a characterization newspapers, TV programs, and blogs rapidly diffused, in effect resuscitating the "Neapolitan question."[117] In October 2006 Minister of Justice Clemente Mastella announced that although he used to feel differently, sending the military into Naples to contain the emergency would not be a taboo.[118] Mastella was prepared to out the state by exposing its monopoly on violence in response to the camorra's own indecent exposure. When he made his announcement, animated public debate ensued. Some Neapolitans exclaimed that Naples needed more jobs and public resources, not more rule of law. Others complained that people who perennially vilified Naples would begin to avidly collect the new, camorra edition of the Neapolitan postcard.

Parliament transferred one thousand police from other parts of Italy to Naples and one thousand video surveillance cameras into the city's streets and piazzas. Meanwhile, new exposés appeared in print. In Naples the large chain bookstores Feltrinelli and Fnac set aside a table dedicated to the new genre, incorporating even pre-*Gomorra* works into the growing niche market it had identified. Some years later, a larger table was needed to include exposés on Berlusconi and the Vatican.

During this time Isaia Sales, economic adviser of the Campania region, and the sociologist Marcello Ravveduto gave a highly publicized presentation of their book, *The Streets of Violence.* In their book, a study of Campanian organized crime, they implicate neomelodica music. They write that the neomelodici "affirm the identity of an urban minority that seeks, through these songs, cultural recognition of their way of life." At the same time, the authors argue that neomelodici lyricists write songs only for "their" publics. They emphasize that neomelodica music emerged in the same period that Pino Mauro performed his canzoni 'e mala, to an "exclusively local" and "neo-plebeian" audience, which they describe as having been a pool of potential affiliates of Cutolo's NCO. Neomelodica music, they write, continues to endorse the "values typical of the Neapolitan periphery in which illegality is often confused with daily life and daily life with the camorra."[119]

The book presentation also featured Minister of Interior Giuliano Amato, who was in Naples on a promised monthly monitoring visit. Amato echoed the authors' sentiments by denouncing the neomelodici for "exalting" camorristi as "heroes."[120] The denunciations triggered protests from many camps, from politicians to artists to the neomelodici themselves. Raiz, former leader of the dub group Almemegretta (whose song "Hannibal's Children" invoked Italian "blackness"), defended the neomelodici as "neorealists."[121] The novelist Erri De Luca said in an interview that as "First Policeman," Amato's denunciations carry the weight of proper indictments. Sarcastically, he suggested that the minister also indict Martin Scorsese and Francis Ford Coppola. Amato's behavior, he said, is reminiscent of the fascist-era "Miniculpop" (Ministry of Popular Culture).[122]

As an alternative culture industry, the neomelodica scene consolidates, like the dominant culture industry, a political economic culture whose internal consistency naturalizes it from within and makes it seem impenetrable from without. This apparent impenetrability perhaps contributes to fears that neomelodica music threatens state hegemony. Or another way to interpret the strong reactions of politicians to neomelodica music scene is that it "deforms" dominant culture industry. When boss–impresari dictate market tastes, they perform with parodic literalness the practices of dominant culture industry elites. Commercial liberalism as the basis of a stable democracy rests on the free pursuit of "interests," the new name assigned to one of the "passions" during the rise of modern capitalism.[123] Neomelodica music enacts a rogue commodity culture that reveals through mimesis the "magic" and fraud of the state and lures people away from a sense of national belonging.[124]

Verismo

The "secret of publicity" is that it continually reproduces "suspicious subjects."[125] Repeated revelations about the horrors of Naples have produced an overexposed world, a stereotype. The blood-spattered postcard has become a symbol that no longer references the world; instead, these representations are currency in consumer markets and in politics. The aesthetics of exposure incites people to adopt a hermeneutics of suspicion as a consumer–citizen practice.[126] Tano Grasso, an entrepreneur from Palermo who in 1991 denounced mafiosi extortionists and founded the Italian Antiracket Federation, calls this *Gomorrismo* (Gomorrism): feeling civically engaged simply by reading.[127]

Or by watching a film. The dialogic phenomena of publicity versus exposure are useful for making sense of the affective–aesthetic atmosphere captured and generated when in 2008 Saviano's *Gomorra* became a feature film. The film is composed of three alternating narratives, one of which takes place largely inside the housing project known locally as Le vele (The sails), located in Scampia. About shooting in this neighborhood, Garrone said, "When you cross the line and go inside that community, it's very hard to tell who's good and who's bad. . . . It's a big gray zone."[128]

Discoveries about the cast of the film after its release brought this big gray zone into relief. Three actors, two of whom played crime bosses and the third a hitman, were identified as fugitives and arrested for drug dealing and camorristic association.[129] One of these "reality actors," Giovanni Venosa, has a record for extortion. In the film, Venosa's character is based on the Casal del Principe crime boss Francesco Schiavone, a.k.a. Sandokan, who orders the murder of two young men who attempt to become independent mobsters.[130] The two young men steal cocaine from African dealers and go to a remote location where they snort the coke and listen to a neomelodica song about advice to a woman whose love is unrequited. The younger of the two, played by Ciro Petrone, Pisellino (Little pea or Little dick), dances and serenades his friend: "But if he comes tonight / don't be a fool / and if your heart beats fast don't kiss him."[131]

Matteo Garrone, the director, said that he made the film by capturing life and its sounds as he found them.[132] When his production team tried to find Rosario Buccino, the author of "But if he comes tonight," they discovered that his actual name is Rosario Armani, a fugitive.

In another scene, the two discover a cache of weapons of the Casalesi boss (Venosa) and commit a *sgarro* (affront) by stealing them. They stand dressed only in their underwear in the shallow water of a lakeshore, showing each other how far they can shoot the(ir) guns. They compare themselves to Brian De Palma's depiction of the Cuban drug trafficker Tony Montana, a.k.a. Scarface. In 2010 police raided a wedding banquet at Villa Cupido, a top venue for private parties where neomelodici perform. Attending the banquet were several affiliates of the Prinno crime clan (linked to the powerful Sarno clan), a neomelodico named Rosario Miraggio (the performer of "But if he comes tonight"), and Ciro Petrone, the young actor of *Gomorra,* who was armed with a 9 mm pistol.[133]

People living in the gray zone that Garrone entered (and well beyond this zone, Saviano writes) have erected a closet at the threshold between knowing and unknowing. Whereas the "homosexual" hides in the closet from a hegemon who holds the privilege of unknowing, the becoming-hegemons in Gomorra's "Scarface" scene emerge from an inverted closet.[134] The camorrista enjoys the privilege of being unknown and coming out is his (or her) act of terror. Self-exposure is not denuding but titillating. He performs excessive manhood like a striptease. In their coming-out becoming-Scarface scene, the two characters also enjoy the privilege of excessive fraternizing. Petrone sought that privilege in real life.

In effect, organized crime affiliates collaborated on the film's production. They took active roles in producing globally circulating representations of their lives and setting these representations to a soundtrack. It is reasonable to suggest that the soundtrack was one of their areas of influence; in a fiercely competitive music scene dominated in part by

Gomorra's narrative centers on these two characters to tell a "coming of age" story, but with a perverse and ultimately destructive end: they visit a strip club and fail to consummate with women who work there because they are thrown out by bouncers, and their excessive fraternizing is their demise. Garrone also uses scenes of perversity to enframe the camorra in *The Embalmer* (2002), in which a beautiful young man is "lured" away from his fiancée when he strays into the workshop of an extremely short and unattractive taxidermist, for whom he becomes an apprentice; the taxidermist, also the mortician for fallen camorristi, is infatuated with the young man.

organized crime, it is not unlikely that a crime boss claimed the opportunity to get songs and singers under his purview into bigger media circuits. Indeed, that a crime boss made sure some songs were privileged over others would have been in perfect keeping with the film's verist aesthetic. Most importantly, the crime boss and the singer would have been giving a virtuosic performance of success for their intimate public.

Gomorra, in a sense, incorporates neomelodica music and the criminal associations that are linked to it in dominant culture industry while exposing the material work of incorporation in jarringly veristic ways. Diffusing the lurid discovery that the camorra infiltrated the cast and soundtrack of an internationally acclaimed film derived from an anti-camorra text, the infotainment industry has intensified this camorristic special effect. In the process, Campanian organized crime affiliates have used the dominant culture industry to mediate their protagonismo and circulate their self-depictions within their territories and transnational circuits of control. Meanwhile, Gomorrismo's audiences, a.k.a. Gomorristi, are complicit in these veristic performances.

Neomelodico singer Antonio Fischetti, a.k.a. Antoine, told the journalist who interviewed him during the faida of Scampia and Secondigliano, "Many singers . . . become famous only because they buy airtime on local TV channels. Moreover, in order to achieve rapid success, they speculate on delicate themes, putting into circulation trashy lyrics."[135] Fischetti's words discretely convey that many of the neomelodici who become famous speculate on la malavita. He is describing an aesthetic of excess: when organized crime figures in neomelodica song lyrics, it also figures in the entrepreneurial life of the performer. Similarly speculating on la malavita, the producers of Gomorra have also engaged in an aesthetic of excess: excessive realism.

The neomelodica scene is a contact zone enlivened by a continuum of tolerable and excessive arts of making do. In this contact zone, anomalous aesthetic forms and practices emerge. Neomelodica music is a remix of "traditional" and outmoded modern musics. It combines contemporary dialectal lyrics with ornamentalism. The music, when observed from the perspective of stable meanings and unity, is perceived as the refuse of a perverse modernity. Many neomelodici simultaneously appropriate this perversity as an identity form (in synch with their entrepreneurial hustle) while continually projecting this sense of trash on each other. They perform a variation of who am I and who are you? When dominant culture industry mediates this performance, it becomes an indeterminate part of it.

Assunta Spina (dir. Mario Mattoli, 1948).

THREE

The Sceneggiata
Melodramas of Manhood, Allegories of Violence

IN JULY 2009 two men, one in a car and the other on a Vespa, collided. The driver of the Vespa was knocked to the ground. He was not physically injured, but he suffered a moral offense. Enraged at having been thrown off his everyday ride down a familiar street, the Vespa driver shouted an insult at the car driver. According to *Il Mattino*, it was *"the* insult *per eccellenza"*; it was the kind of insult "that can raise the blood pressure of even the most astute and levelheaded."[1] The word was *cornuto* (cuckold). If a man is cuckolded, it is implied that he is physically and sexually impotent. The word makes sex and gender trouble. It conjures up the figure of a man unable to protect his property from other men and unable to satisfy "his" woman so that she doesn't wander off with other men. In Naples a cuckold is also described as *fesso,* a word derived from the slang for vagina, meaning dim-witted. The opposite of fesso is *furbo* (crafty, streetwise) or *sveglio* (awake). In this figuration, the ideal man holds sovereignty over his personal domain and demonstrates sexual potency, crafty preparedness, and the capacity for violence.

The moment he heard the Vespa driver shout "Cornuto!" the car driver lunged at his enemy, beating him brutally. When the police appeared, he got back into his vehicle and sped off. The Vespa driver, still on the scene, gave the police his account of the incident. When the police finished their report and left the scene, the car driver returned. This time he was on foot, and he was accompanied by several relatives. At the same time, the Vespa driver's relatives had joined him as well. The two families launched into a violent brawl, a *maxirissa* (maxiriot), as *Il Mattino* called it. The result was chaos. The "Far West."[2]

These events unfolded on a hot summer afternoon near Piazza del Plebescito, or Plebiscite Square, at the center of Naples (where the plebiscite for unification in 1860 took place). Bloodied combatants and terrified bystanders, some of them tourists, fled to the nearby Royal Palace (now the National Library) and others to the art nouveau Caffè Gambrinus, where during the belle epoque people came from all over Europe to watch variety shows composed of skits, poems, and Neapolitan songs.

This violent performance of guappo versus guappo was activated and even appears to have been necessitated by the convergence of bodies, circumstances, and affects. The collision occurred on a high-traffic piazza frequented by tourists and residents, some of whom became active participants in the scene. Presumably, the collision and the insult took place near the quartieri where the drivers live, making it possible for both of them to swiftly summon the support of relatives. Because it occurred so close to home, the collision intensified the perceived challenge to each man's personal sovereignty.[3] Moreover, as *Il Mattino* indicated, the uniquely charged word *cornuto* reverberated through the scene and intensified the collision's impact.

The two drivers felt "honor-bound" to use violence to communicate to one another, to the public, and to themselves their sense of personal sovereignty.[4] And their kin came to their aid, supporting their "autological" acts with "genealogical" force.[5] But the collision and its effects do not constitute a discrete, enclosed event. Rather, they are part of an open-ended performance that traverses day-to-day life in the form of communal, public negotiations about what kinds of masculinity, femininity, and shared spaces are recuperated from the past and produced in the present. At least this is the case in the milieu I frequented (and the quartieri where I lived, Piazza Garibaldi and the Quartieri Spagnoli).

This does not mean that personal sovereignty is necessarily grounded in honor, violence, or even manhood. The honorable man is a *figure* who "collects up and reflects back the hopes of a people . . . the sense of the possibility of fulfillment, the possibility of damnation, or the possibility of collective inclusion."[6] The honorable man uses his personal force to realize and maintain his sovereignty against the *sopraffazione* (oppressive bullying) of others, without the aid of the law.[7] He's an allegorical figure who inspires excessive exegesis: he's the brigand, bandit, lazzaro, and scugnizzo. He's Robin Hood and Masaniello. He's an extraordinary man of the *popolino* (little plebe), an "aristocrat of the plebe," the ancient hegemon, the Prince.[8] He's the nineteenth-century *guappo,* a word likely derived from the Spanish *guapo* (bully, tough guy). Much of this ambiguous figure's potency is built on appearances. He dresses like a gentleman who lives a life of leisure, but his modest wealth comes from managing the conflicts of others. He does not use violence frivolously, yet he appears strong and courageous, inspiring fear and respect. He is not a camorrista, but he does not live a life of legality. He makes his own laws, and he makes his own way in the world. He needs neither the Law nor a criminal organization like the camorra because he is his own source of power and *sapé fà* (know-how). He is 'O mast, the maestro, master of himself.[9]

The ongoing everyday performance of personal sovereignty is instantiated in the myriad practices encompassed by l'arte di arrangiarsi. The performance is enacted in many modalities, such as inventive bricolage, entrepreneurial *furbizia* (craftiness), or violence. These practices and modalities share a somewhat consistent set of affective–aesthetic qualities. These include hyperbolic acts (material, speech, and otherwise) of self-display; binary oppositions that surge in intensity and split the world into opposing forces; high-stakes ultimatums that mark a tipping point; a sense of moral injury and the demand for justice. At their excessive limit, these affective–aesthetic qualities concretize as violence.

But these performances once followed a different, less quotidian narrative than the travails and triumphs of l'arte di arrangiarsi. The figure of the personal sovereign is the main protagonist of the allegorical narrative called the *canzone sceneggiata* (staged song) or simply the *sceneggiata* (staged). The sceneggiata is a century-old Neapolitan melodramatic musical performance genre that has taken the form of theater, film (silent and sound), and music videos. It heavily influenced neomelodica music, which shares with it many aesthetic features and conjures some of the same sensibilities, but it is also fascinating in its own right. In its early life, the sceneggiata was a potent force in popular culture in Campania and in Italian diasporas. This force waned across decades of political economic change. Now the sceneggiata is staged only as fragments in Neapolitan popular culture and performances of everyday life. The reasons for this change are registered in both the waning potency of allegory and the allegorical narrative itself.

Allegorical Figures

The figure of the guappo has an ambiguous relationship to the figure of the camorrista. Like the camorrista, he is a self-realized sovereign, a man of honor who uses violence as a form of capital. Both figures are above the Law, but the guappo exercises restraint and the camorrista knows only excess. Unlike the camorrista, the guappo is not a businessman; he

Pasquale Squitieri's *I guappi* (The guappi, 1974). In this picturesque representation of late-nineteenth-century Naples, the law and the Law confront one another, embodied in the two main characters, played by actors who appear in many polizieschi films: Fabio Testi (the guappo in this image) and Franco Nero, a young man studying to be a lawyer who discovers he is from a family of camorristi. The two men butt heads but eventually become best friends. When the guappo kills the police inspector bent on capturing him, the lawyer defends the guappo in court, arguing that the murder was a crime of passion and honor because the inspector had cuckolded him.

never expands his political economic power beyond his quartiere. Unlike the camorrista, the guappo uses violence primarily to mediate violent situations; otherwise, he cultivates his power as his violent potential.

The figure of the guappo is an imperfect symbolization of a "premodern" golden age; he is "marred by the grit of reality" and grounded in the "mournful spectacle of history" and its ruins.[10] This is because he's dedicated to an impossible form of honorable manhood, which relies on personal force without recourse to the state authority and, if necessary, in opposition to it. His figuration is about a "collective yearning" that looks "backward in time, as if puzzling to remember an original meaning that has been lost."[11] Today the guappo is an anachronistic figure in

the era of the "new camorra" where camorristi collude with state authority in a limitless pursuit of private interest.

La Sceneggiata

"Formalized" in the early twentieth century, the sceneggiata is defined
in Italian dictionaries as the Neapolitan melodrama *per eccellenza,* where
a dramatic plot is spun from the song it showcases, and often songs are
composed with a three-act sceneggiata in mind.[12] It consists of a formu-
laic plot described locally by the phrase *Isso, essa, e 'o malamente* (He, She,
and the Evildoer), the drama's three archetypal protagonists. A hetero-
sexual couple is violated by a male interloper. The boyfriend or husband
is betrayed or perceives that he is betrayed by his girlfriend or wife. He
vindicates himself by killing her lover and her, or giving her a sfregio, or
a scarring gash across her cheek. Violent self-vindication is the only way
to recuperate and safeguard his manhood and honor. By marking "his"
woman with a sfregio and literally defacing her, he puts his potent manhood on public display.[13]

When a man wages violent self-vindication against his unfaithful
woman and his male competitor, he commits "crimes of honor" in accor-
dance with the "law of the vicolo." However, his acts of violence provoke
a confrontation with the Law, and he is imprisoned.[14] Imprisonment
(one form of personal sovereignty sacrificed for another), in turn, means
family fissure, provoking a lyrical lament within the drama:

> My mamma is ill
> How she calls out for me and waits for me
> And because I am imprisoned, I cannot save her.[15]

Significantly, it is the "wife-whore," the unrestrained and undomesti-
cated woman, who severs the contact between her husband or fiancé and
his innocent mother.[16] The role assigned to the mother in a man's life
mirrors the privileged role of the Madonna in Italian Catholic worship.
In the sceneggiata, the suffering and sacrificing mother overshadows her
son's fiancée or wife. *She* is becoming-mother and perpetually risks failing to fully complete her transformation. *She* is oversexed and promiscuous, and her uncontrolled sexuality provides the Evildoer entry into the
family. Her body is the family's weakness, inviting moral ruin to fall on,
in particular, the man of the family.

The sceneggiata is an allegory for the conflicts that a corrupt power creates in the everyday life of ordinary families in the Neapolitan popular classes.[17] Allegory is a "way of seeing" that endows signs with a unique power "that makes them appear no longer commensurable with profane things," raising them to a "higher plane."[18] The unique power of the early sceneggiata as allegory is that it enabled ordinary individuals to transfigure daily life in terms of a "higher level" code of honor.[19] In the early sceneggiata, the guappo figured honorable manhood. The guappo was a man of superior force and style; he was a sovereign who paid attention as much to his presentation of self as to his realization of self under the expectant gaze of his milieu. The sceneggiata achieved its enormous success because it provided audiences with clear-cut justice not found in real life:[20]

> According to the law of the theater, she has to die
> The audience, in delirium, has no choice but to applaud.[21]

Targeting women enhances the gendered potency of men's violent performances. As the song "The King of the Sceneggiata" claims, the audience is delirious when that force is unleashed. They not only applaud wildly but also hitch themselves to that force and participate in the performance with shouts that become a repartee between performers and audience, eventuating at times in physical violence.[22] The heightened emotions of melodrama have the capacity to carry participants to a level of "truth," even if the spectacle is not necessarily "real."[23]

Neapolitans recount episodes of audience members climbing onstage to slap or punch the Evildoer. In fact, to stop the bleed between the true and the real, one theater constructed barriers to separate actors from audience. The barrier, however, did not deter spectators from waiting menacingly for the Evildoer at the exit after the performance.[24] In 1920, when Eliva Notari's film-sceneggiata 'A legge (The law) was screened at Salone Margherita in Galleria Umberto I, the police were called in to quell the riotous crowd.

The potency of the sceneggiata is that it achieves "iconicity of style." Style is composed of shared conventions of form that are "empirically real" but "also necessarily general, vague, and physical, feelingfully ingrained in affective time and space." Style becomes iconic when the aesthetic metaphors people use to refer to it feel "naturally real, obvious, complete" and when the aesthetic beliefs they make manifest seem "natural, proper and moral."[25] People take up cultural forms as a lived sensibility, allowing highly predictable aesthetic formulas to retain social potency over time.

Staged Histories

The sceneggiata genre has undergone changes over its discontinuous century-long history. These changes do not merely reflect material history or perceptions of history. History is not merely registered in the sceneggiata as aesthetic form; history is also *made by* this allegorical sensibility, as its retrospective narratives follow sceneggiata plotting. This happens in texts, songs, images, and their patchwork, a.k.a. everyday, life. The guappo and the "old camorra" are nostalgic figurations that come to life and are elided in the contact zone where scholarly and popular histories intermingle.[26]

According to popular perception and some scholarly accounts, when the "new camorra" began trafficking drugs and accumulated unprecedented capital, it became "modern." The modern camorrista does not know the value of self-limitation; he replaced the values of honor and tradition with purely economic value and pursued it in alliance with state authority. The modern camorrista, no longer concerned about the popular classes, sought embourgeoisement. This figuration is partly produced by the desire to stage popular resistance against the crimes of modernity, disavowing the fact that nineteenth-century camorristi were already entrepreneurial moderns. Their contemporary, the writer Marc Monnier, did not share this desire because it is intrinsically nostalgic. He emphasized their apolitical self-interest, reporting the proud declaration of a camorrista: "We squeeze gold out of lice." A camorrista's "honor" came not from the respect of his milieu but from the money he extorted from even the most abject.[27]

The sceneggiata, like these staged histories, drew some of its early inspiration from the *canzone di giacca,* which itself was inspired by the work of poets such as Ferdinando Russo in the late nineteenth century.[28] The sceneggiata emerged from the *café-chantant* scene of the belle epoque and became musical theater around 1916–19.[29] In the 1920s it was entwined with Neapolitan verist cinema, its silent contemporary. During the projection of films by Elvira Notari and Nicola Notari and other directors, singers often performed live with an orchestra in front of the screen.

The projection was synced with the music, rather than vice versa. These were "film performances" in which songs carried the images, actualizing them anew with each live screening.[30]

In contrast to the studio-shot epic narratives produced in Rome, a mixture of spontaneous and performed outdoor-life scenes dominated Neapolitan cinema. The Notaris shot scripted arguments on city streets and had the camera crew film from hidden locations. The staged arguments attracted the participation of passersby, and the scene became a blended dramatic–realist performance. On one occasion Notari's crew came across a group of young children playing the game Italians versus Turks. They asked the children to start from the beginning while they filmed them, and the children played so hard that they injured one another.[31]

Sceneggiata cinema faded after the 1920s and, after a small revival in the 1940s, returned in full force in the 1970s with the films of singers such as Mario Merola and Pino Mauro and lasted until the mid-1980s, with singers Nino D'Angelo and Carmelo Zappulla. The 1970s was also the decade of the *poliziesco* (crime drama). Like the late sceneggiata-film, the poliziesco was low budget. As with the verist cinema of the silent era, the poliziesco was often filmed in public places without clearly marked boundaries. While filming a crime scene for Umberto Lenzi's feature *The Manhunt,* actors were shot at when the actual police arrived.[32] According to Stelvio Massi, director of both film-sceneggiate and polizieschi, film crews and actors were professionals of the "art of making do."[33]

The art of making do was not only a mode of filmmaking. It is also a narrative force in the films themselves. In the poliziesco, the art of making do goes far beyond its excessive limit, offering scenes of spectacular violence in a chaotic world of boundless corruption. In the late film-sceneggiata, the art of making do remains the modest practice of workaday people who are threatened by the excesses of others. What is distinctive about both kinds of films is that the romantic guappo figure recedes into the background and the camorrista figure takes his place.

While in the early sceneggiata, la malavita was blended with everyday life among the popular classes, in the late sceneggiata the life of crime is more clearly marked as "the camorra." In the late sceneggiata, neither the camorrista nor the ordinary man follows the tradition of *guapparia* (guappism). The camorrista derives honor from the wealth he acquires through sopraffazione, and the ordinary man derives his from the sovereign art of making do. They confront one another in the contact zone, where a new melodrama unfolds in the twilight of the camorra's golden age.

Assunta Spina: Disfigurement, Murder, and Manhood

Before the twilight, Salvatore di Giacomo's 1896 play *Assunta Spina* was adapted to the silent screen in 1915 by Francesca Bertini, who also plays the title role, and Gustavo Serena. The story is the tragedy of a Neapolitan *stiratrice* (ironer at a laundry) and her undying devotion to her fiancé, Michele the butcher from across the vicolo. When the couple goes to the elegant and romantic neighborhood Posillipo with its extraordinary panoramas of the Bay of Naples to celebrate her name day with friends and family, they encounter trouble.[34] Raffaele, an old suitor of Assunta's who has not yet given up on her, shows up at the celebration. With languid sidelong glances at Assunta, he wanders like a cunning leopard around the animated table of dining and drinking guests. Michele, who has already expressed his turbulently jealous side a few times over in the story, is now inconsolable. "But I love only you," Assunta declares while stroking his cheek and kissing him. Achieving no effect, Assunta makes one last attempt by putting her arms around Michele to coax him back to his loving self. When he shoves her away, the proud and beautiful Assunta lingers for a moment, as if thinking something over, before walking off. Michele paces back and forth alone at the far end of the terrace.

Assunta, to spite Michele, coquettishly asks Raffaele to dance. An intertitle reads, "And thus the inevitable happens." Michele's jealously is unhinged, and it propels the plot of the sceneggiata along its expected course. Michele rushes in on the dancing couple and tries to jump Raffaele, but his friends hold him back. When Assunta throws her arms around Michele in a desperate effort to calm him, he pushes her away even more violently than before and storms off. As the party disperses, Michele's mother belligerently confronts Assunta: "You've ruined my son's life!" she shouts, lunging at her. The condemnation overwhelms Assunta, who weeps wretchedly as she is led home by a group of women from the party.

Making their way through the city streets, the women are surprised by Michele, who bursts out from a nearby doorway. Running straight into the small entourage, he aims for Assunta with his razor and slashes her cheek before running off. Assunta collapses into the arms of her companions, who help her into the nearest dwelling. Still clutching her right cheek, she is eased into a chair. Suddenly she shouts, "A mirror! I want a mirror!" Then, taking her hands away from her face and holding up a mirror, she sees a deep, bloody gash.

Assunta's disfigurement tells a public secret. It makes explicit "that which is generally known, but cannot be articulated."[35] The incident that drove Michele to attack his fiancée was one that he read as an encroachment on his public image as a man capable of "domesticating" the sexual impulses of his fiancée by properly satisfying them; otherwise she would not stray to other men.[36] By disfiguring her, he seizes control of her betrayal, the public secret that threatens to efface him, making him an *omm 'e niente* (man of nothing), a cuckold. He tells the secret himself, using violence to expose it, and restores his honorable manhood.

Significantly, Michele reacts to an incident that is not an actual betrayal but a semblance. Moreover, he reacts to Assunta's intentional performance of this semblance. Nonetheless, "the inevitable happens." An apparent correspondence between the signs of betrayal and actual betrayal materializes in the embodied sign of the sfregio. Michele's allegorical way of seeing produces "a world in which the detail is of no importance," where exact relationships between signs and their referents are immanently spurious and therefore superfluous.[37] For him and the other men of his milieu, it is the "higher plane" of honor to which the signs of betrayal, true and verisimilar, point. It is also on this plane that signs have a peculiar potency that men harness to become men of honor. A man of honor recodes his world in this manner.

The sfregio was punishable by law, but the "law of the vicolo" affords men the right to commit such "crimes of honor." This is how Michele attempts to defend himself in court in the 1948 remake of *Assunta Spina* by Mario Mattoli, starring the Neapolitan playwright and actor Eduardo de Filippo and the famous actress Anna Magnani. Michele claims that a man has the right to do what he wishes with his "property," invoking the unique fusion of interests and affects that make violations of personal property an intense offense to honor in his milieu.[38]

Assunta shares this allegorical way of seeing. She defends her fiancé by telling the judge, "But he's jealous, he has always been jealous." However, she fails to sway the court in Michele's favor. The next scene summarizes the full narrative with striking economy. Assunta nervously waits under the long portico of the courthouse courtyard, holding her black headscarf over her scarred cheek. The jailers escort Michele down the portico and when they reach Assunta, the couple exchanges glances. As the jailers continue along the portico, Assunta begins following them, as if tethered. Coming to her senses, she stops and huddles against the wall. Then she hears Michele's distraught mother, shrieking as she reels down the passageway in pursuit of her son. Three women, a man, and a child brace her, all of them moving together in a tangle toward Assunta. Michele's mother lunges at her, but her crowd of guardians holds her back. Suddenly remembering her sorrow, Michele's mother turns back to desperately chase her son down the portico.

Just then Federigo enters the scene. An elegantly dressed prison official, he's been present during the trial and its aftermath. He stops near the cringing, shrouded Assunta and murmurs something in her ear. It takes Assunta a moment to respond. She turns her pained face toward the man. He has just offered to arrange for her fiancé to serve his sentence in Naples so that she can visit him. Now interested and determined, she asks, "Really? . . . How much will it cost?"

"Nothing," the official responds, simply and calmly.

Incredulous, Assunta asks, "What do you mean nothing? No one does these things for nothing. They require money, I know. . . . How much?"

Still calmly, Federigo repeats, "Nothing," then adds, "Nothing yet."

A look of disturbing recognition passes across Assunta's face. Disappointedly, she replies, "Aaah. Thank you very much, but no."

The plot of the sceneggiata is distilled in a sequence of bodily movements within just two brief consecutive shots. When Michele is escorted past Assunta, we see the magnetism of their jealous love as it tugs at her and leads her a few steps toward imprisonment. Immediately following is Michele's mother, wavering between pursuing her son and attacking Assunta. In the long, centuries-old portico of the courthouse, Assunta is physically wedged in the middle of an intense dynamic between mother and son. When Federigo arrives, Assunta is also caught in the middle of another potent relation: between her fiancé and his rival.

In the first dynamic, the "virgin" mother disparages Assunta's alleged uncontrolled sexuality, the cause of her son's ruin. Essentially, she accuses Assunta of betraying the implicit understanding that "relations between husband and wife [are] just part of that network of family relations which [bind] the complex together."[39] Sex within a marriage may create a family, but it cannot thereafter interfere with it. Furthermore, marital sex is not an appropriate topic for public discussion.[40] Assunta's first infraction of the law of the vicoli was to generate public signs that could be taken to refer to her (questionable) sex life with her fiancé. Michele's mother assails Assunta for failing to behave like a proper future mother, one who will uphold her husband's honor and, by extension, his capacity to maintain the livelihood of his family.

Michele's capacity to produce a family with Assunta or any other woman is put into question by Assunta's performance of a betrayal. This is the significant feature of the second dynamic in which Assunta is caught, between her fiancé and his true interloper, Federigo. As the narrative progresses, we learn that Assunta finds no other recourse than to give in to Federigo's extortion of sexual favors. And in so doing, she becomes attached to him. Federigo, however, has a wife and kids and grows tired of Assunta. Abandoned for several tortuous weeks, she begs him to come to her for one last dinner. He concedes her wish, but just before he arrives, Michele walks through the door. He's been released from prison early. Assunta finds no way to avert the impending disaster. Resigned, she confesses everything to Michele.

The inevitable happens. When Federigo arrives, Michele stabs him. Honor is performed through personal force without and, if necessary, against the authority of the state. The Law in this sceneggiata is corrupt and *prepotente* (arrogant and oppressive). It not only punishes Michele for the sfregio he rightfully inflicted on Assunta, it even cuckolds him in the person of Federigo.

When the police arrive, Assunta tells them that she is the murderer. She obeys an implicit expectation to repeatedly sacrifice herself to save the man who loves her and to protect her potential family. Self-preservation is not necessarily the man's prerogative, but it is defined in relation to a man's concerns, the first of which is the maintenance of his honor and through it, the honor and longevity of his family.[41] *Assunta Spina* is about the law of the vicolo, where violent self-vindication is perceived as a necessary social fact. It renders justice through an allegory that refers to a "higher level," where the moral life of personal sovereignty transcends the "details" of state Law.

Betrayal: Melodramas of Making Do

In the early sceneggiata, 'O malamente is either a philandering solitary guappo or a corrupt state official. In the late sceneggiata, from the 1970s onward, the Evildoer is more often a camorrista, the boss of a criminal organization. These family dramas are driven not by crimes of honor but by crimes associated with l'arte di arrangiarsi and its excessive limit, organized crime. In this new sceneggiata, the conflict centers on the *sgarro* (challenge) against the camorra, and frequently there is no unfaithful woman to mediate the conflict. In the early sceneggiata the "unjustice system," or the Law, punishes good men who safeguard their honor.[42] In the late sceneggiata this system is an unwanted intrusion into the everyday art of making do, which at times requires excessive acts and moral compromise.

The late film-sceneggiata *Tradimento* (Betrayal) typifies this moral political economic family drama. Merola plays Gennaro, a vendor who sells octopus broth without a license, struggling to support his wife and kids. The film begins with scenes of Gennaro wheeling his cauldron while singing "Acquarello napoletano." The song begins with a melodious call-to-sale, executed as a *canto à distesa* (extended song): "I'll have you drink a broth of real octopus / full of pepper."[43]

Gennaro's modest earnings attract the interest of a camorrista who demands a tangente. When Gennaro refuses to pay, the camorrista has the police bust him. When Gennaro continues to challenge his authority, the camorrista entraps Gennaro by concocting a scenario that incites him to attempt to carry out an honor crime.

Meanwhile Ruotolo, a young, aspiring singer played by D'Angelo, is courting Gennaro's teenage daughter. Ruotolo commits *scippi* (purse snatchings) to save up the money he needs to produce his first album. For Gennaro, Ruotolo plays at the threshold that separates *scugnizzi* (young petty criminals) from organized criminals, and he forbids him to have anything to do with his daughter. Ruotolo is presented as a likable ordinary man. In one scene, he expresses remorse, returning to a poor old woman the handbag he stole from her. The woman, moved to tears by his gesture, calls Ruotolo *figlio mio* (my son).

Both Gennaro and Ruotolo are everyday Neapolitans who commit crimes in the service of l'arte di arrangiarsi. However, the two men differ in their interpretations of that art. Gennaro judges Rutolo for his excesses, and Rutolo expresses disdain for Gennaro's interpretation of personal sovereignty as honorable self-restraint: "The world is for those who take it," he shouts at Gennaro. "Look at this," he continues, showing him a fanned-out wad of lira notes. "This is money . . . . Don Gennà, I have liras and you're dying of hunger!"

Tradimento (dir. Alfonso Brescia, 1982).

One way to interpret the dramatic tension between Gennaro and Ruotolo is to take it for the inner conflict of the popular classes, forestalling class-consciousness before the characters can even begin to enunciate it. Such an interpretation might come from the politicizing impulse of the dominant mainstream culture industry to redeem and incorporate the sceneggiata genre. However, the kind of political economic identity at the heart of *Betrayal* and other sceneggiate is honorable manhood or womanhood as family members, not as members of a class or of society. A more plausible interpretation of the conflict between Gennaro and Ruotolo is that it is an inner drama of the everyday family, this time wagered between pure fathers and "unhonorable" men. The moral political–economic drama introduces a new conflict for men, women, and families in which family health and stability are imperiled by the choices of men (the father–husband and the father–husband-to-be), as well as the contaminants that oversexed women carry into the family nucleus.

The dramatic tension in *Betrayal* and other sceneggiate from the same period is the desire for a better life for one's family and the moral compromises made necessary by the ever-present and ineradicable camorra. Once having ventured into the "shadow" economy, thieves such as Ruotolo would eventually be enticed by the greater riches to be had through organized, rather than freelance, petty criminal activities.

Gennaro's wife, Carmela, who is a juice and granita vendor in the same piazza (and obediently pays the camorrista his regular tribute), secretly solicits the help of a powerful lawyer who patronizes her stall. He tells her to visit his studio. When she finds him, she pleads with him to wipe out the charges against her husband. She underscores how it is an uncomfortable situation that she should earn money while he cannot. However, the lawyer is uninterested in Carmela's husband. His goal is to bait Carmela and have his way with her. He grabs hold of her and kisses her. When she resists, he pounces on her. She kicks him in the crotch and scrambles toward the door. Just as she reaches the threshold, he grabs hold of her skirt. Carmela wrests herself free and runs out into the street.

Once she's outside, Carmela realizes she must quickly regain her composure; after all, her visit to the lawyer was illicit. Adjusting her rumpled outfit, she notices a piece of fabric has been torn from her skirt. The lawyer, still lying on the floor of his studio where Camela left him, is triumphantly holding the missing fragment. The piece of fabric becomes a concrete sign of Carmela's betrayal when it shows up in the hands of the local boss who has had it in for Gennaro. The circulating fragment traces the outline of a conspiracy. The camorrista teams up with the lawyer, whose deepest injury is that Gennaro's wife, an uneducated and poor woman in need, has spurned his affections. The two male villains spread rumors about Carmela's promiscuity. People begin talking. The camorrista then calls Gennaro directly, turning rumor into reality. When Gennaro confronts the camorrista face-to-face to defend his honor, the camorrista makes his coup de grâce. Waving before Gennaro's face the fragment of Carmela's dress, the camorrista provokes Gennaro to commit a crime of passion. Gennaro stabs the camorrista, and the police arrest Gennaro.

The title of this sceneggiata derives from its central conflict, his wife's betrayal or perceived betrayal. Her interference in her husband's sovereign performance of l'arte di arrangiarsi, just like Assunta's interference in Michele's, is an emasculating transgression that is likened to and elided with adultery. This inspires Gennaro to sing:

Cold like the blade of a knife
the truth entered my heart
At once the world goes to pieces
you kill me without a thought.[44]

Faithful to the early sceneggiata, the late sceneggiata is centered on the family drama. The "oversexed" and "fragmented" woman is blamed for ceding to 'O malamente and endangering her husband's honor and the vitality of the family. This is the case with Gennaro's wife as it is with his teenage daughter, Titina. When she comes home one evening wearing a new, trendy jacket, her father grabs hold of her and demands to know its origins. When he learns it's from Ruotolo, he assumes the jacket is the fruit of his petty crime and insists that she return it. Both the daughter and her mother—there is also Gennaro's pained mother who must helplessly observe the unfolding conflicts, as well as Gennaro and Carmela's prepubescent daughter, who becomes the conduit for gossip the crime boss has spread about her mother—endanger the family with the allegorical fragments worn on or torn from their bodies.

In this sceneggiata, the camorrista cuckolds the everyday man by getting into bed with the Law. In a sense, the camorrista disfigures the guappo; the camorrista sullies its own sublimated form. He entraps the everyday man with the traditional code of honor that everyday men and camorristi shared in the early sceneggiata. In the new order of things, similitude is not reality and allegorical signs are their own betrayal. In *Betrayal*, as in *Assunta Spina*, apparent betrayal and actual betrayal are equally burdened with the freight of affect. But in *Betrayal*, the true betrayal is the decaying allegory of honorable manhood undone by its overly polysemic signs. It marks the attenuation of the allegorical mode of attention itself. Rather than elevate everyday life to a higher plane, the allegory gets caught in the "grit of reality," the base truth that the camorra and the Law are conspirators. Without the guappo to figure it, honor gets lodged in the profane everyday world as a moral political economy, and the sceneggiata becomes the melodramatization of l'arte di arrangiarsi.

The Stage of Life

The double face of the sceneggiata as aesthetic form and sensibility, as an allegorical sensibility, shows up in both Italian and Neapolitan dictionaries, which give the word a second meaning: "an exaggerated and often insincere display of sentiments and emotions,"[45] "a fictitious situa-

When Mario Merola died in 2006, thousands crowded into Piazza Mercato around the church Santa Maria del Carmine (the same church commonly associated with Masaniello) to say farewell. Antonio Bassolino, then president of the Campania region, and Rosa Russo Iervolino, mayor of Naples, attended the ceremony. In 1999 Merola costarred in Ninì Grassia's film-sceneggiata *A Hundred Years* with Gigi D'Alessio, who becomes the representative voice of the contemporary form of the sceneggiata, neomelodica music. I talked with Merola twice, the first time on the set of the satellite broadcast Napoli International. When I asked him how he felt about the neomelodici, he answered, "My son, Neapolitan song will never die."

tion created in order to confuse or affect."[46] The sceneggiata is a mise-en-scène, a performance that makes protagonists and puts them in the scene. The sceneggiata is an "aesthetic event of the senses" where matter shifts into image shifts into matter.[47]

A sceneggiata is an event that occurs when aesthetic form and sensibility collide for performers and publics. The collision conjures an iconic figure who gives back to them their collective affective investment. The more participants expend and give themselves over, the more they get back in pleasure. To critics of the sceneggiata, the full-bodied participation of spectators in a melodrama that "exalted" violence was alarming. They attacked the "retrograde" moral code it sustained and blamed it for inciting people to carry out violent vendettas. They also attacked its aesthetic form, popular melodrama. Like the criticisms of melodrama that circulated in other parts of Europe and the United States in the early twentieth century, these critics emphasized the sceneggiata's facile reduction of complex situations to simple (and problematic) binaries and its sacrifice of character multidimensionality to cartoonish hyperbole.[48] These aesthetic features encouraged people to engage in the affective fallacy of reading from the heart.[49] Indeed, critics seemed never to be able to divorce their aesthetic criticisms of the sceneggiata from participants' moral–affective investments in it. The sceneggiata, they believed, triggered irrational, passional excess and made characters rush toward fatefully emplotted ends.

Participants of the sceneggiata, and its descendant neomelodica music, appraise performances with a recurring metaphor: whether the performance "comes from the heart." The first criterion for a successful sceneggiata is that it moves its spectators, even making them cry. Commotion, being moved together, far more often than the sceneggiata's content, is, for fans, the purest expression of Neapolitan identity. The sceneggiata's narrative and lyrical content follow highly conventionalized forms that tend to steer "meaning" away from its linguistic referentiality toward what links all sceneggiata performances: the public's full participation, such that they are both affected and affect the performance in return.[50] People feel they are participating when the sceneggiata stares back at them.

In 2003 I attended the premier of the film-sceneggiata *Il latitante* (The fugitive), a film based on Tommy Riccio's overwhelmingly popular song of 1997 by the same title. Cinema Corso hosted the event behind the central train station at Piazza Garibaldi. The crowd slowly leaked in—the singers, the actors, the film crew, friends, fans, and others who wanted to be seen. Women wore lacy, semitransparent, tight-fitting blouses that revealed ample cleavage, long fishnet stockings half-submerged in tall black boots, thick lipstick, and demure expressions that tried both to repel and to attract. The men had more gel in their hair than usual. Some captured small windstorms in the styling—whirls of hair that finished in sticky, protruding points at the top back of the head and at the temples, or strands that dripped down toward one eye. Some had last year's long black leather coats on, and as it was late October, they had on their padded sweaters—white fabric with pleather patches placed like lungs and kidneys. The men and women walked into the movie theater lobby and languidly scanned the room to see who was seeing them. As the space filled up, people who recognized one another clumped together and talked fervidly about those they had already seen, who should still be coming, and what about this fucking rain.

When Riccio walked through the door, the theater's lobby speakers that had been murmuring some barely inaudible tunes briefly stuttered before surging with the song that had made him a local star. He moved through the now-crowded lobby, greeting people with kisses and a couple of words. He was headed for the projection room upstairs. A young blonde mother whispered to her two small boys, "Look at him there, that's the singer from the movie. That's the singer there . . . look, look!" The children did not respond to her excitement as one might expect. One boy began singing along with the song that had brought us all together: "The least important friend becomes the most important / to give a gift to the child who awaits Papà."[51] The mother smiled with embarrassment and told him to lower his voice. Instead he raised it, laughing as he continued to sing.

Apart from this singular micro-outburst, most of the guests at the premier stood or moved about with restrained and frustrated hyper-performativity. It was a big night and Riccio's song ordinarily incites pathos, but the implicit demands of the event's exclusiveness bore down on the guests. The reason I was included among them was because the managing editor of the neomelodica music magazine *Sciuè* (Quick), Antonio D'Addio, had invited me. When I first contacted Antonio in 2002 I didn't realize that he and *Sciuè* were a major node in the circuit. We spoke at length, and although thoroughly entrenched in the scene, he was refreshingly candid, not at all like the acritical populist celebrant of neomelodica music that the *Il Mattino* journalist Federico Vacalebre had made him out to be. The two journalists had engaged in a brief back-and-forth in 1997. D'Addio had written in a letter from the editor in the August 1997 issue of *Sciuè* that he hoped critics (like Vacalebre) would stop labeling neomelodica music as *sottocultura* (subculture) or as a *televicolo* phenomenon—that is, TV-broadcasted yet confined to the vicoli.[52] In response, Vacalebre wrote in *Il Mattino* that D'Addio was right to demand greater respect for the genre, but he accused D'Addio of helping inspire the criticisms by his "silence in the face of the scarce professionalism that reigns in a circuit that continues to live mostly on weddings, piazza festivals, and pirated CDs."[53] If the neomelodici want greater respect, Vacalebre wrote, they have to improve both artistically and "organizationally."[54]

Antonio made a significant impact on my research. He invited me to accompany him on several important events, including music festivals and national and satellite television broadcasts. He also introduced me to many of the scene's key players. On these occasions, he encouraged me to use my video camera, often prompting my "interviewees" to play their role. Although Antonio understood that it was never my intention to conduct interviews, his special status as a journalist rubbed off on me and elicited many glossy interview performances. When I couldn't bear another kitschy *this is the land of Partenope, the siren who lured Ulysses,* I told people I was shooting a documentary and that, in the spirit of cinema vérité, I wanted them to "be themselves." Unfortunately, others before me had shot documentaries and made-for-TV docu-vignettes about the neomelodici, so the scene's protagonists had even polished their day-in-the-life performances.

Antonio not only had an impact on my research but also helped me affect the circuit. With Antonio's help, I became plugged into the neomelodico scene at more entry points than many of the people I met. To be seen with Antonio meant to share his influence. Over time, when I arrived at an event, a growing number of the scene's protagonists recognized me, even anticipated my arrival. This made fieldwork intrinsically political. Sometimes situations developed when I failed to notice people who, spreading their feathers like peacocks, wanted to be noticed.

The premier of *Il latitante* overlapped with one such situation. Antonio and I stood among the other guests in the lobby joking fondly about whether we should fetch the songwriter Maestro Chiarazzo, who lived just a couple of blocks away. We speculated about the dramatic insults he would hurl at the crowd in his old-school sceneggiata style. "They're dogs!" I was saying, just as a singer and one of the scene's very few music video directors approached us. I immediately recognized them both. I had met the singer on the set of the TV show *Kaos,* produced by the Marigliano brothers, who also put on the most prestigious neomelodica music pro-

Kaos was a competition where a "Big" and an "emergent" singer, usually split by an age difference of ten to fifteen years, formed teams and competed against other teams, running up to a gong and striking it when they could "name that classic Neapolitan tune." The winning team sang two songs, one each for the Big and the emergent. Emergent singers paid to be on the show, and the Big were paid as guests. The show offered exposure—a chance to sing, a chance to be heard, a chance to hang on the arm of a Big. One of the Bigs wanted to be seen and heard by me.

gram called *Villa Cupido,* a live broadcast from the extravagant provincial banquet hall by the same name. Antonio had invited me to *Kaos,* where I was talked at by several vociferous singers. One of them, as Antonio pointed out to me at the time, was a man who wasn't afraid to tell the truth. "Because that's what you're looking for, right?" Antonio reminded me.

But the real truth turned out to be the same real truth everyone revealed when prompted: *'a munnezz,* trash. "This scene is all shit. Everyone will drag the other down before they let anyone make it out, and *I* know what I'm saying!" the singer bellowed, grabbing my hand to shout into my audio recorder.

That was the sixth interview I had had that hour, and I was wiped out. When Antonio offered to introduce me to yet another singer named

Carmelo, I politely declined, "I think I have enough now." What I didn't realize was that Antonio had already intimated to the singer that I wanted an interview. He was waiting for me to approach him. Another half hour passed, and Carmelo, as if jilted, got visibly upset. He moved jauntily about the set to speak to this person and that person with a command, a question, a word of advice. He circled and zigzagged and by pure kinetics amplified his presence. To me he looked like a cross between a cat in heat and a poodle with its nose in the air.

The man accompanying Carmelo to the premiere of *Il latitante* was also a character from a prior situation. Several months earlier, I reached something like documentary burnout. Because fewer people on the neomelodico scene acted out for me the canonical picturesque postcards of the Bay of Naples, Vesuvius, and the happy ragtag scugnizzi lolling about in the vicoli, more people were now *overacting* in their eagerness to make it real. Exhausted and perplexed by how little control I had despite being on the shooting side of the lens, I took another tack. Instead of negotiating with people *about* the spectacle, I could negotiate with them *within* it: I started shooting music videos. I began with pro bono work. My first video was for a young singer and his family. After I handed the completed video over to the family, an associate of theirs asked me if I wanted to earn some money shooting a TV commercial for a pastry shop. Things were happening quickly, and I was feeling the thrill of sheer momentum. Armed with a growing portfolio, I started to solicit clients to hire me for pay, and things barrelled forward from there.

Naively, I decided to get to know the other music video directors on the scene. Maria, an avid neomelodica music fan I had befriended, told me she knew just the person to contact, Paolo Vannucci. She even had his number. I asked her to call him. When Paolo picked up, Maria announced herself like a close friend, "Ciao Paolo, how are you? Listen, I have a friend here who's writing a book on Neapolitan music and he wants to talk to you. I'll put him on."

I repeated to Paolo what Maria had told him and added that I was making a documentary, too. I said that I had seen a lot of his music videos and wondered if I could talk to him about his work. "Maybe we could meet at your studio so I could see what kind of equipment you use?" I asked. As soon as I spoke, I realized my mistake—at least one of them.

"You want to come here? I don't know. I'm pretty busy." People at recording and photography studios often had intense relationships with their equipment. Many were hyperproud, demanding that I get it all on video. Others were hyperpossessive, demanding that I promptly put my lens cap back on. In this second group, sometimes the equipment was "hot" and sometimes it was a matter of intense privacy, even intimacy. Paolo was clearly part of this second group. I could hear the edge in his voice.

My biggest mistake was not asking him about his equipment, however. The truly grave mistake was to call Paolo at all, being that I already had developed a reputation as a budding music video director. Calling him up with such levity and asking to get a shot of his equipment was the equivalent of an attempted sfregio.

Paolo decided to take on the challenge right then while still on the phone with me: he asked me about my equipment. "So you're making a documentary? Then you're shooting on film?" The edge of his voice became a blade.

"No. Video," I stuttered. Then, scrambling to recover, "But I have some people interested in it." My reflex was to vaunt my abilities. How else was I going to convince him that I was worthy of his time and that I knew what I was doing?

Perhaps my dumb bluff (but not any dumber than the many bluffs I heard coming from the people around me) convinced Paolo I was worthy, or conversely, it assuaged his anxieties that I might be terribly furbo, because he invited me to meet him at his studio the following day. "Come with Maria," he said. "Till tomorrow."

It was a hot autumn weekday at rush hour when Maria and I trekked across the chaotic city on several buses, the metro, and on foot. After an hour and a half we were near our destination when Maria decided to call Paolo to alert him of our arrival (appointments had built into them up to an hour or more of lateness). No answer. She tried again every few minutes. No answer. She tried texting. No answer. Finally, she closed her phone, put it in her handbag and looked at me with that look of knowingness I've seen on the faces of people who are simultaneously defeated and impressed. "He made sure that we would have to travel all this way at this busy time just so he could stand us up."

"But why?"

"To give us a sfregio," Maria said. "He's jealous of his territory."

We didn't hear from Paolo again until the film premier, when I found myself face-to-face with him, my sfregiatore (disfigurer), accompanied by my *sfregiato* (disfigured man), Carmelo. The two men greeted Antonio warmly with a kiss-kiss and, with notable skill, passed their gazes right over me before walking on.

There is no sfregio in the film-sceneggiata *Il latitante*. As in *Betrayal*— and my scene with Paolo and Carmelo—the sfregio is metaphorical, not allegorical. It is an injury alone, without an emblem to transform it, to elevate it. In *Il latitante*, a man's personal sense of justice is pitted against the Law. The main protagonist is Nicola, a young man whose father is dying. Unable to come up with the money necessary for his father's treatment at an American hospital, he approaches boss Don Antonio. Don Antonio tells Nicola he'll help him, but only if he'll get his hands dirty by helping Don Antonio intimidate business owners and extort tangenti. On one occasion, Nicola accompanies one of Don Antonio's camorristi on a visit to a business owner who's late with his payment. The camorrista beats his victim and then kills him. Nicola and the camorrista use Nicola's motorbike to flee the scene. When the police find a piece of paper on which a witness has written down Nicola's license plate number, Nicola becomes their number-one murder suspect.

When Nicola learns that the police are looking for him, he makes a late-night run home to say good-bye to his wife and children before beginning his new lonely life as fugitive: "That evening I set off on that long road of fear that you're not sure ever ends."⁵⁵

The film's entire cast was present except for the fugitive's wife, played by Barbara Chiappini. In *Il latitante* she's extravagantly beautiful—long, dark hair that contours her high, sharp cheekbones and almond hazel eyes, full lips, big breasts, and a curvaceous body. Her character's fugitive husband, Karim Capuano, equals her in beauty. He is tall and has black wavy hair, a strong forehead, black eyes, a square jaw, full lips, and a broad torso. The pair seemed better suited for a Gucci advertisement. Karim sat in the movie theater next to Tony Spereando, the actor who plays Nicola's avenging nemesis, Inspector Sarnataro. Spereando wore a red suit and sucked on a lollipop.

The conflict between Nicola and Sarnataro happens outside Nicola's house, where one of Don Antonio's clan affiliates, a peripheral character played, surprisingly, by Riccio, awaits him in a car. But while Nicola is making his family good-byes, the police surround the camorrista. He fires several shots at the police, and, just as Nicola arrives on the scene, the camorrista kills an officer.

At that moment the movie theater audience shouted, "Oooh! Uàaa! Vai! [Go!]." Sperandeo sucked harder on his lollipop and smiled.

The fallen policeman is the nephew of Inspector Sarnataro, who, crying out with rage and pain over his kin's body, swears to seek revenge. With tragic misrecognition, he is convinced that the murderer is Nicola.

Nicola hides under the protection of Don Antonio's allies in Caserta, Rome, and Sicily. Time passes, and Nicola misses his family more than he can bear. He decides that he'll return to them at any cost and face whatever consequences await him. He meets his wife and embraces her. She tells him his father died while he was in hiding. Upon hearing this news, the despairing Nicola exclaims that he did everything he could to save his father—he even became a camorrista. And he regrets none of it.

In the final scenes, Don Antonio tells Nicola to go to Morocco, again without his family, where he'll be safe. Nicola, not realizing that Don Antonio is leading him into a trap, tells his wife to meet him at a landing strip, where a private plane awaits him. When he reaches the rendezvous point, he finds Inspector Sarnataro. Sarnataro and Nicola duel with their pistols, and Sarnatoro prevails, claiming his revenge.

Il latitante echoes the early sceneggiata drama of family scission, but with one important difference: the love triangle and the crimes of honor that it provokes—disfigurement and murder—have been replaced by the moral political economy of the vicolo and the crimes of making do. "'Nu Latitante" and other neomelodiche songs that echo the early sceneggiata tend to linger on the threshold between individual criminal acts and organized criminal conspiracy.

Contemporary neomelodica music inspired a handful of other musical films in the 1990s and 2000s. While theaters in Naples will occasionally stage sceneggiata performances, the few performances there seem to be mainly on satellite television aimed at audiences throughout southern Italian diasporas across Europe. More than a performance genre, the sceneggiata lives on in Naples as an affective–aesthetic sensibility.

The sceneggiata works as a backdrop, a receding infinity point in the past, as a romantic memory of a golden age when people respected the value of honor and when the camorra was an association of men of honor. At the same time, the sceneggiata also does the work of figuring a future where romantic and familial love can be safe and honor secure. It makes less sense to look at the sceneggiata as an aesthetic object or cultural artifact than as a thing in the world that affects people and with which people affect each other. A sceneggiata is a crystallization of colliding circumstances, people, and affects that brings on the shock of recognition. This recognition is sometimes willful and knowing, and sometimes people simply tumble into it and get carried off. A sceneggiata is not a thing that reflects life or perceptions of life, nor is it enacted in life. The sceneggiata is an orienting allegorical sensibility whose figures— honorable men and women, the humble and loving family, the camorrista, and the Law—offer imperfect reference points of historical truths and future promises.

FOUR

Family Affairs
Coming of Age Onstage

IN THE NEOMELODICA SCENE, family life takes on the affective and aesthetic qualities of a sceneggiata, a figural male life course. "Becoming a man" begins early with a young son's economic education. In the first act, a boy and his father speculate on opportunities in the neomelodica scene, and in the process they brush up against malavitosi, who try to seduce the boy into becoming their filial client. In the second act, a son must make the transition to husband and father by marrying. The art of making do becomes for him a deeply personal and public performance of the personal sovereign providing for his family-to-be. He is tempted by the enticements of malavitosi—money, power, and protagonismo. In the final act the son, now married, tries to seize more than the meager share of well-being available to an ordinary enterprising man engaged in the art of making do. When he performs manhood he exceeds the boundaries of performance. The figure of the personal sovereign is an impossibility that lures men into its shoes. Some men end up on its narrative path while with other men, only moments of their lives begin to resemble the life of the figure.

Act 1: The Ventriloquist's Ventriloquist

Things were not going right for Fulvio Girardi, *nome d'arte* Giulio. I watched as the angelic twelve-year-old boy kept stumbling over his words. He was hosting his live pirate broadcast at Telefantasy, the clandestine TV studio in Santa Teresa, a neighborhood in the center of Naples. Standing before the live camera, Fulvio began to announce, "The next song is dedicated by Anna to Nunzia—" until his father, Pasquale, barked at him from the balcony above: "Nunzi*o*, *not* Nunzia! . . . *Mamma d' 'o Carmene!*" Roberto, Fulvio's sixteen-year-old brother, also joined in, shouting his own directives: "Just sing, Fulvio! Go ahead and sing, because you *don't know* how to talk!" For a few moments Fulvio stood there, frozen, while the males in his family verbally assailed him before stomping off to the cramped, unsupervised control room (the owners, Rosa and Mimmo, were on the balcony arguing with a client about a payment). Fulvio remained standing before the live camera, an expression of confusion and pain washing over his face. When he turned toward me, standing off-stage to the left, his expression turned to shame and helplessness. I stared back blankly, incapable of reassuring him. What could I say or do?

Suddenly the sound of "Innamorato" (In love), one of the songs from Fulvio's premier album, began to fill the small studio (Mimmo was back in the control room).[1] Fulvio was still confused and upset. His father shouted at him again: "Go on, sing! Sing!" A synthesized brass melody blasted through the studio and onto the airwaves, but it seemed that Fulvio would not be able to pull it together in time to lip-synch when the lyrics began. He looked up at his father and brother, who had returned to the balcony, and he looked at me, off-stage. He looked everywhere but at the live camera (operated by Mimmo and Rosa's son) and the inestimable number of viewers watching from their homes within the one-mile radius of Telefantasy's signal. But when his recorded voice began to sing, Fulvio indeed managed to mouth the lyrics:

> A flame of love has been ignited that burns every day in my heart
> I'm not sleeping at night, but why?
> I have bags under my eyes; my mother has begun to worry
> She called the doctor, but he doesn't have a cure for me
> I am already in love; I hear my heart go "boom"
> Even though I am so young, I already want to kiss you

Pasquale composed the arrangements for "Innamorato" for his son's first album. Just one month prior, with the hired help of Fiorilli, who owns a small suburban studio, the father and son recorded the album *Sett'anne fà* (Seven years ago), which featured original songs and classic Neapolitan covers.[2] The selling point, Pasquale hoped, would be Fulvio's *voce bianca,* or "white voice," the pure, sexless voice of prepubescence. To promote the album and, more importantly, Fulvio's services as a live performer at private parties, Pasquale brought both of his sons to Telefantasy, an illegal TV studio in a moldy garage in a small labyrinth of narrow vicoli. Nearby was the archaeological museum, at the time hosting an exhibit of Pompeii's lurid frescoes and mosaics whose most prominent leitmotif is men with impossibly large erections. It was past 1 a.m. on a Tuesday.

During a pause between songs, Fulvio took the opportunity to catch up with the dedication requests and greetings he had no time to address during his previous broadcast. Sitting on a narrow polyester loveseat before a painted mural of the Bay of Naples, he read from a sheet of paper: "A special hello to Domenico of San Giorgio from Maria; a big kiss from Franco and Ida for Luisa and her husband in Bagnoli; a kiss to Jennifer from her grandmother Flora; a special greeting from Sasà for the Rea family, wishing that young Fabio return home soon; many, many hellos to Gigi and his brothers from their cousin Danilo; a big kiss from Rosanna for Enzo, wishing him a swift return home."

Fulvio read the incoming calls of affection with the tonal monotony of a rosary. This ritual, pervasive in many TV transmissions of neomelodica music, seems to routinize expressions of affective contact and separation, which include people's longing for their "temporarily absent" loved ones—a euphemism in Naples for prisoners and fugitives. Many people suspect that their ordinary sentimental greetings and song dedications have been infiltrated with the business talk of la malavita. However, what is being communicated when and to what effect remains indeterminate; performers like Fulvio serve only as unknowing conduits. The everyday ritual of telegreetings and musical dedications sometimes serve, beyond their intention, as business talk's affective–aesthetic encasement.

Pasquale has undertaken the difficult task of educating his sons in the art of making do, or the entrepreneurial arts of independent employment in the informal economy. "Independence," in this instance, means achieving forms of economic success while remaining sufficiently clear of entanglements with organized crime. Pasquale explained to me that because "the work situation is so bad in Naples" he feels he is doing both his sons a favor. His eldest son, Roberto, used to work full-time as a cashier at an auto mechanic for a mere 500 euros per month (around U.S. $700). "It was senseless," Pasquale complained. Then there was hope Roberto would get work in a small shoe factory, but his mother was resistant: "It's hard work," she said dismissively. Instead, Roberto helped his father manage Fulvio's career. Pasquale argued that he was providing both of his sons with a future by building a sort of family business.

When he was finished reading the list of greetings, Fulvio regained the inflections of his voice and announced he was ready to take the next caller. After a brief pause, Rosa patched someone through to him.

"Hello? Hello? Giulio?" asked a young female caller, using Fulvio's stage name.

"Ciao, buonasera. What can I do for you?" Fulvio answered. Although he looked down at his shoes while talking to the caller, his voice conveyed remarkable composure and self-confidence.

"Giulio, don't you recognize my voice?"

"Uh . . . ," he searches his memory. "Ah, Giusy! How are you?" he asked, remembering.

"I'm good. And you, Giulio? How are you, Giulio?" the caller returned.

"*Tutto bene* [All is well]. So how is your Aunt Maria?"

"She's fine, Giulio. We're waiting for you to come by again, Giulio."

The boy reassured her, "I'll come, don't worry, don't worry. So, what do you want to hear tonight?"

After a pause she said, "Giulio, will you sing 'Cari genitori' [Dear parents] for my friend Ciro?"

"OK, no problem, Giusy. A big kiss to you and say hello to your Aunt Maria for me."

As if to conjure his presence in her home, the caller repeated Fulvio's stage name for the eighth time, before hanging up, "Thanks, Giulio, you're great."

Upstairs in the control room, Rosa, a tall black-haired woman with pale, pockmarked skin and crooked teeth, took a drag on her cigarette and nodded, seemingly bored, at Mimmo. Mimmo, in turn, shouted, "Go!" Pasquale, passing the cue on to Fulvio, leaned over the balcony and shouted, "Go! Go! Now!"

Fulvio, confirming to Mimmo, Rosa, and their son's teenage friend who was now operating the camera (the son ran out for cigarettes) that he had heard the cue, shouted, "Go! 'Cari genitori'!" The music began to play, and Fulvio began lip-synching:

Dear Parents
I can't wait any longer
This time I have to say something
Listen to me
I see mamma crying
and who can reason with Papà?
understand me
I don't understand you two anymore

We can't live like this
Be done with it

Do you love each other or not?
Embrace each other
Do it for me

What are you two arguing for?
And you lock me in my bedroom
I know how it ends
You two always make peace in bed
And I'm crying but no one thinks of me
But haven't you noticed I've grown up?
You shouldn't have to suffer at age thirteen
And you, especially, Papà, you refuse to understand?

Pasquale quit his job playing piano in a successful music ensemble to manage his son's singing career. He spent about 2,500 euros on Fulvio's first album and hundreds more on airtime at Telefantasy and other TV and radio stations. However, Pasquale's entrepreneurial gamble was not going well. His son's gigs were still only earning them 80, sometimes 100 euros each. The gigs, moreover, were erratic or inconveniently co-incident, requiring a race between multiple distant provincial weddings and baptisms on a single day. Car fuel was a significant additional expense. Rita, Fulvio's mother, is the breadwinner. She works in customer service at Enel, Italy's largest power company. She and Pasquale have borrowed against most of her pension to launch Fulvio's career while they struggle to raise their two other children.

Pasquale and Rita's particularized interest in Fulvio is interwoven with their intense love for him. The disproportionate amount of attention they pay to their youngest son oscillates, in its extremes, between obsessive pampering and abusive exploitation. On the one hand, Fulvio is the prince of the family. When at home, he lacks nothing: he wanders up to the kitchen table between bouts with his Playstation in the bedroom that he shares with his older brother. The platter of fried squid, shrimp, and *triglia,* and the pan of baked ricotta-filled pasta, all converge his way through the signals of his father and the deft hands of his mother. His older siblings, Roberto and Stefania, must repeat their own requests again and again, and usually to no effect: "Can I have a knife? Is there any bread? Can I have some more pasta?" Receiving no response, they lay their hands flat on the table and slump farther into their seats.

Moreover, Pasquale recounted how Fulvio, when he was an infant, had severe asthma and was put in incubation. Pasquale prayed and prayed that God would take the illness away from his son and give it to him instead. "And that's just how it happened," Pasquale said. Now, over a decade later, Fulvio is completely healed and Pasquale is the one with asthma. Pasquale's love for his youngest son is immense.

At the same time, however, Pasquale's concern for his son's well-being seems inextricably entwined with his interest in the natural resource his son embodies: his voice. This suggestion emerged one evening at another pirate TV station called TVP (TV Partenope). Pasquale drove us to an apartment building on a dimly lit street near Porta Nolana. When he parked, he turned to me and said, with a mixture of embarrassment and bemusement, "This TV station is *abusiva* [illegal]." With Fulvio we entered the building, took a tight elevator ride to the third floor, and buzzed a door. When we walked into the studio, I was surprised to find that we were in someone's home. Several people were eating dinner. Each had a plate with one large meatball covered in tomato sauce. *Friarielli* (fried greens) sat in a pan on the stove, ready to serve for the next course. There were four people sitting at the table: a woman in her late thirties with dyed blonde hair and a red sweatsuit; a tall, sunlamp-tanned teenage singer with gel-spiked hair and a chain and medallion hanging around his neck; and two middle-aged men, one short, skinny, and gray haired, and the other tall and broad shouldered. Pasquale greeted all of them, but he did not immediately introduce me. The broad-shouldered man, sporting a fat, gold-chain necklace, gruffly asked him who I was. "He's American," Pasquale answered. His response was both identifier and explanation: I was not a threat because I was irrelevant.

Down the hall in what was formerly a bedroom, two men squeezed by each other to operate the digital camera, stereo, mixer, and computer that crowded the space. They were broadcasting the last few minutes of a film-sceneggiata starring Nino D'Angelo and preparing for the start of Fulvio's transmission. One of the men, a neighbor from an apartment on another floor of the building, was the station manager. Pasquale got him to pause for a couple of minutes to tell me about his work. The manager explained that he had been pirating signals since the 1980s. "He was one of the first," Pasquale chimed in, supportively. The manager said that

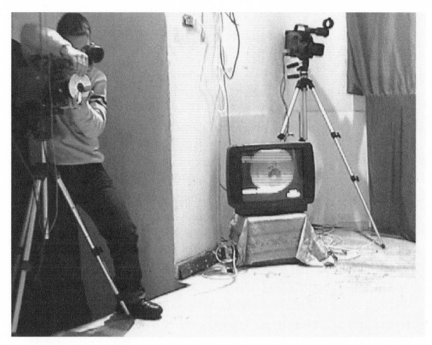

The cameraman, about sixteen years old, makes a peephole frame for a singer's live transmission by holding a CD over the lens. He also swung the camera around the studio, tracking various people coming in and out the main door.

what he was doing was good. He was providing *gente dei bassi* (people of the popular quarters) a cheap service and broadcasting the kinds of programs they want to see.

My conversation with the manager distracted me from Fulvio's show, which had already begun. With a mic in his hand, Fulvio sat on a stool before a bright blue curtain that had been tacked to the wallpapered wall. His amplified young voice filled the room as he repeated TVP's phone number and invited viewers to call: "081.77.56.##. *Pronto!*" Cell phones rang, the door buzzer squealed, and various people, many with cigarettes dangling from wrinkled mouths, shuffled in and out. In every room of the apartment, men pawed and hugged each other, some near enough to topple the active camera, as they talked in the typical manner of aggressive affection pervasive on the scene. One of the men—a skinny, wrinkled, greasy-haired, and nearly toothless character—was a popular comic. In a loud, cloying voice, he mimicked Fulvio, mocking what he perceived to be Fulvio's sense of self-importance while taking phone calls from his fans.

The comic's behavior was linked to an ongoing polemic that involved him, the station manager, and Fulvio's family. The nieces and nephews of TVP's station manager were fans of "Giulio" and said they wanted him to perform at their family's next communion celebration. The station manager decided that instead of paying Fulvio he would invite him for two months to participate on an upcoming TV show that the comic was producing at TVP. The comic objected. "What do I care about Giulio?" he exclaimed to the station manager. The manager pleaded with the comic until the latter conceded, "Well, then this is a favor for *you*—and I'm only hosting the kid for *one* month." Rita was angered when she heard about the affair: "It's simple: Fulvio should be paid for the gig and that's that. No show, no favors, no discounts!"

During the second half of Fulvio's hour-long transmission, I wandered between the studio, kitchen, and foyer. At times I felt like an intruder; it was unclear to me what I could or should not know. When Fulvio's transmission was over, Pasquale, Fulvio, and I began to take our leave, but we were stopped by a walrus-moustached man with a Marlboro in his mouth. "Can we talk?" he said to Pasquale, "I wanna talk to you about your boy's career." Pasquale was not eager to listen, but the man put a hand on Pasquale's shoulder and started to give him his advice. In a hushed mumble that lent intensity to his words, he told Pasquale that he should lower Fulvio's price so that he could get more gigs and therefore more experience and exposure.

Pasquale looked furtively at me out of the corner of his eye to gauge how much I understood. His response to the man was markedly emphatic. Stepping back from him, he gesticulated wildly and loudly declared that he did not want to overwork his son.

The man answered with bafflement, "What? Why not?"

Then, as if correcting himself, Pasquale explained, "I mean, I don't want to destroy his voice by overworking it."

When I heard these words, I understood that Pasquale was talking about protecting Fulvio's voice and not his childhood. I must have looked visibly disappointed, because when Pasquale, Fulvio, and I got in the car, Pasquale continued with his fervent explanations, this time performing them directly for me (and maybe also indirectly for Fulvio?). "You know, it's for him, I'm thinking about him, you know," Pasquale said almost pleadingly. He said that the only way Fulvio's singing career would go forward is if he took it out of Naples. Maybe he could get his son hooked up with Rai, he said. "I gave up on being a musician because there were too many compromises to be made. I'm not interested in it for myself. But Fulvio *has to* make it, he *has to* make it big!" As Pasquale spoke, he got louder and louder, and eventually he was hitting the steering wheel with his fist. Then, pausing for a couple seconds as if catching himself, he said calmly, "You know, this has nothing at all to do with *me*. I'm doing this for my *son*. *I* don't even matter." We were still parked outside TVP and it was late, but Pasquale had more to say. He returned to the subject of Naples and the urgency of "getting out." He talked about Rome and Milan and New York. He went on like this, wistfully and breathlessly, for fifteen minutes of frantic soliloquy. Finally, when he was finished (or when he noticed my silence), he turned to me and asked beseechingly, "So, when are you writing this book, Jason? And will you remember us?"

I was well aware that Pasquale and his family were eager to help me with my research because they anticipated many indefinite returns. When was this not the case during my years of fieldwork? I was included in the opportunities and risks of the neomelodica music scene in which Pasquale and many others were gambling. As was the case in many other relationships I developed, Pasquale valued me for my perceived status, not as an anthropologist or researcher but as a "journalist." I represented a link to the potentials of publicity and the dangers of exposure. Ironically, when an actual music journalist who writes for the cultural insert of the nationally circulating communist newspaper *Il Manifesto* proposed that I contribute an article about child singers on the neomelodica scene, I could no longer deny the special status people had been conferring on me. This resulted in a disorienting and revelatory entanglement of privilege, power, and intimacy.

Pasquale was driving me home after another evening at Telefantasy. Everything was going well until Fulvio's cell phone rang (the ringtone was the melody of "Sett'anne fà"). Fulvio took the call and spoke briefly and confusedly to the person on the other end of the line. After he hung up, he told us that a girl had just phoned to ask him about Piccolo Pino (Little Pino), another young singer whom Pasquale and his family considered Fulvio's rival.

Pasquale was instantly enraged: "What! And you talked with her? What's wrong with you? You gotta tell someone like that to fuck off!"

Fulvio cringed. In pained frustration and with tears in his voice, he protested, "But what can I do? How do I just tell her to fuck off?"

"It's a figure of speech. You tell her you don't know *who* she's asking you about and that you don't know *what* she wants from *you!*"

I turned to look at Fulvio in the backseat and saw that he had tears in his eyes. He looked distressed. Feeling culpable for not having intervened on his behalf in other similar instances, I decided I would now defend him. Does an anthropologist (or a journalist, for that matter) never take a position? "But come on, Pasquale! It's difficult for a child to respond just like that, on the spot. How is he to know?" My comment, however, seemed to have no effect on the interaction. Pasquale continued to berate his son, who got more and more upset. Instead, it was the newspaper article I had written for *Il Manifesto* that seemed to defuse the tension.[3] The article, titled "The Broken Dream of the Ventriloquist" (the editors changed my original title, which was "The Whisper of the Ventriloquist"), had just come out in print, and I had brought a copy for them. When we reached my apartment, I handed it to Pasquale. First, Pasquale and Fulvio admiringly commented on Fulvio's photo (which I had taken from his album cover). Then Fulvio pointed at the photo of Piccolo Pino and shouted "Che cafone! [What a hick!]." Then, without reading the article, they both scanned the text for any mention of "Giulio." Twice finding his name, they laughed triumphantly. Pasquale asked me if the article mentioned Gigino, another young rival singer, but he already knew the answer. Before I could respond, he and his son hooted with glee. Embarrassed by their gloating, I tried to extricate myself from the interaction. I clarified that the reason for the omission was simply that I had not yet met him at the time of writing. I wanted to draw a line, for myself as much as for Pasquale, between following Fulvio's career and promoting it.

Ironically, had Pasquale and his son actually read the article, they would have realized that I was quite critical of the pressures a young boy endures when he is put to work as a neomelodico singer. The article was a companion piece to an article on la canzone classica, written by the journalist who had invited me to write mine. In mine, I refer to Friedrich Kittler's idea of the "discourse network," or a system of people and modes of communication. Kittler argues that until 1800, prior to the invention of the gramophone, mothers, children, and unmediated oral communication constituted the primary discourse network for language acquisition. I argued that the dominant discourse network on the neomelodica music scene is composed of fathers and sons, pirate broadcasts, and synthesized neomelodica music about love, sex, betrayal, and imprisonment. I suggested that in this new discourse network between fathers and sons, the process of language acquisition resembles ventriloquism. That is, the embodied integrity of voice and personal sovereignty comes undone as fathers teach their sons the(ir) language of commerce.[4]

One Sunday afternoon, after finishing lunch at Pasquale's home, I struck up a conversation with Rita. "So you have two jobs: one at Enel and then you come home and work again." I made a sweeping gesture with my arm to cover the dimensions of the kitchen. Rita nodded and said, "Sì-sì," but it wasn't clear how much she wanted to agree with me. Was I too forward? Was I too feminist? If there was any agreement on

A father–manager waits for his son to finish his song so he can give him more cues. They are in the control room of a private TV studio in a provincial town just outside Naples. The studio is in the upper-floor apartment of a residential building.

her part, it was from a different perspective: in her mind, housework and parenting constituted her first job and customer servicing was her second. Family labors were affective imperatives, and, perhaps, they also made her feel comfortably "identified" as a Neapolitan woman.[5]

Over the course of the afternoon, Rita made a few comments, in the presence of Pasquale and the children, about their lack of money. These included half-subtle recriminations against her husband, whom she believed should do better at making money with his musical pursuits. When Pasquale chuckled over how he had crowded their living room with recording equipment, keyboards, and several guitars, Rita interjected, "Yeah, we should sell it all." Was she tired of this chase after musical success? It seemed to her the venture with Fulvio's voice was a crippling expense and a gamble on an uncertain future. But was she also concerned about the heavy responsibilities Fulvio shouldered in this affair? She was proud of his talents, she told me. "But the only thing is that the others on the scene, those who do favors for one another and hire each other's children to sing, try to keep Fulvio from rising. Remember that singer we talked about the first time we met—the young boy with the beautiful voce bianca who came to a violent end? Patrizio. Fulvio has been compared to Patrizio. Now they're afraid that their own sons will be out of the game, so they keep Fulvio down."

Rita had faith in Fulvio's potential, but she was pessimistic about his possibilities. One reason for her pessimism was that Pasquale was already intimately familiar with the playing field. He used to perform classic Neapolitan music for publics overlapping with those of neomelodica music. Occasionally Pasquale pointed out performers appearing on television programs on the national networks: "I know those two, we used to work together, and one of them used to be a pickpocket," or "That one—it was always cocaine with him. Once I threw him out of my house."

When I asked Pasquale about his past colleagues, he suggested that their success was inauthentic or simulated. It was not talent that distinguished them from him. Instead, their success indicated another distinction altogether: they had *certa gente dietro le spalle* (certain people backing them). When Pasquale worked with them, he felt increasing pressure to follow the same trajectory. It seemed that once the distinction between them and him became clear, they were adversaries. But Pasquale did not simply dissolve his relationship to his colleagues; he gave up his career.

Was this because his former colleagues, with their newfound support, monopolized the market?

Pasquale now led his youngest son into the neomelodica music scene, which overlapped with the same *giro* (circuit) he had been so determined to avoid. Did he believe he could manage the inevitable entanglements better as a ventriloquist? The answer was not clear, but the precariousness of the situation was manifest when he got his son and the rest of his family embroiled in economic and potentially violent collisions. While I hung out with Pasquale, there were several such instances. For example, Pasquale arranged with the pirate VesuvioRadio to have them play Fulvio's albums a few times a day for a couple of months. He had been told that the manager of TVP had a long-standing favor exchange accord with VesuvioRadio, in which each would send the other clients. Additionally, TVP and VesuvioRadio agreed to give each other's referrals first-time freebies. However, when Pasquale went to VesuvioRadio, they charged him 150 euros (U.S. $200) for the airtime. When Pasquale told the manager of TVP, the manager contended that Pasquale should not have paid them. Pasquale also complained that VesuvioRadio was not even providing the service he shouldn't have paid for. "Disgraziati! [Good-for-nothings!] They don't play Fulvio's music often at all, and when they do, it's late at night." The manager of TVP grumbled about the affair alongside Pasquale, but the manager never intervened.

Pasquale had a conflict as well with his co-composer, Carnevale. Carnevale claimed to have made a gift of some of the songs he and Pasquale composed together to a couple of singers when, in fact, he had sold them and pocketed the money.

"Strange he should suddenly behave this way after two years of partnership," I said.

"No, no, he's done this before, years ago. Back then I distanced myself from him," Pasquale explained. What he left out of his explanation was in the ellipsis: *But now I'm back in business with him and it's all fucked up again.*

Rita was frustrated with Pasquale's habit of doing business with people who already proved themselves unreliable or dishonest. She pointed out that it was not surprising that the station manager at TVP had gotten them ensnared in a baroque deal with the comic, because the manager had already revealed himself as an *omm' 'e mmerda* (man whose word is no good). She recalled how in the very beginning of their business relations with TVP, the manager was supposed to give airtime to

Fulvio's music videos but never made good on the promise. People like that, she said, shouldn't be counted on again and again. "Pasquale knows only about music," she said to me, shaking her head.

When he poured a few thousand euros into the hands of a two-bit recording studio proprietor, Fulvio's second CD did not materialize in time for the wedding season, costing them potential CD sales and further self-promotion. Fulvio's mother explained that the producer ran off with the money because he had trouble with *gente e' miezz' a vì* (lit. street people). When I asked her what she meant by this unnecessary code (we were entirely alone in her apartment), she said, "How can I make you understand? . . . There are certain people . . ."

When Pasquale conducts the family into treachery, it is Rita who has the fight in her to put things back to the way they were before. She recounted how she went to the home of the seventy-year-old father of the two-bit producer and demanded to know the whereabouts of his son. The old man refused to answer, so she threatened him. Rather suddenly, the old man managed to get his son on the phone. Rita said she snatched the receiver and told the son she'd smash up his studio—and his old man—if he didn't show up with the money. "He came right away," Rita said.

One day, while walking near the central train station, I spotted Rosa, the crooked-toothed owner of Telefantasy, and her son. They were riding a blue Vespa, carting groceries. I shouted out to them, and they puttered up to me. "I called the station many times, and then I looked for you on TV, but I couldn't find you at all. What happened?" I asked.

"Well, you know . . ." The two faces looked at me for help in filling in the ellipsis, but I didn't know how to help.

"What happened?" I repeated, this time cautiously.

With something like a smile on her face, Rosa said, "They shut us down."

"Oh shit! Did they fine you? Was it a lot?"

Rosa kept her eyes on me and said nothing, still with her slight (sardonic?) smile. I looked from her to the other pair of eyes on her teenage son, and they, too, looked back at me, impassive. Finally, I caught on; they suspected that I had turned them in.

Unfortunately, I confirmed my suspicion of their suspicion when I ran into Mimmo the day after Easter (Pasquetta, or Little Easter) at the extravagant procession to the Madonna dell'Arco in Pomigliano, a village ten kilometers outside Naples. Teams walk the full distance (the females wearing nothing on their feet but multiple layers of socks) to the chapel where a miracle apparition was said to have taken place. In the fifteenth century some men were playing a game of *pallamaglio* (pall-mall). One got angry and threw a wooden ball at an aqueduct archway adorned with the image of the Madonna. The Madonna's cheek bled, the man was hanged, and an annual religious procession was born. In some ways, the procession feels as if it keeps alive the violent spirit of its origins. Divided into teams, men hoist onto their shoulders large floats with paper-mâché models of the Madonna and child and vertical banners depicting the hanging of her offender. Then the men charge through the vicoli before assembling at Piazza del Carmine to prepare for the hike to Pomigliano (without the floats). The long walk was surprisingly "profane." Team members flirted or joked and punched each other, and they tore laundry off people's balconies. Vendors paid tangenti to camorristi for the right to sell religious paraphernalia along the route. In the evening after hours of walking, we converged on the church with thousands of others where we waited for our turn to see the Madonna. Ambulances stood by for the rapturous "faint," as did carabinieri. People wept and I, too, wanted to weep, enchanted by exhaustion, torture, and then, finally, release. My vision of the Madonna lasted two minutes before I was ushered out the backdoor to make room for the next person.

Just before the trek I saw Mimmo. I decided to approach him first, in order not to seem shifty. But when I walked up and said hello, I sensed he had already noticed me. When was this not the case in this milieu? After a brief exchange of greetings, Mimmo asked abruptly, "You know, they shut us down?" He looked angry. Was he trying to catch me off guard in order to figure out whether I was guilty?

"Yeah, I saw—and then I ran into your wife." Not knowing what else to say, I decided on a research question, although I wondered how appropriate it was: "Did they make you pay a fine?"

"Yes," he said, nodding seriously.

It took enormous effort not to defend myself at that moment, but I felt certain that restraining myself was the best way to avoid intensifying his suspicions. At any rate, the matter of my guilt or innocence never arose again or, depending on how one interprets the situation, was never resolved.

Not much more than a month passed before Rosa, Mimmo, and their son reopened, this time in another space, in another neighborhood. They formed a joint venture with TVP, which had also been shut down by the cops that same week. The manager of TVP, in the few minutes he took from his chaotic broadcast to talk to me, had explained, "They shut us down before and took all our equipment, but we've reopened a few times over." TVP, Telefantasy, and other stations treated raids as if they were frequency problems. TVP often lost its signal to malfunctioning equipment or adverse weather. Once during his heartfelt lip-synched performance of the classic song "Reginella," Fulvio's transmission—sound and picture—turned to blackness, as did the cramped apartment. When TVP managed to get back on the air, Fulvio calmly resung the interrupted strophe after a quick and simple apology to the public. These vicissitudes of mediated presence seemed to be of the same order as the sporadic police raids. The owners of pirate stations absorb the costs of replacing sequestered equipment and paying off fines as general operating expenses.

The moment I told Pasquale about my encounter with Mimmo, I immediately regretted it. Pasquale was already skittish and self-doubting; my comments would only exacerbate the wariness with which he had for years been navigating this environment. Indeed, he fell silent with alarm, responded with no more than a grunt, and never again referred to the matter. Months passed before he would let me accompany him to any TV station. Many obstacles suddenly cropped up—no room in the car, not enough time to pick me up—but Pasquale did invite me to Fulvio's performances at private parties and public festivals. That is how I learned just how reasonable were Pasquale's fears.

It had taken us the better part of an hour to find the venue in Guadagno. It was Fulvio's third engagement that Sunday. Pasquale and Roberto asked people for directions at cafés and restaurants all over the seaside town. It seemed everyone was celebrating communions, baptisms, and weddings. People were made up in their Sunday best: men in shiny and double-breasted or long-tailed suits, some with gold chains and slick, gelled hair; women with red- or blonde-dyed hair, wearing tight-fitting blouses; little boys in oversized suits and bulging tie knots with angelic faces framed with stylish prickly-gelled haircuts and fading sideburns; little girls with ringlets, scarves, long dresses, and a light touch of lipstick. Neomelodica music emanated from several banquet halls where patrons were ensconced in the palms and large ferns, and from restaurants that flanked the edges of the flat streets. A thicket of signs stood at each crossroads, arrows pointing to myriad venues for private parties.

"Where is L'Incanto [The Enchantment]? Where the hell is it? That omm' 'e merda, why did he tell us to come all the way down here? It's not here and he knew it wasn't here, so why open his mouth at all?" Pasquale was angry and exasperated. We had been working for five hours, running here and there, meeting with impresarios, organizers, and other singers, getting chummy and stroking egos, laughing and reassuring, defending, asserting and bargaining, and prompting and prepping Fulvio, giving directions to Roberto, and positioning me with my video camera.

As usual when I was with Fulvio in the backseat of the car or waiting with him in the foyer of a banquet hall, I tutored him in English. He studied it in public school, and I wanted to be sure he performed well at least in that subject. Meanwhile, Pasquale went into the banquet hall to discuss business with the organizer. This was important for announcing our arrival, ensuring that Fulvio would perform soon and, most of all, that the organizer would pay Pasquale 100 euros now, in advance. "Otherwise, there's no show," Pasquale had announced to Roberto and me while we were still en route, as if rehearsing the ultimatum. At a previous gig, the same organizer had said he would pay "next time," but next time never came. While we waited for Pasquale to return from his confrontation with his adversary, Roberto said that, knowing what a *stronzo* (shit) the organizer is, it was possible the afternoon's performance would not happen at all.

But Pasquale apparently won the battle. Voices from the banquet hall began to call for Fulvio to go in and perform. Part of Pasquale's victory was due to the fact that the news of Fulvio's arrival had quickly spread among the children at the communion. Pasquale was still talking to the organizer when five or six small fans, followed by a constant flow of others, ran outside to see Fulvio. Like a rock star pulling up to the backstage door by his driver, Fulvio was thronged from where he sat in the backseat. The little fans competed for a chance to touch him and talk to him. One girl, who could not have been more than ten or eleven, said to Roberto, "Your brother's cute." When Roberto asked if she liked Fulvio, she answered matter-of-factly, "But I already have a boyfriend."

Roberto and I got out to stretch while Fulvio remained in the car, surrounded by his young fans. Some of them climbed in and sat down next to him or in front of him, all wanting one of his photo-postcards and his signature. Fulvio wrote in an illegible, extravagant script as the kids held out their hands for their postcards, one by one, saying a single word: Gennaro, Luisa, Gianni—the people to whom he was to dedicate a phrase or two. A very small blue-eyed boy, who was too short to reach Fulvio's window, shouted with his tiny voice, "Fulvio, do you have a Playstation?" Another boy, pudgy and ruddy-skinned, took a look at me and asked Fulvio, "Is this your brother?"

"No, this is our friend the American, the journalist," Fulvio corrected him.

We entered the restaurant and followed Pasquale past several dining rooms to the party that had hired Fulvio. Sometimes the swinging doors of the other rooms burst open and white-jacketed waiters bustled out, carrying lunch remains—fried fish, mussels, linguini and clams, grilled eggplant with capers and roasted red peppers, or bouquet-like armfuls of mineral water bottles. Each time, a blast of song sprayed out of the room. I lingered as we passed these rooms to peer into the momentarily exposed dining rooms. I met the eyes of several people looking back at me, many with inexplicable animosity.

As we approached the dining room of Fulvio's party, we encountered a short, balding man who stood before the swinging doors as if waiting for us. He wore a poorly fitting blue suit: the long jacket hung down to his knees and several inches of cuff-slack pooled at his ankles. The man greeted Pasquale briefly but meaningfully; his voice and his gaze were weighted by some implicit gravity that only Pasquale would be able to explain to me, provided he was willing. As we entered the dining room, I turned back to get another look at the ill-dressed man. Despite his awkward attire, he walked about the wide corridor measuredly and self-assuredly, greeting people with every few steps he took.

We entered the dining room to find a young man performing the last song of his set. Strikingly, the guests had stopped most of their conversations and carousing to watch and listen with rapt attention. "Listen to that! He sounds just like Gigi D'Alessio," Pasquale shouted excitedly, referring to the one neomelodico who had truly "made it" on the national music scene.

"It's true, he sounds like D'Alessio!" a woman standing near us agreed enthusiastically.

I pulled out my video camera, but I felt unsure about using it. Pasquale looked at me several times as if about to say something to me. At first I thought he was unhappy that I should take interest in another singer, but something else made me uneasy. Pasquale looked at me longer and longer until finally he said what was on his mind, "It's not a good idea to use that here. You could raise suspicions."

I began to look around me and suddenly everyone was implicated. I read an incoherent mix of signs, but of what? What was I looking for? A scene erupted on the dance floor with a woman in her midfifties. She had heavy bags under her eyes and wore a lavender pantsuit. Several people tried to coax her onto the dance floor, but she struggled energetically. Her abductors resorted to dragging her clumsily and violently. They almost let her wriggle away, leaving red fingerprints on her skin and disheveling her hair and her outfit in the process, but then a man caught her. He was short and had olive skin and dark, narrow sideburns. He began slow-dancing with her, one of his arms bracing her neck against his chest. They continued this way until she no longer resisted. The short man was the only male dancing, so he took turns with a number of female partners. His main partner, it seemed, was a tall, slender, dark-haired woman, with tight black polyester pants, a chain belt, and a tight white sleeveless top with an open neck displaying a gold chain. She danced at the hips, moving her body like a wave. Someone during the evening undid her long black hair, which was tied behind her head, and out fell dozens of tight corn weaves. Laughing, she tried to bundle them up again.

The men sat around at their tables, many of them scanning the room, focusing on the women and each other. At times they looked at me with what seemed like resentful curiosity. One side of the room was oddly demarcated by a row of potted ficus trees, where a young man in a tight black suit was on his knee before a woman in a slinky, low-necked blouse. The woman gestured with her head in my direction and said something to the man, who then looked at me, too. A sullen balding man sat with another man—he had a bulbous nose and narrow eyes. They ate mussels and drank white wine that stood in a chilling bucket swathed in white serving towels. They never once moved from their table.

Finally, there was a table of women in unusually provocative attire. One had dyed-blonde hair and a low-cut blouse that revealed impressive cleavage. Another woman, full-figured and toweringly tall, wore enormous hoop earrings and dark purple lipstick that she had outlined in black. She was dressed in a tight white polyester shirt and white pants that barely veiled a tiny pair of red panties. Each time she stood up or sat down, she left her ass lingering in midair for a moment, sometimes looking about her with a sultry, I-dare-you expression.

What, I wondered, was the significance of these signs of aggression and sex? Were these the signs of the camorra one should look for? They were certainly consistent with the general aesthetics of excess manifest in many expressions of "camorra style," including some neomelodica music.

Once Fulvio finished his set, we left in a great whirl, seemingly leaving pieces of equipment, and some of our group of four—namely, Pasquale—behind. As Roberto, Fulvio, and I raced to the car, a tall man stopped us with a question. He had a golden music staff pinned to his lapel. In garbled Neapolitan he asked me if Fulvio worked for an organizer. Before I could answer him, Roberto stepped in and said,

"No, we were just called here by the host."

"Well, maybe we can arrange something. I need a singer."

"OK, let me get our appointment book," Roberto said, pulling a leather-bound day planner from his backpack.

Once Roberto and the new client fixed the date and decided on the price (100 euros), I asked the man if he was an impresario.

"No, why?"

"Your pin," I said, nodding toward it.

"No, I just love music. My wife gave it to me. But I separated from her because I couldn't get a blowjob out of her. Now I have a lover."

Fulvio was with us when he said this. When we got in the car, I noticed he was disturbed. "These are strange people," he said.

"Why?"

"Because they are strange."

"Do you not trust them?"

"Not exactly. It's the things they say."

When the four of us—Fulvio, Pasquale, Roberto, and I—were driving home from our last engagement for the evening, Pasquale seemed inordinately irritable. He shouted at Fulvio, "You sung like a *chiavaca* [fuckup] this evening. What's wrong with you? This is work. This is *not* play. You play *afterward*. Why do you keep making the same mistakes? I told you already that you have to sing "Palcuscenico" *without* that elongated note. You don't *hold* it there—you need to finish and then move on. Why the hell do you keep making that mistake? You made us *fare una figura di merda* [make a shitty impression]. You sung like trash!"

The argument escalated when Fulvio responded in defense, "OK, OK, I forgot. Just drive! Go!"

His anger now inflamed, Pasquale yelled, "No, you *don't* forget! We are *working* here. And *you*," he turned now to Roberto in the front passenger seat, "You can't hurry me like that! What the hell do you think you're doing? It's impossible to work like that. You don't know the meaning of work. You're going to find yourself in the middle of the *street*."

These words triggered Roberto, who both raised the volume and lowered the pitch of his voice, menacingly. He gesticulated heavily in front of him, in the small space the front passenger seat provided. "What am I supposed to do? I don't know!"

Finally exasperated, it seemed almost a fake Neapolitan that Pasquale spoke, theatrical, dramatic, "But you can't work like this!" He repeated this sentence three more times, enunciating each syllable with lamenting stretched vowels that finished in a nasalized sound that other Neapolitan speakers—critical of this pronunciation—describe as "Arab."

Pasquale went on like this for fifteen minutes, until it seemed no one would be able to take it anymore. Roberto, wanting to stop him, said in a soft voice, "Dad, come on, you shouldn't."

This irritated Pasquale to no end: "What? *I* decide what to say, not *you!*"

I turned my face toward the window so as not to be seen. Fulvio offered me one of the sugarcoated almonds from the small gift the host of the communion party gave him. I took it from him and grasped his small shoulder for half a minute, trying to express to him that he can count on me to see things his way. Fulvio, however, seemed perfectly unscathed by the whole drama.

Later that night in Pasquale's kitchen, I tried to learn more about why my video camera could have raised suspicions among the guests at Fulvio's last gig. Pasquale was surprisingly candid with me; ordinarily I had to take what I could get, which usually consisted of the cryptic remarks he made in situ. But then I remembered why this communicative shift would be happening. During the months of pirate TV transmissions, provincial family celebrations, and all the dealing, arguing, boasting, and joking, there were a few other times when we reached this breaking point of exhaustion. A lot goes on in a full day for a boy on this scene: the expanding promise of something within reach and the struggle to plan for and bargain with the encounters that paved the way to it. A lot goes on as well for an anthropologist who follows him, because merely following or "hanging out" is never the only thing the anthropologist does. It was at the end of these runs of "excessive" hanging out, at the brink of exhaustion and on the threshold of revelation, that it seemed *something* was *really* about happen.

Pasquale explained that the guests at Fulvio's gig in Guadagno were malavitosi and that among them there could be fugitives who dared to make an appearance on the occasion of their kin's wedding or communion. He said it must have happened at least five times in his career that police raided and captured fugitives at private parties while he was performing. Upon hearing this, I understood something I had observed during Fulvio's performance. Pasquale had been operating the sound equipment while talking with the host of the party. Then something Fulvio announced to the audience made Pasquale laugh uncomfortably and transformed his conversation with the host into an intense and animated discussion: "This next song is called 'A tangente' [The bribe]. It's dedicated to all the *detenuti* [prisoners] who could not be here today." Ironically, from one perspective, Fulvio was referring to the detained kinspeople who had not succeeded in evading the police and attending the family celebration. By logical extension, he was also referring to those who had at some point become fugitives of the law and were now present.

Capitalizing on our exhaustion and Pasquale's openness, I also asked him about the man in the ill-fitting suit who had greeted us at the restaurant. Pasquale said the man was an organizer named Mariano Durante. "Durante has his own giro. He shuts Fulvio out because I don't want to be involved in his activities," he complained bitterly.

"Do you mean that you don't want to have anything to do with his circle or that you would like it if Fulvio could sing for his circle, provided nothing more were expected of him?"

Pasquale did not seem too comfortable with my fine-spun distinctions. By giro did he mean a "clique" of intimates, or did he mean a "circuit," in the sense of a business network? Was Pasquale saying that he wanted to be a part of the latter, but not the former? He seemed to suggest that the two were potentially separable. But Pasquale evaded my question: "Fulvio has been shut out for years, but now that they [individual clients] are calling him directly, he doesn't have to go through any organizer. This proves that Fulvio has something."

What I made of this statement was that Pasquale believed Fulvio's talent was the "something" that might enable him to survive outside the nucleus of malavatiso paternalism and filiation. A week later, Pasquale told me about an encounter that directly challenged this hope he had for his son, himself, and the rest of his family. Alone in his car on the way to fetch Fulvio from basketball practice, Pasquale asked me for advice about a certain problem. A family had invited Fulvio to sing at their wedding party the following week in Trelingua, a town just outside Naples. The Cimino crime clan runs Trelingua, and the capoclan's brother, Raffaele, runs a music agency. Pasquale says he wants nothing from Raffaele Cimino and that he has never asked him for a thing. In the recent past, different residents of Trelingua wanting to hire Fulvio to sing at their weddings twice called Pasquale. Each time Pasquale took the job. After the second gig, Cimino called him and announced, "You gotta go through me when you take these gigs, you understand?"

Pasquale claims that in response he challenged Cimino (but it is more likely that Pasquale said these words only to himself, in his head): "Why? They weren't gigs that *you* landed for me. They have nothing to do with you."

Cimino elaborated, "Everything that happens here has to do with me. If you have a gig here, you make sure you tell me next time."

I asked Pasquale what would happen if he didn't tell Cimino about his son's next engagement. His answer, which he kept repeating, as if trying to convince himself of its truth, was "What can this guy do?" Paradoxically, or simply realistically, Pasquale supported his defiant statement with defensiveness: "From a thirteen-year-old kid he wants to rob 20 euros? What is he dealing in such small change for? I can't believe he would be interested. There are singers making six or seven hundred euros a gig—that's where the money is, but Fulvio? It's like stealing from a kid."

"It's not the money that matters, it's the principle of it," I told him. I was amazed that we were having this conversation, that I should have to explain these things to him.

"But why should I give him a cut? What is he giving me? Nothing!" he declared.

"That's right. Nothing. That's how it works. He gives you nothing."

"So what should I do?"

"Well, go calmly on this next gig, and then . . ." I wanted to tell him to let Cimino know, but Pasquale was not really asking me for advice.

"It's not even in Trelingua, it's in Cardarelli," he said with exasperation.

"Which borders Trelingua?"

"Yeah."

"And the people who are hiring you are from Trelingua?" I was thinking about networks as much as I was about territories.

"Yeah, but how will he know?" Pasquale asked, this time with more concern than exasperation in his voice. He realized I might be onto something with this line of reasoning.

"He'll know, don't you worry," I said with surprising finality.

It took incredibly long to find La Conca d'oro (The Golden Conch), the restaurant where Fulvio was to perform in San Biagio. We asked groups of old men sitting at tables outside bars, various pedestrians, and a gas station attendant. Each had a different story, causing us to literally drive back and forth along the same main street. Finally, two young sunglassed men on Vespas said that we should follow them. They led us down the main street until we were out of the town center and then pointed at a left turn. Pasquale had just taken their cue when his cell phone rang. It was the organizer.

"Where are you?" the voice said at the other end of the line.

"We're here, we're arriving now, don't worry," Pasquale answered deferentially. After he hung up he said, "These people are precise," as if trying to justify his lateness.

When we arrived, a man stood waiting for us in the parking lot of the restaurant. It was Luigi Ippolito, whom I remembered from another of Fulvio's gigs in a village at the foot of Mt. Vesuvius. Luigi remembered me, too. After greeting us, he took Fulvio under his arm. He walked with him slowly, talking with fatherly deliberation, to the front door of the restaurant. I trailed behind.

Luigi wore a blue pinstriped suit, a white shirt, and no tie. His pale face was tranquil; he seemed good-natured. When he was on his feet, he moved around slowly and never raised his voice; he seemed never to betray a sense of urgency. "You wait here," he told Fulvio when we reached the restaurant entrance. Then he went inside to announce Fulvio's arrival.

Once Fulvio began singing, I sat down at an empty table near Luigi's. Fulvio looked at me occasionally during his performance. He smiled when I looked back at him. What made him happier—that he had a new friend or that an American "journalist" was interested in his career? While I wondered about the question, Luigi suddenly moved over to the empty chair beside me.

"I'm going to make this boy grow," he said in a variety of provincial Neapolitan with which I was unfamiliar.

Trying to sidestep the problem, I responded in Italian, "Yeah? So you're an organizer?"

When he answered me, the only word I could make out was the word "command." Unable to come up with a graceful way to tell him that I only understood the varieties of Neapolitan spoken in Naples, I simply reminded him that I was not Italian.

Luigi repeated his answer to my question, but it sounded exactly like it did the first time.

Unwilling to just get the gist of it (I still hoped for precise listening even if I no longer hoped for precise speech), I said, "I'm sorry, but I still don't understand."

He turned to look directly at me with a hint of impatience. In clearly enunciated Italian he declared, "I am a camorrista. I control these parts."

I paused, wondering if he was joking. Never had I met a person who openly pinned himself down, just like that.

Deciding *this is play,* I adopted an ironic tone. "So these other people here—do they work with you?"

"They're my relatives," he said plainly.

I was not entirely sure the man was ironic. I started to think he was *raddoppiandosi,* "doubling himself," puffing up. Or was he playfully puffing up? Did he want me to acknowledge and play with his vaunting, or did he simply want me to be impressed? I decided on the former: "And what kind of businesses do you operate?"

"Cose illecite [illicit things]," he said, now with a slight smile.

Did he smile because I played well? Or did he smile because my boldness impressed him? Or were both possibilities the case? And, I wondered, from his perspective, what kind of boldness was I demonstrating? Was it the boldness of a "real player"—*nu most',* a monster, as Roberto would call me—or was it the boldness of a Pulitzer Prize–winning investigative reporter?

Of course I could not dilate time any longer with such endlessly recursive thoughts—timespaces with self-professed camorristi were so rare in my experience, and I did not want this one to end just yet. I decided to continue playing, but by deciding I instrumentalized play, unintentionally turning it into a different kind of challenge: "Yeah, and what specifically?"

Luigi smiled widely and said, "Various things." It seemed he was dismissive in the paternal manner that meant to say, *There's no need for you to worry about all of that.* Then with two hands he took hold of my forearm in the form of an affectionate handshake, got up, and moved back to his own table.

For the remainder of Fulvio's performance, I watched Luigi as often as discretion permitted in order to detect any residue from our interaction. Maybe I had crossed a line with him, and I would catch him observing me or talking to someone else about me. I was relieved and perhaps a little disappointed to notice nothing of the sort. Was I once again irrelevant? Or was our strange interaction his way of verifying my irrelevance? Neapolitans generally "loved" Americans (as their liberators and as inventors of the American Dream), but not many Americans hang out at crime family celebrations in provincial towns. Maybe he identified himself to me because he thought that through me he could get to Fulvio? Did he want me to convince Fulvio and his father that Luigi Ippolito could "make that boy grow?" Even worse, did it seem to him I was responding with sarcasm to the claims he made about his power?

One Sunday, Rita was preparing *pasta al forno* for our large afternoon meal. I had left Pasquale and the boys in the sitting room to be alone with her in the kitchen. I hoped to learn some new recipes and to learn more about her. She answered a few of my queries about cooking, but then it became clear that she, too, wanted to learn more about me. She interrupted me to ask, as she often did, if I was going to get married. My usual answer—that I first needed to settle down in one country—seemed never to satisfy her. This time Roberto, who had come in the kitchen for his cell phone, answered his mother's question for me: "No, he's like me—he wants to be free." This version sounded more appropriate. It redefined my "procreative lack" into a surplus of "masculine potency," making me out to be a Don Giovanni.

Relieved but not entirely comfortable with Roberto's intervention, I quickly took the opportunity to redirect the conversation: "You don't have a girlfriend, Roberto?" I asked.

He shook his head.

"But you had one last year . . . what happened? You got rid of her?"

He smiled.

Stefania walked into the kitchen, returning from the pastry shop with a large tray of delicacies. I asked her, too, if she had a boyfriend. She, too, said no.

"So no one is marrying and leaving home anytime soon," I said to Rita.

Rita looked at me with feigned misery, "No, no one will ever leave, it seems."

"Jason, 'a zezzenella è doce [the teat is sweet]," Stefania declared. When I repeated the saying to demonstrate I had understood, everyone laughed.

Rita and I had known each other two years, spending nearly every Sunday together at their house, as well as evenings at Telefantasy, TVP, and other broadcasters in the suburbs of Naples. But that was no matter, as I learned from our conversation the following week just after the ragù. Trusting is not merely "a matter of time."

We were in the kitchen, Rita at the stove, and Fulvio and I seated at the table. Fulvio looked at me and touched my ear. "You still have such small ears," he said affectionately, pointing out, as he had once before, my physiognomic peculiarity.

"You know what that means?" Rita suddenly interjected.

"That I'm mean," I answered, repeating what a Neapolitan friend once told me, long ago.

"No, that you're going to die young."

"Don't tell me that!" I said, raising my voice.

"I'm only repeating what they say."

"But I don't like hearing that."

Fulvio joined in, too: "No, don't say that. That's not right."

Fulvio's protectiveness was comforting. "It was better not to know," I said, ready to leave it be and move on.

Then Rita changed the subject slightly. She said to Fulvio, "But did you hear what he said?" Then turning to me, "You said that it means that you're mean. So then, you're mean?"

I felt offended. "No. Do I seem mean to you? Do you think I'm mean?"

She didn't answer.

"You hesitate! So after all this time you can't tell whether I'm mean or not?"

Again she didn't answer. In silence, she returned to cleaning up in the kitchen.

Now I was angry. "You're a bit diffident, aren't you?" I said to her, taking a stab at being personal—something I rarely did.

Then finally Rita spoke, but only after an additional disconcerting moment of silence: "You see, we are a bit different—"

"Than us Americans?" I interrupted, irritated that she might be referring to some stereotyped radical difference between us she believed I was unable, particularly as an American, to overcome.

"No, we're even different than the northerners here in Italy. We open up quickly, so it's always possible that we let a bad one in. So we have to be careful."

I had asked Rita whether she could see that I was good. But to her, good and bad had nothing to do with appearances. Rather, they were wrought by circumstances, most of which, people often seemed to think, were still to come. In my experience in this milieu, it is a common practice to ask a person the same question a number of times over time. It is a technique for getting at the unrevealed truth. I use the term *unrevealed truth* to avoid what is usually implied by the word *lie,* a word I have rarely, if ever, heard uttered in Neapolitan. It seems that people commonly take for granted that what is said is never entirely the truth. Rather, they assume that what is said is more an intimation of what is left unsaid.

Leaving truths unrevealed is a form of indirect speech, a form of discretion or prudence. The philosopher Torquato Accetto wrote in 1641 that "honest dissimulation" is a "veil of honest darkness," not where lies are produced but where the truth is given repose so that it may show itself later, at the right time. Dissimulation, provided that it is honest, is a "rhetorical expedient" that has nothing to do with ethics.[6]

Many people in this milieu have the capacity to anticipate and sense truth in facial expressions, gestures, and silences, which are all folded into a "situational proprioception." This practice is not the same as reading or scanning signs in order to arrive at a "deeper" interpretation, or "the hermeneutics of suspicion."[7] The people I got to know are indeed suspicious of people who are not intimate "family" (biological, conjugal, or fictive), but this doesn't mean they are engaged in "paranoid reasoning."[8] In other words, suspicion is a form of relation and not an interpretive procedure. Suspicion may saturate encounters outside the nuclear membrane of the family, but it does not overdetermine them.

People do not engage in these encounters according to any *code* of conduct, and they certainly don't take the deconstructive approach of "always already." Suspicion, rather, is the mode of attention "always potentially anything." That I should persistently reply the same way to Rita's repeated question about my intentions was perhaps more suspect to her than if my responses had varied over time. She anticipated locating unrevealed truths in the slippage between my accounts of myself. But I inadvertently confused her expectations, which perhaps felt to her like cunning resistance.

Rita and her family had indeed "let me in." On the one hand, I had intimate contact with their lives, particularly their sporadic dealings with malavitosi. I was also the recipient of their abundant generosity. Yet I reciprocated fully with my computer and video camera skills, my contacts, and even with gossip. Generosity of the heart works fast. It is how people communicate good feelings and the desire to be close. It is also the way to solidify economic alliances and open new exchange routes and eventually exchange groups. Letting each other in feels like an inexorable hurtling toward complete transparency and total two-world exchange, yours and mine: me and my skills, resources, and network of contacts, friends, and family, and you and yours. Everything that is at my fingertips becomes, through me, accessible also to you. Our trade routes are open and unlimited. Trade unions of this kind are extreme, near total, teetering on family making. This is one reason why simple interactions can already feel like inevitable entanglements, which in turn give one a sense of inevitable calamity, like the breakups and reunions of familial and romantic relationships. Total union becomes indistinguishable from collision.

After another Sunday lunch at Fulvio's home, Pasquale, Rita, Stefania, and I were sitting around the kitchen table watching one of the regional TV channels. A series of music videos by a young singer were aired. Rita turned to me and said, "This kid, I really don't like him, and I'll tell you why. One evening we were at Telefantasy and he was on before us, so we were waiting. So was his father. His father came up to me and said, 'I spent 50,000,000 lira on him [about U.S.$28,000], but you, what have you done for your son?' I just laughed, and I laughed, just like this," Rita cackled for me in demonstration. "'And what the hell are you laughing about?' the father shouted at me. 'I'm talking about something serious.

That's a lot of money, 50 *millioni!*' I looked at him and I said, 'I can laugh, what's it to you? If you felt like you had to spend that kind of money . . .'"

Pasquale and Rita have chosen to promote their son's career without the backing of malavitosi, as Rita implied with her anecdote, because *where there's money, there's the camorra.* Pasquale had an anecdote of his own to drive home this implicit message. He told me about a young singer who couldn't sing for the life of him. "He was launched [by a clan affiliate], and then he was pushed on people within the boss's giro," Pasquale said with increasing disgust. "Whenever he finished his short performance he would say, 'Well, I'm going now, so let's hear an applause.'"

Pasquale threw a look of incredulity my way. "What an embarrassment, can you imagine? *Canta 'na chiavaca* [he sings like a fuckup], so when he finishes, there's only silence in the audience. When Fulvio sings, the crowd goes wild."

Pasquale seemed to be referring again to Fulvio's talent and the "fraudulent" success of performers backed by malavitosi. In this case, the singer simulated a successful performance by extorting praise from his audience. He performed both song and the threat of violence in a voice that was not his own: it was the voice of his ventriloquist—arrogant, bristling, vulgar. Pasquale's and Rita's anecdotes show that "like boss, like son." The fictive filiation of boss–patron and boy–singer is made public in parallel forms of excessive manhood—belligerent, narcissistic self-display.

It was in the late afternoon in July that we finally decided to shoot the music video I offered to make for one of the songs on Fulvio's new album. As a gift, it was reciprocation for their generosity. But it also had other functions; like their gifts to me, it was self-interested. The benefit for me was twofold. First, coparticipation in a creative process gave me access to their aesthetic world. Our collaborative project created contexts for engaging each other about aesthetics and, through aesthetics, about other dimensions of everyday social life.[9]

Second, I wanted my music video to become part of a portfolio that I could use to convince Gaetano, an alleged boss–impresario who was opening a neomelodico talent agency, to take me as his in-house videographer. For many months, I felt I had reached an unsatisfying threshold in my study of the scene. I knew intuitively that the only way to cross the threshold was through deeper intimacies nurtured by shared interests. As a participant who bartered with concrete local resources, rather than just my inadvertent influence as a journalist, I began to understand and apply local value theory. The people with whom I worked located most value in relations that were simultaneously affective and interested. And affects and interests were interdependent, mutually reinforcing, and mutually destructive.

Pasquale, Fulvio, and I were looking for a parking spot at Piazza Carità (Charity Plaza), from where we would walk to Piazza Montesanto to shoot the music video. A middle-aged man with a cigarette in his mouth and a baseball cap on his head waved at Pasquale while approaching the car. "Two minutes," he mumbled to Pasquale. The man then walked toward a cluster of parked cars, motioning us to follow with the car. The man communicated in gestures—first wagging his hand palm-downward by bending it at the wrist, then raising the palm of his hand toward us, telling Pasquale "stop" and "wait with the car idling." Pasquale got out of the car to pay the man, who had already begun attending to a second "customer" across the "parking lot."

The man in the baseball cap was a *parcheggiatore abusivo* (illegal parking attendant) who, with the authorization of local clan affiliates to whom he paid tangenti, extorted fees from drivers wishing to park in public spaces. In Naples everything about this transaction, at the time commonplace across the city, was ordinary. The parcheggiatori, with their gestures and the bodily sense of spatial proprietorship they conveyed, were clearly visible, as if they wore reflective yellow vests. Drivers understood this language implicitly and automatically. If drivers ever resisted, they argued with the amount of the fee, not the fee itself or the principle behind it. Drivers, moreover, trusted the quality of the service provided: "protection" against vandals and thieves (likely to be associates of the parcheggiatori or even the parcheggiatori themselves). Although resigned to the forced transaction, they inevitably received reliable returns.

Fulvio and I watched the transaction from where we remained seated in the car. It was one of the rare instances when he and I were alone (by his parents' design?), if only very briefly. I had waited patiently for opportunities to speak to him without his parents responding for him. But it was Fulvio who seized the opportunity first by asking me a question: "Jason, is there the camorra also in New York?"

Fulvio seemed to think of the world as one great, big place where the camorra was always present and encounters with "it," especially when you had to work hard to avoid it, were inevitable. In the world as Fulvio imagined it, people took "the camorra" for granted as if it were a natural disaster that seemed always on the verge of overwhelming and transforming everything into something else.

Act 2: Betraying Secrets

In 2003 the neorealist-style movie *L'isola* (The island) was released in Italian theaters.[10] In one scene, Teresa, a ten-year-old tomboy, suddenly bursts into tears because her grandmother has given her a horrible haircut. She wanted to look good for the new older boy who had recently come to live and work at the grueling job of tuna fishing on the tiny Sicilian island. Her grandmother tries to console her. "Don't worry about your hair," she says in soothing tones, but Teresa continues to weep. The grandmother repeats her words, now almost pleading with the child, but still has no effect. Her tone gradually escalates: "Don't you remember your grandfather [now dead] saved you when you were drowning, when you were just a baby? Don't you realize that he's protecting you? And you cry? Why should you cry? You make me cry, too." She begins to cry along with Teresa, who soon stops, looking through her wet eyes at her sobbing grandmother with a strange sort of recognition that she's not alone.

I asked a Neapolitan friend what was going on between these two characters. His response was automatic: "How do you console a person who's crying? The only thing to do is to give the other person company. What better way than to cry along with her?" In the milieu I frequented, the family is a deep pool of confluent affects and interests. The late sceneggiata allegorizes threats to the family as the leaky affect of She who cedes to the Evildoer. In reality, the family fissure is often the handiwork of the overgrown son who wants to get married and get out. When he tires of the art of making do and follows instead the lead of camorristi, he makes waves in the family's pool of affect. Rather than look for the content of secrets, this story follows how people use the force of secrecy to create human entanglements. The account below suggests that in moments of crisis families may tell secrets to stir up affects and draw each other, and sometimes other people, into deeper sympathies. Betrayal, secrecy, and the betrayal of secrets are forces that contribute, at times independently of human intention, to the reproduction of families and networks.

This was the case with Giuseppe and his family. Giuseppe created musical arrangements for singers in a small office above a tiny recording studio on Via Tiberio run by forty-three-year-old Pino, with whom he works in tandem. Pino recorded the voices once Giuseppe had produced the arrangements. Each did his part to pull in the clients. Giuseppe was thirty, with dark hair, pale skin, and sharp, watchful blue eyes. "People are shit. It's only animals you can trust," he often concluded after we had gone round in circles talking about the dirty music scene. What for me meant probing the hidden relations that kept (apparent) enemies and friends associating (apparently) intimately and frequently for him meant repeatedly circling the same simple point: treachery. This time we were talking about how mobster impresarios used to get "their" singers hooked on coke, one of the currencies in which they paid them for the wedding performances to which they pimped them out. Eventually payments exceeded the service, and the singers became indentured. And to be indentured to a camorrista means to be indentured indeterminately, indefinitely.

Giuseppe was speedy and agitated, with sparks in his eyes. He was talking fast and aggressively rattling off his consonant-less Neapolitan as if it were water. I asked him jokingly if he had blown some coke earlier, since we were already on the topic, but he said no, "This is the real me. I'm influenced by the weather and now that the heat is gone and it's cool and cloudy, I'm myself again." Suddenly Giuseppe announced that he was going to marry his girlfriend, Annalisa, next fall. I was confused about this decision, which seemed sudden and out of place considering everything I knew about his feelings and ambiguities. Only recently he told me, "Annalisa is a good girl, but she's not the kind I want; I like them blonde, fair, and *porca* [lit. piggish or voluptuous]. Besides, after ten years it's boring with the same girl. You want something fresh." Similarly, often while driving and honking at a girl, he shouts, "*Uàaa!* What can I do? What can I do? I can't stop this desire. . . . I just want another woman so bad. I can't stop looking and wanting to take her and then that other one and the next one." He complained that it's tiring to see Annalisa every night, the same thing again and again. "No freedom, you feel trapped, you know what I mean?"

When I asked him why he decided to get married, his explanation was tangential and long. "I can't go on like this. If something doesn't change, if I don't get this job that Matteo's brother Giovanni's friend can get me, the city job, because of my invalidity [he had a leg ailment that caused a painful limp], if nothing comes of it, then I'm going to change lives from one thing to another—completely." He said this in a threatening tone, loud and staccato, while gesturing with his flattened hand, turning it over once with deliberation, showing both its faces. "In three months, if it doesn't happen, I'm going to make a big change and do something really evil," he added with a squinting stare. He was not offering a lot of clarification, but I knew more or less the way people communicate heavy things here, so I foresaw that he would eventually arrive at it, on his own terms, taking his time. He had to first talk around it, partly setting it up with justification and background, partly to ease the impact by accumulating hints toward it. More importantly, his presentation style melodramatized the situation, working to stir up uncontainable apprehensions and a palpable sense of the incalculable force of things brewing.

"So if nothing works out, I'm going to get my alliances together and take charge of *l'ambiente* [the scene] here," he said, his eyes seeming bigger and bluer than before. He said this while gesturing out the kitchen balcony at the lot flanked with the other pockmarked and sagging 1950s four-story apartment buildings, their facades completely disordered with balconies, laundry, and different kinds of faded or stained canopies and blinds. His hand swept past this scene and toward the small cloud-covered mountains in the distance behind them, beyond all the other, equally trash-strewn lots. "And I'm capable of it, too. I know how to bring the money in. All you need is to be *sveglio* [awake] all the time, see everything around you, and know what people are. And I know how to get things from people."

We were still not getting to the topic of his marriage, and now I had questions about this tangential topic, which I gradually realized was not at all tangential: "But what about Gaetanino? Doesn't *he* control things here?" Gaetanino is the local boss with/for whom (often I didn't know which) Giuseppe and I worked. He brought in the talent by casting his net and "inheriting" the singers who used to work for his father, a camorrista who ran his own talent agency up until the last decade.

"Listen, Gaetanino wants out. He wants to start this music agency and quit that other stuff. He pushes coke, it's true, but he wants out. *I* want in, though. But I don't want to mess with the drugs," he explained. "What do you want to do, then?" I asked. Gradually, Giuseppe's words started to sound like *chiacchiere* (chatter), or the big talk of plans that get continually deferred into nothingness: "Prostitution and extortion."

I knew something about the neighborhood, so decided to put him to the test. "Is there prostitution *here?*"

His answer was immediate: "No, but there are where my cousins live, in Boscotermini. There you go and take your pick, they're all along the streets, just like in Germany, you go out to a club and all you need to do is look at a girl and she's yours." It seemed we were veering back toward the paradox that his plan to marry and his wandering sex drive generated. Why did he want to marry? I gradually realized that Giuseppe was telling me that organized crime was part of the answer, but I could not yet understand how.

I decided to probe farther into Giuseppe's interest in the camorra. "I get it: so you're going to align yourself with your uncles," I said to him, referring to the big fishes that are supposed to be a threat to Gaetanino. They swam up to the surface just the day before as the reason why Giuseppe did not worry about Gaetanino trying to move in on him and Pino and take over the studio space, and them, for his new talent agency. I had listened to a heated conversation between Giuseppe and Pino, and a lot of dancing around between the two of them and Gaetanino over whether the landlord of the building would be able to rent the adjacent space out to Gaetanino to set up shop. Pino was squirming with rage and fear that Gaetanino would colonize them.

After a couple of hours, the five of us had walked a few blocks to the bar for an espresso. It seemed as if we had all slipped into a comedic intermission from the tense negotiations back in the studio. This shift in modes gave me time to think and to catch up on what I didn't understand. Trailing behind the others, I said to Giuseppe with a hardened face, "You have some explaining to do." Giuseppe was my best confidant on the scene, and now we were in business together; he therefore understood what my accusation meant. I was entitled to know the nature of his contact with the camorra, which would inevitably become my contact as well.

Although, or because, we were in the company of the very two people about whom I wanted to have a "private" discussion, Giuseppe signaled me to go ahead: "Go on, ask me." Still unwilling to let everyone hear me, and unsure how much Pino and Gaetanino were hearing, I said in a low voice, "Pino is totally against all this and wants nothing to do with these people, but you are ambivalent about it for some reason." Giuseppe answered plainly, unworried, "Because Gaetanino will eat Pino up, but once my uncles arrive, *they* will eat Gaetanino up." I was surprised not only with this new information but also that its "veracity" was necessarily proven, or even produced, by its now semipublic nature. *Pettogolezzi* (gossip) in Naples is often performed in the earshot of the subjects in question. Part of the reason for this is that Neapolitans distinguish it from *'nciucci* (possibly related to the slang *ciuccia,* or vagina), which they define as gossip with malevolent ends. Gossip is acceptable, expected, and not a secret matter. Furthermore, "open" gossip is often intentional. Gossip, when it is the semipublic, eavesdropped speech that Giuseppe was performing with me, functions as an indirect message to the eavesdropper.

"Oh really? After a year and half you tell me this about yourself?" I said to Giuseppe, hyping up my indignation at not having known how powerful he considered himself. He laughed at me while our animated group on the busy sidewalk that Saturday afternoon contorted in on itself as conversations crisscrossed and gestures extended outward and backward, as some of us stopped dead in our tracks to create dramatic moments in our declarations, and as we grabbed each other by the arm or put an arm around the other's shoulder for emphasis. Sometimes these sudden and complicated movements absorbed innocent passersby who gracefully slipped back out once again and went on their way in the other direction, as planned. Giuseppe and I also found ourselves suddenly reintegrated in the mix, effectively ending our semiprivate exchange.

The next day, as Giuseppe and I sat alone at his kitchen table, I could ask him all the questions I wanted. "I get it: So you're going to align yourself with your uncles," I said. "No, my cousins . . . that's who I'm gonna align with. They come from my mother's side, and they are a family *per bene* [a good family].[11] They're clean people. But for some reason these two cousins are total criminals. I don't know why. And they're younger. And then one day they were here in Rione Alto and we ran into this big boss in the area and I watched the boss kiss one of my cousins when they greeted, and he said, 'Hey! How you doing!' and was all happy and intimate. And I said to myself, what is this? *Uàaa!* So I think me and them, we can do business." After a brief pause, Giuseppe concluded with a decisive air, "But they don't know how to do anything here, *either.* That's why I can get in on this."

"But isn't the territory all covered now? How are you going to get in?" I asked. Giuseppe gestured to me dismissively, tossing his hand out to the side, as if shaking off dirt, "Naw, these people are stupid, they don't know how to do things, and there are so many people involved in their little worlds and no organization." He continued now with a look of disgust on his face, "They're nothing. About twenty years ago, that's when they were the real shit. Brutal. I remember on this road right here [he gestured out the window to the narrow road that flanked his apartment building—the road his bedroom faced] there was a war with bullets everywhere, cutting up the tufo stone and brick walls and breaking all the windows.[12] You wouldn't believe it. Back then the real bosses were around, real bosses who were famous and ran off to places like England, South America, and France and started business there. Others had good relationships with the Sicilians. . . . That's how big they were. But then a whole mess started and they shot each other all up, a chain reaction of vendettas, and they either died or ran off and the power fell into the wrong hands—and too many of them. Now it's these idiots who don't know how to do anything. If the kid of one boss beats up the kid of another or disgraces him in some way, these days there is no retaliation, because maybe a boss's family is not sure of its own strength and fears the other boss. And they divided the power a hundred times so it's a mess now.

"The camorra is not like the mafia; it's more dangerous. Here, you don't know who's in charge. You think that guy there's the boss and you stick with him. But if he dies, then you're on your own. Or, in order to disrespect your boss, someone will shoot *you*. No, it's not like that with the mafia. In Sicily you know who the boss is and as long as you respect him, everything is quiet and calm. They have a tradition and things are within the family. Here it's not like that.

"They don't know a thing about selling drugs. Here there are couriers who are risking huge prison sentences bringing coke in from South America, Peru, and Colombia, but they're not the ones getting the good cut of the profits; it's the distributor. And he gives it out to the dealers and says he wants from them a thousand a week or so, whether or not they sell. If one dealer's doing good and sells a lot all the time, maybe he knows more people, knows how to make more friends, knows how to stick with the heavy users—a lot of them don't know shit; I wouldn't sell it to people who use it every now and then. No. I go for the ones who are real cokeheads and I stay on them. And the dealer who does that and does good, maybe he gets shot by another dealer who doesn't like the competition, seeing that he's making more than him. And the distributor, the boss, doesn't give a shit about one or the other. No, I would do it all differently, giving the courier a good 40 percent, because the dealers are out in a matter of months if they get nabbed, but a courier, that's a real blow they take. And then the distributor gets thirty, and the rest goes to the dealers. I would get a whole organization together, keep it tight and kill off all the rest, cleaning it all up."

At that moment there was a knock at the door. Giuseppe went around the corner from the kitchen and down the short hallway to see who it was. He spoke for ten seconds with a young female voice, and then came back into the kitchen alone. "Mamma mia, *'a faccia d' 'o cazzo* [lit. the face of a dick]. She's so fine, that one." I asked him who it was and he answered, "Gigi's daughter," referring to his neighbor of about forty, a soft-spoken, tall, slim man with carved facial features. "She's eighteen and *bona* [fine]. And just think, I used to hold her in my arms when she was five. Damn! There was no thinking about it then, . . . but *now*."

Gigi sometimes joined us for a coffee. His usual performance is to outdo Giuseppe in front of me by calling him ignorant and explaining to him the importance of studying Neanderthals, Egyptology, and Zulu rituals. Giuseppe, however, knew when it was futile to argue and took his anthropology lessons in silence. The last time we saw Gigi was just the week before. He stopped by Giuseppe's after lunch and asked me sheepishly if I would give English lessons to his daughter. I made the mistake of veering toward a no, which only paved the way for his persistent attempts to convince me to change my mind. People most often do not say no; it is perceived as abrupt and cold if it is the response to a request to perform a favor or an invitation requiring presence. Once, when Giuseppe was dropping me off at the subway after our last lunch together before I was to leave the field, he asked me if he was going see me again before I left. I told him it was unlikely.

"Oh no! Don't say that! Tell me 'yes' instead," he told me, visibly upset.

I defended myself by asking, "Even if it's a lie?"

His answer came quickly, "Even if it's a lie. Otherwise it sounds ugly, like you don't *want* to see me."

Presence and good-heartedness are the kinds of contact that people expect from one another such that their absence must be coded as the result of unwanted or unforeseen obstacles. And when people have a par-

ticular interest in each other, they are not adverse to exploiting the affective tug provided by the culturally enforced laws of contact.

After finally catching on, I gave Gigi the right answer, "OK, we'll
see." Finally Gigi said good-bye and left, closing the door behind him.
Giuseppe then started to talk about something that by the tone of his
voice sounded important, but stopped suddenly and crept up to the door
and listened to find out if Gigi were still lingering outside. Satisfied that
we were really alone, he went on, this time staring me down hard. "In
my world, if you break a secret, it's really the end, a bad end, if you know
what I mean . . . and *I'm* going to tell you a secret."

"I had Gigi's wife for two years." Here he paused and smiled, waiting for my reaction. I smiled and nodded, appropriately acknowledging
his sexual prowess. "And you know, she disgusted me. She was attractive back then, don't worry about that—even though now you can't
even look at her—but it was the way she behaved. She would call him
up in the middle of us and ask him what he wanted for lunch. 'Pasta and
beans? OK, I'll make it just how you like it.' She would do it because you
would never know if he was on his way home, that way she could figure
out where he was. But it disgusted me. Not the cheating; it can happen, it
can happen to anybody."

"Even Annalisa?" I asked him, referring to his girlfriend and trying to
provoke him.

"Yeah, anyone. But with this woman you have a double life. You either stay with the guy or you tell him, look, it's not going on anymore,
it's not working."

Meanwhile, I wanted to know more about Giuseppe's extended family.
His family had its own double, its own bad copy. I began asking Gianni,
Giuseppe's father, "You know, Giuseppe told me that you have *certi parenti*
[certain relatives] who are a little particular."

Gianni had shown up at the apartment late for lunch. When we were
finished eating, he railroaded me into spending the afternoon with him
in the car, running work errands. I thought I'd take advantage of my
time alone with him and ask about his family's involvement with malavitosi. I had learned not to toss the word *camorra* around as if it were
like any other, and my ellipsis, certi parenti, was well taken. Speech in
this milieu often trails off into inference and obliquity, if it is not already
swathed in irony or hyperbole. It is not appropriate to ask, "What do

you mean?" Asking for clarification incites even more indirectness. An interlocutor is expected to infer the gist and respond from there; it is no matter that this joint operation can be highly approximate. Often, significance does not inhere in any specific content that one wants to communicate or that one wants to have communicated to them. Rather, it is meaningful nonsignifying meaning, the "idea-force."[13] This is especially true with talk that comes into close contact with the camorra.

Gianni answered me flatly, "It's my brother who lives just above us." Now it was all connecting. This part Anna had left out when she and I were talking "privately" in the kitchen (Giuseppe had gone to the bathroom) at lunch. I told her that Giuseppe had told me that there were certain relatives in the family.

She crossed the room and closed the shutters on the balcony before answering me, "It's the one who lives above us."

I wanted to know more, so I told her what I already knew, "Giuseppe says he used to sell contraband cigarettes."

Feeling more comfortable knowing she wasn't revealing too much new information, Anna said, "Yes, that's right, but he was foolish. He didn't know how to handle money. While the others he was organized with bought a billiards hall and brought in a lot of money, he just kept on spending and didn't invest in anything. He could have been settled and happy with the money, but instead he squandered it." Anna, probably because I had cornered her into talking about this man as the upstairs neighbor, talked about him as if he were a distant relative. Similarly, Gianni was telling me that the camorrista in question was his very own brother, but without ever mentioning that he lived in the apartment above them.

"Information" or the "truth" is a precious and dangerous substance in this milieu; it is hard to come by, and it pins things and people down to the concrete. This encumbers the mercurial movements so highly valued by people who are continually dodging identifications, which they ultimately associated with entrapment, violence, and the general potential for moral and economic disaster. To ask for or to respond with information can lead to imbroglio, the excessive limit of contact.

Gianni was taking me to Caserta, the third stop in his series of errands, but lunch was finished and Giuseppe was heading back to the studio. I wanted to follow Giuseppe and continue talking. There were a lot more questions to ask, and Giuseppe was particularly expressive today.

He and I were really getting to the bottom of things, it seemed. "Giuseppe is in love with the camorra," Gianni suddenly announced. "But I don't think it's anything more than that. He's not one of them," he added, after a pause. It was uncanny that he and I should be having this near-duplicate conversation when Gianni arrived at lunch long after Giuseppe and I had finished our "private" conversation about his intentions to go about making a living the *other* way. Maybe it really wasn't a new turn in the road at all; maybe this was a single turn that had been taking years and years for Giuseppe to make. Maybe it never really was a secret to his father.

Because I too am "in love with the camorra," Gianni managed to entice me away from Giuseppe with the claim that he had something camorra-related to show me. The week before, Gianni had promised to take me to San Giovanni, where he knew a group of camorristi with whom he had celebrated a baptism with a roasted pig and other delicacies. They were associates from his work at a trucking company that shipped prosciutto, Molisano milk, San Marzano tomatoes, and other typical products of the Campania region. However, his promise now turned out to be an empty one; instead, he took me hostage on his long drive from warehouse to warehouse. Ironically, we were merely driving farther and farther from my real interest, the meeting Giuseppe had set up with Gaetanino, a *real* camorrista who I could be sure existed.

Gianni then picked up a conversation started earlier when we were still all together in the kitchen. The topic was Giuseppe's marriage plans for next year. The cost was going to be something extraordinary. Giuseppe was saying, "I have nothing in my pockets, and I don't know if I'm going to have money next year. I need to get settled first. Otherwise, how am I going to do this?"

In response, Gianni turned away from the steering wheel to shout at me, his passenger-seat hostage: "Now how am I going to explain this to Annalisa when she comes to me asking, 'Don Gianni, but please, when are Giuseppe and I going to get married?' We already told her when, and now you want to change it! Listen, I am at your disposal. If you want to get married, I'm ready." This meant financially, as it was customary for the groom's father to pay the bill for the reception, probably the costliest part of it all. The car's interior seemed to become even more compact as Gianni's volume, pitch, and gestures occupied more and more space. Gianni, like most others here, required no less than an athletic listening.[14] It is common for reported speech to take on an affective charge equal to its "original." What better way to get your ersatz interlocutor involved than to shout at him, too?

"Why can't he be better behaved? Why can't he be different? Giuseppe doesn't know the meaning of work. I can't say that he takes advantage, but he leans too hard on us. It's not as if it weren't our fault, Anna's and mine, either. I should have explained to him what the problems were. Part of it is his illness. You know, many years ago, Anna and I lost our first child—he died soon after birth. Then Giuseppe came, but after a few years, we noticed he was ill and had a limp. In school they said he was faking it, but it kept going on, so I had an X-ray taken of his leg and they found out that a huge part of his femora was eaten away, but had grown back, but badly. He spent four years immobile, with casts and going through physical therapy, and now he's OK, but he has this bad limp."

He paused for a second, and I took the opportunity to ask, "Couldn't he get assistance from the state?"

"No, because it wasn't serious enough, his ailment. We thought the best thing was music, because it didn't take any movement, and that's where he is now."

Is it possible that Gianni doesn't know that the local music scene is a zone of contact with la malavita? Perhaps that is not the point at all; many unregulated work opportunities are assumed to bring a person into contact with organized crime. The real point lies in foreseeing and forestalling the moment when brushing up against becomes crossing over.

Gianni had large hands and fat fingers that were stained with grease and dirt, truly stained in a permanent way. They gestured to me and to the road before him, in between shifts of the gears and turns of the steering wheel. He was a short and stout man with just a few gray hairs at the back of his head. His large dark-blue eyes were alert and sincere, open and inviting. "Giuseppe is in love with the mafia," Gianni said to me again, point-blank. It seemed almost out of context, if one thought about it logically. We were talking about work, the upcoming marriage, the costs, the things that didn't work in Giuseppe's life, and then this sudden declaration. But at the same time, it fit perfectly; it was the missing piece. It was the piece Giuseppe put in when he and I were alone in his home, before his parents arrived for lunch: his secret plan to make a life change. It was the secret both Anna and Gianni kept about the occupant of the apartment above theirs; it was the concrete fact that only the words of the two of them put together could reveal. Together, Giuseppe,

Anna, and Gianni were telling me that Giuseppe was using his upcoming marriage as an excuse to fully enter into the camorra through his uncle. If an ordinary man wants to start a family, he needs the financial means to do so. Giuseppe's parents felt just as strongly as he about this goal, but they could not unhesitatingly channel their pool of affects into the plan Giuseppe was considering.

I asked Giuseppe if Annalisa knew about this plan.

"Naw, she doesn't know."

I imagined that eventually she would, though, if he did what he claimed he would do. I thought about Gaetanino's wife and his mother, the two hardest women at his sons' birthday party that I filmed for him. They scowled at me through my lens as I meandered here and there in the sparse, fluorescent-lit room with folding chairs and card tables, graffiti on the walls, plastic cups and plates, sagging mignon pastries, bags of pretzels, stale mini pizzas, and a big, blue birthday cake with a brownish food-dye photo reproduction of Mario and Salvatore, his two sons of one and eight years. Gaetanino didn't introduce me to anyone at the party. It was unclear if anyone knew why I was there, only that they had seen me walk in with Gaetanino, who then told me he had "errands" to run and would be back soon. His wife, who wore a strapless bright red dress on her dark body and a severe look on her face as if she were continually about to argue, smiled only twice the entire evening. Once was during the "happy birthday" song all the kids performed for her sons; the other time was when I showed her the digital photographs I had taken of the party guests, including her. Gaetano's mother was equally unfriendly. She looked directly into the lens as if she were about to say something in protest, but then left it alone. It was on film that I noticed that she and most of the other women at the party had small tattoos behind their right shoulders.

I thought of Gaetano's wife and mother while imagining Annalisa married to Giuseppe, years down the line. Annalisa already seemed to be a cheerless woman whose shyness came off as an aggressive repellent. She didn't mince words or make idle talk. I thought of Gaetanino's mother, who knew her son dealt coke, just as she knew her other ten sons worked in various sectors of organized crime. A mother's love for her son is like no other love. When police enter the hood, everyone notices. Heads turn, people stop, the word spreads. If the police are on a chase, mothers toss chairs into the streets to create obstacles and set fire to dumpsters. If kin are apprehended, mothers punch and slap the police. Then, it is the women who perform the "work of pain." They labor to assimilate the family's grief into the community by making their private crisis public through ritualized lament, a spectacularization that, although "true," resembles a sceneggiata.[15]

Gianni knew that Giuseppe was intermittently involved in the camorra. Gianni also knew that Giuseppe was at times on the threshold of a greater commitment than that. "Giuseppe is involved with the mafia," Gianni said to me, almost in non sequitur form. It seemed he was reasoning with himself. Or was he? Maybe he was trying to get something out of me, Giuseppe's friend and confidant. After a pause—probably the pause I was supposed to fill with some kind of reassurance—Gianni added, "But he's not like them." This same sort of internal dialogue that spilled out and invited me to participate, should I catch on, happened several times during our never-ending day of errands dealing with Mack trucks, warehouses of boxed prosciutto, highways and provincial coffee bars in the vicinity of Caserta with friendly but studious management who carefully examined us "strangers." Giuseppe had told me during lunch that Naples is nothing now when it comes to the mob. "The real shit is outside, in Aversa and Caserta." That's where the fiercest of all camorristi are and where their reach is capillary. The unknowable yet significant presence of something severe in fact thickened the air that Gianni and I breathed during our brief pit stops for coffee and pastries. The polite exchanges between Gianni, the barmen, and the cashiers were rendered sinister with overcharged smiles through which peered eyes of scrutiny. "What does it mean if you fuck somebody up—shoot them or cut them up in a fight? Then you're the guappo in Naples!" Giuseppe had nearly shouted at me, taken in by his own rhetorical revulsion. "That's bullshit. It doesn't happen like that, so easy, *outside*."

At last Gianni and I were back in Naples, where, according to Giuseppe, the mob was just as two-bit as is the neomelodica scene. Gianni and I inched in his car down Via Tiberio to Giuseppe's studio. It was half past seven. "And this music stuff, this studio, we do it for him because it keeps him occupied. But it's a waste of time, nothing conclusive, and all wrapped up with people who are inconclusive."

Finally I mustered up something to say, taking a chance. "I think Giuseppe realizes it, too," I said.

"Yeah? I hope that's true. That would be good," he answered. It was the input Gianni was searching for. That was the reason for taking me on his errands, after all.

"Who is it that you have to meet?" he asked me, referring to the appointment I warned him I had at seven with "clients" of Giuseppe, before we set off on our long journey all over the region.

"Andrea and Gaetano. I need to get to know them. Gaetano is an example of a camorrista for me," I said, choosing not to use the diminutive *Gaetanino* while talking to Giuseppe's father.

"Gaetano is not a camorrista," he responded in a dismissive tone.

"Well, I don't know," I answered. This way I could send a signal for Gianni to follow in case the dramatic performance his son gave me before lunch had any truth to it.

I couldn't imagine Giuseppe as a boss, but it was clear the money was seducing him. Surely it was humiliating for him to ask for fifty euros from his father in my presence. It was the last fifty he needed to pay the rent on his studio, and his father had decided not to make it easy. He had wanted to give him a loud lesson in front of me, the unwilling audience. "Why did you tell the landlord maybe you'd have the money today? There is no *maybe,* or 'I'll do,' or 'I'll say'; that's *not* how things work. *First* you have the money in your pocket, *then* you talk!"

Although I was only trying to help, it seemed strangely abusive to talk about "the camorra" with such directness to Giuseppe's father. I had felt the same way earlier even when I used a synonym in my conversation with Giuseppe's mother. Feeling I had actually leaked la malavita into their family by naming it, I tried to repair the breach by recalling that on her side of the family tree there had been a bourgeois gentleman she called a "nobleman."

"Yes, it was my maternal grandfather," Anna answered, easily engaged in the new topic. "He had the vice of gambling though. He was always in Monte Carlo and he squandered it all. Nothing came down to me," she said ironically, but not bitterly.

Then she opened a subject that interested her more. "I knew it would only be a matter of time before our neighbor Gigi came by and asked about you. I was amazed he didn't come sooner. Those people over there, they're users. The wife, she puts *herself* to good use, now that I'm on the subject, if you know what I mean. I'm sure Giuseppe has told you."

That afternoon everything tumbled into the realm of the uncanny. Once again, the same conversation was happening in triple time, with

Giuseppe and each of his parents. I let them talk it out. They had a lot to say today.

"You know about it?" I asked her cautiously.

"Yes, I know," she said, reassuring me. "The thing was, she was my friend. She had a key to the apartment for when I was at work. She used it to come in and give Giuseppe a bit of . . . coddling in the morning," she said with irony. "OK, Giuseppe is a man and has his experiences. . . . But if you're my friend and you're ten years older than him—" she paused for a few seconds, waiting for me to react. I nodded in agreement. "And you know what she said to me when I found out and was unhappy about it? She said, 'What? It's not as if you were my husband. What's it to you?'"

This time I shook my head in agreement and tsked once with my tongue.

"And when she realized that I wasn't just 'getting over it,' like she wanted, she invented some excuse to distance herself from me, telling her husband that I went around talking badly about her. I didn't talk to anyone, but it's all right. She did the work for me and took a distance. That's how our friendship ended." Gigi's wife, seeking to preempt her exposure, "told" her secret in her own way and put the betrayal of her family honor on Anna.

In the car, Gianni and I talked about this act of family self-preservation. This time we approached the topic from Gigi's point of view. Gianni called Gigi *'o cornuto felice* (the happy cuckold). Expressing disgust, he elaborated: "There really are no cornuti, in the end. A cornuto always knows, and he decides to be what he is. But then be what you are! He listened to his wife's tales, and maybe he was right to take sides with her, but then take that road all the way. If you come back I can't have respect for you."

According to Gianni, Gigi fears that if his family secret was exposed, it would unleash a force he could not overcome. The secret would expose Gigi for who he really was: the cornuto who is unable to respond "honorably" to betrayal.

Gianni, Anna, and Giuseppe each criticized how Gigi's family failed to contain its affects. Giuseppe accused Gigi's wife of straying from her own family. Giuseppe's mother charged her with coming too close to her own family and creating an imbroglio. Gianni accused Gigi of secreting away the imbroglio because he was unable to overcome it. All three told me the secret of Gigi's family betrayal, but the telling was embroiled with the tale of another betrayal: Giuseppe's plan to affiliate with a crime clan, another Family.

Although no one felt Giuseppe had any responsibility in Gigi's family betrayal, the sceneggiata tradition points to Giuseppe as the true betrayer of families. He even betrayed his own future family by using his upcoming marriage as legitimation for binding himself with a crime clan. As a single man, this bond would render him rapaciously self-interested: 'O malamente. As a married man, the bond is a forgivable compromise in the service of making do and family making. Giuseppe's parents acknowledged their son's ambiguous contact with organized crime and his "secret" plan to deepen his associations. All families in the contact zone share this secret. Everyone "knows": they are all happy cuckolds.

Act 3: The Erotics of Self-Exposure

One day a local music journalist named Francesco said I needed to talk to the Faletti family if I really wanted to understand neomelodica music from a fan's point of view. While accompanying me to their apartment in the periphery, he confided, "I want you to know that the wife, her name is Maria, she's a fan of the star singer Fabio. She is completely obsessed with him. Both she and Fabio have families. Knowing Maria, it seems impossible that she would be unfaithful to her husband. Knowing Fabio, however, it is not easy to say the same for him."

I asked the journalist a few basic questions about the family. He told me that Maria works on and off in a shoe factory while her husband works part-time as a security guard. Together they provide for their four sons.

We reached a two-story apartment building at the end of a cul-de-sac and found Maria already waiting for us in the lobby. She was an attractive, full-figured blonde in her forties. She wore tight-fitting black polyester slacks and a low-cut blouse out of which peeked her ample chest.

"Fabio is the only artist for me," Maria told me in a cooing, breathy voice when we began our interview, inside. She and the singer had developed an intense relationship over the past five years that seemed, under all appearances, to be a love affair. She gave him gifts, wrote him poems, and submitted romance stories about him to *Sciuè*. She also sent him poetic praises via cell phone text messages that he read to his audiences while conducting his live, viewer-call-in private TV broadcasts.

Fabio was a swaggering, long-haired, self-proclaimed womanizer in his midthirties. He dedicated songs to Maria on live regional TV. Sometimes he invited her on his transmissions and sang her dedications face-to-face, complete with longing gazes and expansive gestures. Maria was timid before the camera but held herself together. Their relationship took on the quality of a romance novel. Something about their combined performances when they were broadcast for their local public felt generic, such that no one would ever think it was the truth.

Maria loved Fabio's music. She loved Fabio as a singer, which is one step away, or beyond, loving him as a man. Fabio made his manhood partly through his emotionally charged musical displays. As a sceneggiata performer, he played the role of the betrayed. As a neomelodico performer, he played 'O malamente, the *prepotente* (bullying), philandering male. He had made two music videos with female porn stars, one of whom he serenaded as the Rondine napoletano (Neapolitan Swallow) who taught him things he didn't know about love.

Maria tirelessly recorded every TV transmission on which Fabio appeared, regularly adding new videocassettes to her vast archive of recordings, concert posters, CDs, letters, and newspaper articles all stacked up in the bedroom next to the porcelain Madonna poised on a tall, white, faux-marble Corinthian column. In fact, these items seemed to share some auratic quality with the Madonna, as if she were the cause and they the effect. Maria looked at my admiration for her piles of Fabio and said, "Sometimes he calls me three times a day because maybe he needs a copy of a videotaped performance or a newspaper article faxed to someone. Other times he calls to ask me to act as ambassador to someone he needs to meet. He calls me without hesitation, even after midnight, when he finishes a performance: 'Maria, I sang *alla grande* tonight. I hit it big. I gotta tell you about it, Maria.'"

During our interview, it was almost embarrassingly obvious to me that Maria was having an affair. Yet I doubted my perceptions because it was too direct, too close to the truth to be the truth. And no one else, apparently, was scandalized. Could Maria be so shameless for so many years and not be having a *real* love affair with Fabio? Perhaps Maria found the perfect guise, the most effective form of dissimulation: obviousness. Could the spectacle she made of the affair actually be camouflaging it?

The room we sat in was in polished disuse. It contained only a few objects. One was a tall glass display case filled with various show-plates and ceramic figurines. The striking absence of things, of objects, in humble Neapolitan homes can be disconcerting. There one finds only the cold sparseness of the polished cement floors, the blank white, thick concrete walls hung with just a crucifix, or glittery scenes like the Bay of Naples, its fishermen, and the looming volcano, rendered in the foil analogue to velvet paintings. In the bedrooms there are faceless armadios, and in the kitchen there are little shelves propping up lonely objects like a decorative coffee pot, a white ceramic cat, or a cane basket containing nothing. Usually there are only these few things, lit by harsh fluorescent light. And then there's the impeccable cleanliness.

However, such objectless rooms can fill up on a moment's notice with the voices and animation of its inhabitants, who rarely sat still and remained quiet, at least when I was around. And they never let me, for even a moment, sit still and quiet. Questions, requests, and friendly tugging demands: *Come here and see this! How do you say that in English? Let's hear you say it in Neapolitan. Do you like* babbà? *That's a real Neapolitan dessert, you know. Is New York near Florida? Is California* bella?

This also happened in Maria's home. Her family was waiting patiently to talk with me, and make plans with me. Now that Maria was done with her interview, they had their chance. Finally, amid the excited shouts and questions of the four sons, Maria's husband, Antonio, put his hand on my shoulder and smiled warmly, "We'll see you back here for dinner this Saturday."

When I returned with Francesco to Maria's home, I was curious to hear her husband's side of things. I was surprised, however, to find another guest: the eighty-year-old songwriter, Alfonzo Chiarazzo. Il Maestro, they called him. Maria had already laid out the appetizers on the patio table— pickled eggplant, rice and tomato croquets, mozzarella slices. Il Maestro dominated the conversation. "Unlike other songwriters, my sceneggiate don't talk about love that is disrupted by betrayal. No cuckolds in my songs, for Christ's sake, sweet Madonna, no. *My* lovers suffer from problems on the *inside* instead," he said dramatically, waving a croquet in the air with one hand and hitting his fist against his heart with the other. "Nowadays singers want betrayal in order to *far 'o guappo* (play the thug). And they can't do *that* right anyway."

Just then Maria's oldest son, the sixteen-year-old Sandro, came home.

The handsome, surly-faced boy approached the table and greeted us. Sandro was eager to talk to me about his own favorite singer, whose songs were *untroubled* love stories. When I brought up his mother's favorite, Fabio, he became uncomfortable and cautious. "Some like to sing about love and some sing about the *ugly* side of Naples. And some are successful because they have talent, while others are successful because they have help from *certa gente* (certain people)," he went on. Finally, almost unwillingly, he added, "Some singers even put certain *faccie brutte* (ugly faces) in their music videos to show off their power." He had a hint of anger in his voice.

Our discussion was suddenly interrupted by shouts that Sandro stop badgering me and let me eat the first course of pasta and chickpeas. The dinner was full of other Neapolitan delicacies and included more discussion by Maria about Fabio, by Il Maestro about the sorry state of today's music, and by the four children about their new Playstation. Maria's husband was strangely silent. It was only much later, past one in the morning, that Antonio spoke. Everyone else was inside. The kids sat in front of the Playstation and Maria and Il Maestro stood in the kitchen, winding down with scraps of conversation, getting ready to say their goodbyes. Antonio and I were alone on the patio.

Antonio, with his average build, graying beard, and frequent silence, seemed like a mild-mannered family man. Now speaking to me in a violent whisper about Maria's obsession, he revealed quite the opposite: "So I put a stone over it and moved on, then another stone, then another stone. . . . So many that they're breaking my back. And I'm supposed to live this way?" He cocked his head and stared at me with wide black eyes, "At a certain point I couldn't reason anymore. . . . I wasn't understanding anything. I have to think about myself, you know. I have a family. Four kids. I do it for them. I try, but if it continues much longer, I'm gonna have to think about *myself*."

Antonio clenched his fists, "This guy is trying everything. He's sick. And you know, I went after him once to kill him," he said with a menacing glint in his eye.

"When was this?" I asked, incredulous.

"In December. I got in the car with a friend and drove to the TV station where he was performing live. I had my pistol on me, and when I took it out and started going inside, my friend realized what I was about to do and stopped me."

That evening had an uncanny resemblance to a sceneggiata. Everybody seemed to be playing their roles perfectly. Maria was engaged in what appeared to be blatant adulterous behavior, everyone made Fabio out to be the perfect "Evildoer," and Maria's husband appeared bent on resolving the matter through violence. Then there was Il Maestro, who preferred love stories with *internal* bleeding. He, like Antonio and Sandro, were expressing their resistance to 'O malamente of this family drama, Fabio.

Antonio was the "happy cuckold" who knew of his wife's betrayal but could not respond with any form of personal potency; denied access to the sceneggiata's allegorical powers, he had neither material nor symbolic violence at his disposal. The force of his male competitor, ambiguously affiliated with a crime clan, posed too formidable a challenge. Sandro found himself in the same impotent state.

Il Maestro, however, took the route of metacommentary. He was pointing out the flaws in the Evildoer's "performance" while making a comment shared by many others of his generation on the current state of the camorra, the ordinary Neapolitan family, and contemporary ideas about making do. He lamented that today "making do" also includes behaving like a two-bit camorrista. Il Maestro knew Fabio well; they collaborated regularly until something unpleasant happened. Fabio decided he wanted to cover Il Maestro's famous song "Malufiglio" (Bad son), which he originally wrote for the "king of the sceneggiata," Mario Merola in 1963:

> "He's street," I hear them saying
> That's what I've become since I've been in your embrace
> Malufiglio mamma calls me[16]

But the music video Fabio shot for his rendition of the song shows him riding around on his motorbike with a well-known camorrista holding on behind him. They're driving through the streets of Naples, checking up on his "perfidious" girlfriend who's always out and about. Finally they approach the billiards hall to hang out with other well-known "ugly faces."

Il Maestro was enraged by Fabio's decision to put a camorrista in his music video. In doing so, Fabio elided guappo with camorrista, blurring a distinction that Il Maestro believed only the older generations knew how to maintain. Essentially, for Il Maestro, you can be street without being a mobster; you can be furbo as you engage in the art of making do, but you don't have to be an organized criminal. Il Maestro didn't mince words when he spoke his mind to Fabio, who bellowed back at the old man with an even angrier response, "I can do what I want to the song. *You,* instead, are *no one!*" Later, Fabio took down the picture of Il Maestro he had once hung on the wall in his parents' bar.

"'Naples is getting too small for me,'" Il Maestro snorted, now mimicking for us one of Fabio's many self-aggrandizing assertions about his singing talents. "Well, I say they're *dogs*—that's what they are! Howling! Oh! Don't make me talk! *Don't make* me talk!" Il Maestro shouted generally, to us all, as we sat at Maria's dining table. Condensed in his criticisms of the lost aesthetic of the sceneggiata, there was also the vitriolic charge that the sceneggiata as allegory had collapsed. That is, musicians were now not only performing the part of mobsters in their music videos and stage and film performances of sceneggiata songs but also playing the part in everyday life. And, according to Il Maestro, both performances were second-rate. For him, two-bit musicians were now indistinguishable from two-bit mobsters; no one had the talent to be good at one or the other. With this, Il Maestro summed up two related social critiques that Naples's older generations commonly express. The first is that the neomelodica music scene shows no respect for Neapolitan song traditions. The second is that contemporary crime clan affiliates no longer understand that "honorable manhood" is made not merely through potency but also through restraint. Excessive flamboyance, philandering, and violence make a slipshod performance.

Il Maestro's critiques also implicitly denounced this form of excessive performativity as "excessive manhood." In a sense, he was also referring to the life course of a male gone wrong. In the story to which Il Maestro was privy, Fabio's decision to publicly announce his association with crime clan affiliates was intimately linked to his philandering and, ultimately, to the role of 'O malamente that he played offstage in the everyday life of an ordinary family. These excesses are the vernacular of the sceneggiata; Fabio's greatest excess was to give a magisterial performance of his own melodrama, but without the ironic frame of *this is play.*

When Fabio began jealously questioning Maria about me, I realized that *both* of our performances were getting out of control. "Who is this American?" he asked her.

"I told you already, he's D'Addio's friend and you met him, too. He interviewed you," Maria said.

"I don't care. I don't like this," he told her.

Fabio remembered me from many years back, when Carmela the impresario introduced me to him in 1998. When I thought about this, it occurred to me how utterly strange it must be to him that I was still hanging around. I had no evidence of a job, and I was not independently wealthy (somehow people believed me when I told them so). Journalists and "researchers" stick around only until their last interview, and whatever documentary I was supposedly making should have been completed long ago. I hadn't made any neomelodico famous in the United States, and, as far as he knew, I was neither a musician nor a singer. It made perfect sense that he was suspicious.

But Fabio was not only suspicious of me; he was also enticed by what I might have to offer. Suspicion and hope are both speculative. For many people in this milieu the two are consonant, even entwined. Fabio, it seemed, resented that I had such an effect on him.

When Maria told me she thought it would be a wonderful surprise for Fabio if I showed up at his next performance, I knew I had to do it. He was bothered not so much by the attention I paid "his" woman as the attention I wasn't paying *him*. The problem was that I had already booked a research trip to Palermo.

"Then we'll send you a greeting on Napoli International," Maria reassured me. Her reassurance, however, had for me quite the opposite effect.

FIVE

Ethnographic Imbroglios

IN THE LATE 1990S a small chain of stores called Napolimania began to dot commercial districts of Naples. The stores sell an evolving collection of souvenirs for tourists both "foreign and Italian" that represent the "imagination and genius" typical of Neapolitans.[1] For some months, Napolimania's windows showcased a sweatshirt with the word *Verace* (authentic) printed across it in large letters. The word is immediately recognizable to Italians as the name of the fashion designer Versace without the "s." Ordinarily, the counterfeit good is the vendor's secret irony. In this case, the vendor was selling irony with the counterfeit: the sweatshirt is a true Neapolitan fake.

In the late 1980s a young Neapolitan building surveyor, tired of the frequent business trips his company required of him, invented a way to connect with his beloved Naples from afar. He began making fake postal stamps that contained messages about events in his everyday life. He affixed them to postcards and letters and sent them to his best friend in Vomero. The stamps worked every time, so his friend in Vomero began making stamps and using them, too. Amazed to see that the stamps never failed to do their job, another friend of the building surveyor, also in Naples, joined the game. They sent postcards and letters, some of them priority, from not only Italy but also France, the UK, Spain, Switzerland, and Germany. An early stamp read "Second auto theft of little Luca," announcing their exasperation that in the span of merely six months Luca (one of the three philatelic counterfeiters) had been the victim of two car thefts in Naples. The stamp inspired another stamp, "First international stolen car show," and then the series, "Most stolen cars."

Maurizio, another of the three counterfeiters, told me that they used the stamps to publicly denounce the ills of Italian society and of Naples.[2] One stamp read "Bicentennial of the Campanian camorra" with an image of a smartly dressed, nineteenth-century male figure standing with his hands in his pockets before a distant Vesuvius. Another read "Endangered animal: the pig" above an image of pornstar Moana Pozzi, the Love Party candidate of 1991 who was elected deputy minister.[3] The caption below her image read "Toste italiane" (Hard Italian women), substituting a "T" for the "P" of *Poste italiane* (Italian Post). Another stamp read "Yes to the deployment of nuclear missiles in Iraq and in Naples" crowned with the seal "Lombard League," one of the founding parties of the pro-autonomist and "anti-South" Northern League.

"It was disappointing, every stamp passed through the postal service, even stamps we drew directly on the envelopes. . . . We weren't having fun anymore," the United Counterfeiters, as they came to be known, later told reporters.[4] Determined, they started circulating stamps they were sure would call attention to their gaffe: "The law is rewarding dealers in fake stamps"; "Check stamps more carefully" (with the image of a giant magnifying glass); "This one could be a fake"; "First postal forgers' strike—no to the automatic franking of stamps."

After nearly four years, the three young men at last revealed their game to *Il Mattino*. The minister of the Italian Post was enraged. The three young men were charged with fraud, counterfeiting, and criminal association. They hired Avvocato Siniscalchi, the same lawyer who that year had represented Naples's soccer star Diego Maradona.[5] Fortunately for the United Counterfeiters, Siniscalchi, who was looking forward to a trial that promised to be entertaining, got their case dismissed.[6]

When asked what they had hoped to get from it all, the three men said they wanted jobs at the state printing and minting agency. They said they would also settle for publishing their collection as a book.[7] They admitted that they had been motivated, in part, by "protagonismo"; they were seeking attention, publicity. But they were also engaged in a social experiment: "We made jokes about painful realities. We wanted to exasperate them, invert them."[8]

The United Counterfeiters, like the creators of Napolimania, make the art of making do a public spectacle. They display their creations and the process of their fabrication in a singular performance of personal sovereignty qua ironic craftiness. Their performances are inspired by the "operational aesthetic."[9] The performers are not truly performing until they expose to people the artifice of their performances. It is performing performing, or the process of performing, that provides aesthetic pleasure.

The contact zones I frequented bluster with the disorderly conduct of representations and referents, and of performances and their affective–aesthetic effects. It is impossible to separate "truth" from the entanglements of everyday life without it looking like a cheap knock-off. Rather than expose the truth behind people's representations and performances, I treated them as "true"—and as real as counterfeit stamps that make it through the post. I engaged affective and aesthetic facts, sometimes appropriating and exasperating them in melodramas of my own manufacture.

Interpretations of Culture

The people I got to know on the neomelodica scene rarely, if ever, presented their world to me in any way compatible with the conventions of ethnographic realism. To honor my presence they poured on the thick shellac of *napoletanità* (Neapolitanness), glossing over even the intimacy of family, like during the many smilingly argumentative, aggressively loving, and always indulgent family meals, replete with pasta, ragù, wine, pastries, and singing. There is plenty of that kind of folklore in Naples, and much of it is related to song.

Most of the singers, composers, recording studio owners, and TV managers I approached were immediately effusive. They expressed strong opinions about Neapolitan music and they were eager to buttress them with cultural analysis: "Neapolitan music is like the poetry of the popular classes. It's all that we have. We sing to forget our miseries" (the functionalist explanation popular among those who are either old enough to remember postwar Naples or are familiar with its representations in nostalgic neorealist cinema, theater, and literature); "Vesuvius reminds us that all we have is *today,* and so we sing" (the cultural–ecological explanation preferred among those wishing to invoke a nineteenth-century central-northern Italian view of the "volcanic South");[10] "Our music is like an emotion. We sing because it's in our hearts" (the biological determinist explanation for those who dare dredge up the racial discourse championed by the "father" of criminal anthropology, Cesare Lombroso).[11]

In nearly all of my conversations about the scene, people rehearsed recitatives like these. They demonstrated that they too could play culture-as-text. They were more than familiar with the academic search for "meaning" behind the "signs" and "patterns" of cultural worlds. They trafficked in representations about themselves, and like Pulcinella, the Neapolitan archetype of the commedia dell'arte and the greatest of all folkloric invocations, they performed the oppressed Neapolitan with expert irony.[12] The depth of our encounters seemed to be only as deep as these representations—unless, that is, if I made more of these representations. Ironically impressed by the artfulness of these communicative performances, which were no less (and sometimes more) artful than their musical performances, I began paying more attention to the craft of semblance and dissemblance.

Life, Live

Self-folklorization in Naples is arguably a reaction to recurrent northern Italian (and European) desires dating back to the eighteenth century for a premodern, picturesque "Italian South." An event I attended in 2003 brought these desires into relief. Invited by a Neapolitan journalist called Francesco, I observed and videotaped the live national TV broadcast of the Rai 1 program *Life, Live*. Each week, the show's host tours a different Italian town. Naples was this week's highlight, coinciding with the city's annual Pizzafest competition. Comme il faut, the set was populated by proud *pizzaiuoli* (pizza makers) in clean white hats and aprons who presided over displays of ruby red San Marzano tomatoes, bowls of milky *mozzarella di bufala,* and an assortment of freshly baked pizzas. Resting on one display was an ostentatiously framed image of Naples's patron saint, San Gennaro, whose blood annually decoagulates, warding off the wrath of Vesuvius. When the cameras began rolling, three women walked on the set to model nineteenth-century wedding dresses. Following them was a Big, Luciano Caldore, who began singing, with maximum expressivity, not a neomelodica song but a classic Neapolitan song called "Funiculì Funiculà."[13] The producers of Rai 1 chose a classic song for its international cachet. The Neapolitan singer, like most, if not all, of his peers, did not hesitate to exploit it as well.

As Caldore performed the refrain, five young pizzaiuoli encircled the neomelodico singer as they spun large flat discs of dough high above their heads and between their legs. "This is what people in the north know about Naples, and so this is what they find: pizza, singing, and weddings," Francesco the journalist later said to my camera with a sneer. Yet he and everyone else in the neomelodica scene were willing to partake in the spectacle, including the music's fans.

The very moment the neomelodico finished his rendition of the classic

Neapolitan song, Maria, who the journalist had also invited to the taping, rushed on the set. She moved so fast that when she embraced the singer, they were, just for a moment, on national television together. Afterward, I asked Maria if she enjoyed herself. Victoriously, she looked directly into my camera lens and declared, "Now I'm satisfied. Now everyone will know that I did it and that I matter." She was referring not to Italians but to the Neapolitans in her milieu. Many people in the neomelodica scene regard Italy's national media as an opportunity to perform for other Neapolitans their "mastery of form."[14] That is, they demonstrate to each other their deft execution of the self-folklorizing performances that production teams of the national "Italian" media often expect of them. Appearances in these media spaces may not win them success among national publics (quite the opposite), but it certainly affords them cultural capital among others in their Neapolitan milieu. By wearing the mask of Pulcinella, people in the neomelodica scene create an ironic "space of habitation" with room to maneuver.[15] They create a space with a different temporality than the palatable timelessness of regional-culture-as-aesthetic-object.[16] Rather, participants of the neomelodica scene communicate with one another with an affective immediacy that invokes the demands and desires of their intimately shared world. In the case of *Life, Live* the show's participants, and the people of their milieu who watched, shared the irony of "being Neapolitan," caught in a place where their needs and hopes are met with rejection yet having to perform napoletanità, the stereotype of the passionate and spontaneously creative, but sometimes crafty, premodern folk. In this way, fans transform Italian national media into Neapolitan-style narrowcasting.

Video Provocations

Every Sunday from May to July, videographers recorded family gatherings as they enjoyed neomelodica music performances at their weddings and baptisms. Without fail, they included shots of the family embracing, kissing, and dancing with the singer. All year round, young singers and their associates shot rapid-fire music videos throughout the historic center and any spot with a panoramic view. Without fail, they framed the singer's face so that it was at the center of most shots. Every evening until the wee hours, in tucked-away garages or the back bedrooms of humble family apartments, neomelodica music narrowcasters aimed their video cameras at anyone anywhere in the studio. They toggled freely between music videos, viewer telephone calls, off-camera guests, and center-stage live lip-synched performances. My own video camera was welcomed in these contexts because, rather than an intrusion, it was received as an opportunity for interaction. People on the scene interact with video cameras (and TV) in ways that are consistent with their own performance aesthetics. Performance, for them, is less an act or artifact of (re)presentation than a mode of social networking.

Although I shot from the sidelines, people drew me into their performances. Some singers looked in my direction while lip-synching on live TV. Some announced to their viewers that I was in the studio and told the camera person to turn the shot on me. Other singers told me to put my camera down and join them center stage. It was impossible to remain on the sidelines, but my impulse was to resist their pull. My goal, I told them, was to document neomelodica music performances, not join them. Perhaps I sought what I perceived to be authentic pristine performances, unchanged by my intruding video camera. But after some months I realized that something significant about their performances would emerge *only if* I participated in them.

Whether they courted or deflected my lens, people emphasized the video camera's ability not to (re)present but to provoke and intensify social and economic engagement. Indeed, even after many months in the field, I found I had invited performances that make for good footage, and thereby artifactualized what was happening.[17] Instead of trying to capture on video the secrets of a contact zone where people fear and resist capture, I began paying attention to the "aesthetics of use" incited by the video camera itself.[18] That is, the video camera was far more effective when I used it to mediate "live" social entanglements on both sides of the lens.[19]

Entrepreneurial Arts

This principle—that TV and video are used for social networking—fuels a little economy within neomelodiche artistic practices. When I shot a music video for Fulvio and his father, this economy came into relief.

It was a weekday when we walked through la Pignasecca in Montesanto. Some of the passersby looked inquisitively at the three of us—me with my tripod and video camera, Pasquale with his boombox, and little Fulvio with his perhaps recognizable face. After walking a few hundred meters,

Pasquale spotted a short vicolo that ended in a long set of stairs leading up to another intersecting vicolo. "Here?" he asked.

"Yes, that's good," I said. Fulvio looked down at his feet. I marched ahead of them into the vicolo and set up the tripod. Fulvio took his spot, but he was surprisingly begrudging. Was he tired? His eyes looked puffy and half closed with sleep, yet he didn't seem tired otherwise.

In the vicolo there was an old woman sitting in a kitchen chair outside her basso. She watched with interest as we set up, knitting her hands in her lap. As we began shooting, a few passersby entered into the frame behind Fulvio, and soon they realized what was going on. They watched impassively. When the song finished, a girl approached a wicker basket hanging by a long string from a balcony several stories above. She steadied the basket and emptied into it the contents of her shopping bag—dishwashing liquid, sponges, and the like. When she was done, the woman at the other end of the string began pulling the basket up. Pasquale shouted to me, "Get that, get that! Did you get that?" He was thinking folklore.

For the second half of the shoot, I had Fulvio perform the song again, this time in the center of Piazza Montesanto. The piazza worked for me for a couple of reasons. First, it was "ethnographically picturesque" to my documentary eye. It was devoid of the usual splendors of crumbling baroque architecture; instead the piazza was crowded with tables packed with random merchandise (toilet seats, ceramic giraffes, flip-flops) presided over by Sri Lankan and Senegalese vendors and crates of gorgeous fruits and vegetables (bulbous white fennel, seductive softball-sized pastel peaches, curly vines of fat blood-red cherry tomatoes) hawked by elderly, wrinkled Neapolitan vendors. Second, I could frame Fulvio amid the entire scene from the tall platform of the funicular and the Cumana, a regional rail line, at the head of the piazza.

When we were all in position—Fulvio in the center of the piazza, Pasquale standing with the boombox off to one side, and me with my tripod up above—we ran through the song one more time. When we finished, some of the old vendors approached Fulvio and spoke to him, shook his hand, or patted his head, smiling at him encouragingly. I wondered if they recognized him or if they were simply congratulating him on his effort to make a career. I could see in Fulvio's reaction, however, that he was very upset. Ordinarily an exceptionally friendly and forthcoming boy, Fulvio now was reserved and reticent. It was then that I realized how uncomfortable the shoot must have been for him. How strange he must have felt in the middle of that busy piazza, lip-synching to the music of a boombox while looking upward at me on the elevated platform of the Cumana.

As I walked toward Fulvio and his father, I could see that the boy was completely disgruntled. He and his father were arguing. "But *this* is not how you do it! I felt like a gypsy out there in front of all those people walking around me!"

Pasquale, I could tell, wanted to silence his son, but he also couldn't hold back. "Well you are really a shit, aren't you? Be quiet!" he growled.

I felt terrible for Fulvio. I insisted we get *gelati*. Fulvio ate his in silence.

When I got home, I had already planned in my head how to make the best music video on the scene. Fulvio deserved it. I pieced together a rich montage of street scenes from the Quartieri Spagnoli and shots of Fulvio lip-synching at Piazza Montesanto. I packed fifty cuts into the three-minute video. I took care to match images with lyrics, but without being overly rhetorical. I even added some fast zooms and wide panning, shooting practices I noticed in many music videos. These were not my style, but I wanted to please Fulvio, who might otherwise not know how to relate to the other, "newer" aesthetics I was introducing.

When I presented the completed video to them, neither of them liked it. They politely described it as documentary style.[20]

"Everyone is doing the same thing all the time," I told Fulvio's father, trying to convince him the video was good. "What you need is to make your son stand out," I said in the big-talking entrepreneurial register I had heard other protagonists on the scene use. Pasquale, however, couldn't be convinced.

"They want to see only the singer close-up and all the time," Giuseppe the composer, my close confidant, later explained to me. "Only the singer," he repeated. Recorded video, like live video, is intended, in some way, to augment social interaction. Neomelodica music videos, like the live pirate TV narrowcasts that air them, are a source of face time with the singer. My video was cluttered with Naples.

The video was not only my heartfelt gift to Fulvio and his family. It was also intended for the work portfolio I wanted to develop. I had made plans with Giuseppe that together we would court business from singers and then each of us would do his part: Giuseppe would write the songs and compose the arrangements and I would make the music videos. I was disappointed that Fulvio and Pasquale didn't like what I had made for them, but I was also concerned that they wouldn't use it. Fulvio was hosting a weekly program on TeleP; it was critical for me that he and his father air the music video. To ensure that it would happen, I told Fulvio and Pasquale that I would be happy to go on the show to introduce the video myself. Pasquale hedged. *They didn't want to air it,* I thought. But I sensed room for maneuver. I remembered how much Fulvio's criticisms of the video shoot angered him. Pasquale probably feared they appeared indecorous.

Perhaps I reactivated that fear by once again offering to present the music video on TeleP. Without warning, in the middle of a commercial break in his transmission, Fulvio and Pasquale began shouting at me (to be heard over the screaming kids), beckoning me to stand before the camera. I passed my video camera to Pasticcio, an impresario who had bought up blocks of TeleP airtime and was reselling them at a premium to people like Pasquale and Fulvio. I asked Pasticcio to videotape us. Taking the mic from Fulvio, I announced to the cameras, "And now I want to present to you a music video I made for my friend Fulvio. I hope you like it."

Doing fieldwork in the neomelodica scene became less about representation and more about mimesis. To practice the art of making do in this scene, you conjure up a spectacle, or leap into one that is already underway, or stretch its boundaries to include you. Sometimes this means usurping the narrative from its protagonists or even derailing the narrative altogether. Such tactics are a source of exhilaration for us in this milieu. We derive pleasure from seeing how things work and who makes things work to their own advantage—or how we can make things work for ourselves.

Instead of sorting things out and summing them up, I adopted a mode of attention that does not distinguish between theory, ethnographic practice, writing ethnography, and even reading ethnography.[21] Instead of attempting to get to the stable structure at the bottom of it all, I began tracking "the vitality or animus of cultural poesis in the jump or surge of affect (rather than the plane of finished representations)."[22]

However, I kept getting hung up on finding the potent center of things. When people outside the scene asked me, "So are they camorristi or not?" I couldn't give any clear answer. It wasn't a question I was pursuing (most of the time), but it did seem (sometimes) strange to "conclude" these years of research without having found certain answers. For all I knew it could be a phantom, a figure.

Who Am I and Who Is She?

In the typical vague manner of plans and activities that undergo sudden radical revisions and dissolutions (accompanied by shifting or entirely lacking explanations), I thought Tony was taking me to Piazza Garibaldi to go to the local TV broadcaster Televesuvio. Instead, we were driving a long distance out toward Vesuvius and into the village Boscotrecase. Tony and I had known each other for nearly two years and had just encountered one another after a three-month hiatus. We were both charged up by the prospect of doing business together. I was now shooting and editing music videos and wanted new clients. Tony was interested in getting a good package deal from me and decided that our friendly history was just the leverage he needed.

While driving, Tony and I quickly launched into negotiations, implicitly deciding that, to begin, he would have to take me on his gigs. However, I also wanted him to act as my ambassador to particularly difficult acquaintances such as female singers and camorrista impresarios. When he offered to bring me to the Televesuvio broadcast, I jumped. I had been shut out of the pirate TV circuit for some time, after two stations had gotten raided and shut down. There were some rumors that my presence and my video camera had something to do with it. I decided I would kill two birds with one stone by regaining access to the pirate TV circuit while gradually working on Tony to agree to acquaint me with certa gente.

But instead of driving us to Televesuvio, Tony was taking us on an epic journey to a place much nearer to Vesuvio. We were going to that infamous spread of marble and frond I had visited only days before with little Fulvio and his father–manager Pasquale: the Villa Cupido. Tony parked on the street outside the sprawling complex of banquet halls sitting fatly behind spraying fountains and a throng of leafy palms.

Attributing the sudden change in plans to my own miscomprehension, I hid my surprise. Instead, I decided to try out a new strategy to get Tony to focus on my needs. I engaged him in what was acceptable and expected gossip about my long-term confidant, another singer called Raffaele. I knew that gossiping would further embroil Tony and me with one another, which was what we both wanted. We would come into closer contact and each would be able to discern how the other distributed value across his life. On his side, Tony was finding out in what manner, other than money, he could pay me for my video work. I, on my side, was showing Tony by bad example what he could do better than Raffaele. That is, if he wanted a discount on my work. "Raffaele never opened up to me and he even lied a lot of the time," I told Tony.

Tony wanted to know what my life was all about, why I was doing all this in Naples when I could be in New York instead. I often found it hard to answer those questions, because of my interlocutors and because of the domains I represented—university, anthropology, documentary film. How to explain this in clear terms to people who don't see the practical use of "research"? Tony preferred to think of me as a journalist—someone who's doing "reportage" to bring back to America. The ends were clear in this case. I work for a paper, and they want me to find a scoop.

"So, in the end we want the same thing," he said flatly. "You want a scoop that's going to bring you success and money. Just like me, like us, you want to make it big. Everyone is looking for the same thing, everywhere."

My instinct was to fight off this characterization: "No, it's not the first thing, the only thing. This is really interesting stuff that I'm learning here and bringing back with me. When I present this stuff to people in the U.S., they look at it with their eyes wide open. It's not as if I'm going to get rich."

"But, if you find a good scoop, you'll get somewhere with it," he said bluntly.

I had no more arguments. All that was left to say was, "Yeah, I'll get a good job in a well-paying university and I'll be comfortable."

Tony repeated himself, driving it home: "So we are looking for the same thing, in the end. All of us."

Before getting out of the car, Tony called Pasticcio on his cell phone, and they shouted to each other in their gruff, contracted, elided, and elliptical Neapolitan. Apparently communication between them was not much clearer than mine with Pasticcio. Pasticcio came from the "hinterland" town of Volla and spoke another version of the Neapolitan I had learned in the city's historic district. He, like many Neapolitans of the popular classes, understands Italian but feels discomfort and intimidation when confronted with such a formal "code." This is true as well for listening. People like Pasticcio not only feel like poor performers of Italian but also feel incapable of understanding the language when it is spoken to them. When I had engaged in some short-lived and ignominiously ending commerce with him several months before, I learned that I compounded our linguistic problems with my American accent. Through our mutual friend Pasquale, Pasticcio and I argued over the price his buddies at a local pastry shop should pay me for the commercial I shot for them to broadcast on pirate TV. Pasticcio had procured for me the gig and was obviously skimming off my price. "I'll get you ten more gigs like this if you lower your price to 30 euros," he told Pasquale to tell me.

"Why would I do that when I know I can get 100–200 euros per commercial?" I told Pasquale to tell him.

"If you lower your price, you'll get more work," again he told Pasquale.

"If that's the way it is, I'm not selling the commercial to you," I returned to Pasquale. As if we were performing a comedy skit, Pasticcio and I argued through our interpreter about two-bit ads destined to air during live lip-synched neomelodica song transmissions on pirate TV, standing under the great nineteenth-century arcade Galleria Umberto I, where famed singers like Sergio Bruni once transacted with impresarios. Clearly it was not only linguistic recognition that was lacking; I was refusing to participate in an economy of the *sciuè sciuè* (quick-quick) and refusing to account for the flexibility of value fueling l'arte di arrangiarsi. In the end, I rejected Pasticcio's paltry offer of 50 euros, partly on principle, partly just to see what would happen. Pasticcio seemed baffled and irked by my refusal.

"I *said* I am outside in the car. . . . Pasticcio?" Tony shouted. Another moment passed before a garbled response could be heard on the other end. Tony, satisfied with the response, replied, "OK, I'll come in."

We parked in the lot and walked into the glittering chandelier-bedecked foyer on the other side of the electric whoosh of sliding, frosted glass doors embossed with "Villa Cupido" and a floral flourish. We walked across the varnished pink marble floors, past the Louis XVI mirrors and hall tables, standing vases, and gilded armchairs, up three steps to the end of the corridor to the main banquet hall. I saw Cinzia and her scantily clad girl dancers (one of them prepubescent) waiting on the ornate crème divan just outside, the hot orange of their halter-tops adding an uncannily appropriate splash of color to the tableau.

"Fulvio just left," Cinzia said to me. Her sheepish smile indicated that she wanted to put on public notice the fact that I had come to the wedding party not with Fulvio but Tony, the next singer on the schedule. I was just as much the property of Fulvio and Pasquale as they, in their eyes, were the stars of my research. Cinzia, on the other hand, is Pasticcio's principal confidante. She provides Trio Dance! to Pasticcio, who acts as the impresario of a special entertainment troupe consisting of Trio Dance!, Giulio (Fulvio's *nome d'arte*), and sometimes Tony.

"Oh, he was here?" I answered Cinzia, concerned about my perceived betrayal. Was this going to be misinterpreted and circulated? It looked bad, and it hadn't even been in the plans. Tony and I were supposed to be at Televesuvio.

When Tony and I walked into the main banquet hall to look for Pasticcio, we saw a man in his midtwenties with ruddy red skin and brown hair singing sloppily but exuberantly to a large and lavish wedding party. Tony led the way through the agitated yet happy crowd straight up to the small ensemble that accompanied the singer's off-key rendition of the classic song "A Postcard from Naples":

> "How can you be happy" mamma tells me
> "far from Naples, far from your mother?"
> . . . .
> There's a thorn in my heart
> when I compare America with this postcard![23]

Suddenly I noticed a black-haired woman in a dark suit standing amid the musical ensemble, waiting to greet me. "Four," she said, staring me in the eye and holding up four fingers. She paused long enough for my reaction (inquisitively wide pupils) and then continued, "Four husbands, I had, and they're all *dead*," she declared, now smiling seductively and threateningly.

"Oh, yeah? Then you'll have to tell me how you killed them," I returned, gesturing "you" and "kill" with a finger that I first pointed at her and then drew across my own neck like a straight razor.

Carmela was in her midforties, not more than a decade older than me. She had long and thick straight black hair, full lips, and a slim body. The jacket of her black pinstriped suit cut sharply inward, accentuating her breasts. Her white blouse was unbuttoned to her tanned cleavage, over which hung a silver chain and an enormous, glittering rhinestone crucifix. Although she understood that I found her attractive, Carmela likely did not know that I was ultimately impervious to her seductive performances. She, like everyone else on the scene, never heard me say, "I am gay." However, it was possible that my sexuality, like many things a person may or may not want to know about another person in this milieu, could be sensed through less-finalized forms of capture than linguistic self-identification. At any rate, having encountered frequent homophobic epithets (*Ricchiò! Femminell'!* [Faggot! Fairy!]), some of which were directed at me "in jest" (or did people know?), and having heard accounts of sporadic hate violence in Naples, I feared my access to the field would be restricted if I did not stay in the closet. When people asked me if I was married, which was rather often, I usually told them that I was waiting until my travels were over before settling down. Eventually, when I began writing my own neomelodiche songs, I found the opportunity for passing with my autobiographical song, "Ammore senza voce" (Love without a voice). The song recounts *un'amore illecito* (an illicit or adulterous affair) that, when the watchful eyes of the neighbors take notice, can continue only through cell-phone text messages:

> That other guy already married you, but I saw you, too.
> You were at Piazza Montesanto in the middle of all those people
> And I noticed *you*; you were texting some other guy
> I called you once, but you didn't want to listen to me
> The second time, you turned to look
> Without a voice, only text messages, this love keeps growing
> Because they're only memories and fantasies
> I got off my moped in order to get closer to you
> To take your hand, I don't know, to have a coffee
> Antonella, Antonella, you whispered this name to me
> Antonella, Antoné, now I know only this name
> There never was a second word
> Without a voice, only text messages, this love keeps growing
> Because they're only memories and fantasies

The song was my ironic commentary on the prominent role cell phones play in deep attachments in the milieu I frequented. For my neomelodici associates, the true irony was my infelicitous lyrical Neapolitan. In one stanza, I thought I had written "I brought you to the studio where I made figurines for *presepi* [nativity scenes]," but to my fellow musicians, it seemed I had written that "I brought you to the feces laboratory." Despite my linguistic blunders, the ultimate irony was really mine: "Antonella" was, in actuality, a man from Forcella named Antonio.

Taking hold of the microphone, Carmela announced Trio Dance! to the wedding party. Still looking bored, the three girls walked on the dance floor in their orange bikini-like ensembles, light blue eye shadow, and bright red lipstick. They began to move, in synch, with heavy steps and lazy jolts in what Pasticcio called *latinoamericano* style to the sounds of salsa-inflected neomelodica music.

My eyes followed their movements as they plodded through their routine until I noticed Pasticcio sitting at a nearby table with his wife and some other middle-aged men and women. I wasn't prepared for this chance meeting, especially not now, coinciding with this chance meeting with Cinzia and her girls, and Carmela to boot.

However, when my eyes locked with Pasticcio's, he greeted me with sweeping hospitality. "Jay-Soan!! Come here, come here! Sit down!" he said in his bellowing voice, accompanied by a gesturing hand that struck the cushion of an empty crimson-and-crème upholstered chair with a serpentine wooden back. Brusquely welcoming, he pulled the chair out for me and cleared a space on the table amid the half-filled wine glasses. When I sat down, I nodded to the others at the table. Pasticcio and I didn't talk, except for one short exchange.

"Be careful, she had four husbands," he said to me.

"I know," I returned, wondering if he was interpreting it as a come-on or a threat. Maybe he was simply enjoying making things more confusing for me.

The nickname Pasticcio means pastry (he used to own a pastry shop), but it also has a second, metaphorical meaning: "a sticky mess."[24] I had tried asking Pasquale and Fulvio if Pasticcio was known for creating imbrogli, but I could never get a straight answer. If his nickname meant what it resonated, then I wondered what it meant for me. So far, Pasticcio seemed unchanged by our smeared history. But then again, how often do people let on that they have unfriendly feelings for you? Certainly not when it's potentially disadvantageous to do so. Pasticcio, like most people I got to know on the scene, was likely ensuring that my potential value remain available to him. Or was he, like some people I had met, maintaining a pleasant performance while preparing a terrible, artful act of revenge? Pasticcio seemed to get around quite a bit on the scene, and it was unclear what that might mean. Was he merely acquainted with many players in the industry, or was he more substantially associated with them? One never knew the full extent of another's network or his or her willingness to activate certain nodes for certain effects. Pasticcio's wife poured me a glass of white wine. I drank it in large gulps, hoping it would help clear my head so that I could quickly sort out my own, current web of relations.

After chatting with several different guests, Carmela approached our table and sat in the chair next to me, putting me squarely between her and Pasticcio. "You came by my store before. You're the journalist for *la Rai*," she said not only to me but to everyone at the table. It was no mistake she was making. More precisely, it was an intentional mistake meant to inflate her social capital.

As I had always done when frequently faced with willful misunderstandings of my work, I answered with a corrective, "No, not for *la Rai*, but yes, you're right, we met a long time ago." No sooner had I corrected Carmela's statement than I began regretting it. I doubted that my words did any real damage to her public face; people in her milieu expected exaggerations, elaborations, and even what outsiders might consider outright lies as part of a person's public self-production. However, what concerned me about my thoughtless decision to expose Carmela's *raddoppiandosi* (self-doubling) performance was that it signaled to her my unwillingness to play. I wondered, *Why was I unwilling? If this is how people engage one another* . . .

I feared a spell was broken, an opportunity for contact lost. Still worse, Carmela might have interpreted my sudden unwillingness to play, after the intensity of the beginning of our encounter, as an act of open aggression. My only hope, I thought, was that I merely seemed like the clueless, harmless, and ultimately endearing American *ca tene 'a facc' d' 'o scemo* (who has the face of an idiot).

Now, sitting with Carmela at a table at the Villa Cupido, I found her a lot less enthusiastic about my interest in neomelodica music. "So I hear you'll be visiting us at the studio during the broadcast of my TV show this Sunday," she said to me in a smilingly accusatory tone. Indeed, just that week I had met a singer called Andrea, and I had asked if I could accompany him to his upcoming TV performance. Andrea was a new client and confidante of mine who wanted me to shoot a package of four music videos for his new album. My negotiations with Andrea over the deal had splintered my asking price of 500 euros across the variant values of friendship and favors. He knew that his flirting and overtures about our *sintonia* (harmony) wouldn't work as well to lower my price as letting me accompany him to the live transmission on Televesuvio that he conducted with Carmela. I didn't want friendship; I wanted to learn more about pirate television.

But Matteo showed hesitance: "Well, she's difficult, you know," he tried to explain.

"I know Carmela. I met her a long time ago. She won't mind me coming along," I asserted.

Reluctantly, he agreed to meet me late that night at the central train station, where he would pick me up and drive the short distance to the clandestine TV studio.

"And who invited you?" Carmela asked, still with her unfriendly smile.

"*I* did," I answered bluntly, feigning as much self-confidence as I could.

Saying nothing, Carmela turned her gaze to the young singer, who was between songs and using the mic to chat with his audience.

Pasticcio's wife refilled my glass, and I drank in large gulps. Earlier, I had noticed a table just to the left of the main doors toward which all of the room seemed drawn throughout the night. There, a forty-year-old man of average build wearing a tieless, crisp, white button-down and a dark blue jacket sat straight and still, leaning against the wall behind him, never moving from his seat. He eyed my video camera when I walked in, and I immediately felt lucky to have come to a wedding with Tony and not Pasquale and Fulvio. Pasquale was neurotic and often prevented me from videotaping. "You just keep that in your bag. Don't take it out, not here," he would say. When I asked him why, it was always, "I'll tell you later." Although in this milieu "later" usually meant "never," I managed one day to get it out of him. "Because these are usually *gente malfamata*," he said in that just-barely-toss-him-a-bone manner I encountered whenever I thought I managed to corner somebody with whom I could *pigliar' 'a confidenza* (presume a level of intimacy) and talk about "the camorra." But no one was happy to name it, let alone talk about it. They substituted *gente malfamata* (people of ill repute), *gente 'e miezz' 'a vi* (street people), *strana gente* (strange people), *certa gente* (certain people), *faccie brutte* (ugly faces), and so many other terms for a force that pulsed somewhere in the ellipsis not only in speech but also in knowledge. Most people didn't know the concrete, but rather, the general contours of identities and actions of "the camorra." Specific knowledge is not only dangerous but also difficult to come by, for a great deal of the camorra's force emanates from its production of indeterminacy.

The expansive hall was filled with some two hundred guests. The ruddy-faced singer sang a love song, unable to stick to the key. Unperturbed, a small phalanx of about ten men in wedding suits danced in the direction of the singer, who shared the dance floor. The men playfully held each other's hands, clutched each other at the waist, and cradled each other arm in arm. They moved forward and back again, performing an improvised, erotic line dance while the singer stepped back and forth in synch with them. One dancer added a flourish to his routine by putting one hand behind his head and the other on his waist and thrusting with his pelvis. Seated guests clapped their hands in rhythm to the flamboyant parade of their friends and kin. Here and there, the dancers' choreographed sensuousness unraveled in smiles and laughter.

Although their behavior was not common from what I saw at the seventy-five celebrations I attended throughout my research, it was not inexplicable in a context dominated by "men of honor." Sicilian mafiosi engage in homoerotic and gender-bending performances at banquets, but typically in the absence of women.[25] Months later, when I reviewed my video footage, I found a possible explanation for the anomaly at Villa Cupido that evening. For only a few frames, I noticed a subtle exchange that seamlessly blended with the dancers' extravagant movements. In a swift and fluid gesture, what looked like a small plastic bag of cocaine passed between the hands of two men. The significance of the exchange was underscored by the interested glances of the surrounding dancers. Apparently, the men had been too coked up to worry about their excesses.

Others sat at their tables and watched, some clapping their hands in rhythm to the music. They were flanked on three sides by heavy crimson-and-crème drapes with a Florentine pattern, hanging grandly over the windows lining the banquet hall. Each was like a stage curtain waiting to be swept open. And soon enough they were, when Carmela took the mic and announced the beginning of the countdown. At once everything halted, and the entire party rushed to the windows. A crescendoing thunder overcame us all, and a helicopter landed in the sprawling gardens below us. The bride and groom had arrived.

When Carmela took the seat next to me at Pasticcio's table, I tried to make conversation. "So what other singers are you managing besides Matteo?" I asked, disinterestedly.

After a long pause, Carmela slowly nodded her head. I had received that response from many people before her. Semantically, it was nonsensical, but it had the force of a brush-off.

Anxiously sensing foreclosure and at the risk of creating contention, I repeated my question.

Carmela did not look at me. She pursed her lips and smiled slightly. "I'll tell you about it later," she said, beginning the endless deferral to which I had become so accustomed. This time I knew it would take many arts to get beyond the ellipsis. My relationship with Carmela suddenly took on a new charge, and I became intensely interested in her. When I first met her in her music shop, she instantly activated her wide network for me. Encountering her now, six years later, as a significantly networked protagonist on the scene, I triggered her diffidence. The only way to get anywhere with her, it seemed, was to play. Play is a contact zone. The rules are suspended and no one is safe. Play, histrionics, and threat shade into one another and it is up to you to make sovereign decisions.[26] When *this is play* you maneuver with simulations and dissimulations. Outside the frame, nothing appears to be any different, but inside, everything is potentially not at all what it seems. I wondered, *Was Carmela the boss–impresaria I had been seeking all along?*

Who Am I and Who Is He?

I told Maria and Francesco the journalist that I was planning on contacting Salvatore Riccobono to produce my neomelodico album. They both looked at me in shock. Francesco seemed concerned. "Maria, tell him what you think of Salvatore Riccobono," he said with an insistent charge to his voice. I noticed this habit of his, but not only his, to defer to others rather than express a strong, precise opinion. But Maria responded with willful imprecision. She began with a long pause and a frown, and then, "No . . . *non è una persona stabile* [he's not a stable person]."

"In what way?" I asked.

"Naw, . . . he's not stable. He's not a stable person," she repeated.

I turned to Francesco, "He's not a camorrista, is he?"

This time Francesco turned sharply to look at me. His face seemed flushed. Then with an oddly glittering smile he exclaimed, "What strange questions you ask!"

"You mean naive," I added, asking as much as affirming. It felt important that I at least pretend to be fully getting it, that I be in on it, whatever the message was. But like many times before, our conversation ended there. I now knew the subject of Riccobono made them uncomfortable, but I could not confirm why.

That was the end of a very long night at the Festa della Sanità, a.k.a. 'A festa ro munacone (festival of the big monk), an annual two-day neomelodica music series at Piazza Santa Maria della Sanità, the church that houses a statue of the quartiere's patron saint, San Vincenzo Ferreri. Don Antonio Loffredo, the parish priest, described it: "His finger is pointed upward because he teaches us never to lower ourselves before anyone. . . . And then he has a trumpet because we're noisy, we make ourselves heard. But above all, his wings enable him to fly. He therefore has enormous potential."[27]

With Francesco's press pass, Maria and I went with him backstage, where there were several singers, including Stefania Lay, Antoine, and Biagio Izzo, the comic. There were also relatives or friends of singers, sound technicians, stylists, cops, and idlers talking with members of the pressing crowd just meters away. I had the impression from the beginning that it was going to be a long night. Neapolitan performances were always long, for various reasons. The organization of events is never very tight, so there are often a lot of empty pockets of time. Performers tend toward extreme exhibitionism and want to remain onstage as long as possible. The public is more than willing to remain for such long periods of time, because they feel involved, and, on some level, protagonists just like the performers. Performers and the emcee (there always has to be a very ceremonious emcee) love to talk, and a lot of what goes on onstage consists of talk. Long introductions, anecdotes, analogies, sweeping statements about culture, ethnicity, traditions, emotions, and of course elaborate thank-you's to the performers, organizers, and sponsors. The thank-you's, comprehensive and carefully intonated to excess, are then repeated somewhere in the middle and at end of the performance.

Persistent, I repeated my declaration when Francesco, Maria, and I were together again several months later at the Festival di Napoli in Castellammare di Stabia. This time I received no response. The two just smiled and moved on to another topic. Later, when Francesco went off on his own to attend to the festival (he was one of the organizers), Maria urged me to drop it. "He's a millionaire and they say he's retired, but I don't know."

"Retired from what?"

"He was involved with certain people . . ."

"What do you mean?"

It was difficult to watch Maria squirm in discomfort, as many others had done when I insisted with such questioning. I was not a cooperative conversationalist by any standards. I was expected to interact inferentially, not to demand full-on literal exposition.

Maria rechanneled the conversation. "I have no problems with Riccobono. He has always been good to me, because he has known my family forever. He sometimes gave me gifts, *delle buste* [some envelopes], you know, with money, and he was always very respectful."

Her statement still didn't answer my question. In fact, it only triggered more, but too much was going on that evening for me to pursue it any further. The festival was taking place in the lush thermal baths on the coast south of Naples, near Sorrento, under the shadow of Vesuvius. I had gone two days earlier at Francesco's suggestion, and he arranged to have me put on the press pass list as "an American film director," a title he chose. The old thermal baths were shut down, and the Circumvesuviana (the regional rail network) no longer stopped at the stop I needed. I found myself stuck waiting at the wrong stop with a young journalist for *Napolipiù* (More Naples), the Campanian paper formerly called *La Verità* (The Truth). From the question he was asking the station manager, I understood the young man was going my way. When I asked him, he said, "Yes, there's a sort of press conference going on this morning," as if he were explaining it to an outsider who might not be able to follow what he was saying.

"Well, then we're going the same way," I responded, dispelling his assumption.

He introduced himself as Teo and asked me what my role in the festival was, if I was a journalist. I told him I was a film director and that I was covering the Neapolitan music scene. He was interested in learning more, but he was careful not to be indiscreet with his questions or betray his interest. I noticed it more and more clearly as we waited for the train. As we talked about his work at *Napolipiù* I demonstrated my knowledge of the paper, its history, and I even named one of its former journalists, whom I had met at a dinner party.

This made Teo feel comfortable enough to ask me questions about my own work. Eventually he asked me if the film was at my own expense or if I had some sort of production behind me. I told him it was my own show, but that there were people interested in it. Because conversations about my work rarely extended this far in the neomelodico milieu, I had the uncanny feeling that I was approaching with a stranger a level of familiarity that had become unfamiliar to me. At the same time, I wanted to keep things vague, partly because I was tired of telling my story and partly because I didn't want too much familiarity to develop between us too quickly. Disentanglement is not a terribly easy thing to undergo. You fall into a network of friends and colleagues and associates who now know you. People to greet emerge, people who now have an alibi to talk to you. People often want something from me. Money, contacts, a link to America and all that that represents: sex, knowledge, novelty, wealth. People on the neomelodico scene also complain about the excessive demands their associates make on them. At the same time there's a great deal of generosity on the circuit. Food and hospitality, transportation—these things are crucial for your circulation on the scene. You are *tirchio* (cheap) in the material sense if you don't put things in circulation and you're tirchio with your heart if you don't put yourself in circulation. Such gifts can quickly become gray with favors and services.

I didn't want anything more from the people I met because I already had all the knowledge whose cost I was willing to endure. At least I periodically thought I had reached my limit. Even though information, knowledge, and gossip are not commonly recognized commodities in this economy, people immediately recognized and capitalized on my need and desire for these things. They acknowledged my desire as a sort of exchangeable value, and by default the objects of my desire—their knowledge—became valuable to them as well. I was tired of the games, the suspicions, and the endless deferments. You press someone to give you something, and you are sure to get nothing.

Often people retract simply out of instinct, just in case, or simply because they sense desire on the circuit, and that therefore there *must* be value located somewhere. So then they feel it's best to wait and see why, what it's worth, and what they can get out of it—never mind what it is. Desire, the presence of desire, tips people off, sets off alarms to both gains and risk. If someone has a desire for something, then surely someone else has something to lose. You may not know what either of these are, but you'll hold off until you find out.

Teo seemed to want nothing from me, but why? This was probably not a good question to ask. For one, we were on the same side of the irony. This circumstance created an interesting process in which we tried to figure out each other's irony quotient. The ironic will be careful not to betray themselves (I knew this firsthand). Giuseppe has irony, but he's not ironic in *this* respect; he is too much a part of the neomelodico scene. He can incisively criticize the scene and its players and masterfully hide these feelings when interacting with them to do business (all interaction is business), but in the end he works in the scene, composes songs for them, and, it seems, is pulled in aesthetically by some of the work he produces. However, maybe this is understandable behavior for a guy who hates the music for which he contributes arrangements, because it's work he can do, it's the people he knows, because there are limitations to his survival. The irony becomes intertwined with everything; it's not a rupture but an accent. In contrast with Teo and me, Giuseppe cannot really walk away from it. Teo and I were affiliated with universities (Teo studied communications), but Giuseppe's life is threaded through the scene, not out of love, belief, or conviction, but out of necessity. And then remastered with irony.

Teo and I wanted to know the same thing: can we laugh about this together? Can we share a complicity–duplicity? We shared a sort of dance on the narrow platform at a station near Castellammare di Stabia. It was nearing one hundred degrees Fahrenheit, and the cool but airless station was a great relief from the boiling world just outside. Where we stood we could see a sliver of lush landscape, a road, and a little granite cart managed by a short, old, sweating man in a white tank top. Behind him were olive and lemon groves, craning palms heavy with fronds and fruit, and beyond the trees, the still Mediterranean, now the warmest it has been in three thousand years, according to yesterday's paper. I was thinking two thoughts as I gazed at the scene: how soaked in sweat we would be by the time we found the bus that would take us the last leg to the press conference, and when would it all be over so I could take a swim in that shimmering blue. Distractions are always good when you want something. If, like me, you haven't yet learned the art of wholly dissimulating your desires, their betrayal will screw up your business. But this time, because I was indifferent yet amicable with this young man, he felt at ease with me and was willing to talk. Better yet, he was more intrigued by *my* story and the information *I* had to offer.

"So you cover exclusively the neomelodica scene for your paper?" I asked Teo.

"No, no, entertainment in general," he answered, and I detected a slight, wry smile. He noticed me observing him and looked into my eyes.

"And you, why this interest in the neomelodica scene?" he asked almost challengingly, as if to say, *Why don't you admit it first?* Or as if to say, *Come on, when are you going to drop it and tell me what's really going on? You can't be one of them. You're not even Neapolitan, for one.*

"Well, my real profession is anthropology. I'm conducting research on the scene here."

"OK, OK," he said, with an air of knowingness, as if to say, *Now I get it.* Because I smiled and looked down as he said it, the deal was sealed. We were partners outside the frame.

We got there after twenty minutes, wet with sweat. There was a flurry of activity in the parking lot—cars pulled in and paused at various confused angles and people got in and out of them while heatedly discussing critical matters: when to go into the spa, what to bring, who will park the car, who will accompany the person entering now, who managed to see whether so-and-so had already arrived. Teo and I picked up our press passes and entered the complex. We walked along the snaking paths through clusters of lemon trees and laurel bushes and along the white cement colonnades until we reached a garden clearing roped off with police tape. There, in the hush of foliage, a live press conference was taking place on a small stage hosting a semicircle of seven seated men and women, with a banner in the background sporting the words *Festival di Napoli* and *Radio Kiss Kiss Italia* on the lower border. The audience was a small and motley group of seated and standing individuals: some dressed in shorts and muscle T's and some in suits and ties; some wore summer dresses, high heels, and Anastasia-style sunglasses, and some dressed conservatively in slacks and blouses. A caterer's table to one side was lined with assorted minipastries like *babbà, bigné, sciù*—a sort of Neapolitan éclair—and profiteroles. A bowl of orange punch sat at one end of the table, and a young, overheated, and tired woman stood before it in uniform, waiting.

The press conference seemed to have been well underway already, a surprise, as we were only forty-five minutes late, just about the same length of built-in confusion time customary to the opening of such events. The small group onstage was composed of reasonable, smiling admirers of Neapolitan song, all of them thanking the festival's organizer and numerous others for making the event possible. Then they conveyed what they felt was different about this year's festival, despite the fact that it held on proudly to its long and important history: its taking place in these beautiful gardens, with a highly professional and organized staff; its opening up a space for new trends in Neapolitan music, exhibiting its major and emergent protagonists. Mediaset covered the event with a wonderful new presenter from Rai, a tall woman showing lots of cleavage.

The press conference closed with a statement from the festival's organizer, Rocco Buonanotte, who thanked a number of people for making the event possible and underscored the festival's long history. He then suddenly raised his voice, "And I will stand up for this next thing I want to say . . ." He stood up and continued to address the audience, "This year the word is *transparency*! Complete *transparency*!"

After the taping had finished, I approached Teo and a colleague of his, Piero. Clearly Teo had told Piero that I was "one of them," because they both wanted to joke with me about the event. I noticed they weren't making any moves to gather more info for the article they were going to write for the newspaper. I, however, was still on duty, so I eased myself away from them and mingled with the other guests.

I returned with Maria to Castellamare for the last day of the three-day event. I first took the bus to her neighborhood, where her husband was waiting for me with the car. We drove back to their home and picked up Maria and her eight-year-old son, and then drove on. It was still steaming hot, and the traffic intense. We arrived around 10 p.m., and Maria's husband and son left us there and drove back home. It was impressive, the amount of driving her husband did for her.

We entered with our press passes and greeted Francesco. He was cordial yet busy, flying in and out of the small, open-air foyer set up to filter arrivals as they came in claiming to be this or that. This time the selection process seemed more stringent, but the door personnel were polite and genuflecting as they scrambled to find lists and match peoples' names with their preprinted ID cards.

It was early and the festival hadn't yet begun, but people were filtering in to the roped-off stage and seating area, looking for their assigned seats. Two tall and extramuscular guards stood by to keep order, and several other stagehands, presenters, performers, and their kin moved about behind a veil of light chaos, giving you the slight suspicion that maybe things would not be pulled off as planned.

Maria waited for me impatiently as I took shots of the audience members filing in. They were the friends, family, and managers of the contestants, and they were dressed up more than usual. When I paused for a moment, I found her immediately hanging on my arm, telling me things like, *Did you see Luciano Caldore? Did you interview Merola? Did you see how Cinzia Oscar is dressed tonight?* At a certain point I happily found myself alone with Teo and Piero from *Napolipiù*. I complained about Maria.

"Does she want to marry you?" Teo asked. He had seen our dynamic from afar.

"She's already married. Her husband even brought us here!"

The two guys laughed. I warned them not to wax ironic around Maria because she was a part of the scene, and then just at that moment she called me on my cell phone. I cursed before answering it. "Where are you?" she asked in her cooing voice, "I've been looking all over for you for the longest time."

"I'm working right now. We can meet up later at the bar."

There was a dead pause before her answer came. Clearly she didn't like this plan. She wanted me to accompany her. "Are you going to be long?" she asked helplessly.

I felt guilty. "I'll meet you there in ten minutes. How's that?"

At once the pitch of Maria's voice kicked up a few tones: "OK, in ten minutes."

By the time I reached the bar, Maria had already been in and out several times, talking to people, wandering around, feeling unaccompanied, lost. She told me that Angelo Buttafuoco was there and that she had told him that I was launching a record. "He has a big record company, Angelo, and it's better you go to him than Riccobono."

"I know Angelo, but I didn't know he had a record company." I wanted to say more, like that I didn't like or trust him, that not only did I hear bad talk about him concerning a major theft (a vanful of Rai broadcast-quality video cameras), but I also had my own bad experience with him the year before. Through a chain of acquaintances that began with my roommate, I had found myself with a small group of individuals who worked in a hair salon in Mugnano, in the periphery. The owner of the salon, Giancarlo, had arranged a deal with a local shop that sold wedding dresses and tuxes. Giancarlo and his staff were to provide models, do their hair and makeup, and bring them to a studio where they were to wear the garments from the shop. In this way, the shop owner had "top models" to don his clothes and Giancarlo had extravagant clothing to accentuate his hairstyles. The models served as the backdrop to a live TV transmission hosted and produced by Buttafuoco at the local private (and maybe pirate) TV station, TVT (Television Taitanic).

Angelo's show, *Emperor for a Day,* consisted of a song competition between emerging singers, who all paid, of course, to sing a song of their choice, original or a cover. Various guests of honor included the "Big," as they were called, who engaged in a bit of chitchat with Angelo and then sang a song, goaded on by a seated onstage mini-audience occupying a semicircle sofa à la Merv Griffin. The sofa guests were in their teens or younger. Some of the girls dressed up in multistrapped backless, shoulderless, sleeveless tops, short, tight skirts, or skintight black polyester slacks. Their hair was spun in thick cornrows or piled in curls and twists interrupted by large silver hoop earrings. The guys had on an assortment of T-shirts with numbers and British and American city names written on them so that they resembled basketball, baseball, or rugby shirts. Some wore simpler T-shirts with a faded-as-if-painted Union Jack. They wore cotton or fleece sweatpants or bell-bottomed jeans with a low-rise waist and tight at the thighs, and Puma running shoes in bright solid colors like orange or baby blue. These young guests rocked back and forth in unison to the music when it was particularly rhythmic and not melodic. It turned out that many of them were actually singers that evening, or their friends or relatives.

When we first entered the TV station dressing room, Giancarlo introduced me to Buttafuoco. He presented me as a journalist who had come to follow the show and do some videotaping. Without even greeting me, Buttafuoco cried out, throwing his arms up in the air in supplication (or was it resignation?) before the saints: "Oh! Why do *you* have to happen to *me* of all people, why to *me*?"

What this meant, I didn't know. I could only guess that he was saying outright that he didn't want me poking my nose around. I had never before encountered such a direct warning or expression of displeasure when I entered someone's realm with my video camera (after that, I had quite a few such encounters). I decided to just go along with it, but with caution. Buttafuoco left the dressing room and engaged in conversation first with the camera crew, then audience members, then others, looking frenetically busy.

It turned out that one of the male models was missing. In the car ride over, Giancarlo and his staff had told me to keep an eye on him. "Tell us what your take on him is. Ruspoli (the shop owner) always brings this model. Why this fifty-year-old would want to model the wedding tuxes of a local shop on a local TV station, I don't know. Does he think he's going to make it big? And he never talks; he just sits there, stern and silent. He's not a bad-looking man, and has his charm, but what does he get out of this? It seems like it's some kind of favor to somebody. He just sits there, not with us but off on his own to the side of the stage, but always on camera."

However, the mysterious man didn't show up. We had two beautiful female models, both in their teens, and a young and very dashing Dane, a visitor who was the adopted brother of Giancarlo's boyfriend, a Danish man living in Naples.

"Would you try this on and see if it fits?" the shop owner asked me, handing me a hangerful of black garments.

I stuttered, "I—don't know," and I looked at Giancarlo, as if asking for help, or at least an explanation.

"Don't worry! It would really help us out," Giancarlo said soothingly. "We can use safety pins to make it all fit."

I really wanted to observe and do some shooting, but instead I was obligated to offer this favor. They dressed me up, and since they hadn't provided me with black shoes—I had on brown leather shoes—we just decided that the camera should not point down below my shins. I was doubtful that this decision would actually be carried out. For one, communication among all parties on a production team was always poor, and this new bit of information would certainly not circulate among all involved in the short amount of time remaining. In fact, one could already hear the deafening sounds of melodic quartertones from the bulky speakers, indicating that the show had already begun. Even if the information had circulated successfully, it was still no guarantee that everyone heard or listened to it, or that they would implement it with care.

We managed with pins and a belt to keep my wide-waisted pants up. I felt in danger of losing them to my ankles at any moment, so I moved

around stiffly and awkwardly. Fortunately there was no movement involved when it came time for the live on-air modeling. The four of us
stood side by side, the men behind the women. The women sat on stools
with the frills of their white dresses spread on the floor around them.
I made sure "my wife's" frills covered my shoes. Buttafuoco positioned
us next to a black Yamaha grand piano. A couple of meters in front of
us the singers performed, some of them hopping about pop-style, others
concentrating most of their movements in their sweeping hand gestures.

Midway through the show Buttafuoco came over to us, the cameras
still rolling, and pointed us out to the home viewers. "Tonight we have
some guests who make up the modeling team that has presented for us
the garments of Casa Ruspoli, located at Via Mondragone in Mugnano.
Let's hear who these people are." Buttafuoco first introduced the shop
owner, whom he had asked to join us before the camera, and then one by
one the models. He chatted and joked and flirted with the two women
for several minutes before turning with his mic to me.

"And this one I'm not going to introduce to you because *I just don't
like him.*" And with that, he moved on to the Dane. I expected Buttafuoco
would return to me after making me squirm a bit; it seemed that making each other uncomfortable, consciously or not, was the game we were
playing. But he didn't even look at me again. Instead he introduced the
next singer.

I was confused and irked. Earlier, while the stylist and the other models were fitting my oversized garb and styling my hair, I had texted my
roommate to tell him I was going to be on TV and that he should record it on the VCR. The recording was important for my documentary.
I envisioned a reflexive documentary about my efforts to track the art
of making do on the neomelodica music scene, a melodramatic spectacle that gradually engulfs me. I also wanted to craft my public image on
the scene. I already knew many people, and many people I didn't know
already knew me. Buttafuoco reminded me that I needed to take more
control over whatever reputation was preceding me.

There was yet another reason I wanted my roommate to record my
TV appearance: *protagonismo.* When I was a teenager I had modeled
for fashion designers in Milan. The money was great and the admiration I received wasn't bad either, but I didn't like my superficial, pawing
colleagues. Two decades later I found myself in the *periferia* of Naples,
modeling an ill-fitting wedding tux—and brown shoes—on a private

television channel. I was making an ironic comeback, and I was only half-ironically enjoying it.

Midway through the transmission, Buttafuoco returned to us, this time to talk about the women's hairstyles. Again, he asked the stylist and the shop owner to join us before the camera. Again, he went through the introductions. When he came to me, I mistakenly assumed his game would be over, but he said, *"This one* is simply unlikable. He's an imposter and he shouldn't even be here among us, so we'll just move on . . ."

That's when the shop owner protested, *"Uè!* Let him talk! Let him talk!"

Grinning, Buttafuoco turned back to me and handed me the mic. Without smiling, and probably scowling, I took it from him. I tried to quickly regain my composure, then looked into the camera and presented myself to the viewers. I explained that I was writing a book and shooting a documentary on the Neapolitan music scene. "So if you see me around, you'll know that's what I'm up to."

Buttafuoco finally let up on his mock antagonism, luckily, because I was getting pissed. I thought the special confidence he had with Giusy, the younger of the two models (seventeen years old) who was my wife in our commercial performance, might have something to do with his behavior toward me. Buttafuoco was a little shorter than me, with a rather handsome face, big dark eyes, and a full head of black hair, and he also had a large belly, as he himself frequently pointed out. He was in his mid- to late thirties. Maybe my athletic build gave him an urge to compete, and maybe he feared an incursion on "his" Giusy.

When the night was over, we—Giancarlo, the other models, and Buttafuoco and an older female singer in her early thirties, very thin and heavily wrinkled from tanning—drove to an all-night *cornetteria.* Inside, great baking sheets of nutella and cream-filled croissants and brioches were pulled regularly out of the hot, wide ovens and sold to end-of-the-night crowds coming from parties, nightclubs, or from work, like us. Buttafuoco treated us all to pastries. We stood at one of the several standing tables placed on the sidewalk before the shop and struggled to eat the hot cornetti, the nutella falling out in large, stretching lumps onto our wrists, the table, and the pavement. I noticed that although the show was over, and although it was late and the others were tired like me (the difference being that I had had to struggle with Buttafuoco's confusing games, my reputation management, the incomprehensible Neapolitan some people spoke, and the deafening volume of the music, a lot of which was simply not good by anyone's standards), Buttafuoco was still not relaxed, and his performances were not entirely over. He had trouble looking into my eyes for any decent length of time, and he addressed me offhandedly, peripherally, quickly, and only when needed.

When I was finally alone again with Giancarlo and his staff, driving back home, I commented on Buttafuoco. "I think I made him nervous," I said. "I think he has something to hide. I don't know about him."

Giancarlo answered, "You think? Naw, he just likes to play."

"But he was joking pretty hard with me—to the point of aggression."

"Naw, that's a compliment. It means he likes you. You know how Neapolitans are. They like to play, and the more attention they pay to you, the more they like you, even if it means making fun of you. If he really disliked you, he would have ignored you altogether."

I thought about it, but I was unconvinced. What was there to like about me? Buttafuoco and I had no interaction of any substance. He truncated any attempt I had made to talk to him, preempting it with aggressive dismissals.

Over a year later at the Festival of Naples matters concerning Buttafuoco became clearer. "I didn't know he had a record label," I said to Maria, unsure of her relations with him and what I could or couldn't say. I also wanted to warn her not to go around like that, indiscriminately talking about my upcoming stunt, to become the next neomelodico. But I also enjoyed her talking about me. I was starting to realize that she was a significant personage on the scene and that her home was a sort of salon for singers and their associates. Maria was already doing a lot to stir things up around me, stimulating my fieldwork like a fluffer, making it happen *to* me.

We went inside the bar and waited on the sweaty confusion of a customer line—more like a continually morphing crowd—to order drinks, which were mostly sold out. Water and espresso were good enough. Maria engaged with some other people at the bar, and I told her that I was going outside for some slightly cooler air. As I walked in that direction, I heard my name called out. To my right was none other than Angelo Buttafuoco, seated in a semicircle with a group of young women and somewhat older men. He beamed at me as I moved in closer to greet him. I didn't expect such a welcome, and I was curious to see what was up. I stood before the seated grinning man with a boisterous voice and grabbed his hand in a casual handshake. I nodded to the others whom Buttafuoco informally introduced to me en masse as "friends." They nodded back, most of them with polite smiles and only one of them with that studying, detached, surly look that said, *And who are you?*

Buttafuoco then turned to me and grabbed my balls. Somehow I didn't react with surprise; maybe it was something I had read in his eyes just moments before. "So what is this, this physique? Then you say you're an anthropologist one day, a journalist another, then a filmmaker, and *now* you're making a record?" He held on as he said this to me, tauntingly and with a touch of sweetness.

From my standing height I stared down at his seated figure without flinching. Miraculously, I maintained my composure while his hand still clasped my balls. "So you want to produce me?" I responded.

Still grinning, but pausing for just one more fraction of a moment, he let his hand drop from my crotch. "Sure, I'll do it."

I was done with our interaction, and I was happy to bring it to a close. I was done with this man and his unfazed company who all witnessed an act so over the top that probably no one knew how to make room for it in the meaning of things. It was a typical tactic of dissimulation, the kind Maria perhaps had practiced with her favorite singer Fabio, hiding the truth by shouting it out in all its obviousness.

"Then we'll talk," I told him. "Arrivederci." And I walked outside.

I was mulling over what had just happened while waiting for Maria, watching passersby, and listening to the music booming from the distance. The festival was already well underway, but it wasn't what was onstage that interested me. Being at this far distance, back in the bar on the other side of the spa's grounds, seemed to me like being at the heart of matters.

And it sure was. Soon Maria came out from the bar, as well. She approached me quickly, visibly upset. She looked down, her eyes were narrow, and there were extra lines on her face.

"Maria, what's going on?"

"I don't know, but I don't like it. Maybe I made a mistake, but when you're joking it's just a joke . . . joking is all right?"

"What happened?"

"Buttafuoco offered me a job, told me I should be his secretary, that I should be his shadow, just like I was for Fabio."

"So? What kind of work does that entail?"

"He said, 'Maria, you need to follow me in everything, like my shadow, all the time . . . but,' and you know what he said then?"

"What?"

"He said, 'But Maria, you have to know that my wife is a jealous woman.' So I said, 'And so? My husband is a jealous man.'"

"This doesn't sound good," I murmured.

"No. And maybe I made a mistake and gave him too much confidence. What should I *do*?"

"You mean should you accept the job?"

"Yeah."

"Of course not! It sounds like a proposition and only that."

"I think you're right," Maria said. "I think I shouldn't do it because he might want something else."

"That's what I'm *saying*."

"Maybe I gave him too much confidence, but everyone knows that he and Fabio are like rivals. Buttafuoco was always competing with Fabio for me."

"Really?" That was news to me.

"And now that Fabio is out of the picture, maybe he wants to do him wrong by getting close to me."

"Well, he definitely wants more than work from you," I said, half-enjoying my private irony.

"I think you're right. So you don't think I should take the job?"

"No, of course not." I wanted to tell her about my experience with him, but I decided against it. I needed to know if I could trust her and know how much of a gossip she was. I wasn't ready for word to get around and then for it to come back to me in the form of retaliation. I eventually did tell her, but months later after another, oddly related encounter she and I had with a singer and a composer at her home one evening. To test her, I asked her who else knew about *her* run-in with Buttafuoco.

"Only you and Francesco," she said.

If after a month of opportunity Maria had told only the two of us, then I could believe she was sufficiently discreet. I decided to tell her about *my* run-in with Buttafuoco.

"I didn't know that about him," she said in response.

"I didn't know that either," I echoed, "but it should stay between us, right?"

"Yes, of course," she said.

Imbroglio

The people I got to know engage in a lot of highly charged talk, whether in the recording studio or in the entryway to it, backstage at piazza festivals or even onstage during wedding performances, on live pirate TV transmissions, or just at the dinner table, while riding side by side on Vespas, or paying the fruit vendor. This talk involves hands that grab arms and genitals, lay themselves heavily on chests, thighs, and other hands, and stroke the cheek and pinch the chin. It involves arms that hook around necks and waists, barricade and push, and actively gesticulate. Bodies lean in close, block, jerk away, and pace. Voices rise and fall in pitch and power while extending themselves across elongated and ebullient or frustrated and angry vowels as in *Uèee!* (Hey!), *Oooh!* (Hey!), and *Nun si può faticàaa acusìii!* (You can't work like thaaat!). The main content of this talk is elaborate and often rabid plans to collaborate on business ventures and scams like launching a televised song competition or luring tone deaf (and even deaf) young men and boys into recording their debut album.[28] Once I grew accustomed to the spectacular sensory dimension of this talk, I was able to follow the details of the plans it articulated and carefully track many of them over time. I found that they almost always led to their own dissolution, and often instantly. The reasons varied—*We didn't have any appointment!*; *I said that I wanted to think about it first!*—and often involved put-downs and generalized condemnations: *He's a man of shit!*; *To accomplish anything in Naples, you have to leave Naples!*

The people I got to know often engaged in exuberant project planning and contests of wills, less for any concrete result than to generate imbrogli. The definition of the anglicized version of this word retains only one of the original meanings of its Italian root: "a state of great confusion and entanglement; a complicated or difficult situation (esp. political or dramatic); a confused misunderstanding or disagreement, embroilment."[29] Imbrogli are makeshift atmospheres in the neomelodica scene, where protagonists stage with and for one another their dramas of personal sovereignty. This is a melodramatic mode of attention.

These dramas, too, are staged in imbrogli. But they also remain faithful to the word's second Italian meaning, lost in the English translation: "cheat, swindle, fraud, trick."[30] These ethnographic dramas honor and exploit the simulations, dissimulations, and the frauds of field encounters. They are not resemblances that predicate themselves on a model that they must return to and reveal.[31] They don't identify a sovereign truth and crown it at a remove. These ethnographic dramas *are* truths— transversal truths lying across the arts of the contact zone, their reenactments in writing, and the art of reading. These stories are not, cannot, or do not necessarily need to all be "verified." There is no prenarrative truth.[32] Truths are made by the pressure these melodramas apply to the surface of real situations.

These melodramas happen in ethnographic atmospheres—in the jangle of loud melodies, jarring words, flamboyant gestures, pressing bodies, and *them* and *me* sizing each other up. These atmospheres hover with potential, hang like a fog, or simply dissipate. They don't allow events to be followed to their completion or depletion. We make our way using the melodramatic mode of attention. And with a sliding scale of irony, we reach for personal sovereignty.

SIX

Who Am I and Who Are You?
The Promise and Threat of Contact with the Camorra

In Naples you hear the expression "to weave one's net with thick yarn" instead of the usual thread. The yarns people weave in the contact zone are made of twined affects and interests. They are melodramas freighted with promises and threats of total contact. Total contact is where overdrawn hopes for a better future meet inflated fears that nothing will be separated out and spared. Suspicion and hope are both speculative.

Like many others on the neomelodica scene, I wove a net of thick yarns. Then I tried casting it over a contact zone, wanting to capture it. Gradually I realized that what I had woven was already a contact zone and that *I* was an object of capture.

Act 1: Lying Together

On the neomelodica scene, affects, aesthetics, and interests interweave in moral and political economic practices. Network building and bargaining are performed through affective–aesthetic contact in the communal reproduction of iconicity of style. People attune themselves to each other's sensibilities to weave a contact zone. People tell lies together, outwardly performing the implicit operations of aesthetic experience.

"We're not interested in that," Gaetano, a.k.a. 'O lione (The lion), said to me calmly, almost under his breath, when I was loading the video work I had done for him on my laptop. He was responding to what he saw on the desktop while I was booting up: a photo of three cops standing up against a wall, all looking off somewhere to the right of the frame. I had taken the photo at the Festival of La Sanità, where my journalist friend Francesco told me, "Look, it's the irony of Naples: there are three cops standing there looking at the stage, just looking, and on and around the stage are four or five people who should be in prison."

Every year, neomelodici perform in a two-day piazza festival partly funded and organized by the daughter of the late Totò, Naples's famed comic actor and poet who lived and performed many of his roles in the neighborhood La Sanità. A stage is set up on the main piazza in front of the statue of the neighborhood saint Vincenzo Ferrer, "The Big Monk," who stands grand and spotlighted in the massive foyer of the striking baroque basilica, Santa Maria della Sanità.

Every year an "official" political representative of the neighborhood attends the festival. This year he spent a lot of time backstage with the singers, the press, a few privileged fans, and me. Did he know which of us were fugitives from the law? Very few of us knew how this amazing feat was being pulled off, the spectacularly public appearance of fugitives who, for a couple of nights, enjoyed immunity. The craft and yarn-weaving it would take to get to the right people and the information or facts that would explain the mechanics behind this event would generate too much contact.

Paradoxically, the fugitives were spared by the event's intensely public and spectacular nature. Diego Paura, a journalist who writes for the performing arts page of the daily *Il Roma,* has noted that sometimes protagonists of this milieu who have trouble with the law organize "official" events by inviting journalists who, by their very presence, double as guarantors of the event's legality.[1] It is likely that the press, the politician, and the police provided, and not necessarily or entirely willingly, the fugitives' cover. Singers and journalists have both said that sometimes bribery and intimidation play a role in their relations.

Francesco and I were experiencing the irony of Naples in its full regalia: the most public display of fugitives and foes celebrating together before an audience knotted up with them in the thick yarns of an affective–aesthetic economy. Many of the performers were residents of the neighborhood; with their network of family and associates, they peopled the stage, backstage, and the audience. Some peopled the main boulevard that spilled into the piazza, selling roasted nuts, blocks of nougat, and bottles of beer. These vendors were likely required to pay the local boss for their "operating licenses" during the festival. The singers were the privileged few who were given the opportunity to perform (many of them for free) at such a significant event. Performing on the festival stage was like performing their managers' hegemony.

Those of us in the roped-off backstage space found ourselves in a high-density contact zone. Networks were baldly exposed, and new network formations were in the making. This meant entanglements. In my case, singers were miffed when I didn't court them (with my video camera). "Spies" watched Maria and me and reported back to Fabio what they saw and imagined.

The audience, instead, seemed attuned to the affective surge of neo-melodica song. There were ecstatic teenage girls with large hoop ear-rings and the latest hairstyle (long and straight, with multilength bangs hanging to the side). They wore billow sleeve blouses, or black-and-silver sequin tank tops, or minidresses. There were amped young men in basketball tank tops, Napoli-blue soccer shirts, or cowboy button-downs with cut-off sleeves and sweatpants, Capri pants, or short shorts. There were as well several adults with excited young children sitting atop their shoulders, calling out lyrics with the rest of the crowd when singers beckoned them.

I didn't want Gaetano to see the picture I took of the three cops at the music festival. I had been holding my laptop out of his sight while waiting for the video program to open up on top of the desktop pic-ture. It was Giuseppe who, catching a glimpse of the photo, laughingly insisted: "Let him see, let him see it!" At that point it would have been worse to hide the picture after so much attention had been drawn to it, so I brought my laptop back over to Gaetano. He was sitting at the large, empty desk in the corner opposite to Giuseppe's keyboard workstation. There was once a time when everyone would crowd around the other corner of the room, hugging, pinching, slapping, chattering, and sing-ing around Giuseppe as he worked out new arrangements for the lyrics they brought by. Since Gaetano began coming by, the swirl and surge of minor activities centered on him, his empty desk, and the blank red date book he flipped through absentmindedly as he listened to what others were saying. When he spoke, the swirling increased, consisting of def-erential pauses and glances, heads that bent and craned in response to his words, and bodies that leaned in his direction or made way for his movements.

"We're not interested in that," Gaetano said in a slow mumble, with-out raising his glance from the picture of the three cops on my desktop. My collection of photos and film footage didn't faze anyone. He and everyone else coming in and out of the studio knew I was "making a documentary on Neapolitan music." To hang around and ask questions as an anthropologist proved suspect; even confidants whom I'd known for years "jokingly" told me they still wondered for what police task force

I worked. Paradoxically, only confidants would confide in me such suspicions; the others kept their suspicions to themselves. Even after nearly two years Giuseppe thought he would trip me up by saying: "I think that there's something going on with you, that you've come to Naples for another reason that you won't talk about . . . but I'm gonna find out. I'm gonna ask some questions, so don't you worry. I'll know the truth." He spoke while his mother, Anna, dumped the pasta in the boiling water. The challenge had an everyday quality, slipped casually into the routines of work and talk, the heat, meals, espressos, and Neapolitan mothering.

I decided not to take it too hard: "Oh, so you're returning to your original thought—" I started to say, referring to the suspicions he and his friends had when we originally met that I worked for 'a finanza (the treasury police), but he cut me off:

"Look, you come from New York, the best city in the world—"

At that moment a new voice entered the conversation: "From *your* point of view," Anna said, stirring the zucchini and prosciutto into the pasta.

Giuseppe ignored her, continuing, "—where life is easy and you don't even realize how lucky you are because you can work and have money. But instead you come to underdeveloped Naples where people are ignorant, where there's no work. Why? There's something wrong with this. I think you were sent here to look into the camorra. Someone sent you to break the camorra, and you say you want to study the neomelodici because you realized it's the closest thing to the camorra you can find."

Giuseppe was extremely quick and acutely observant. One of his favorite games was to imitate me—my accent, the way I gesticulate, the way I move my body—making me realize just how carefully he watched me and other people. And he watched unnoticed. His face never seemed to be occupied with the task of observing, showing neither a tensed brow, pursed lips, nor eyes that focus a little too hard. Nor was his body ever arrested in its movements and activities for the sake of assessing whom or what to target. He talked, smiled, completed other tasks with ease and eloquence while gathering, compiling, and processing signs, traces, and hints. I was impressed with how close he veered to the truth, just mixing up a few signs and inverting it. "I came to study neomelodica music and only later did I realize it was connected to the camorra," I corrected him.

Giuseppe only looked at me ironically and mumbled, "*Sì-sì* [Yeah, sure]." It was clear he was joking this time—at least almost entirely. About a month later, while we were alone in his car, he said to me sternly, "You know, don't you, that if anyone ever sees you showing your footage to the police, they will find you and they will kill you?"

After I began to video-document my field research, people got so used to my video camera that they assumed I was making a documentary. This was mainly because "a journalist with a video camera" made more sense; as an anthropologist I didn't seem to have any concrete objectives, besides obtaining "information" and "data." I quickly learned that such an objective was perceived as a threat. Likewise, "curiosity" and that perniciously vague "pursuit of knowledge" proved suspect dispositions. Had I made frequent daytrips to nearby Pompeii, participated (more than once) in the annual ten-kilometer pilgrimage of violently ecstatic worshippers to the Madonna dell'Arco, or made field recordings of roaming musicians along the promenade of Naples's port Mergellina, people would have regarded my behavior as more appropriate.

Many people in the scene regarded the work of journalists in the same manner. Journalists, in their eyes, did not go on fact-finding missions to Naples, but rather dropped in for a bit of folklore and sensation, only to quickly leave again.

On many occasions, the camera lens was essential in binding me to others in circuits of exchange, for it made me apprehensible. As if they were looking back at me through my own lens, people sensed my motivations in relation to their own. By getting at my career goals, they could locate what it was I needed. This entailed constructing my career with me: the journalist with the video camera. People typed me in order to barter with me; by giving me, unsolicited, what I needed, they could pressure me down the road for favors in return. My imposed vocation made me less suspect, and my habit of observing, listening, and sometimes recording more credible.

On many other occasions, however, it took an artful repartee to cull from people performances that went beyond talking in postcards. That's one reason why I decided to compose postcards with them. If I worked beside and for people, I thought, I could learn (and record) pragmatically and laterally. I began a partnership with Giuseppe, shooting the videos for the songs he arranged. This entangled me within the shared web of interests that bound participants of the scene. More specifically, I was now "interested" in the monetary sense as well.

Giuseppe and I decided to set my price at 500 euros for a package of four music videos and 150 for one. A singer I hadn't yet met who had been working with Giuseppe for a few months became our first shared client. His name was Andrea, a short, dark-haired, good-looking man in his late twenties. One morning I came to meet Giuseppe in Pino's dimly lit recording studio below Giuseppe's office and found them both sitting and chatting with Andrea. The latter greeted me with unusual enthusiasm: "So *this* is Jason," he said with a big smile and a concentrated gaze. He pronounced my name with such unusual accuracy that he immediately put me on guard. Even Raffaele, a shifty singer I had been following around for five years, still called me things like Joseph, Jackson, and Johnson. It seemed everyone excepting my true confidants called me by some misinterpretation of Jason, including the more improbable variations of Jane, Josey, and Gesù (Jesus).

Andrea was very charming, or was he putting on the charm? I wasn't sure what the difference was. I was drawn in and wondered if I was about to be had. There was a sort of twinkle in his eye that made it seem he was flirting. "So you do videos?" he asked.

"Yeah, I do. Are you interested?" I volleyed back bluntly.

Without missing a beat, he nearly sang the words, "It would be an honor to work with you," finishing it off with a dripping gaze and a smile so slick it seemed soaked in irony.

"No, the honor will be all mine," I returned, reflecting the same ironic, flirtatious smile. He cocked his head to the side, intrigued and perplexed.

Giuseppe then interjected, "If you go upstairs with him, he'll also do an interview with you on camera."

Andrea was now even more intrigued: "An interview? But what kind of questions are you going to ask?"

"I will ask everything possible to put you to the test," I answered Andrea in mock challenge. Most people I encountered in this milieu were eager to play. The art of conversation rapidly expands into playful bodily interaction, and it can often draw even the most diffident strangers into animated engagement. For example, while many shop owners and market vendors will languidly grumble their way through a transaction, if the client launches into play, often everyone present immediately follows suit. This form of contact often consists of personally addressed irony and indexical references to one's own and each other's bodies.

But when I pushed play to another level in this first meeting with Andrea, a hint of uneasiness flickered across his face. I smiled and reassured him, "No, we'll talk about whatever you're interested in." I hadn't planned on conducting an interview, but now that the wheels were in motion, it was going to be next to impossible to escape without satisfying his inevitably triggered exhibitionism. When I asked people why, according to them, Neapolitans were so eager to be in front of the video camera, the response was often, "We are all like Farinelli," referring to the eighteenth-century Neapolitan castrato, whose physical beauty and spectacular vocal abilities afforded him a renown of mythic proportions all over Europe. "We like the attention." Accordingly, I was often the voyeur by default.

It wasn't long before Andrea and I met again upstairs in Giuseppe's office. After engaging with him in a bit of autopilot prattle about the differences between Naples and America, I decided to take out my video camera. Immediately Andrea puffed up like a peacock and seamlessly slipped into marked performance mode, conducting a self-interview in Italian. As if the camera lens were asking him questions (I certainly wasn't), he began talking about his childhood, and then the early years of his career, at last waxing big about his goals for the future. He rattled on about how song had always been in his heart and how he was different than the run-of-the-mill rabble clogging up the channels of the local market. He believed in quality and originality, and most of all, he had to feel something about what he sang. Andrea looked directly into the lens, conversing with it reasonably, gesturing to it, talking sense to it, and explaining to it in plain terms what it wanted to know.

I suddenly turned off the camera and put it down. Having finally pulled his attention back to me, I said, "Well, you know, my job is really difficult because I have to deal with a lot of people who don't act naturally in front of the camera. It takes time before I hear about the real stuff, and believe me, I know what the real stuff is."

Andrea stared back at me with evident discomfort, but then quickly recovered, "No, no! Wait! Put the camera back on! I can tell you that I argued last night on the air with the people on a show at Televesuvio because I didn't like how *l'ambiente* [the scene] was there." He spoke in Neapolitan, his code switch indicating that now it was "just us talking" without the mediation of that stiff language Italian and that third eye, the video camera.

Just then Giuseppe barreled into the room, his booming voice leading the way, "Jason, show him your video work. Let him see it!" Giuseppe was followed by Pino and a friend called Sasà, who had promised to put me in touch with a guy who peddles audio equipment and pirated software. I needed a better video-editing program if I was going to convert footage from American to European format. Just as I began preparing Andrea for the presentation, Sasà interrupted with a question, "Hey Jason, so what is it you need from Erry the audio guy?" I ignored him so that I could finish what I was saying to Andrea. Clearly Sasà knew I was working on a business deal—word travels fast in this environment when it's a matter of gain—so I thought he would wait a few moments. I was just about to launch the video for Andrea when Sasà called out again, "Hey Jason, what programs do you want me to ask for?" Although I had already explained it to him in detail, I did so once again, as it was customary among men in this milieu to repeat instructions several times in several different ways. In doing so, the listener can translate them into his own terms and demonstrate both to his interlocutor and to himself that he understands. Oddly, the exact opposite can also happen: the interlocutor claims quickly, even before hearing all the instructions, to have fully understood them. Here, men feel they are supposed to already know without ever having been ignorant.

But Andrea was still waiting for my presentation, and Sasà was delaying it. I decided to begin even before he finished repeating my instructions to me once again. Sasà nevertheless continued to interrupt us with his repetitions, competing with Giuseppe and Pino's loud conversation about putting together a TV program. Miraculously, it didn't hinder Andrea from focusing on the video. I realized that he, like most people I met, was capable of optimum concentration during moments of disturbance and light chaos. When he finished watching, Andrea started to barter with me. "So you've made other videos?" he asked.

I tried to make my response brief. "Yes, I made this one for that young boy Fulvio and a couple of others," although, apart from Fulvio, there had been no "others."

Unfortunately, Andrea asked the question I was dreading, "For whom? You have a name?"

Now I felt under pressure. I had inflated myself to maintain my price. I wanted to convince Andrea that I didn't only do pro bono work but had also sold music videos for money. I remembered then that the lies that function best are those closest to the truth, so I searched my memory for the name of a real singer, but one that no one would know. "Ciro is his name," I said, hoping it would suffice, but of course it didn't.

"And his last name?" Andrea insisted, no longer smiling.

"Ah, Ferrucci, yeah, Ferrucci is his name," I answered, wondering what the consequences were going to be.

Inevitably, Andrea knew who I was talking about, "Oh, from Capodichino," he said, referring to the neighborhood on the hill near the airport.

"Yeah," I said, "that's right," now afraid that Andrea and Ciro had some form of contact and that the truth would eventually come out. I was having a hard time with my lie, which was taking on a kind of permanence in our interaction.

"And what happened to the video?" Andrea asked, his curiosity now at its highest.

Concerned that Andrea was unintentionally following me into a cul-de-sac, I mumbled strategically, "I don't know what he did with it. . . . you know, I've been looking for the right software to convert from American to European format and I can't find it anywhere," remembering that another good lying tactic is to change the subject and bury the lie among the banalities of the day-to-day and its relatively unimportant truths.

But Andrea lingered back where I left him: "Ah, I can't believe it. What's wrong with that guy? You make a video with an American and then you just put it aside? Some people . . ."

In addition to doing business, Andrea was engaging me in a common ritual of mutual identification through a kind of verbal GIS tracking using the parameters of *zona* (area), quartiere (neighborhood), associates, and kin. Almost without fail, when two people of any socioeconomic and educational level meet for the first time, they engage in the elaborate science of position plotting within the fluid, intermingling networks of a city of one million inhabitants. If the two navigators come from vastly different socioeconomic levels, the calculations often begin and end with zona. If one of them names as her home an area prohibitively expensive for her interlocutor, the mapping stops and polite, distanced interaction ensues. When the socioeconomic levels are more similar, *campanilismo* (lit. church bell-ism), or a parochial attachment and loyalty to one's home neighborhood, historically marked by the sonic reach of the church bell of the nearest piazza, emerges in the interaction to determine where the finer differences lie.[2]

Campanilismo is an affective and interested relationship not so much to the neighborhood as place as it is to the neighbors themselves. Networks begin with the family and then branch out into the neighborhood community, with much overlap between the two. The process of naming who you know can go on for a long time. In such cases, the participants in the ritual seek to describe and identify an associate or even kin they have in common. Once they've located such a node, they begin slowly zooming out once again, to review the secondary, internodal links surrounding them. This step enables the participants to verify their own and each other's claims at having nodes in common. If you know Gigi the glassmaker, then you must also know old Luisa, his neighbor the *sansara* (DIY apartment broker) who's been doing his washing since his wife died.[3] Still more, you of course would know that great pizzeria just two doors down from Gigi's shop, you know, Nennella, where they make the best *capricciosa* (lit. capricious, meaning pizza topped with prosciutto, mushrooms, artichokes, and olives)—No, I've never had one there, I'll only eat a *margherita* (named after the Savoy queen for whom it was invented upon her visit in 1889)—Well, when *I* want a margherita I go to a place on Piazza Sannazzaro (grinding his knuckles in his left cheek as a gesture meaning *Madonna, that's good food*—The one that serves mussels? —Yeah, that one; Giorgio the pizzaiuolo is my wife's nephew—You mean the bald guy with the missing tooth? I go to him on Mondays and Tuesdays when he fixes cars—No, that's the restaurant next door—Oh yeah, yeah, I know, you're talking about Da Enzo where there's that young kid, the one who's father . . . (realizing now that his interlocutor's brother-in-law is the guy who was nabbed last month for armed robbery) —Uh-huh, that's him—Oh, so then you know Elena, his girl. She works in the handbag factory in Campanelli with my wife. She's the one who told us about the mussels.

In this way, the participants of the ritual reel each other in using the strands of common affect and interest by which they are ultimately connected. Their GIS talk scans the pattern of networks and reconfigures them so that they can shift the focus on their relationship to one another. In effect, they create through talk a new network by twining together as many shared threads as they can find and creating thick cords to conjoin their day-to-day lives. By the same token, the participants may also locate reasons for backing off from one another, finding that there are already some severed fibers between them. Broken contact is a form of social trauma; in this milieu it is an excessive and violent act. The connective strands of affect and interest between individuals fray because of neglect more often than they are snapped by conscious acts of separation.

The ritual, if all goes well, will round itself off with a hearty session of gossip. At this final stage, participants take the opportunity to gather missing pieces in their knowledge of the third-party players in their recently established mutual network. Gossiping also allows each of them to further test just how strong the strands of affect and interest that connect the other to these third-party players really are. By assessing each other's store of gossip material, they also assess the intensities of contact that have made their accumulation possible.

Fortunately, the new topic I introduced about video formats helped me move the conversation with Andrea away from my fabricated client. Although I still worried about the future consequences of my lying, I realized I was behaving like most people of this milieu who exaggerate, dissimulate, and replace with ellipses "information" about themselves, their work, and their position within the city's networks. "Lying" is in fact an accepted and expected strategy in bargaining; it sticks to the practice and not to the individual. If I lie while showing off my wares, people of this scene do not regard me as untrustworthy. Instead, they take it for granted that participation in an economy of scarcity, secrecy, and the fear of violence necessitates corner cutting such as lying. The delicate yet aggressive approaches people take to one another in matters of interest contain within them the implicit knowledge that they are both sifting through each other's gray matter in search of the bottom line: nontransparent jealous interests.

It suddenly seemed that Andrea had already detected my lie when he announced, "Well, I've already started my new album, so I don't know about making videos for the last one. But, on the other hand, you *could* do a video for the last album just to get your name out there and get some more business. After that we can talk about you doing the current album." Andrea was telling me indirectly that he knew I had little experience. His strategy was to claim that both he and I needed me to shoot a sample video before there could be any "formal" commerce between us. According to him, he needed to have proof of my abilities before investing in them, while I needed any opportunity I could get to put my videos out on the airwaves.

Because my greatest skill in talk is to not prevaricate about the bottom line—something regarded as quite the opposite of skill in this scene—I said, dryly, "Well, for a package of four videos I'm asking 500 euros, and for one it will be 150."

Andrea did not comment on this artless and disengaged response. He only looked at me, waiting for me to say something more. When I didn't, he changed the subject. Not surprisingly, he found another opening about a quarter of an hour later, amid all the cell phone ringing, bargaining, and joking carried into the small office by various men who had come upstairs for reasons that seemed would never become concrete. Andrea came and stood noticeably close to me. He was only tall enough to reach my shoulders, so he turned his chummy smile upward at me: "You know, when there's good *sintonia* [harmony], you don't need to know a person a long time, and I already know that there's sincerity between us." His overture to me had the strange effect of being simultaneously laughable and convincing. It wasn't that he wanted me to feel guilty about my lying; he was letting me know that we were lying together and for that reason, in synch. It was likely there were lies I hadn't detected in his part of the script that would emerge only through time.

More importantly, Andrea was also opening up a new realm of contact between us; now that the moral pretense of truthfulness had fallen away, thanks to his initiative, we could begin the contemporaneous practice of bargaining and getting to know each other as we "really" are. Affective contacts such as aggressive declarations of friendship or anticipations of long-term relationships comprise an economy of friendship. Andrea had located me in his same moral–political–economic universe and wanted to welcome me with affection. The bargaining was not replaced by this new recognition but deferred for the time being until it could become more subtly woven into our "friendship."

Dealing Affectively

Affective contacts such as aggressive declarations of friendship or anticipations of long-term relationships activate an economy of friendship. My bartering session with Andrea was like a bad copy of my transaction earlier that week with Tony. Tony and I shared an actual, particular intersubjective history spanning nearly two years, in contrast to the weak symbolization of one that Andrea tried to sing into being through talk of our "syntony."[4] According to Andrea's claims, we were singing in tune, as do the market vendor who chants his call-to-sale and the patron who barters with him. Andrea employed a good strategy, invoking presence as a way to establish contact between us; he used all means available to him through flirting, physical contact, and the immediate impact of a declared mutual "feeling." However, these tactile qualities of the exchange, while they lent it a certain density, could not create for it the "depth" and "interiority" that my exchange with Tony possessed.[5] Tony, not Andrea, knew that I had a greater goal than selling music videos. I ultimately wanted to get a "scoop," as he called it, using the English word. Tony and I had long been directly linked in our shared network, and we both had had the opportunity to learn a lot about each other. Quite simply, he was more aware than Andrea of what was truly valuable to me.

But not totally. He didn't know I had an even greater goal of developing relationships with people who could link me to their links to boss–impresari. I couldn't make this objective clear, because no one else was willing to be clear about the camorra. After nearly two years, I still hadn't gotten to know a single boss, not because I didn't come into contact with them or that they were in short supply, or even that they were somehow inaccessible, hidden, or exclusive. I had met a number of bosses in passing, but I hadn't yet had the opportunity for sustained interaction with them. The situation had to come of its own, organically. If I showed too much enthusiasm about meeting and getting to know a boss, I found resistance. Whenever I expressed my interest in the camorra, I drove others away from me. They didn't want to be associated with someone so pointedly concerned with camorristi as camorristi.[6] Of course, more or less everyone knew or knew of someone who had expressed interest in a particular boss, but for a specific purpose, such as obtaining production support for their music or finding out who had stolen their car. For example, a videographer named Mario with whom I later worked told me that his associate Angelo had borrowed his shooting equipment, only to claim a week later that it had been stolen from his car. Suspicious of Angelo's story, Mario decided to verify with the boss of the neighborhood of the alleged robbery that it had actually occurred. The boss told him there were no such thefts at all that week and that furthermore he knew that Angelo had pawned the equipment to someone else. Bosses are simultaneously police, judiciary, and executioners who identify, prosecute, and sometimes punish. That I should express interest in "the camorra" and the identity "camorrista" seemed too close to the sector with which the "other" police and judiciary dealt.

Despite their aversion to the topic, people certainly did want to find out my objectives, taking what appeared to be their own circuitous routes to get there. Suspicions about my activities put me on the defensive, especially when police raided in a single week two of the pirate TV stations I had been frequenting. People were afraid of what I might be connected to, and I feared their fears. A fine game it was, as if both they and I were avoiding the descent to "the dark at the bottom of the stairs" where our inchoate fears lay.[7]

Tony was a short and good-natured forty-year-old father of two. He worked in a leather handbag factory and lived in Secondigliano in the housing projects nicknamed "167." The last time I had seen him was with another singer called Raffaele, a hyperactive, good-looking, curly-haired man in his early twenties who always had a new thing going, often in words alone. His latest thing was a TV transmission on the more costly regional/pirate stations TeleP. His fast-talking and listen-to-this-grabbing-hold-of-your-arm-and-talking-into-your-face style both turned his temporary collaborators off and enchanted them. One afternoon he had managed to rally up a songwriter named Gennaro, a performer named Enzo who sang in the classic style of sceneggiata king Mario Merola, and me. He had us all crowded around him in the parking alley outside Giuseppe's office, frantically building up to towering heights a show like no other, with singers and comics, fine painted backdrops, guest appearances each week from a different "Big" (one of the ten or fifteen singers on the scene of greater fame), and my American accent from offstage reading faxes from fans—"Yeah, we gotta have faxes instead of wasting all that time with phone calls saying, 'Ciao mamma, a hug to grandma and a kiss to little Mary.'"

Everyone competed with Raffaele for his own attention, trying to interject in his narcissistic scramble toward fame that didn't take him a single step out of that alley, and in doing so, they became just as enthused. They named others on the neomelodica scene who, according to them, were going to be equally inspired. Our little throng in the decrepit parking alley became a confusion of gesticulating arms, grasping hands, shoulders that blocked others to get to Raffaele first with overlapping, repeating shouts like, "But listen to this! But listen to this! But listen!" We seemed to be brawling. The parking attendant who liked to play cards near the gate with stray singers when they took a break approached the scuffle with his twenty-year-old son to watch and toss like poker chips a few words into our boiling-over talk. A couple of sullen faces appeared on the surrounding balconies to sneak sidelong glances while pretending to focus on the drying laundry or potted jade plants and geraniums.

The names Giuseppe and Tony came up, and in no time their collaboration on the TV show also became a natural fact. Ironically, it was Giuseppe who began to unravel the entire project over the hours and days that followed, leaving only Tony as the last collaborator to also abandon Raffaele to his own wits. Giuseppe refused to participate from the outset, saying that it was all two-bit and second-rate in his eyes.

Gennaro, later in the car with Raffaele, blew up in a rage because he felt Raffaele was demanding too much time and money from him, a grown man with two kids to take care of: "You only care about yourself, but I have responsibilities and you don't want to understand that!" Enzo, instead, just faded from sight, doing his own thing elsewhere and not returning to the studio until the entire project had dissolved once again into day-to-day chatter.

Tony was the last to back out, after he and Raffaele had bargained for the time slots and hourly rates and shot a two-minute ad for the show at TeleP's studios. "Singing is my hobby," he told him in what was to be their last conversation about the matter, "and so it comes *after* I take care of my family."

Raffaele complained to me later, when he decided to relaunch the project all on his own, "These people are strange. They make appointments and promises, and then they don't come through. That's not how I want to work. It's better to just do it all alone."

Now, after a three-month hiatus, Tony and I encountered each other again in Giuseppe's studio. Tony wanted me to make his music videos. "So you dumped Raffaele?" he asked me, surprised not to see us together, as if I could come into the studio only while hanging on Raffaele's arm. Tony was one of several people to ask the same question in various ways, each making it sound as if Raffaele and I were lovers. They asked, actually, with the hope that I now felt the same way about him as they always had. I told Tony that Raffaele always behaved jealously with me, signaling in subtle and not so subtle ways to the others to keep their distance from me because I was *his* friend and *he* had found me. Raffaele and I had known each other the longest, for five years, and this had become his claim on me. We were an item and he owned me, according to him. He had great plans for us all of the time, but strangely enough, they were always more useful to him than to me.

One morning my cell phone rang with Raffaele on the other end. "Josey, I'm downstairs. Get ready and come down because we're going to a film audition." He knew I liked film and theater auditions in Naples because if one neomelodico singer attended, then tens more did as well. Talk gets around fast, and competition grinds its gears without any prompting. It turned out that although tens of other singers and their associates were present at the event, all puffed up and roosterlike, with hair gel and biker glasses, long black leather coats, and slow strutting, none of them wanted to engage me in conversation for more than a minute because I was there with Raffaele, who was making it clear that his American was there with *him*. Just as I had *my* ambassadors to some of the rougher neighborhoods and residents of Naples, I was Raffaele's ambassador to the legitimate world of media entertainment that extended, ultimately, to America.

Raffaele's possessiveness was not at all anomalous behavior. Just a month earlier when I hung around Piazza del Carmine on Pasquetta, looking for a team of pilgrims to follow on the ten-kilometer trek to the sanctuary of the Madonna dell' Arco, I was claimed by another young man with a similar sense of ownership. Seeing me with my video camera hanging around their float was all the information Piero needed before he announced, "You're going to come with me like this," taking my right arm under his left, "all the way to Pomigliano, you understand?" The procession attracts thousands of participants, and, Piero told me, the confusion can provide an opportunity for pickpocketing. I needed his protection, he said, gesturing at my video camera. I accepted his offer, but I soon learned that it came with a cost, for if anyone else spoke to me, Piero charged at them with the warning, "Don't you even think of talking to him. He's *my* friend."

I told Tony that, in effect, everyone responded to Raffaele's possessiveness by keeping a distance from me whenever I walked into the studio with him. I also told Tony that on the few occasions when I showed up without Raffaele, others were much more willing to approach me and talk to me. "But the problem was that all that time I spent exclusively with Raffaele was a waste, because he never opened up to me and even lied a lot of the time," I complained to Tony, performing the hard gossip I had heard others engage in on countless occasions.

Tony responded by shaking his head slowly with commiserating disapproval. "The thing about him is that he never has a single word; there's always another after that and the thing changes. And then there's nothing concrete."

I summed it up for us, "*Chiacchiere* [chatter]," I said.

"Yeah," Tony returned.

I was opening new channels between Tony and me. Paradoxically, I was making direct contact with him by telling what I was all about and what I wanted through analogy, through external example. Understanding in this milieu is more potent when it is indexical, and what better way to make a convincing, concrete reference than by gesturing toward shared experience, particularly relational experience. The circuitry of the networks that crosscut this world is alive with gossip and *'nciucci* (gossip with ill intentions), but not because they are the inherent vices of milieus that compete over scarce resources. Nor is it because the infrastructures of interpersonal mediation "on the market" that are commonly perceived as the natural topography of more "developed" and "rationalized" economies like that of northern Italy—with its bureaucracy, professional associations, the law, and the standardized aesthetic ideologies of dominant culture industry—are ill-matched with the desire for the unmediated immediacy of clientelism and familism. In the neomelodica scene, people communicate with people through gossip and 'nciucci because this indexical mode of communicating by example aids in mutual recognition—and entanglement. In a scene where affects are rarely, if ever, considered to be separable from interests, recognizing the person you're dealing with is part of the deal. It's another way of playing *who am I and who are you?*

I didn't just point to what I wanted; I also began searching for it specifically, telling him what pieces were missing from my puzzle and asking him pointed questions. Tony had initially begun our bartering by using the friendship card, but I swiftly tore it up by responding in Neapolitan, for emphasis, "Yeah, but you gotta pay." Knowing now that he'd get nothing out of me for free, he looked for other ways to pay me, in favors. I told him I needed to get to know a couple of female singers and at least one camorrista who channeled money into the scene and squeezed it back out again.

"With that last one, I can't help you. Sorry," he said dismissively and with a look of disgust and the I-take-my-hands-off-the-table gesture (in this case off the steering wheel). "Do you want to meet Cinzia Oscar?" he offered.

"Yes, in fact I just got her number from Antonio the journalist, but I wanted to reach her through an ambassador," I said, making up my own variation of the expression *far 'na mmasciata* (to deliver a message). Fear of collision is pervasive, and the approach of people with whom no prior contact has been established triggers what appears like paranoia. However, because people often puff themselves up with claims of contact, I had reason to doubt Tony. "Who do you know?" I asked him bluntly.

"Well, I know her, I've worked with her. She has a show at Televesuvio and she invited me to go on a few episodes. When I went, the people who hung around backstage were making me uneasy, and I just don't feel good around those types, so I had to stop going and decided to distance myself. She wanted to do more work with me, but I kept my distance.

"You know, she's difficult to contact," he said, as if dangling a carrot before my eyes. He and I were already bargaining, and we both knew. He was promising the lady, and I was already gathering data around his promises. "Because she's a camorrista?" I asked. Tony was quick to answer, which made his words convincing, "No, but she has them *dietro le spalle* [backing her]," he said, trying now to trail off into an ellipsis, but I looked at him and waited for more. He went on, "She has the help of a well-known millionaire who apparently doesn't work with the mob anymore," he said, making an implicit connection between money and the mob, as most people of this milieu tend to do. "But now he has his money and that's the end of it, they say, but I don't believe it. I think there are still some links there. So this guy funds her activities like her television appearances, and he promotes her. He is also the main point man for wedding gigs." Tony could see I was riveted by his account, which was more detailed and direct than most because we were doing business. He looked at me and noticed my piqued interest. As if to calm me down, he warned, "And she won't tell you a word about all that, so you can just forget it."

But Tony's talk did more than establish routes of exchange between us; it also told me about his own career and character. "But you know what happens when you get that kind of help; I could do the same and

questo che vorrei che Marco non crescesse mai. Sono egoista, lo so, ma non mi importa, finchè potrò voglio godermi mio figlio a tempo pieno, infatti lo porto sempre con me e spesso balla con noi."
Un tuo parere su Franco Calone... "Come artista è unico, ha una voce particolare, piace tanto, è un esponente della tradizione classica e moderna, è tra quei pochi che si salvano, come uomo è fantastico, premuroso, buono, sensibile, affabile, dovrebbe essere meno impulsivo, però."

Antonio D'Addio

Cinzia Oscar is a "veteromelodica" of the earlier generations. She took first place at the 1979 Festival di Napoli. She is married to the neomelodico Franco Calone, and in this page from *Sciuè* she says that her husband has a command of both classic and modern music and is a wonderful man, but he could be less impulsive. She also hopes her young son never grows up: "I'm selfish, but I don't care," she comments.

become successful in a couple of days if tomorrow I went and knocked on some doors. But I prefer to struggle and make it on my own, because then the success will be mine. I may not make it, but at least I'll be clean."

I nodded and made agreeing sounds, expressing that I knew he was clean and encouraging him to go on talking.

"Otherwise, you end up having vices to satisfy. You have to compete big with the others and it costs money, paying to be on more and more TV transmissions, doing a better CD at a more costly record company, making more and more videos, pouring more and more money into it, all of this in order to make the money to pay them back. And they own you because you owe them. Then it's better not to sing anymore at all if you really want out."

"And what happens if you just want to quit and not sing anymore, if you'd rather do something else?" I asked, wondering what lay at contact's limit.

"Then you'd better not sing anymore," Tony answered with uncompromising finality.

Our conversation was fired with excitement and a sense of mutual understanding because we were both eager to find level ground between us where we could stand and make a deal. Tony was now asking me how I supported myself, and I explained my struggling situation of grants and loans from friends. Once again he shook his head with commiserating disapproval, this time not of Raffaele but of my "employers" for not paying me enough for what I was doing. I corrected him by telling him that the reason I did my work was because I cared about it, because it was more than work. I wanted to let him know that, in the end, I was like him; I had gone into debt for a passion, hoping to realize the dream of eventually earning a living doing what I loved. Tony took the time to understand all this not out of a genuine interest in me but in the interest of figuring me out. It was of course flattering to have the attention of that rare someone who wanted to understand the reason I found myself in this odd and somewhat dangerous scene, bearing economic hardship, occasional surges of violence (I was once held up at gunpoint on Piazza Garibaldi), and the frustrating inscrutability of diffident, ironic, and often dissimulating people. But I would have been naive to think that recognition necessarily had to come, if ever, from a position of disinterest.

Act 2: Seduction and Colonization

Contact happens near a potent center, like the source of determination and force embodied in a camorrista. Sovereignty, in this milieu, is performed through individual force. It is also the ability to breed fear among other individuals. Camorristi generate fear, in part, through the indeterminacies surrounding them: the unknown extent of their power and their never fully realized potential for violence. These indeterminacies are also self-regenerative. They reverberate in the talk of the quartiere, leaving ellipses in their wake. Many residents—in fear, loyalty, indifference, unknowing, or . . .—make do with these dynamic gaps. Some people, however, try to fill the gaps by drawing closer to the center of determinacy.

"We're not interested in that," Gaetano said to me calmly, almost under his breath. Showing him the photo of the three cops seemed precisely the wrong thing to do—as reckless as putting the photograph on my desktop in the first place. It was Giuseppe's idea to create this dangerous incongruence by pushing me to show Gaetano the photograph. He was having fun now that he had finally been able to introduce me to a camorrista. It was as if he were bringing into the open the uncomfortable doubts that would inevitably swim between Gaetano and me. Giuseppe knew that Gaetano would need to take some time to get to know who I really was, just as he knew that I was afraid of the still-opaque consequences of doing business with a camorrista. Unlike anyone else with whom I collaborated or bartered, Giuseppe not only talked to me freely about my goal of getting to know a camorrista but even made me fear that my wish had come true. This, of course, was play.

It was on a particularly hot afternoon that Giuseppe arranged my first introduction to Gaetano. I had just returned from a few weeks in Palermo and the Aeolian Islands to attend a wedding and find respite in the tranquil waters of paradise. We first picked up Giuseppe's friend Lello to join us for lunch with Giuseppe's mother at home. We pulled up in front of a graying cement building with a cement garden and a thick-rodded green iron gate in front. Giuseppe honked, and after about twenty seconds Lello, an overweight guy in his early thirties with pale skin and receding light brown hair, appeared at a second-story window. Giuseppe shouted in his nearly incomprehensible version of Neapolitan, which did away with consonants, instead opening and closing vowels just barely when they were needed: "Why don't you come over, it's cooler at my house, and there's someone with me." Giuseppe then signaled me to show myself to Lello, so I stuck my head outside and raised it over the roof so that he could see from the other side.

"How's it going?" I shouted.

Lello answered by slowly lifting his hands while turning his palms upward to say, "It goes." Lello ate a lot, slept a lot, and sometimes worked in construction under the scorching heat. Up until last year he worked at a telesales company pushing counterfeit antique furniture, until the business got busted. He was Giuseppe's best friend, but there were periods as long as months during which Giuseppe saw no sign of him. It seemed today the unbearable heat was bringing us all together for an afternoon of commiseration. The paper that morning announced that according to meteorologists the West African rains had caused the Central African climate to shift north, covering northern Africa and southern Europe. The claim of some northern Italians that "Africa begins after Rome" was becoming true. Rampant fires were spreading across southern Italy, Spain, France, and Portugal because of the parched, flammable terrain that the incessant weeks of heat and dryness had been cultivating since June. Now nearing mid-August, we all had a right to complain and even imagine conspiracy.

"I think the CIA is hiding something—" Giuseppe said once Lello was in the car with us.

"Always," I interrupted, but Giuseppe continued with his theory, "—because there's something going on. . . . This is dangerous, this heat, and they know something." As Giuseppe finished his sentence, half of it under his breath, we pulled up in front of another graying building crouched behind a tall, thick black gate. This time no one answered Giuseppe's honking. "It's the king of bingo I'm looking for," Giuseppe explained.

"Why?" I asked.

"Because he's producing a song for us. It's about debts, and he'll sponsor it if we do some advertising for him," he explained.

"And who's going to sing it?" I asked.

"Matteo. He's friends with the boss of this neighborhood and with this guy Mimmo, who owns a big bingo joint in Agnano. The boss is going to produce the CD."

I was impressed with all the new activity that had gone on during my absence. "What does he get out of it?" I asked, referring to the boss.

"A hundred euros whenever Matteo sings," Giuseppe answered with a kind of nonchalance that indicated he was offering only an approximate figure. I found this kind of investment to be extraordinary, considering that everyone complained there was a deep recession in the neomelodica music market. It was a gamble for both Matteo and his patron boss, as Matteo may land only a few gigs and not get much more than a hundred euros per gig.

"Gaetano knows people," Giuseppe reassured me, referring to the fact that the boss could easily convert his wide network into a wide market.

"And you?" I asked Giuseppe about his role in all of this.

"Giuseppe's doing the arrangements on the CD," Lello said, answering for him.

"And how did you get all this together?" I asked, still looking at Giuseppe in the driver's seat.

"I've known Matteo for years. Matteo knows them and they took a liking to Pino and me," Giuseppe explained, referring to the recording studio owner with whom he shares clients. "This one will really do you good, this one," Giuseppe said, finally turning to me with glinting eyes and a flattened palm that chopped slowly up and down diagonally in front of him. The gesture is often accompanied by the expression *te faccio novo novo* (lit. I'll make you new-new, i.e., I'll beat you beyond recognition). He wasn't threatening me directly; he was letting me know that if I fucked up, there could be serious trouble, and not only for me.

That midday seemed like an interminable, boiling prelude to the crowning moment of my research. Slowly, we made our way to Giuseppe's apartment building and upstairs to his first-floor apartment. Finally inside, we sat around in the kitchen, stoned by the excessive heat while Giuseppe made us coffee. "Let's sit in there. It's cooler," he said, motioning with his eyes to the living room. We sat down in front of the standing fan that swiveled back and forth in front of us. A small portrait photograph of Giuseppe's great-grandfather, leaning against the wall behind him, stood on a small shelf. He was a gentleman with a suit and tie of the period, a gallant and demure expression on his face. Giuseppe's mother had told me she came from nobility, if you went back far enough. The only difference now, she continued, is that she lives in these conditions, here, in Civitanova. This neighborhood, when I mention it to others, merits those typical sounds of exclamation that tend to replace words altogether—*Aaah!* or *Oooh!*—along with a shaking of the head or a raised hand that swats the air away, my utterance included.

"Oh, here it's really cool and fresh," I said ironically when Giuseppe followed us into the sitting room with three small glasses of espresso.

He looked back at me crookedly. "Really? Here you are at the hottest point in Naples. This is hell."

His religious reference reminded me of another afternoon when Giuseppe's father told me, "Instead of visiting the church in la Sanità," referring to the folklore pit-stop—a favorite among visitors—where residents of the neighborhood each take charge of one of the skulls displayed in the anteroom and, with morbid obsessiveness, gives the skull a name and cares for it by washing, adorning, talking, and praying to it, "go to the church where the priest didn't want an altar set up for the fallen camorristi of the neighborhood, so in the parking lot on the outside wall of the church they created an independent altar for themselves that they care for." Civitanova, in the grip of camorristi like the one I was about to meet, was to Giuseppe and his family an inverted world of demon-saints. Self-interested, they adapt religious feeling to this-worldly affairs in a black market of devotion, sacrifice, and gains.

Another never-ending, listless hour passed before we found ourselves in Giuseppe's studio, waiting for Gaetano the boss to arrive. I was well into presenting Giuseppe and Lello with the song I had written called "Ammore senza voce" (Love without a voice) when we were interrupted by a shout from outside the window. "Oh! Giuseppe!"

As he got up to go to the window, Giuseppe turned to me and said with excitement, "It's him, the last son of eleven in a family of killers."

The voice outside now shouted with greater emphasis, "Giu-Sep-Pe!"

Giuseppe shouted back, "Uèla!" as he leaned out the window. "I'm here with my American friend."

I went up to the window to show myself, and saw two guys sitting on an expensive-looking red Vespa, one of the latest models. The driver was a thirty-year-old blond, with his hair nearly shaved to the scalp around the sides and a bit left on the top. He wore a small silver earring, a sleeve-less white T-shirt with a hood, and a pair of blue and white floral short-shorts that jarred with his tanned and muscular arms. His bright blue eyes were so alert that they seemed to glare like spotlights. We looked at each other while Giuseppe spoke to him.

"Matteo said he's coming. I'll give you his number if you want."

Gaetano nodded in response and turned to say something to the guy sitting behind him on his Vespa. His companion was a much younger guy of around fifteen wearing a baseball cap and a gray T-shirt with "ENGLAND London" printed across it.

Giuseppe nudged Lello with his elbow at the sight of him. "That's the Pirelli boy," he said with muffled amazement, referring to the other major family who controlled with Gaetano's family a second territory, Rione Basso.

When the two were finally upstairs with us in the studio, Gaetano introduced himself with an extended hand and an intent gaze that he aimed straight into my eyes. "Gaetano," he said, announcing his name. Often I did not merit either a handshake or eye contact—for example, the Pirelli boy greeted me only by quickly nodding in my direction—but because Gaetano and I were about to engage in business, things were different. He turned to Giuseppe and Lello and after some talk and joking, updates and promises, spoke to me once again.

"So, the song is about bingo. I know the owner of the bingo hall and I'll tell him to let us in to film; he doesn't let anyone in there because . . . [he looked down for an instant, his intense blue eyes letting up on me for a moment] . . . they don't have a lot of time for us, so we will have a half hour there and that's that."

The music video I was going to shoot pro bono for Gaetano was about a guy who heaps on himself heavy debts because of his passion for bingo. Bingo halls in Naples, the latest extension of the oldest recorded lottery system of Europe, have sucked in countless individuals and their incomes.[8] Some even go to the plush, carpeted halls dressed in bathrobes and slippers, prepared for a long night. The bingo song for which Gaetano wanted me to shoot the video also describes how the indebted man goes to a usurer to get himself out of his mess, only to make it all worse. The same inner network of associates both rake in their clients' bingo losses and loan-shark it back out at deadly compounding rates, in effect getting payment three times over. On top of it all, they are investing in a music video that will feature their bingo hall, advertising, ironically, the tragedies they can procure for you.

I was soon to discover that there was a similar gang-bang profiteering—that is, the spoils of colluding profiteers who gang-bang the same clients or, as Neapolitans say, *I give them a blowjob and they go and put it in my ass*—occurring between Gaetano and me. Giuseppe and I had devised the plan that I offer to do pro bono work for Gaetano in order to convince him with a good sample music video that I was worthy enough to get on his regular payroll. Gaetano had intentions of launching a talent agency and producing and promoting several singers, in addition to

Matteo. His "good name" afforded him the automatic inheritance of his father's talent repertoire, as 'O lione senior had also been an impresario in his day until about a decade earlier. It was my alleged interest to get on board an agency destined for success. According to everyone—Gaetano, Matteo, and even Giuseppe—I had to pay *now* for those future returns. It was the same principle most people, Giuseppe included, followed when buying city jobs with money, favors, or by pulling on the cords of affects/interests that bound others to them in friendship: pay now for a secure future. In this environment of scarce resources and high and crafty competition, survival is indeterminate even when momentarily accomplished; the more enduring kinds of security provided by the state and the camorra are the privilege of only a few who manage to weave themselves close to such nodes of power. Those who are thus networked and have access to or sit fatly at any such node will inevitably sell their access to others. These people "double themselves" when they make it a privilege for others to engage them in such transactions and put a price on the privilege itself. In doing so, they also double their profits. It was according to this principle that Gaetano decided that I should do preliminary video work for him to prepare for my privilege to do pro bono work on the bingo song.

Specifically, he wanted me to film and edit a vignette of him singing Matteo's latest song, "Your dressed heart," right then and there in Giuseppe's studio. There was no refusing Gaetano. Giuseppe had to tie up all his equipment and play the arrangements for Gaetano while he sang, and I had to shoot it. Gaetano doesn't know how to sing, yet his delight and whim became our imperative; we worked in the service of his limitless display of self. It was enforced "play":

> What good is a wedding dress if your heart is already dressed?
> I'm tired of living alone. My bed is bigger than me.
> I only want a drop of true love. Give me a part of you.[9]

And so, unexpectedly, we found ourselves in Giuseppe's overbearingly hot studio laughing with, but not at, Gaetano. With the bottom half of his T-shirt rolled up to expose his belly, he sang indiscriminately across several keys the lyrics to Matteo's song. He was shy yet determined to take hold of the mic. He instructed Giuseppe to make a sound recording on his equipment and me to record it on video while the shirtless and sweaty Matteo guided him, strophe by strophe, through the song.

Gaetano's performance and our cooperation lasted for over an hour before we could put it aside and wind up our meeting with summaries and some final closing chatter. Gaetano, of course, conducted the conversation; he initiated each new topic, held the power to ask questions and have them answered, and claimed his turn merely by opening his mouth and speaking. The usual peacocklike competition among men was visibly absent, the chaos of color and feather giving way to the single voice, gaze, and gesture of the boss. Every now and then during the conversation Giuseppe winked at me in a gesture that said, "See what I mean about Gaetano?" I smiled back at him each time, quickly and cautiously.

Gaetano's demands were as great as his largesse. At one point during his song recording he turned to Giuseppe and complained, "You have a mic that doesn't work too good. You can't hear good," while shaking it in his hand and looking up at Giuseppe for a response.

Giuseppe joined him in complaint by answering, "This equipment is giving me more trouble than you know . . . like the cost . . ."

Gaetano immediately picked up on the tone that Giuseppe was pretending to be using casually, with indifference. "What? How much do you owe?" he asked with sudden alertness.

"I have this guy I buy stuff from, but he still wants another 1,500 euros. Man," Giuseppe elaborated, still maintaining an air of nonchalance.

Gaetano's expression was that of someone about to fix a problem. He listened attentively, absorbing what Giuseppe was saying, thinking of the solution, which would come to him later, when it could be imbricated in more of his own demands. Similarly, when Matteo was admiring the fancy cell phone the young guy who had accompanied Gaetano—later it was revealed that this was his cousin—pulled out of his pocket, Gaetano asked, "You want it, Matteo? You want one?" When Matteo didn't answer but instead continued to ask Gaetano's cousin questions on how to use it, Gaetano insisted in a louder voice: "Do you *want* one?"

Matteo tried to quell Gaetano's excitement by responding, "Naw, naw, that's all right."

Giuseppe, in fact, had initially told me that Gaetano's impulse to help could be easily excited. He told me if I were to announce to Gaetano that I had a video format compatibility problem because I used an American video camera, Gaetano would have asked me what I needed to overcome the obstacle. Even if I had told him a PAL video camera would solve the problem quickest, he would have put one in my hands the next day.

Although Giuseppe had the foresight to imagine such potential benefits, he forgot for a moment that Gaetano's capital was magnetic, ready to attract and bind through its force. As we were all saying our good-byes, Giuseppe mentioned a resident in the area who complained about the way he parked his car. "Who is it?" Gaetano immediately asked, sitting up straight in his chair, now more alert than ever.

"No, no, it's just some idiot," Giuseppe said in an effort to deflate the quickly escalating issue. Each of us—Giuseppe, Matteo, and I—were hesitant to enjoy too much of Gaetano's largesse, struggling not to gamble beyond a dangerously shifting threshold where contact becomes association, indebtedness, or capture. We had a business plan to work out, but Gaetano repeatedly tried to splinter our exchange into realms beyond the music. But the truth of the matter was that the passionate affects in which Gaetano's largesse was entangled and the avaricious interests that puppeteered his multiple demands were all part of the same netting that he cast over those around him.

It wasn't long before Giuseppe and the others were calling Gaetano by his endearing diminutive, Gaetanino (Little Gaetano); by the same token, it wasn't long before Gaetanino took his own share of confidence. That is, he took liberties with the boundaries between Giuseppe and Pino's business and his own.

One afternoon Gaetano was sitting at the large, empty desk in Giuseppe's studio, flipping through the blank pages of a red date book that had been lying there for months. Several other people encircled him: Giuseppe, his friends Lello, Pino, Matteo, and another singer called Antonio. All of them were heatedly discussing the idea of opening a music agency called 'O Lione Music in the office space adjacent to Giuseppe's and above Pino's small recording studio. Gaetano didn't say much, but when he did, it seemed only he had the power of illocutionary speech. However, the flow of conversation was noticeably pooling around the obstacles Pino kept tossing in its path. He repeatedly named the landlord of the building as an insurmountable obstacle, but said that he knew of other spaces to rent farther down the street. Gaetano effectively removed these obstacles with a dismissive wave of the hand, an elongated vowel, and brief, self-assured declarations such as "It's not a problem" and "I'll take care of it."

Matteo, Gaetano's singer sidekick, talked double-time, clearly irritated by Pino's resistance. "Ah, naw! Don't go saying that! The landlord will agree to rent to us; there's no reason he shouldn't. Don't even say something like that!"

Giuseppe, clearly the craftiest protagonist in the room, played both sides by tossing doubts and ambiguity in either direction: "It's true the landlord is a little funny . . . but you know, Gaetano can pay—and he can also pay some extra in advance. . . ."

Giuseppe's position, just like his strategy of continually repositioning himself among competing adversaries, was based in ambiguity. On the one hand, he was excited to finally get in on the big bucks that could come only in the long-term security of a city job or in the potential profits of a gamble with the camorra. On the other hand, he was frustrated by the fact that the city job and the gamble in crime were inextricably intertwined in a single knot that was itself a game of ambiguity; how much and for how long was Gaetano going to "take confidence with us" before giving something back? How long could Giuseppe continue to invest in this relationship without getting any returns? Who was going to give the first returns—Gaetano with payment or Matteo with a city job through his brother Giovanni's connections? Lately Giuseppe had been getting fed up with the constant invasive presence of Gaetanino and Matteo, who appeared in the studio night after night, wanting to try out this song, change that other, and chatter a lot in between, never accomplishing much at all. In addition, Giuseppe was getting heat from Pino, who had to endure the same interruptions and demands in his recording studio below. Pino resented Giuseppe for having enticed the whole ordeal into their territory to begin with, courting Matteo and Gaetano and the alleged money and city jobs they had in their pockets, ready to pull out. So far no one had seen a cent or a job.

Just a few days before, Pino and Giuseppe had a heavy and heated discussion in which Pino told Giuseppe he didn't like those two guys coming around all the time like they did. Giuseppe was defensive through most of the discussion, clearly trying to protect certain interests of his own. "This is work, I need the money, but don't you think that I'm fed up with it, too? This is how I make my living, and they're not paying me, wanting *this* and *that* all the time. I don't have time for it." It was a complicated conversation where Giuseppe slid between, on the one hand, a challenge to Pino's latent, mounting declaration that Giuseppe would have to somehow dissociate himself from Matteo and Gaetanino and, on the other, a concession to Pino that the situation was intolerable. Part of the complication was due to the fact that the two of them were essentially powerless, in the long run, and they seemed to know it. They could only deal with the situation as it developed, rather than ending it altogether. The wheels had already begun turning, and now they had to ride.

Something was building in Giuseppe while the pressures stacked up on the outside. That something grew in the narrow space for maneuver left to him by his impending marriage, zero financial stability, and the simultaneously real and elusive prospects of making it on the music scene or making it into a city job—if only he invested more time and patience in Giovanni, Matteo's brother, by first investing in Matteo, but not before investing in Gaetano. "So if nothing works out, I'm going to get my alliances together and take charge of l'ambiente here," he said to me later that week, his eyes seeming bigger and bluer than before while he gestured out his kitchen balcony. Giuseppe, like many others who found personal sovereignty in the art of making do, was, unlike many others, considering that organized crime might be the highest of all such arts.

The fact that Giuseppe was getting nothing of what he wanted while he continued to give a lot to Matteo and Gaetano, all the while struggling to pacify Pino, made him more agitated than ever. He raised his voice many times with a tone of dead certainty at Pino, Matteo, and even Gaetanino during the next week. "I need to work . . . but it's *not* going like that. You ask me to do *this* and *that* when I got things to *do*! We gotta work on one thing at a time, finish it and then let me do *my* work!" Things got so bad that one day he decided he wasn't going into the studio at all. "I need a vacation," he said to me, point-blank. We decided to drive around Naples with his friend Lello, touring the *zone malfamate* (infamous neighborhoods) for my benefit.

Before beginning our tour after a lunch of linguini and clams, fresh *mozzarella di bufala* and *bresaola,* the air-cured, spice-rubbed, thinly sliced beef produced in the Alpine valley of Lombardy, an extravagance in Civitanova, Giuseppe announced, "I better let Gaetano know that we're not coming to the studio." We were in the car driving toward Gaetano's corner of the neighborhood while Giuseppe took his usual fast and reckless turns, often onto the wrong side of the street. With each entry into a new street, it seemed the neighborhood took a turn for the worse, becoming more and more dilapidated, trash-strewn, grayer, desperate.

Finally we pulled up to a three-story building with a chipped and graffiti-marked face, pockmarked with laundry-swathed recessed balconies with unadorned, straight square bars. Each balcony had its Persian blinds lowered to a different height, adding to the disorder. When Giuseppe shouted out, "Gae-tan-o!" a woman eventually appeared.

Her age was camouflaged by the hanging laundry from which she peered and called back to us, "He's not here."

"You'll tell him I won't be at the studio?" Giuseppe called out of the car, across the lot of weeds, trash, and dust, to the half-obscured figure now leaning out between the immaculately clean drying sheets and underwear.

"All right," she answered, and then, after a strange pause in which we all participated while looking in her direction, she went inside.

Giuseppe drove us away, past a similar but larger building that looked as if it were under construction, tucked behind a mound of trash and dirt. "It's under *de*construction," Giuseppe corrected me. "It's where they sell drugs."

When we reached the main boulevard of the neighborhood, Giuseppe mumbled something and suddenly honked with several small punches to the horn. "Is it him?" Lello said from the backseat.

"Yeah, it's him," responded Giuseppe, turning into a school parking lot and honking once again. A few seconds later, Gaetanino pulled up in a shiny car (not a Smart Car or Mini Cooper) with air conditioning—the windows were closed—and Matteo in the passenger seat. We all got out and huddled around Giuseppe while he talked to the driver. He told him he had business to take care of at home and so wouldn't be going into the studio. A noticeable change came over Gaetanino's face when he heard these words, like the disappointment and frustration of a child. Giuseppe of course picked up on it immediately and reinforced his excuse by repeating it, a common practice in Neapolitan talk, adding a bit here and there to touch it up the second and third time around. Absorbing that this was reality, whether or not it was an excuse, Gaetanino started to respond in words, asking if Giuseppe would be around the following day. "Yeah, tomorrow I'll be around, don't worry . . . it's just today."

When we had finally completed our good-byes, drawn out and repetitive, to be sure, Giuseppe, Lello, and I got back in the car and drove off. Giuseppe said only one word: "*Vedi?* [You see?]."

"You complain about the detachment of Americans," he elaborated, "but I tell you, the thing you hate is the thing I miss . . . because here it's just the opposite: They're too invasive, always at you, and you don't know how to get away. You smile at someone and right away they're on your doorstep and you have obligations. The first chance I get I'm coming to America and I'm not coming back!"

Giuseppe's words reminded me to get it into my head that I, too, had obligations now. Ever since Giuseppe had proposed to Gaetano and Matteo that I do a pro bono music video for them in exchange for the (alleged) exposure I would get through having my work associated with them, I was tying myself to them in indefinite, unseen ways. For example, I was required to go into the studio with Giuseppe the next day to present the sample editing work Gaetano had asked me to do the week before. I was catching on that when that time came Gaetano would hold before me yet another hoop to jump through before I could get to my goal of getting to know him.

Recently, however, it was Matteo, not Gaetano, who was holding out the hoops. He had ongoing requests that I take pictures of him for his album cover, that I touch them up with special effects using Photoshop, that I put them on CDs for him, that I take some more pictures downstairs, in front of the recording equipment, outside, maybe do a shoot. . . . In fact, the bulk of our interaction consisted of his quick demands and the expectation that I respond quickly with action. He often interrupted me while I discussed my video work with Giuseppe and Gaetano to tell me to take pictures of him sitting before the large American flag Giuseppe had hanging on his wall. It was becoming incessant, and Giuseppe noticed it, too. "Ah, leave it alone, you're going to spoil him. This guy and his vanity can never get enough," Giuseppe said, not with smiling humor, but with irritation and a screwed-up face.

Matteo ignored him and kept his pose ready for me, leaning up against the flag while looking upward now pensively, now artistically in sidelong, abstract directions. "Come on, come on, let's go!" I noticed Matteo was also pushing Giuseppe around. He wanted one song to be ready faster; he wanted to work on the voice of another piece right now. Gaetano was participating in these demands only by seconding Matteo, who led the way.

Giuseppe eventually took a stand and declared loudly, clearly pissed-off, "This can't go on this way. I have to work on one thing at a time. I don't want to hear about this piece and that piece all at once. I can't play around, I need to sit down and do my work and I can't be answering every demand."

Matteo had a fishy, half-smiling glint in his eyes that betrayed his manipulative designs to inflate his bartered, secondhand power, the power of a boss's sidekick. He was behaving like a two-bit boss, running amok with his demands without the style, calm, and self-confidence that Gaetano exuded. He was like the small child-monster who knew daddy would force anyone to change their no to a yes. In a way, Matteo was more dangerous than Gaetano; he didn't know how to handle his power, how to follow the rules.

It was the same principle that organized the throng of children that attacked me in a small piazza near the central train station one late afternoon. "So you picked a fight with my friend here yesterday, didn't you?" said a four-foot-tall bully of eight while tapping his index finger against my chest.

"I've never seen you or your friend before in my life," I said, pushing the child out of my way before walking across the piazza toward home. Almost immediately, five more children appeared and began hurling an endless rain of broken cobblestones and trash at me while shouting at high volume epithets like *bucchin'* (blowjob) and *omm' 'e mmerda* (man of shit). The commotion was great, and, tellingly, shutters began shutting on the building facades all around the piazza. In most other cases spectators would have gotten deeply involved. On another occasion that I witnessed, a wildly vocal and gesticulatory argument between two men attracted a crowd of twenty people, some of whom argued with each other about the original argument with equal violence. On yet another occasion a husband and wife conducted a dramatic and angry performance in the middle of the busy vicolo outside my window for twenty minutes as I and many other residents came out onto balconies, some with cigarettes to smoke, others with food and drink, just to watch. This time, however, it was clear that these were children of powerful camorristi whom no one wanted to cross.

The belligerent arrogance that Matteo had in common with these children was noticeably absent in Gaetano's behavior. Gaetano made sure to at least make interactions appear as though they were exchanges rather than simple exploitation or extortion. He was genteel, attentive, and interested, almost as if he had gone through workplace management training, or even diversity training, when it came to dealing with me. This came out most clearly one Saturday afternoon when Gaetano, Giuseppe, and I were to meet at Giuseppe's office to discuss a TV commercial Gaetano wanted me to shoot for his burgeoning agency.

I walked down Via Tiberio of the neighborhood Soprascavi toward Giuseppe's studio, but with still a block to go, I encountered Gaetano on the deserted sidewalk, coming toward me. "Giuseppe's not coming today, but since I told you to come at 3:30, I thought I should come here and meet you anyway so you wouldn't be coming for no reason," he said to me with deliberation and emphasis. It was common for appointments to dissolve without warning or to be deferred for hours by the repeated cell-phone promise, "I'm on my way, I'm on my way." Saturdays were particularly susceptible to this inertia, as especially delicious and elaborate meals, followed by card games, visitors, and soccer on TV made the home a snug space for family and other intimates. Gaetano's attentiveness was therefore impressive that afternoon.

We walked the last block together until Gaetano pulled out a set of keys and unlocked Giuseppe's studio door. With this one simple action Gaetano's power welled up and spilled over into Giuseppe's territory. Giuseppe had never given his keys to anyone before; Gaetanino was taking over. Suddenly the office of chaos had completely transformed. We entered to find an unfathomable silence surrounding us, devoid of the usual chatter and interruptions, singing, and blaring music coming from the speakers, the crotch grabbing and the shoving, and the multiple entries and exits of various characters who must always make their presence and leave-taking clamorously known. Gaetanino made his way straight to what had become his desk and opened the red date book and began writing.

He was composing the text that he wanted me to put in the TV commercial in successive flashing bytes: "'O Lione Music / Organizes / Ceremonies / Weddings / Baptisms / for information / contact / tel. 081.233.#### or 327.445.####." Gaetano had told me to bring all of my equipment and be ready to work. I started by shooting him sitting at his desk and then shot a postcard image of one of the four singers he wanted to showcase, Tommy Riccio, whose 1993 hit "'Nu Latitante" (A fugitive) was for a certain crowd a neomelodico anthem. I next dumped the footage onto my laptop and edited it with the text Gaetano wanted me to integrate. When I showed him the final product, the thing that impressed him most was that I knew how to write his nickname, 'O lione.

What in conversations with lesser figures in this contact zone would have been taken for dangerous curiosity was, in Gaetano's case, taken as admiring interest and respect. Gaetano was the first of his kind I was getting to know, and it was immediately clear that the rules of communication were actually more relaxed. Gaetano, unlike most of the people with whom I communicated on the neomelodica scene, was not a moving target. Unlike most others, he had no fear of identifications. Others considered identifying questions, like "information," as high-risk and linked to blame. On the contrary, for Gaetano it was his very identity that generated his power. This was the reason he wanted his historically infamous nickname smack in the middle of his music agency and the TV commercial we were making to promote it. In fact, Gaetano announced that he wanted me to shoot a twenty-minute infomercial. His expansive enthusiasm even eventuated in his own live prime-time regional TV show by the same name, *'O Lione Music,* on which he regularly appeared. Gaetano's freedom of self-identification and the mode of excess in which he indulged were not related as are cause and effect; together they constituted a single loop that he could run with greater and greater speed, if he wanted. The more extravagantly public his self-identification, the more self-assured his power appeared and, therefore, was.

I took the opportunity to ask him what his nickname meant, and he gave me that slightly screwed-up look with eyes that looked off somewhere else, the look I saw often on the faces of men who felt they should know things and have answers to everything, but found themselves challenged. "Well, *Lione* . . . was my grandfather's name, and he was called 'O Lione marinaro [Lion of the sea] because he worked on the docks.[10] Then my father lived in Rione Basso and he was a . . . [here Gaetano drew a diagonal line across his cheek from ear to mouth with his thumb, which was protruding from his shut fist] . . . he was a *pezzo grosso* [lit. big piece]," he continued, after a solemn pause.

I said, *"Figlio 'e bucchin'* [son of a blowjob]," properly participating in our talk by showing him through repetition that I knew what he was saying. I used the expression that meant a man is so crafty that he managed to get conceived from a mere blowjob.

Encouraged, Gaetano went on, "Yeah. So once he knifed someone to death in a fight, and so they called him 'O lione, too."

Giving up on the meaning of the name, I asked Gaetano about his father. He told me he is still in Rione Basso, where he continues to be a pezzo grosso. Then something extraordinary occurred: I asked him to tell me his surname, and he told me without any hesitation or suspicion. "It's Ubaldi," he said, rather happy to talk about himself. I asked him why he lives in Civitanova if his father is still in Rione Basso. "Because he took on another woman and so that the two women didn't mess each other up, he put my mother and us in Civitanova. But *I* am his real son. . . . Those others are just half-sons." This, of course, was not really what he meant; he wanted to underline the fact that they were bastard children, born out of wedlock. "And that's why *I* run Civitanova, because *I'm* there," Gaetano concluded, plain and simple.

Our conversation, revolving around concrete facts that I was later able to verify with other confidants such as Giuseppe and even an anti-camorra magistrate, flowed like no other conversation I had ever had with any participant of this milieu. Gaetano's self-same solidity was equivalent to his impressive power just as his power emanated from this very self-same solidity. I was at the eye of the storm, where the indeterminacies surrounding the moment-by-moment power negotiations of the swaggering, puffed-up pretenders to power gave incessantly unclear answers, fired improbable threats, and staked doubled-up claims of greatness, had no place. Gaetano was the eye of the storm, where determinacy pulsed and from which his incalculable potency radiated. He was one and the same with the core of honorable manhood derived from personal force. Here, at the center of determinacy, there were no secrets to be kept or told. It was only in the vast everyday that radiated out from this core that people shared, kept, and told secrets in the ongoing day-to-day art of tapping into this force that already bound them together in indeterminate ways.

Act 3: Eye of the Storm

Crime clan affiliates seduce people with whom they come into contact. The relationship between an affiliate and a not entirely unwilling associate is built not only on fear but also on the promise of personal power. For many people engaged in the art of making do and willing to make moral compromises, that power initially means moral/political economic sovereignty.

However, as the compromises get bigger, the danger for moral and economic disaster, like imprisonment, also gets bigger. Dealing with this danger effectively requires the use of a different kind of power, the individual force of a capoclan who will also protect and nurture you, your family, and your friends. Clan affiliates mimic the affective fecundity of the family to seduce recruits. Force itself is seductive, registered in the act of a man giving himself over to another, more powerful man in pursuit of "brotherhood" and shared powers of determination.

Gaetano, Giuseppe, Matteo, his brother Giovanni, and I were hanging out in Giuseppe's sweaty, airless studio when Gaetano suddenly turned to me and said, "Jason, I want you to come with me and do some filming at my son's birthday party tonight."

I was more than willing to take him up on his offer to enter the private world of his family life, and I knew it would be important to finally spend time outside the studio alone with Gaetano. However, because I wasn't just an eager researcher soaking up experiences but an "interested" individual with services to barter, I attempted to maintain my sovereign power to make my own decisions. I dissimulated my eagerness by displaying two things: that I wasn't available whenever he simply wanted and that I wasn't completely willing to do work for him when there was no talk of money or some other kind of compensation. "I'll let you know if I manage to free up some time," I told him, casually.

"No! No!" he said while gripping my forearm, telling me that I had it all wrong. "The party's tonight at six o'clock," he said with a raised voice that said, *you can't let me down.* His prosody was affectively persuasive, and it contained a kernel of violence.

"All right, all right. It will work," I answered him.

Immediately I felt I had given in entirely too soon. I could have, for example, pretended I had to make some calls first to rearrange my other plans. However, I wasn't quick enough to come up with the performance, and I regretted it. Sure enough, Gaetano had already self-assuredly filed away our accord and slipped back into the talk, banter, irritation, demands, and complaints that daily shrank the already cramped studio to half its size. However, that he quickly dispelled my feeble facade with little effort gave him no reason to hover over the matter and gloat with the sense of self-possession and authority that I clearly lacked. Instead, he treated his conquest as a matter of course. Apparently, he was concerned only with ultimate, and what he trained himself to perceive as inevitable, effects: the full power to extort what he could from others.

Another half hour passed before Gaetano turned to me and said, "You wanna go now?" He spoke in a tone that was not assertive or demanding like the many others who wanted to either vaunt their new American possession or expressly demonstrate their authority over me by dictating how things were going to proceed. Unlike the many *guappi 'e cartone* (cardboard guappi) I had often found myself mixed up with, Gaetano behaved with gentility. It was because he could afford to do so.

We drove out through the more crumbling parts of the city, where two fleshy older women boiled ears of corn in cauldrons on the sidewalk and sold them on sticks. Ashen faces peered out from the dilapidated, shuttered nineteenth-century buildings, watching and watching. A guy was slumped on a cushion on the threshold of his basso, through which you could distinguish a sweaty bed with an incongruous figure sprawled on it, the blue light of TV flickering in the otherwise lightless, browning dwelling. On the busy streets kids were packed on motorbikes and done up with gluelike hair gel, Anastasia sunglasses, and tight, ill-fitting red T-shirts with *Liverpool* and *Cuba* etched across them, knockoff soccer shirts produced in a *fabbrica abusiva* (unlicensed factory) and pumped out to the low-end chain stores called Pizzeria, Vietato Fumare (No Smoking), and Omonimo (Namesake) for 5 euros each.[11] The last of these stores had a pizzeria abusiva in its basement where you could eat, but not leave with, your promotional margherita as a reward for buying one such article of clothing. Often poor and hungry and needing clothes, I had many lunches there, each time looking a little more neomelodico.

We drove a bit farther and reached an intersection of two narrow residential streets. They met at a small lot hosting a couple of naked trees. The buildings were from the 1980s, with blocklike shapes and faded solid colors like pea-green and salmon-pink layered with graffiti. Echoing out from behind the drying underwear hanging on the balconies were the shrieks of crying babies, the frustrated, angry responses of their mothers, the clanging of dirty plates, and the interminable squealing of a cell phone. There were cars parked in various positions at various angles, and people either leaning up against them or zooming in and out of them on Vespas. Nearly all of them acknowledged Gaetano, and many of them had things to ask and declare: *What did you do about that appointment?*; *I talked to Gigi already*; *Where's Pino? I haven't seen him yet.* The neighborhood swarmed and surged in a small vortex around this thirty-year-old boss, and me, as still more people converged around our car.

When Gaetano started to get out, I began to ask him if the party was in this neighborhood or elsewhere. But he misunderstood because, as is often the case in this milieu, he didn't wait until I finished my question: "Don't worry. I command here," he said to me with a look of seriousness and reassurance. While I looked back at him in silence, it took a few moments for me to realize that he had understood the affective charge of my question—my apprehension—rather than its specific content. And he was accurate nonetheless.

After some brief chatting and walking about the intersection with some of the men and women who had approached him, Gaetano returned to me in the car and started the engine. Before grabbing the stick shift, he looked at the stubble on my face and said that we needed to get cleaned up: "Is it OK if we go and get a shave?" he asked. His apparent deference, however slight, was unusual. Most guys would just grunt something, indicating that there was "a little" deviance from the plan and, without my knowing what happened, I'd find myself in a lavish banquet hall an hour away at the foot of Vesuvius instead of a pirate TV studio at the central train station. It was common in this scene not to plan carefully for things or to separate one thing from the other. It was normal that I should accompany Gaetano on his errands, even the errand that "came up suddenly" before we went into the barbershop.

Just next door to the barbershop was the local soccer fan club. It was housed in a small, shabby building with the word *Ultras* scrawled in graffiti lettering above a wide door. Before getting out of the car, I reached for my laptop.

"I command here. Remember that," Gaetano said to me, putting his hand on my arm, preventing me from grabbing the computer. He then got out of the car and walked inside the pool hall, leaving the doors unlocked and the windows down.

I hesitated for a couple of seconds before following him, empty-handed, leaving the car just as he had left it, unlocked and vulnerable. I followed him into a dark space with a pool table, two video games, some tall wooden stools, and two black pleather armchairs. In one of these sat the president of the club, an overtanned, bald, middle-aged man with about six silver earrings in each ear, shiny against his dark, leathery, wrinkled skin. He wore baggy brown shorts, flip-flops, and a T-shirt. Gaetano walked right up to him and stood before his still-seated figure. "I know what happened," he announced to him.

I leaned up against the pool table and settled in to listen. It sounded as if it were going to be heavy. Once he and Gaetano began talking, the president of the club twitched his leg, jiggling the flesh of his tanned thigh. He looked angry and helpless before the boss.

The conversation was elliptical and difficult to follow, but the main point was clear. A friend of Gaetano's had wronged the club president, and Gaetano was warning him not to retaliate. "I know. I know. But he's *my* friend and you *don't* shoot him," Gaetano shouted twice in response to the angry, frustrated protests of his interlocutor.

The seated man fell silent. Then, as if all were fine and friendly, Gaetano said to me, "Jason, come and meet Lucio, he's the president of the soccer fan club."

I moved toward them and shook Lucio's hand. Lucio said nothing and remained seated.

Gaetano then shouted, "Hey, you should do some filming here! Check this out," as he pointed to photographs of different soccer players and graffiti images of video game monsters on the walls. I panned the room and then went outside to film the lettering on the building. I pointed it at the club president for a bit, and he turned to Gaetano to ask him who I was. Gaetano answered that I was American. Gaetano's answer belied what the question really meant: *What kind of power does this guy have?* Gaetano's answer, which I frequently heard others in this milieu give to define me, meant, *He's OK. And he's irrelevant.*

Gaetano then told me to follow him into the barbershop next door. It was a tiny room crammed with four barber's chairs. Gaetano introduced me to the barber, a tall, balding, heavyset man in his fifties with a thin gray goatee and smiling eyes. Then Gaetano introduced me to another man, much shorter and seated in one of the chairs next to the door. He had a large dirty cast on his right arm and hand. "This is the owner of the shop," Gaetano explained.

I made a special nod with my head out of respect to his authority and my presence in his space. I asked him what happened to his arm.

He started to answer begrudgingly when a young guy with a dark beard, lounging in a barber's chair said loudly, "He took a dive in the toilet." The others laughed, so I did too.

The heavyset barber asked me where I was from. I answered, and it inspired conversation between him and the others, seemingly to my exclusion, as was often the case. Making conversation in this milieu is a contrapuntal performance. You need to assert yourself to participate by raising your voice, interrupting, repeating yourself, holding on to someone's arm to get their attention, and moving up into their face, bodily. As far as everyone in the barbershop was concerned, my participation ended as soon as my response was over. It could continue only if I pushed myself verbally and physically back into the interaction.

"Come," the heavyset man suddenly said to me before putting an apron around my neck and fixing a small cloth collar under it. Once I sat down, he guided my head back on the headrest.

Just then Gaetano asked, "Jason, where's your video camera?"

I pointed to the other side of the room, "It's over there charging. You want to film me?" I asked, surprised at his taking this kind of playful interest in me.

"Of course, we *have to* have a film of you getting a shave in Naples," he answered warmly. He then picked up the camera and asked, "How do I do this?" He held it up at my eye level while searching with his fingers for the "on/off" button. I reached out and opened the LCD screen for him, and he quickly blurted out, "I know, I know that!" pulling the camera out of my range. Realizing he wanted to be in full charge, I guided him verbally through setting up the camera. Meanwhile, the barber had already lathered me up with a thick, pasty cream that he worked with a brush over and over again on my face until it became slick. Gaetano caught the tail end of this process on film, moving about me with the camera in his hands. The barber then took out a straight razor and, with striking casualness, moved the blade fast and choppily against my four-day beard, starting at my left cheek. In the mirror I could see *Cuba* written in white letters vertically along the red-clad torso of Gaetano, who continued to scan me with the camera. My eyes darted from his concentrated, flashing blue eyes to the straight razor scraping under my chin, clearing bristle and cream away in deft, crispy strokes.

"*Jasòo*—Cesare—what's your name?" the barber asked me, laughing.

"It's Jason," said Gaetano, before I could answer.

The barber continued, "Because I didn't know how to say it and Giuseppe over there [he gestured with his eyes to the young bearded guy still sitting behind us] said *Cesare* [Caesar]. Do you understand?"

Anytime someone expressed doubt about my competency in the Neapolitan language, my pride got bruised. I decided to recuperate it by ignoring his question and one-upping him, "No, that would be *Cesarone*." Not only did the name sound more like "Jason" if you mumbled it loosely enough; it meant "Big Caesar" to boot.

"Yeah, that's right, that's right!" the barber responded, laughingly congratulating me on my wit. Neapolitans of this milieu often feel they are the wittiest and the prettiest of them all. They express a special kinship and respect for an outsider who can match them, dubbing him '*nu most*' (a monster). However, not only did I demonstrate a capacity for improvised artfulness; I also entered into street style by engaging in honorific nicknaming. By calling myself Big Caesar, connoting greatness and strength, I took on a nickname that I seemingly acquired through a particularly violent encounter in which I had demonstrated superior power. To add to the artfulness of my joke, honorific nicknames are also given ironically.[12]

When the barber pressed the blade even closer to the flesh on my face, this time the second shave, he mumbled, laughing, "Cesarone."

Gaetano asked me if I wanted my haircut, too. I didn't want all the lines and spikes I was seeing, so I tried to gracefully slip out of the offer. "I'll think about it," I said.

However, without asking and in a fluid movement that blended with the shaving, the barber began trimming my hair, cutting my sideburns, and fixing up the nape of my neck. When he swathed his hands with a heavy gel that he massaged into my hair to make it stand up on end, I tried to look like I was happy with it.

That's when Gaetano shouted, "Uàaa! Look at Cesarone! Look at how he puts on airs. Look at him, the American there in the chair, but instead he doesn't have a cent!" The others laughed loudly at the cardboard American.

Next I filmed the straight razor scraping Gaetano's jugular. He lay there, still, in the same chair I had occupied. He watched silently while the blade cut roughly through cream and bristle to uncover clear, clean skin. I felt a thrill in taking long, close shots of the boss as he lay there, vulnerable. I moved about him with the video camera with a newfound sense of liberty and intimacy. The only sign of life he gave off was in his light blue eyes, which glowed against the blank white of his creamy jaw. They were intense.

When the shave was finished, I started to pack up my video camera. I watched in my peripheral vision to see if Gaetano was paying the owner, who continued sitting in the corner by the door, or if this was free for him, and consequently for me. Something wasn't free, however. He discreetly asked the owner, under his breath, "How much?" The owner, equally discreet, answered with a figure, and I saw a ten euro bill slip into the barber's hand. Gaetano turned away and moved out the door. "Are you ready, Jason?"

When I followed Gaetano to his car, I noticed the bald, tan fan club president outside his shop, smoking a spliff with a buddy. They looked at us without saying anything. Gaetano nodded at them and said, "We'll see each other later."

When we were in the car and had pulled away, I turned to Gaetano and asked, "What happened in there with the Ultras president?"

Gaetano didn't flinch at my curiosity. "Oh, that? The other night he got robbed and the guy who did it is a friend of mine, and he knows it. I warned him not to go and give him a beating. And he knows he shouldn't, because it's what I *say*."

"How much did the guy get away with?"

"About 150 euros," he said without hesitation, with a down-curled lower lip while shaking his head slightly.

I repeated his gesture in words, "Yeah, that's not much," making sure to build consensus so that he'd continue to talk openly. I recalled that "theft" and "cheating" have flexible meanings; often it's a matter of how much and from whom, rather than the principle of it.

Many people blame being swindled on their own lack of *furbizia* (craftiness), before they blame it on the moral turpitude of others. For them, the moral dilemmas of day-to-day life are a given, and one needs to remain *sveglio* (awake). They react by preparing themselves better for the next engagement they are bound to have with their swindlers. Successfully performing the art of making do often requires that people keep their networks intact and continue to engage even their adversaries. Even "adversary" has a highly flexible meaning. Here it is not always the details of making do, but the general arc of it that leads to personal sovereignty.

Some people respond to being swindled by swindling their swindlers in return. When the opportunity arises, some people may do this quietly, content with the private knowledge of their victory. Others do it publicly, giving their adversary a sfregio. They publicly subordinate their adversaries through disfigurement.

Then there are only a certain few who can react to the furbizia of others with direct violent retribution. These people generate and maintain their personal sovereignty through individual force. Gaetano was reminding the Ultras president that he was not one of those certain few.

Finally Gaetano drove us to the community center for his son's birthday party. When we reached a small intersection in yet another rundown corner of town, he parked. People were hanging out in front of two makeshift shops—one a tiny operation that sold cleaning products suspended from hangers and hooks on an open door, the other a kind of mini-deli that sold beer and cigarettes. Many guys went in and out of the second of these shops as I waited in the car with Gaetano. Then, what appeared to be his wife and her friend drove up in a white car with two infants. A guy in his midtwenties with a scruffy beard, tinted brown seventies-biker sunglasses, and thin limbs who had been sitting near us on his flashy chrome motorbike got up and walked to the white car. He reached in the front passenger seat window, pulled out a baby, and showered it with kisses. It was a chubby one-year-old with a big head and quiet eyes called Antonio, Gaetano's youngest son. I filmed the baby once he was in Gaetano's arms, the beginning of my job that night.

Gaetano looked into the lens of the video camera I was aiming at him and his younger son. "He needs to get cleaned up, too," he said. "He got dirty." Months later, while editing the footage of this scene, I noticed that Antonio's filthy, pudgy legs had distracted my attention from a swift, smooth transaction taking place just inches to the baby's right. Gaetano's hand, after having taken a couple of folded-up euro notes from the slim man with the motorbike, slipped them down the front of his shorts while holding his son against his hip with his other hand. Then he carried the baby back to the women in the white car.

"Are you filming?" the slim man asked me as he moved up to me, still in the car.

"Yeah," I answered without peeling my eye away from the video camera. Irritated that the guy couldn't add it up that I was sitting in the boss's car and shooting him full-frontal at close range, I tried to give him the brush-off. *Of course* it was all right to film.

But the slim guy persisted with another question: "Who are you filming? The father?"

At that, I decided to peel my eye off the video camera to look him in the face. He had taken off his sunglasses. He had blue eyes, I noticed, and they looked at me expectantly. "Yeah, him and his baby," I said, pretending to be relaxed about it.

"Who are you filming . . . *the father*?" he asked again, persisting.

I decided to change my tune a bit: "No, I'm filming the baby. . . . It's a job I'm doing for Gaetano: his son's birthday." I turned my eye back to the video camera, trying to brush him off with feigned disinterest. I was irritated. Why the hell was he hassling me like this? Didn't he know I was Gaetano's friend? I felt secure in my position, there in the passenger seat of his car. I didn't want to explain myself to anybody; I thought it was clear that I could do what I wanted.

Gaetano gave me exactly what I'd been seeking for months: access to some of the practices the camorra performed behind the neomelodica scene, the freedom to ask questions and receive straight answers, and privileged access and protection while conducting my research. He provided me with what fieldwork in Naples never could: determinacy. Like the many other men he managed to attract, I was seduced by Gaetano's force. Whereas those others were lured by his power to make things happen, I was lured by his power, in my knowledge economy, to determine what was real.

This portrait of singer Mimmo Dany was taken by the artist Giuseppe Zevola at Casa Zevola, his gallery space and home in the centro storico. We contacted Dany because Giuseppe was taken by his comic sensibility and wanted to offer him a photographic portrait (Dany said he would prefer a portrait painting). Dany came with different jackets and spontaneously assumed a series of poses like the one pictured here. During the shoot, several visitors came by Giuseppe's salon—a gallerist, a painter, and a Buddhist monk. Dany charmed us all. In 2010 Dany starred in the film *A Neomelodic President*, directed by Alfonso Ciccarelli. He plays a neomelodico who runs for Campania regional elections because of his love not for politics but for reality TV: he wants to gain popularity so that he makes it on the show *The Island of the Famous*, an Italian version of the original Australian show *Celebrity Survivor*.

Making Do with Indeterminacy

THIS STORY BEGINS by loitering at the edge of a scene. It registers the impact of atmospheres that for centuries "visitors" (tourists, occupiers, and colonizers) have tried to contain. Their poetic and juridical representations have helped produce murky atmospheres where things such as vibrant folklore and charnel ruination coalesce. This story sidesteps debates about representations of "the South," but it doesn't evade representations themselves. It meets them head-on, not just as forms to be critiqued but as forms to be activated and inhabited. It follows how representations become animate figures that collect up and reflect back "the sense of the possibility of fulfillment, the possibility of damnation, or the possibility of collective inclusion in figures larger than that to which they explicitly refer."[1] Representations do not vanish when they're exposed for what they "really" are. The game of *who am I and who are you?* can go on indefinitely.

The main protagonists in this story are people who inhabit these murky affective–aesthetic atmospheres with the camorra. Outside this contact zone, some people call this complicity. The protagonists of this story are, in fact, complicit, but in the sense that they participate in these figurations, collecting up and reflecting back to their intimate publics and to other publics different senses of possibility and damnation. They enact narratives using allegory, romanticism, irony, and most of all, melodrama. They weave contact zones where representations become animate figures, figures activate becomings, and the boundaries of art, the art of making do, and organized crime become blurred.

This story's narrator made his way into the contact zone, where representations, performances, and matters comingle. He followed people who sidestep debates about representations, try representations on, and become protagonists in melodramas of making do. Many live frustrated narratives stalled between fears of ruin and promises of self-realization. They speculate on futures that seldom come or that they don't really want to come.

But for the narrator, in his moments of excess, this story was too mid-dling. He sought denouement and went to find it in the place to which everyone was gesturing. There, at the eye of the storm, things feel powerfully still, giving you room to be expansive, but storms eventu-ally dissipate. Camorristi are frequently toppled, or they turn out to have been merely or mostly behaving like camorristi.

Or they get arrested for performing figurations of who they really are, as in *Gomorra*. In March 2010 the Neapolitan director Enzo Acri re-leased a "response to *Gomorra*," *The Good Camorrista*. Unlike the camor-risti in the cast of Gomorra, the camorrista in Acri's movie more or less openly exposes himself. Vincenzo Barbetta plays the title role, and his character shares his name. He's a boss of the "old camorra" returning to the scene after serving eighteen years of "416 bis" (camorristic associa-tion). With a "terrorist" he meets in prison, he restores order to Naples by killing off the ruthlessly violent "new camorristi" and allied immigrant crime groups. There are good camorristi, and the bad ones can't muddy Naples, Acri said at a press conference. Months after the film's release,

In Enzo Acri's film *The Good Camorrista* (2010), Vincenzo Barbetta, an actual camor-rista, becomes a boss–impresario who manages the nephew of a Sicilian mafioso. In several shots we see Barbetta as literally the man *dietro le spalle* (behind the shoul-ders, or backing) his patron. In another he is figured as the source of light, and the young singer is his emanation as he "makes the boy grow." In this shot, the singer tele-turns the mic on his boss, a.k.a. ventriloquist.

Ciro Petrone, the young star of *Gomorra* who was mixed up in a raid at a Sarno clan banquet at the Villa Cupido, is also in *The Good Camorrista*. He plays a role similar to that in *Pisellino*: he is the childhood friend of Barbetta who gets too big for his britches and invokes the wrath of the superboss. Barbetta, ordered to snuff out his friend, convinces him to fake a fatal car accident, then gives him a farewell embrace while they stand beside the burning car. Their bond is semiveiled by the flames, like a union of the damned. In a press conference, Acri said that he cast Petrone not because of his role in *Gomorra* but because he, like the rest of the cast, was on Facebook, where he recruited them all.

Barbetta was arrested with over fifty other people in a maxi-blitz against the Moccia crime clan, a powerful and enduring clan that was once allied with Raffaele Cutolo, a.k.a. 'O professor'. The Neapolitan provincial town of Afragola is their seat of power and also the location for most of the filming of *The Good Camorrista*. Barbetta, a high-ranking "Senator" in the clan and the film's producer, said that the people of Afragola were entirely welcoming. In July 2010 he was arrested for intimidation and extortion as a commander in the "triangle of usury" (Afragola, Casoria, and Acerra). Allegedly, his most notable victim was the neomelodica Cinzia Oscar, whom he served as manager. Barbetta is an impresario in the movie as well.[2]

Acting like a camorrista and being a camorrista are sometimes the same thing. However, this apparently is not the case with Carmela, the first impresario I met on the scene. She turns out to be "a foolish woman who's had a lot of misfortune," my confidante Giuseppe recently told me with genuine sympathy. "She's got brothers who are mixed up in some bad business, but she only behaves like a camorrista. Carmela's harmless."

On the other hand, Angelo Buttafuoco, the TV show and record producer, remains fundamentally slithery. Some people have terrible stories to tell about him, while others have nothing at all to report. My sense is that some of these latter have chosen not to talk.

Maria Faletti, who was once light and sprightly, is now blunted and embittered. Her husband died of a sudden heart attack, leaving her to fend for herself and her four boys against economic hardship and overwhelming grief. "He was a security guard, remember? On the day of his funeral, the police all turned their sirens on for him," she recounted, looking down at the floor as she spoke. Now she works full-time at the shoe factory. When her work is over, she returns home and cooks for her kids. "When I get home I don't want to go out again. I don't want to see anybody. No one calls me anyway." Morever, Fabio stopped calling her. She was *sfregiata,* and the Evildoer, not *He,* prevailed. Maria withdrew from the neomelodica scene entirely. We write to each other on Facebook. Occasionally she posts a neomelodica music video on her wall.

Fabio teamed up with his "fraternal friend," Fabrizio Corona, a.k.a. the king of the paparazzi, who was convicted of multiple counts of extortion in the Vallettopoli (Bell Boy City) scandal. Corona loosed cocaine-laced women on famous figures and extorted payment for the exclusive photos his team shot of their encounters. Fabio and Fabrizio met in a nightclub in Sardinia where they butted heads before becoming best friends. Now they share the stage in the sceneggiata *Guapparia* (Gauppism). Corona plays Don Carluccio because, as he told Fabio, he identified with the "arrogant, impudent and bullying" guappo. Fabio told a reporter that anyone who knows Fabrizio knows that this is merely his facade.[3]

Fulvio, now a young man, escaped the neomelodica scene. Happily, he has become a respected jazz singer. He has given small performances with world-famous musicians on Rai and is recording an album in Rome, although the project might fall through. He still sings at private parties, but now they're on the Amalfi coast. "It's a different world," he says. "I don't like to remember that other one."

Recently, Fulvio picked me up at Gambrinus, the belle epoque café near Piazza del Plebescito, and brought me to his family's home, where he went straight to the keyboard. He played me some of his recordings— big band, swing, and mainstream pop. His versatility was impressive.

He then asked me to help him with his English pronunciation. He sang Gershwin's song "A Foggy Day." He sounded like a young Sinatra with an Italian accent. We worked on hardening his r's.

At intervals, other family members came into the room to greet us. Stefania is now a levelheaded and beautiful young woman whom I later saw in New York when she came with her husband on their honeymoon. Roberto, on the other hand, looks older and seems less energetic. While we said hello, a small boy ran up to him and hugged his leg. "This is my son!" he said, holding the child up to me. "I'm separated from his mother. Today it's my turn to take care of him."

Pasquale looked like he's changed the most. He now has gray hair and has gained weight. Although it was a weekday afternoon, he shuffled up to us, disheveled and wearing a wrinkled undershirt as if just waking. "I had a stroke, you know," he said. His frantic pursuits on the neomelodica scene had pushed him past his limit. Ironically, he now had a stable income: a regular disability check. I wondered how this affected Fulvio's mother, Rita, but she never appeared, not even later that evening. Apparently, she was working late at Enel.

I too withdrew from the neomelodica scene—at least as a neomelodico. It was if the album and the artist persona that I had been composing were only a dream. In the space of performance, I was pulled along by the rush of affect, and I even managed to pull others with me. A close friend, a respected artist who does photocollage and performance, co-authored with me "Shpeak a me," a *neoamericano* (our amalgam of *napoletano stretto* and New Yorkese) translation of Destiny's Child's "Say My Name."[4] Rino, the glamrock musician, and I coauthered "Le torre gemelli" (The Twin Towers): "The towers may have fallen but you and I are still standing." I persuaded the violinist from the Virtuosi of San Martino to help compose the arrangements. Rino's band wanted me to open for them at their next show.

Like much of the commotion I followed, this one dissipated—but it didn't dissolve. It resurged in 2009 when Nascar, a digital communications consultancy in Milan, posted on its Facebook profile a neomelodico-style music video titled "Lasciarsi su Facebook" (Breaking up on Facebook).[5] In the video, a counterfeit neomelodico singer named Manuele D'Amore wears dark sunglasses, puckers his lips, and sings a melismatic lament about love and betrayal. He has discovered that during his brief stint in prison, his girlfriend cheated on him and even posted photos of her lover on her profile. In one scene, we see D'Amore behind bars and the words *the police tagged me* scrawled on his cell wall. In another, a couple walks past him on the promenade at the bay, with Vesuvius in the background: "You can't tag my heart. You can't call me 'love,'" he sings. The video attracted tens of thousands of hits on Facebook and YouTube within a matter of hours, and it sparked the interest of regional Campanian television broadcasters, who invited "D'Amore" on their transmissions. They didn't realize that the song, the music video, and the neomelodico singer were all parodic inventions.[6]

Gaetanino, who also uses Facebook (neither of us has friended the other), continues to manage his talent agency, now called Lioneworld, a multiroom complex in a new neighborhood. I recently paid Gaetanino a visit after a two-year hiatus. When he saw me come through the door he shouted, "Uàaa! Jason!" and we greeted each other warmly. "Go and take the tour," he said, before climbing a ladder to a tucked-away loft.

I walked around the soundproof recording studio, a wide bank of high-end recording equipment, a television studio with a ceiling full of stage lights, and three broadcast-quality video cameras. When I climbed the ladder to the loft, I found Gaetano and a young assistant, Vincenzo, sitting before a wall of decks and monitors. Gaetanino told me to sit down and pointed to the seat next to his. Although he didn't say so, he wanted me to look at his show and tell him what I thought. This time it was genuinely easy to find good things to say about the production value. For one, the cameras were stationary and well placed, capturing the singers—a duet—in a harmonious composition with a plain white background, no naïf-style murals of Naples and no incursions into the frame by studio guests and production staff. Also, the screen was cleared of the usual flashing and scrolling cell-phone numbers and exhortations to *book now!* Instead, there was a sleek, narrow line at the bottom that displayed the small logo of Gaetanino's agency and a landline number.

I told Gaetanino what I observed, and he listened attentively. When I finished, he asked me if there was "anything new from America" to give him an edge on the scene. I told him I didn't know of anything. "I think you're on the right track already," I added superfluously.

When Gaetanino took a phone call I initiated a conversation with his assistant. Vincenzo was only twenty-three, the same age as Gaetano's half-brother who was gunned down drive-by style in Rione Basso around New Year's that year. I had read it in the papers. I was afraid for Vincenzo.

Maybe he still had a chance, like Fulvio, to make a better life for himself. I asked him when he started working for Gaetano. He said six months ago. I asked him what he wanted to do in the future. "I want to work for Mediaset, but that's not gonna happen. You gotta know someone."

"That's not true," I protested. "Don't give up. You never know who you'll meet. You've just met me, for example, and I know people." I gave Vincenzo my card and indicated my e-mail address. "We'll talk later," I said.

When Gaetano got off the phone, Vincenzo told him he was leaving. He stood before his seated boss and lingered there uncomfortably for several seconds. Gaetano stared at his monitors, unresponsive. "Uh, can I have some money for the bus?" Vincenzo asked in an embarrassed mumble.

Coming to attention, Gaetano took a five euro note from a bundle in his pocket and handed it Vincenzo. "I'll see you tomorrow," he told him.

When I later asked Giuseppe what he thought that was all about, he said he didn't know. "It's probably nothing," he said. To me it looked like indenture. A couple of months later, Vincenzo friended me on Facebook, and when I accepted, he repeatedly tried to get me to invest in a pyramid scheme disguised as a tourism business.

Giuseppe, at last leaving his parents' home, had moved into Gaetano's neighborhood, where he lives in big new apartment with his wife and a dog. He and I had kept in touch during my absence, and I followed his updates on Facebook. For a long time it seemed the prospect of challenging Gaetano's status in their quartiere was no longer in Giuseppe's cards. In fact, according to Giuseppe, there was nothing to challenge: Gaetano was *no one*. He was never anyone. He was just a laughable ignorant *spacciatore* (drug dealer). This Giuseppe declared to me in a chat on Skype. I pointed out to him that years back he had first introduced Gaetano to me as someone quite different than what he was describing now, but Giuseppe only repeated his dismissals.

This was Giuseppe's take on things until around 2008, when Gaetano launched Lioneworld and Giuseppe joined him as the house composer. He took 50 percent of all song commissions, which came from some of the top singers on the scene. "Because of 'O lione and his number-one agency, I have recognition," he told me in a Facebook chat.

Now Giuseppe works exclusively as the keyboardist in the ensemble of one of his clients. The singer is an old-school neomelodico (in his forties) who has talent and a faithful following. "And they're all malavitosi," Giuseppe said, describing the singer's fans. "Now I can introduce you to *all kinds* of people." Giuseppe knew how to titillate me with the possibility of consummating my love for the camorra. But why should I believe this *imbroglione* (swindler) who had turned me on to a counterfeit camorrista like the market trick *facenn' 'o pacc'* (selling, for example, a boxed stereo that, when you open it later, turns out to be a pile of bricks)?

Giuseppe's mother, Anna, had tried the same scam, I learned, when we had lunch at her home later that week. After she served the linguini and clams and finally sat down, she said, "It's been more than two years! I have to tell you a story." Anna always had fascinating stories, and I was sure they were rarely, if ever, adulterated. I listened intently.

"Last time you were here, you asked me if I had ever had direct contact with a camorrista, but I didn't have any stories to give you. I felt really bad about it. So after you left, I was talking with my husband and we decided we would pull a prank on you when you returned." Suddenly the story did not sound like those I was used to hearing from Anna.

"Gianni has this old friend from childhood," she continued, "His name is Alfonso but everyone calls him 'O mammut [The mammoth] because he's a big man with a big ugly face. I've always known him to be a good man. When we were young, he watched out for me if a guy tried to come onto me. 'You stay away, that's Gianni's girl,' he would tell them.

"For years he came for dinner every couple of months—he was like an uncle to Giuseppe. He always had a funny story to tell—about a big heist or some elaborate scam. You see, 'O mammut was a good man who started out with a small factory, but when he was shut down for not being *alla regola* [legal], he turned to contraband. He drove motorboats that carried cigarettes to the docks. But when that work disappeared, he became a professional thief. He told us some funny stories. One time he was hired to do a job at the Capodimonte museum. They wanted him to steal some ceramic *presepe* [nativity scene] figurines. He said it was the easiest thing."

Anna smiled. "So Gianni and I thought, 'When Jason returns, we should invite him to dinner when 'O mammut is here and then we'll introduce him to Jason as 'boss Alfonso Generoso, a.k.a. 'O mammut.' We knew you'd believe us, because you only need to take one look at him and listen to his stories, and you're convinced.

"When you left, I collected newspaper articles about the quartiere, because I remembered that you said to save anything about the camorra. And you know, *every day* I came across something about those people.

That pile of articles kept getting bigger and bigger, but still you never re-turned. I was getting depressed. I kept thinking to myself, *this is where I live?*

"Then one day I saw an article about 'O mammut. It said 'Alfonso Generoso, a.k.a. 'O mammut, boss of the Pulcini clan shot seventeen times by the Cenerosi clan in Civitanova.'" Anna paused. She looked saddened. "I read it again just to be sure, and it was true, *all* of it: 'O mammut really was a camorrista and now he's dead. I was so sick to my stomach that I took all the articles I had saved and threw them away."

The frustrated (and sometimes fraudulent) melodramas of the contact zone include the ones I enacted. I tried to build trusting relationships, apply pressure to the surface of things, and open channels of com-munication. Failing that, I let myself be taken by a surge of becoming-neomelodico, but that turned out to be more than I could handle. Finally, against my better sense, I made my way to a boss–impresario, my object of knowledge, the source of determination I fantasized would empower me to capture, not unlike he had, the milieu he dominated. Nevertheless, like many people I know on the scene (but not Silvio Berlusconi or 'O mammut), I have been denied denouement.

This, however, is a good ending. By forestalling the moment of crisis when things and people are exposed for what they really are, whether through an aesthetic judgment on neomelodica music or a verdict on the innocence or complicity of people on the neomelodica scene, other forms of knowledge are made possible. When you linger in these atmo-spheres, you allow indeterminacy to make an impact and you get a sense of how people make do with it. Making do in the field for years only to end up with "indeterminacy" doesn't mean coming up empty-handed. The art of making do, for me and for the people I encountered, is not about ultimate achievements, because things often never reach their tip-ping point (sometimes by design), and when they do, they usually aren't final. Frustrated desires for denouement and redemption entice people to linger in neomelodiche atmospheres. For many of us, there are no con-clusions or summing-it-up moments—no happily ever after, nor total di-saster, just the everyday arts of making do, their small accomplishments, and their occasional excesses.

Notes

Introduction

1. A *vicolo* is an alleylike street flanked by four- or five-story buildings with *bassi* (ground-floor dwellings), where sunlight can be blocked for much of the day. In the *vicoli* (pl.), domestic spaces overlap with the semipublic domain of the street, conjuring an affective–aesthetic space and a particular social geography of the popular classes.

2. *Basso* literally means "low."

3. Da Vinci, "La forza di decidere" (The strength to decide).

4. Bakhtin, *Rabelais and His World,* 184.

5. Serao, *Ventre di Napoli.* Serao founded the most important Neapolitan daily newspaper, *Il Mattino.*

6. Stallybrass and White, *Politics and Poetics.*

7. Hirschman, *Passions and the Interests,* shows how liberal intellectuals during the Enlightenment argued that taming all the passions but avarice would yield a productive capitalist economy.

8. Gribaudi, "Clan camorristi a Napoli."

9. Two nonprofits, Legambiente and La Rete Salute & Gusto del Movimento Difesa del Cittadino, reported these findings, citing Campania for the highest number of incidents of incomplete or false labeling in 2004, although incidents are widespread in many regions in Italy ("Pesce Fresco," *Alimentazione News*). See Nordstrom, *Global Outlaws.*

10. In 2009 police raided warehouses containing one hundred thousand pirated copies of CDs and DVDs and duplication equipment (La Penna, "Porta Nolana"; "Centrale dei cd falsi"). Pirated software also circulates among them.

11. Newer urban areas built in the 1960s–1980s are called the *periferia.* Neomelodica music and performers also circulate in Switzerland, France, Spain, and, to a lesser extent, the United States, Canada, Argentina, and Australia.

12. *Neomelodici* is the plural form of *neomelodico*; both are used as adjectives and substantives.

13. There are far fewer female singers and, to my knowledge, no female composers or songwriters, and only two female talent managers. There is an old guard of male (and some female) singers (at the time of writing, in their thirties, forties, and fifties) and a number of "baby neomelodici" as young as eight.

14. In 1994 Naples had 42.7 percent "official" unemployment, and Scampia (of the periphery), 61.7 percent. In 1992, complying with European Union policies protecting fair competition, Prime Minister Giuliano Amato dismantled state–capitalist protectionist institutions, including the Southern Development Fund, created in 1950 to stimulate economic growth. In the 1990s Naples deindustrialized with increasing speed, losing about one-third of its manufacturing industries and employment with the closings of the Italsider steel mill and Alfa Sud car factory. The service economy has not filled the gap. The Agency for the Southern Promotion and Development, subsidizing agricultural and fishing development, the artisanal sector, small and medium businesses, large industry, and infrastructural development, was dissolved in 1993 (Scaramella, "Case of Naples").

15. Stille, *Sack of Rome*, 121.

16. Commissione Parlamentare Antimafia, Doc. XXIII, no. 3 (2003). Between 1991 and mid–2007, seventy-five councils were disbanded in Campania, again significantly more than in other regions (Commissione Parlamentare Antimafia, *Consigli comunali sciolti*).

17. Dines, "Urban Renewal, Immigration, and Contested Claims"; Pasotti, *Political Branding in Cities*.

18. Bassolino, *Repubblica delle città*.

19. People in the milieu I frequented often described moving to northern Italy as "emigration."

20. For ethical practice, see Agamben, *Homo Sacer*. See Pardo, *Managing Existence*, who includes religious ethics in his analysis of everyday economic and social life among some segments of the popular classes in Naples.

21. On figuration, see Haraway, "Birth of the Kennel."

22. Schmitt, "Drei Arten," 23–24, cited in Kalyvas, "Hegemonic Sovereignty," 348.

23. Massumi, "Autonomy of Affect." "Capture" describes the confinement or closure of vitality (potential or virtuality): "Affect is autonomous to the degree to which it escapes confinement in the particular body whose vitality or potential for interaction, it is. Formed, qualified, situated perceptions and cognitions fulfilling functions of actual connection or blockage, are the capture and closure of affect. Emotion is the intensist (most contracted) expression of that capture—and of the fact that something has always and again escaped" (96).

24. Saviano, *Gomorra*, tracks the comingling of Milan-based haute couture fashion houses, undocumented and unregulated factories in Campania, and internationally organized crime networks that manage the circulation and sale of counterfeit goods.

25. Pratt uses the term to describe "the social spaces where cultures meet and clash in often highly asymmetrical relations of power" ("Arts of the Contact Zone," 1).

26. Tsing, *Friction*.

27. Berlant writes that intimate publics shape conventions of belonging and "provide a better experience of belonging partly through participation in the relevant commodity culture, and partly because of its revelations about how people can live" (*Female Complaint*, viii).

28. Gribaudi, "Clan camorristi a Napoli."

29. See Siebert, *Secrets of Life and Death*, and Di Bella, *Dire ou taire*.

30. In an episode of the MTV series *The Vice Guide to Everything*, produced by Alvi Hunter and Ciel Suroosh, the hosts visit Naples, "a city known for pizza, trash and the mob," to follow "the mafia's own music industry" and Alessio, a singer "owned by the mafia." Relatedly, New York City's Little Italy was an early-twentieth-century risqué tourist attraction for middle-class *flânerie* (Gabaccia, "Global Geography").

31. Lamberti, "Così governa la camorra."

32. Italian president Carlo Ciampi, quoted in Phillips, "Fifth Mafia Boss Is Killed."

33. Positivist social hygienists identified two distinct "races": the "Mediterranean" in the south and "European" in the north, the former predisposed to committing violent crimes and the latter, property crimes (Lombroso-Ferrero and Lombroso, *Criminal Man*).

34. Banfield writes that the "backward" society, an excessively inward-looking, kin-structured society (and the predominance of distrust of "strangers") is the binary opposite of "modern civil society" *(Moral Basis)*.

35. Villari's writings, particularly *Lettere meridionali* (1875), influenced many intellectuals and politicians, including Pasquale Turiello and Serao.

36. Moe, *View from Vesuvius,* shows that in the northern European imagination the south of Italy was depicted through both picturesque and denigrating terms.

37. Ibid.

38. Böhme, *Aisthetik,* 45, cited in Pritchard, "Contemporary German Aesthetics," 122. Pritchard summarizes Böhme's idea that atmospheres precede objects, signs, symbols, "physiognomies," and "scenes."

39. Diaconu, "Patina—Atmosphere—Aroma," 136. See also Dufrenne, *Phenomenology of Aesthetic Experience*; Böhme, "Atmosphere"; Anderson, "Affective Atmospheres."

40. I draw on the notion of *Befindlichkeit* in Heidegger, *Being and Time.*

41. Stoler describes ruination as the aftershocks of empire: "Imperial formations persist in their material debris, in ruined landscapes and through the social ruination of people's lives" ("Imperial Debris," 194). Naples was capital of the Kingdom of Two Sicilies before it was annexed to the northern Italian Kingdom of Piedmont–Sardinia in 1860. Political economic developments accompanying Italian unification contributed to a decline in southern Italy's economy and the rise of organized crime.

42. Benjamin and Lacis described the city as "porous" ("Naples").

43. Ibid., 166.

44. Rotondo, "Pallottole"; Rotondo, "Altra pescheria"; Rotondo, "Raid incendiario contro pescheria."

45. Saviano, *Gomorra*. Many of these voices are women's, indicative of their role in the domestic labors of organized crime. Women assist as *vedette* ("lookouts"), cut and package drugs, harbor fugitives, and protect affiliates. Women sometimes take leadership roles in crime clans, issuing orders and exacting violence. See Allum, *Camorristi, Politicians, Businessmen*; Gribaudi, *Donne, uomini, famiglie*; Longrigg, *Mafia Women*; Siebert, *Donne, la mafia*.

46. Taussig, *Shamanism*.

47. Blok, *Mafia*.

48. Saviano, *Gomorra*.

49. De Curtis, "Torna a Surriento"; Capurro, "O sole mio."

50. Depraz, "Where Is the Phenomenology of Attention," calls attention to an embodied modulator of cognition. My understanding of attention draws from philosophy (Husserl, Merleau-Ponty), psychology (Gendlin, James), neuroscience (Damasio), geography (Anderson), and anthropology (Csordas, Desjarlais, Jackson, Katz and Csordas, Geurts, Klima, Reddy, Stewart, Wikan). See also works by Candea, Latour, and Tarde, for forms of social attention.

51. Fernandez, "Dark at the Bottom of the Stairs," calls this zone the "inchoate"; Bateson, "Play and Fantasy."

52. For "meaning effects," see Bakhtin and Emerson, *Problems of Dostoevsky's Poetics*.

53. Stewart, "On the Politics of Cultural Theory." Massumi offers the term *productivism* to describe an alternative to critique that does not disavow its own "inventiveness" (*Parables for the Virtual*, 12–13).

54. Related notions: Herzfeld's "local social theory" in *Poetics of Manhood* and Klima's "philosophical ethnography" in *Funeral Casino*.

55. Stewart, "Arresting Images"; Benjamin, "Surrealism."

56. This work resonates with performance-based and/or embodied ethnographies (Conquergood, Denzin, Linder, Samudra, Taylor, Wacquant) and dialogical ethnographies (Caton, Rouch, Stewart, Tedlock). It also dwells in contexts of uncertainty and ethical ambiguity (Bourgois, Nordsrom, Venkatesh, Williams) and grapples with empathic contagions and entanglements in the field (Behar, Caton, Favret-Saada, Rosaldo), including those centered on gender and sexuality (e.g., the contributors of Lewin and Leap, *Out in the Field*).

57. Fernandez, "Dark at the Bottom of the Stairs," 221.

58. Sedgwick and Frank, *Touching Feeling*, 8.

59. Steinbock calls this "phenomenological reflective attentiveness" ("Affection and Attention," 41); Maurer calls it "post-reflexive anthropology" (*Mutual Life, Limited*, 17).

1. Where There's Money, There's the Camorra

1. Kirshenblatt-Gimblett, "Toward a Theory of Proverb Meaning."

2. Abrahams, "Rhetorical Theory of Folklore," cited in Goodwin and Wenzel, "Proverbs and Practical Reasoning," 142.

3. Sommella, "Potere illegali e territorio," writes that the urban crime clans engage primarily in drug trafficking, the production and trade of counterfeit goods, and extortion rackets, and rural provincial clans infiltrate public procurement contracts and operate businesses. Clans of the urban periphery mediate between these two. Sales, *La camorra, le camorre,* uses the plural form of camorra, *camorre.*

4. I combine Zangwill's ideas on aesthetics with Massumi's ideas on affect and fear.

5. Massumi, "Future Birth of the Affective Fact."

6. Deleuze and Guattari, *Thousand Plateaus.*

7. I draw on notions of authority from Sennett and notions of sovereignty from Schmitt, but unlike them, I refer to personal sovereignty that does not necessarily entail full autonomy. I draw on Hirschman, *Shifting Involvements,* for the notion of interest as "the pursuit of a better life for oneself and one's family, 'better' being understood primarily in terms of increased material welfare" (7).

8. A Neapolitan game similar to bingo, where each number corresponds with a word or phrase and its image.

9. See Zelizer and Ballarino, *Vite economiche.*

10. Agamben, *Homo Sacer.*

11. Pardo, *Managing Existence in Naples,* suggests that the art of making do implies entrepreneurial activity at the margins of formal economies. In this book I use the term in the broader and multivalent manner with which people use it in the milieu I frequented in Naples: as affective–aesthetic sensibilities, as well as economic practices, that traverse open fields of potential where there are no essential margins.

12. I focus on the ways these practices and sensibilities traverse common figurations such as "informal" (and by extension "illicit") and "formal." The art of making do can be spontaneous, guidedly improvisational, or semi-organized, but its organizing principle is opportunity in an economy of opportunity (Peraldi and Manry, "Le lien et le gain"): its practitioners are "itinerant" in the sense that they follow the "continuous variation of variables" in local spaces and situations (Deleuze and Guattari, *Thousand Plateaus*). Rather than conceptualize the informal only in terms of what it lacks, implying that it is an archaism that vanishes with modernization, I follow continuities and interpenetrations across any figuration of the economy, as have others (e.g., Bagnasco, Capecchi, Coletto, Hart, Hirschman, the contributors to Coletto, *Informal Economy* [Portes, Castells, and Benton], Ruggiero, Zelizer).

13. These qualities approach what Deleuze and Guattari call "nomadology," which means not (necessarily) actual movement but "absolute movement" or speed. "Nomads" occupy an unenclosed, "smooth" open space of heterogeneity, a space that is not "striated" or mapped through (state-)regulated circulations and flows (*Thousand Plateaus*, 380–87).

14. Gribaudi writes that the popular classes of urban and rural southern Italy never considered manual labor "sacred" but in fact a "damnation to which they are condemned" and that this was the case with industrial labor as well. Moreover, she argues, when laborers joined unions it was purely for utilitarian reasons, based not on ideological consensus but on tangible and immediate interests (*Mediatori*, 175–78). On entrepreneurship, see Pardo, *Managing Existence*.

15. Gribaudi, *Mediatori*.

16. In fact, these relationships are part of a long "tradition" reaching back to the ruling Christian Democratic Party from the early 1960s through the early 1990s, which distributed jobs in exchange for loyalty.

17. Just over 27 percent of potential students in Naples attended secondary school in 1994 (ISTAT). "Giuseppe" is a pseudonym. In many instances I have changed the names of people, places, songs, and even the lyrics of songs to ensure people's privacy and safety.

18. The atmospheres of "the camorra" are also sensed in housing and business development in parts of Lazio and Calabria (see Lamberti, "Camorra come 'metodo'"). Moreover, Naples is at the intersection of drug trafficking networks between South America, Europe, and North Africa.

19. In 1982 the sociologist and provincial president Amato Lamberti founded a center for the study of organized crime. In 2004 residents of a neighborhood in Naples's periphery launched the Peppino Impastato Center of San Giovanni a Teduccio to provide afterschool programs for at-risk children. After the publication of Saviano's *Gomorra*, new organizations (many funded by regional government) were founded, including Pol.i.s. Foundation (Integrated Politics for Safety); Free: Associations, Names and Numbers against Mafias; and Beyond Gomorra. These organizations conduct studies, provide cultural activities in schools and after-school programs for at-risk children, and coordinate networks of entrepreneurs to resist racketeering. Local rap music groups have also engaged in their own anticamorra initiatives, including Frankie Hi-NRG MC and Lucariello. Grassroots resistance has come from the priest Luigi Merola (under government protection), creator of "Civic Education on Legality" in Forcella's public school and promoter of the Annalisa Durante Association (named after a young resident killed in clan crossfire).

20. Blok calls this atmosphere *omertà*, typically defined as a "code of silence" (*Mafia*). He argues that it refers instead to a general condition or experience rather than an objectified code of ethics.

21. Certeau, *Heterologies*.

22. Former Forcella boss Luigi Giuliano had a sky-bridge built (without a permit) connecting his home (confiscated in 2002) to the building across the vicolo.

23. Saviano, *Gomorra*. Casalesi means "of Casal di Principe" (Home of the prince), a town in the Campanian province of Caserta.

24. Article 416 bis of the Italian criminal code: "A criminal association is considered mafiosa . . . when members of the association use the power of intimidation of the associative bond and . . . the vow of silence ensuing therefrom to commit crimes, to take control of businesses, to obtain the granting of authorizations, tenders and public services or to prevent or obstruct the free exercise of voting rights during elections."

25. Schneider and Schneider, *Reversible Destiny*; Savona, *Responding to Money Laundering*. This law and subsequent modifications criminalized money laundering and instituted provisions supporting transparency in banking and property sectors. Prosecutors "follow the money" and confiscate assets, including legitimate businesses, that help finance organized crime. The Rognoni–La Torre law combines the proposals of Virginio Rognoni and Pio La Torre, murdered by the mafia shortly before its passage.

26. Falcone and Borsellino were investigating relations between the state and the mafia. When colluding politicians could no longer obstruct the course of justice, the mafia waged a war against the state with intensified violence. Their aim was to destabilize the country, which was already unmoored by the Operation Clean Hands trials. During the trials, and during the Berlusconi years that followed, politicians (likely fearful of imprisonment), including Berlusconi, warred against the magistrature by changing laws to limit its power to prosecute politicians.

27. The middle and upper classes have increasingly abandoned active use of Neapolitan since television's diffusion of Italian.

28. Judge Linda D'Ancona, interview by the author, July 5, 2008.

29. Although the term *dangerous classes* was first used by a departmental head of the Prefecture of the Seine, Honore Antoine Frégier, in his 1840 text, *Des classes dangereuses de la popolation dans les grand villes et des moyens de les rendres meilleurs*, it emerged in this field of discourse, which preceded it. Karl Marx defined the lumpenproletariat in terms like those defining the dangerous classes.

30. Bauman, "Ideology and the 'Weltanschauung.'"

31. Jacquemet, "Namechasers."

32. Marmo and Casarino, "Invincibili loro relazioni."

33. Merleau-Ponty, *Phenomenology of Perception*.

34. Machiavelli, *The Prince*, chap. 6.

35. Russo and Serao, *Camorra*; Paliotti, *Camorra*.

36. Benigno, "Dangerous Classes."

37. Marmo, "L'onore dei violenti."

38. In southern Italy, *sgarro* means "offense." I translate the word as "courage"

in this context because piciotti di sgarro obtain their status after a long period of servitude marked by demonstrations of devotion and courage.

39. Monnier went to Naples in the 1850s to manage his family's hotel and later became professor of comparative literature at the Academy of Geneva.

40. Benigno, "Dangerous Classes." Monnier references the novellas of Cervantes as "evidence" of the link between the camorra and the Garduña, established in Seville in 1417. Cervantes, Balzac, Hugo, Sue, and others generated folklore on bandits and underworld criminals that readers of all social classes consumed as *roman-feuilletons* (serialized novels published in newspapers and circulars) and *canards* (satirical or sensational leaflets) (Cragin, *Murder in Parisian Streets*; Matlock, *Scenes of Seduction*).

41. Monnier, *Camorra*; Marmo, "L'onore dei violenti"; Marmo, *Coltello e il mercato*.

42. Monnier published *L'Italia è la terra dei morti?* (1861) in response to Lamartine's 1825 poem *Le dernier chant du pèlerinage d'Harold*.

43. Monnier, *Camorra*, 1. In 1862 Monnier published a book on brigandage. North–south disparities were first articulated as part of a national political discourse by Leopoldo Franchetti, Sydney Sonnino, and Pasquale Villari in the late nineteenth century when they raised "the Southern Question," which Antonio Gramsci took up again during fascism. These intellectuals initiated *meridionalismo*, the political and social project of identifying and remedying perceived differences between the "Italian North" and the "Italian South" and in many ways singling out Neapolitans as a uniquely degraded popolo (Moe, *View from Vesuvius*; Petrusewicz, *Come Meridione divenne*).

44. Monnier, *Camorra*, 101.

45. A discussion of *lazzaroni* follows.

46. Monnier, *Camorra*, 102.

47. The terms *mezzogiorno* and *meridione* both mean "midday" or the "land of the midday sun."

48. Benigno, "Dangerous Classes."

49. Both terms—*lazzaro/lazzari* and *lazzarone/lazzaroni* (big lazzaro)—were in use.

50. Benigno, "Trasformazioni discorsive."

51. The Kingdom encompassed Sicily and the regions today called Puglia, Campania, Calabria, Basilicata, Molise, and Abruzzo.

52. The Kingdom enjoyed relative political autonomy under the viceroyalty. The Neapolitan aristocracy controlled the municipal government of Naples (the most populous European city in 1600 with 250,000 inhabitants), and the barons, with their private armies, dominated the rural areas, where 90 percent of the population lived (Villari, *Revolt of Naples*).

53. Ibid. The distinction between bandits and brigands is explained below.

54. Ibid.

55. De Simone, *Masaniello*. Between 1647 and 1652, thirty-eight books about the revolution were published throughout Europe.

56. Villari, *Revolt of Naples,* 169.

57. After centuries of direct Spanish rule, the Kingdom gained independence in 1734 under Bourbon King Carlo III. In 1759, when Carlo III succeeded to the throne of Spain, his son became Ferdinando IV of the Kingdom of Naples. Ferdinando and Maria Carolina ruled from Naples.

58. Robertson, "Enlightenment and Revolution." Genovese questioned the feudal rights of the Church, Crown, and nobility, and promoted public education that was to include peasants and women. He trained and influenced many thinkers of this new generation.

59. Croce, "'Lazzari.'"

60. Robertson, "Enlightenment and Revolution."

61. Ibid.

62. The origin of Naples is linked to the legend of Parthenope, the siren who threw herself into the sea from the cliffs of one of the archipelago islands Li Galli, a.k.a. Le Sirenuse (The Sirens), off the coast of Positano, after failing to lure Ulysses with her seductive melody and promises to reveal life's secrets. Her body washed up on the rocks of the tiny island of Megaride just off the shores of the quartiere Santa Lucia (Serao, *Leggende napoletane*).

63. Benigno, "Trasformazioni discorsive."

64. Ibid.

65. Ibid.

66. Villari, *Revolt of Naples*. It was more likely, however, that rebels enacted symbolic cannibalism.

67. Acton, *Bourbons of Naples*.

68. Davis, *Conflict and Control*.

69. Ibid., 73.

70. Ibid., 66–90. Davis, like many other scholars, emphasizes that banditry and brigandage had varying qualities across geopolitical and historical contexts in the Mediterranean.

71. Hobsbawm, *Primitive Rebels,* 2.

72. Ibid.

73. Davis, *Conflict and Control*; Villari, *Revolt of Naples*.

74. Davis, *Conflict and Control,* 100–105.

75. Riall, *Garibaldi*.

76. Ibid. Garibaldi explained that his mission was to free the people of the Kingdom of Naples from Bourbon despotism, establish a provisional government, and set the stage for the unification of the south with the northern Kingdom of Piedmont–Sardinia and the Kingdom of Lombardy. He nurtured popular national sentiment from the elite and the hundreds of thousands of poor.

77. Romano and Romano, *Memorie politiche,* 14–20.

78. Ibid.

79. Monnier, *Camorra,* 130. Peppe is the shortened version of Giuseppe.

80. Marmo and Casarino, "Invincibili loro relazioni."

81. Tessitore, *Nome e la cosa,* 92–93.

82. Marmo, *Coltello e il mercato.*

83. Macry, "Borghesia, città e lo stato," 343.

84. Marmo, *Coltello e il mercato.*

85. Ibid.

86. Marmo, "'Processi indiziari.'"

87. Marmo, *Coltello e il mercato.*

88. Ibid. The octopus metaphor renders the dual structure of a core organization that expands through numerous networks, but arguably, it also encourages the conception of upper-class criminality as the effect of a plebeian cause.

89. Marmo, "Città camorrista," 54–55.

90. Marmo, *Coltello e il mercato.*

91. Marmo, "Città camorrista."

92. Marmo, *Coltello e il mercato.*

93. Ibid.

94. For critiques of Hobsbawm's *Primitive Rebels,* see Marmo, "L'onore dei violenti," and Davis, *Conflict and Control.*

95. Commissione Parlamentare Antimafia, Doc. XXIII, no. 12 (1993).

96. Paliotti, *Forcella.* Tobacco was produced in Philip Morris warehouses in Belgium and Switzerland and "officially" exported outside Europe but actually diverted to Marseille, where entrepreneur distributors sold it to smaller distributors or directly to street sellers in Spain, Germany, Poland, and Italy (Ruggiero, *Organized and Corporate Crime*).

97. De Filippo was an enormously popular Neapolitan-language playwright and actor whose work focused on popular and middle-class life. De Sica came from a poor Neapolitan family.

98. Deleuze, *Cinema 2,* 1.

99. Allum, *Camorristi, Politicians, Businessmen*; Saviano, *Gomorra.* For "kin work," see Di Leonardo, *Varieties of Ethnic Experience.*

100. Marmo and Casarino, "Invincibili loro relazioni"; Marmo, "L'onore dei violenti."

101. See Arlacchi, *Mafia imprenditrice,* and Barbagallo, *Storia della Camorra.*

102. Police seized the book, but Cutolo circulated copies in prison and via post.

103. Behan, *Camorra,* 52.

104. Ibid., 53.

105. Commissione Parlamentare Antimafia, Doc. XXIII, no. 12 (1993). The NF, described below, also provided affiliates and their families assistance.

106. Ibid.

107. Gay, "L'Atteggiamento delle associazioni mafiose"; Allum, *Camorristi, Politicians, and Businessmen*.

108. Gay, "L'Atteggiamento delle associazioni mafiose."

109. Lamberti, "Camorra come 'metodo' e 'sistema.'"

110. Baglivo, *Camorra, S.p.A.*

111. Jacquemet, "Namechasers," 734.

112. Gay, "L'Atteggiamento delle associazioni mafiose."

113. Ibid.

114. The Christian Democrats, with brief intermissions, dominated from 1945. In the early 1990s the electoral system was changed by referendum from a proportional to majoritarian vote, facilitating public opinion mobilization (Pasotti, *Political Branding in Cities*).

115. Pasotti, *Political Branding in Cities*.

116. Ibid.

117. Section title borrowed from Donadio, "Berlusconi's Burlesque."

118. Raniolo, "Forza Italia."

119. Stille, *Sack of Rome*. Berlusconi has owned the soccer team AC Milan since 1986. His successes in politics are entwined with the team's successes, and his television empire mediates their relationship. Milan and Berlusconi have received free television advertising, and Berlusconi enhanced his influence through Milan's nationwide fanclub circuit and successes on the field, enhancing also his personal wealth (Foot, *Winning at All Costs*).

120. Ibid., 65.

121. Allegedly, Dell'Utri extorted off-the-books half-repayment of sponsorship money given by Publitalia to the Sicilian Vincenzo Garaffa's basketball team. When Garaffa refused, Dell'Utri had mafia boss Vincenzo Virga intimidate Garaffa. Dell'Utri won his appeal in 2011.

122. Ginsborg, *Silvio Berlusconi*.

123. Tonini, "Personal Leadership."

124. Raniolo, "Forza Italia."

125. Allum, *Camorristi, Politicians, and Businessmen*.

126. Stille, *Sack of Rome*, 60.

127. "Silvio's Sexy Line."

128. Levy, "Basta Bunga Bunga."

129. Owen, "Berlusconi in Racism Row."

130. Berlusconi has also been charged with abuse of office by allegedly phoning the police officers who took Ruby into custody when she was picked up for theft in an unrelated incident, telling them to release her because Ruby was a niece of Hosni Mubarak.

131. Ginsborg, *Silvio Berlusconi*, 84.

132. Stille, *Sack of Rome*, 256.

133. Stille, *Sack of Rome*.

134. Lamberti, "Camorra, come 'metodo' e 'sistema.'" See Blom Hansen, "Introduction—Urban Charisma."

135. In Monnier, *Camorra,* camorristi appear to be the organized elite of the lazzari.

136. Ibid., 98.

137. Ibid. Popolano literally means "man of the popolo."

138. Benigno, "Dangerous Classes"; Davis, *Conflict and Control*; Villari, *Revolt of Naples.*

139. Bauman, "Ideology and the 'Weltanschauung,'" 110.

140. Marmo affirms that the camorra indeed existed autonomously of representations of "the South" and that Spaventa's report was motivated by real problems of public order rather than an interest in representing the evils of Naples, as some contemporary critiques of early meridionalist work suggest *(Coltello e il mercato).*

141. Benigno, "Dangerous Classes."

2. Making Do with Art

1. Biondi, "Camorra o impegno."

2. Saviano, *Gomorra.* Luigino is a diminutive of Luigi.

3. "Boss chiede diritti."

4. Biondi, "Camorra o impegno."

5. Massumi, "Autonomy of Affect," 99.

6. Pratt, "Arts of the Contact Zone," 4.

7. Kendon, "Do Gestures Communicate?"; Kendon, *Gesture.*

8. Brooks, *Melodramatic Imagination,* 72–80.

9. Ibid, 67.

10. The linguist Pietro Maturi taught Neapolitan orthography, but not Neapolitan as a foreign language.

11. This was during a period of regional cultural revival in Naples.

12. Reisman, "Contrapuntal Conversations."

13. Meyer, *Emotion and Meaning.*

14. Naficy, *Making of Exile Cultures,* describes this as "leaky."

15. Popular reality TV show in Italy.

16. Allum, "Politics of Town Planning."

17. There are "167" building complexes in a few quartieri of the Neapolitan periferia.

18. *La bomboniera* (dir. Ricci).

19. See the website of the folk revival group led by the Neapolitan ethnomusicologist Roberto De Simone called Nuova Compagnia di Canto Popolare, which in the early 1990s traced the "Arabian" influences in Neapolitan musical

traditions and in 1997 began to collaborate with members of the Neapolitan hip-hop group 99 Posse: http://www.nccp.it.

20. Burke, *Popular Culture,* employs similar logic when arguing that popular culture of early modern Europe can be traced in the efforts of dominant authority to regulate and resist it.

21. Parallels are found in Calabrian songs depicting experiences in the 'Ndrangheta, the region's organized crime networks, in some Mexican narco-corridos, and in gangsta rap of the United States—all musics that have been subject to censorship—as well as Colombian *corridos prohibidos.*

22. Vacca, "Canzone e mutazione urbanistica"; Frasca, *Birds of Passage.*

23. Assenza, *Giovan Ferretti;* Cardamone, *Debut of the Canzone Villanesca.*

24. Vacca, "Canzone e mutazione urbanistica." See below for descriptions of "popular" vocal styles.

25. Aiello, "Comprensibile esistenza."

26. Term coined by R. Murray Schafer meaning sounds detached from their source, referenced in Feld, "From Schizophonia to Schismogenesis."

27. Leakage in music production happens when sounds bleed across recording tracks so that they are not clearly separated when compared with dominant production standards. "Incorporation" denotes strategies by which a cultural "mainstream" absorbs a subculture, commodifying and diffusing the subculture and/or subjecting it to the discursive categories of ideology, defusing it (Hebdige, *Subculture*). For "world music" and "global beat," see Feld, "From Schizophonia to Schismogenesis."

28. De Mura, *Enciclopedia della canzone napoletana.*

29. See Frasca, *Birds of Passage,* for an account of the flows of music and people between Naples and New York City. Emigrant Neapolitan music also circulated in Philadelphia, Boston, and San Francisco, and in other countries such as Argentina, Russia, France, Britain, and Australia.

30. Vacca, "Canzone e mutazione urbanistica."

31. Silvestri, "Canzone napoletana."

32. Classic Neapolitan song's renown has been so great that many worldwide listeners hear it as "Italian" music. It has also been translated into other languages.

33. Frasca, *Birds of Passage.*

34. De Mura, *Enciclopedia della musica napoletana.* See also "n" museo casa della canzone napoletana: http://www.museoenne.it.

35. Sorba, "Origins of the Entertainment Industry."

36. Palomba, "Storia (personale)," writes that the Neapolitan music industry could have continued to evolve along its own trajectory had it not been co-opted by northern Italian industry giants such as Ricordi.

37. Palomba, "Storia (personale)."

38. Palomba, "Storia (personale)"; Bruni, "Ricerca della perfezione."

39. Bruni, "Ricerca della perfezione," 131.

40. Palomba, "Storia (personale)."

41. Ibid.

42. Aiello, "Comprensibile esistenza."

43. D'Angelo, *Core pazzo,* 17–18.

44. D'Angelo, "Da dentro i violi."

45. *Canzoni 'e mala* might be described as contemporary, grittier versions of the more romantic *canzoni di giacca* (jacket songs), named after the style (jacket and a handkerchief tied around the neck) of the guappo figure that (bourgeois) performers adopted, rather than the usual tuxedo. Sceneggiata songs and theater pieces may have been prefigured by jacket songs, which, in the case of Libero Bovio, simulated three-act dramatic "dark tales" of *guappesco* (guappo-like) passion and violence. These, in turn, were partly influenced by the journalist (and later songwriter) Ferdinando Russo's quasi-ethnographic sonnets and stories of "the underworld."

46. The music of spaghetti westerns and polizieschi films were composed, in many cases, by the same artists (e.g., Franco Micalizzi) and performed by orchestras. Some canzoni 'e mala took on this orchestral sound. By the late 1970s neomelodici performed with smaller ensembles and, with the increased accessibility of music technologies, many eventually performed solo. Tarantino helped curate "The Italian King of the B's" at the 2004 Venice Film Festival.

47. *Corriere della sera online*; *Garzanti linguistica online*.

48. Carmelo Zappulla, Mario Abate, and Mario Trevi also sang in Italian, while Sicilian singers such as Zappulla also sang in Sicilian.

49. D'Angelo, "Da dentro i vicoli."

50. Franco, "Il film-sceneggiata," 184.

51. Neomelodica music and TV and radio broadcasting also have long roots outside Campania. Some of the earliest music videos (early to mid-1980s) are of the Sicilian, Carmello Zappulla. The 1980s TV show *The Guests of Nino Delli,* broadcast in Foggia (Puglia), showcased many Campanian singers, including Merola and Patrizio. In 1966 the Telediffusione Italia-Telenapoli was allegedly the first in Italy to break from the closed-circuit model. In the 1970s Berlusconi paved the way for private TV. In the early 1980s his Canale 5 became a formidable competitor with the numerous private channels that had emerged (Righini, "Storia della radiotelevisione italiana"). The private channel Tele Time of Turin broadcast Neapolitan song transmissions from the late 1980s.

52. The letter "x" is a text-messaging neologism meaning *per* (for).

53. The owners of the top (nonpirate) station Radio Studio Emme said it is too costly to hire consultants to gather the data (interview by the author, July 2010).

54. D'Angelo performed at Sanremo in 1986.

55. Other neomelodici performed abroad (Gianni Fiorellino in Bulgaria) and

signed with major labels, but none have achieved D'Alessio's international reach. This may have changed with the younger generation of singers.

56. Frasca, interview by the author, December 2004. For similarities with Algerian rai music, see Schade-Poulsen, *Men and Popular Music*.

57. For parallel phenomena in Nigeria, see Larkin, "Degraded Images."

58. Pine, "Transnational Organized Crime."

59. De Simone, *Canti e tradizioni popolari*.

60. For example, the *tamurriata*, named after the *tamurra*, the handheld drum that accompanies extravagantly expressive microtonal call-like sounds.

61. Feld, "Aesthetics as Iconicity of Style."

62. On Turkish arabesk music, see Stokes, "Tearful Public Sphere."

63. Bendix, *In Search of Authenticity*.

64. D'Angelo, *Core pazzo*, 14–15.

65. Others analyzing neomelodiche narrowcasts see not intimacy but the distance between their own world and this intimate public, which they characterize as "solitude" (e.g., Franco, "Il film-sceneggiata").

66. Putnam, Leonardi, and Nanetti, *Making Democracy Work*.

67. Banfield, *Moral Basis*.

68. Horkheimer, Adorno, and Schmid Noerr, *Dialectic of Enlightenment*; Pardo, *Managing Existence*.

69. Anzalone, "Tu vuò fà 'o talebano."

70. Nisa, "Tu vuò fà l'Americano."

71. Carosone, *Americano a Napoli*, 54. Resina is in the provincial town of Herculaneum and continues to thrive—now with a mix of "licit," counterfeit, and stolen goods from myriad sources.

72. Ibid., 51.

73. D'Agostino, "Fotomodelle un po' povere."

74. *Bellissima* is the superlative form of *bella* (beautiful).

75. Della Monica, "Sesso e malavita."

76. Giuseppe Junior, "Bellissima."

77. Aiello, "Comprensibile esistenza."

78. Carratelli and Pistolese, *Ciro il nero*, 87–88.

79. Berlant, *Female Complaint*, viii.

80. See parallels in Mexican narcocorridos (Wald, *Narcocorrido*) and Spanish flamenco (Washabaugh, *Flamenco*).

81. Pine, "Transnational Organized Crime."

82. Nazionale, *Una vita difficile*, 58–59.

83. Vacalebre, "MeloGrammy, i fantastici quattro."

84. For example, in 1997 the journalist Carlo Ferrajuolo wrote that the neomelodici are popular because they sing with "pride in their cultural difference that never, however, becomes class consciousness" ("Melodia del nuovo millennio").

85. Ibid.

86. Rossi, "Cuore nero."

87. Moe, *View from Vesuvius,* 164–65. See Gilroy, *Black Atlantic,* for the production of black authenticity.

88. Francesco Linguiti, interviewed in the Rai transmission, "Negri del Vesuvio."

89. Interview by the author, December 4, 2001.

90. Naremore, *Acting in Cinema,* 72; Noble, "Crystal/Charlie."

91. The liner notes of an anthology titled "Music of the Vicoli" issued by the Gramsci-founded newspaper *L'unità* describe Valentina as the "Amanda Lear of 2000." Lear, former model and personality in the 1970s–1980s European nightclub scene, was invited by Berlusconi to host a prime-time variety show in 1982.

92. Affron, "Performing Performing," 42.

93. Bataille, "Big Toe," 22–23.

94. Sontag, "Notes on Camp," 106. Sontag writes: "To name a sensibility, to draw its contours and to recount its history, requires a deep sympathy modified by revulsion" (276).

95. Vighi, "Pasolini and Exclusion," 116.

96. Her autobiography begins with her birth: "It was a summer evening like all the others, hot and eternal. Suddenly, among the voices and noises of the vicolo, one heard a shout. 'She's born. A little baby girl is born. My God, she's so beautiful. It's a spectacle.' I was born" (Nazionale, *Una vita difficile,* 6).

97. Vacalebre, "MeloGrammy, i fantastici quattro"; Nazionale, interview by the author, July 29, 2003.

98. Chiaravalle, "Ragione e sentimento."

99. See Pardo, *Managing Existence,* for flexible notions of "legal."

100. Senior and Mazza, "Italian 'Triangle of Death.'"

101. Assante, "Canto canzoni."

102. Vacalebre, *Dentro il vulcano,* 10.

103. Bianchi, "Parola trash r(esiste)," accessed February 2, 2005, http://www.matteobb.com/letture/008.php.

104. Ranaldo, "Baby neomelodici." See also the blog Munnezza da gente ("trash of the people"): munnezzadagente.blogspot.com.

105. Bomboletta, a notorious cocaine addict with a reconstructed septum, encouraged singers to become dependent on him for drugs. See Commissione Parlamentare Antimafia, Doc. XXIII, no. 46-ter (2000) and Commissione Parlementare Anitmafia, Doc. XXIII, no. 16 (2006).

106. Carratelli and Pistolese, *Ciro il nero.*

107. Del Porto, "Sua fissazione."

108. Sposito, "Arrestato a Scampia"; "Organizzò concerto 'non autorizzato.'"

109. Del Porto, "Sua fissazione."

110. Scarpa, "Chi l'ha visto?" 140.

111. Ibid., 142.

112. Ibid.

113. Ibid, 140–42.

114. Saviano, *Gomorra.*

115. Sannino, "Saviano."

116. Coscia, "Raccontare Napoli."

117. Villari, *Lettere meridionali,* wrote that the Neapolitan Question was "colossal" and that "it is necessary to come here to study and convince oneself that the camorra is born not as an abnormal state of affairs, but as the only possible normal state" (12–13).

118. "A Napoli."

119. Sales and Ravveduto, *Strade della violenza,* 273–76.

120. Lucarelli and Sannino, "Napoli, Amato contro i neomelodici"; Lampugnani, "Amato," 3.

121. "Da Raiz a Tommy Riccio," 2.

122. "Sbaglia," 20.

123. Hirschman, *Passions and the Interests.*

124. Taussig, *Defacement*; Taussig, *Magic of the State*; Berlant, *Female Complaint.*

125. Dean, *Publicity's Secret,* writes that "publicity's secret" is that it holds open a space for the fantasy of a unified public and convinces media consumers that the key to democracy is uncovering secrets.

126. Ibid. The infotainment industry repeatedly exposes the injustices of the world but does little to affect the world.

127. Marasca, "Caro Saviano."

128. Lodge, "Interview: Matteo Garrone."

129. Pisa, "Italian Mafia Film *Gomorrah*."

130. Casal del Principe is a town in the Campanian province of Caserta.

131. Armani, "Ma si vene stasera."

132. IFC Films, "Gomorrah Press Notes."

133. "Da '*Gomorra*' al banchetto del boss"; Tricomi, "Blitz al banchetto."

134. Sedgwick, *Epistemology of the Closet.*

135. Biondi, "Camorra o impegno."

3. The Sceneggiata

1. Crimaldi, "Napoli, maxirissa al plebiscito."

2. Ibid.

3. Gribaudi, *Mediatori.*

4. However, competition for honor outside organized criminal organizations is not necessarily dominated by violence (Schneider and Schneider, *Reversible Destiny,* 114–18).

5. Povinelli, *Empire of Love.*

6. Haraway, "Birth of the Kennel."

7. Arlacchi, *Mafia imprenditrice*.

8. Ibid.

9. Sales and Ravveduto, *Strade della violenza*.

10. Taussig, "What Color Is the Sacred?": "Allegory reminds us that by necessity reality skids away from logic, and it is this gap, this apparent imperfection, that nourishes the sacred as the desire for and the impossibility of the union between truth and meaning" (40); Buck-Morss, *Dialectics of Seeing*, 175.

11. Haraway, "Birth of the Kennel"; Buck-Morss, *Dialectics of Seeing*, 184.

12. To avoid a tax on musical entertainment, sceneggiata producers created dramas around songs.

13. The verb *sfregiare* also means "to deface."

14. There are sceneggiate where the law of the vicolo and the law of the state miraculously coincide, both of them punishing the Evildoer in a conventional "happy ending" (Fofi, "Dalla platea," 19–20).

15. Pisano, "Carcerato."

16. Schneider, "Of Vigilance and Virgins."

17. There are other sceneggiata narrative themes (e.g., emigration) and narrative turns (e.g., the killing of She).

18. Benjamin, *German Tragic Drama*, 175.

19. Ibid. Benjamin writes that through allegory "any person, any object, any relationship can mean absolutely anything else. With this possibility a destructive, but just verdict is passed on the profane world: it is characterized as a world in which the detail is of no importance."

20. Alfonso Chiarazzo, interview by the author, March 2003.

21. Giordano, "'O rre d' 'a sceneggiata."

22. Chiarazzo has recounted how audience members slapped and punched the Evildoer of a sceneggiata (interview by the author, September 25, 2003). The singer Mauro Nardi, when I asked him why the sceneggiata is popular among Neapolitans and not Americans, said, "because American men don't have deep feelings of jealousy and they don't want to see big passions in a performance—they want special effects and action" (interview by the author, September 30, 2003).

23. Brooks, *Melodramatic Imagination*.

24. Runcini, "Tempo libero."

25. Feld, "Iconicity of Style," 76, 92–93.

26. Marmo, *Coltello e il mercato*; Benigno, "Dangerous Classes."

27. Marmo and Casarino, "Invincibili loro relazioni," 396.

28. Lamberti, "'Imposture.'"

29. Sessa and Sebastiani, *Sua Maestà*; Grano, *La sceneggiata*; Scialò, *La sceneggiata*.

30. Bruno, *Streetwalking*, 94–96.

31. Ibid.

32. *L'uomo della strada fa giustizia.*

33. D'Ubaldo, "Introduction," 6–7.

34. The feast day of the saint whose name a person shares.

35. Taussig, *Defacement*, 5–6.

36. Schneider, "Of Vigilance and Virgins"; Blok, "Rams and Billy-Goats."

37. Benjamin, *German Tragic Drama*, 111.

38. Schneider and Schneider, *Reversible Destiny.*

39. Arlacchi, *Mafia imprenditrice*, 28–29.

40. Ibid.

41. Herzfeld, *Poetics of Manhood.*

42. Bruno, *Streetwalking*, 122.

43. Bonagura, "Acquarello napoletano."

44. Palomba, "Tradimento."

45. *Corriere della sera dizionari online.*

46. *Garzanti linguistica online.*

47. Stewart, "Arresting Images," 434.

48. Brooks, *Melodramatic Imagination*; Gledhill, "Melodramatic Field."

49. Wimsatt, "Affective Fallacy."

50. Keeler noted similar phenomena in Javanese ritual speech, where the referential meaning recedes as the link with other such ritual speeches, and the "potency" they express, comes to the surface. When meaning is held "in reserve," the potency of language is felt in its effects (Keeler, *Javanese Shadow Plays*, 138–39).

51. Rossi, "'Nu latitante."

52. D'Addio, "Editoriale."

53. Vacalebre, "Dopo il successo."

54. Ibid.

55. Rossi, "'Nu latitante."

4. Family Affairs

1. Ricci, "Innamorato."

2. The album's title erroneously uses the third person singular of "to do" *(fà)* instead of "ago" *(fa).*

3. Pine, "Sogno infranto del ventriloquo."

4. Kittler, *Discourse Networks*; Connor, *Dumbstruck.*

5. Goddard, *Gender, Family, and Work.*

6. Accetto and Nigro, *Della dissimulazione onesta*, 42.

7. Ricoeur, *Freud and Philosophy.*

8. Ibid.; Sedgwick, "Paranoid Reading and Reparative Reading."

9. Feld, "Iconicity of Style"; Keeler, *Javanese Shadow Plays.*

10. Quatriglio, *L'isola.*

11. *Per bene* ("for good") can mean "bourgeois," "scrupulous," and "proper."

12. A yellowish sandstone composed of compacted volcanic ash used in construction in Naples since antiquity.

13. Bakhtin and Emerson, *Problems of Dostoevsky's Poetics.*

14. Akin to "affective athleticism" in Artaud, *Theater and Its Double.*

15. Magrini, "Women's 'Work of Pain'"; Saviano, *Gomorra,* 171–72.

16. Chiarazzo, "Malufiglio."

5. Ethnographic Imbroglios

1. Napolimania, www.napolimania.com (accessed January 20, 2010).

2. De Fazio, mail correspondence with the author, February 12, 2011. In 1995 De Fazio and a partner opened an advertising agency: www.quidequid.it.

3. Love Party founders described the party as "more horizontal than transversal." Before winning the elections in the spring of 2010, Berlusconi inundated millions of television viewers, radio listeners, and print media readers with his new slogan: "Love always conquers hate and envy." When he won, Berlusconi declared that his Free People Party was the victor because it was the Party of Love (Bei, "Da Moana").

4. Cavallieri, "Gran beffa alle Poste."

5. Maradona was suspended for testing positive for cocaine in 1991. He retired when Siniscalchi lost his appeal.

6. De Fazio, e-mail correspondence with the author, July 11, 2011.

7. In fact, they published two books: *Granchi rosa* (Pink gaffes), a pun on the infamous stamp of 1961 created to commemorate the visit of Italian president Giovanni Gronchi to Peru but was withdrawn because it inaccurately depicted the borders of the South American nation, and *The Postman Always Rings Twice.*

8. Cavallieri, "Gran beffa alle Poste."

9. Harris, *Humbug.*

10. "From the mid-1800s forward, the notion of a natural, earthy, volcanic south will be an increasingly significant part of the geographical imagination of Italian elites. Conceived either as backward and as needing northern civilization in order to progress or as picturesque and as providing northern civilization with a form of nature that it either lacks or that is disappearing, southern difference will be alternatively condemned or celebrated." Giacomo Leopardi in his 1837 poem "La Ginestra" likened the people who lived near Vesuvius to a population of ants whose homes are hollowed out of soft soil and can be destroyed in an instant (Moe, *View from Vesuvius,* 120).

11. In the late nineteenth century, "criminal anthropologists" asserted the existence of a largely "congenital" "violent criminal type," found principally in the Italian "South," who harbors "primitive instincts, like passions for orgies and vendettas" (Lombroso-Ferrero and Lombroso, *Criminal Man,* 213).

12. Pulcinella (little louse) is the "master of two servants."

13. The song's title is a phonic play on *funicolare* (cable car) and was written to commemorate the opening of a funicolare up Mt. Vesuvius in 1898.

14. Baker, *Modernism and Harlem Renaissance.*

15. Ibid. During the Harlem Renaissance, African Americans appropriated the blackface mask and transformed it into an art form. Analogously, Neapolitans engage in the essentially ironic practice of self-folklorization, performing for their peers their mastery of the form.

16. For discussions of the class-inflected Kantian disinterested form of aesthetic appreciation, see Bourdieu, *Distinction.* On folklore as a category serving hegemonic projects, see Kirshenblatt-Gimblett, *Destination Culture,* and the work of Washabaugh on flamenco and Stokes on Turkish arabesk music.

17. Kirshenblatt-Gimblett, *Destination Culture.*

18. Dunne and Raby, *Design Noir.*

19. Pink, *Future of Visual Anthropology.*

20. http://www.youtube.com/watch?v=IFIIHWJIDMA.

21. Stewart, *Ordinary Affects*; Stewart, *Space on the Side.*

22. Stewart, "Cultural Poesis," 1027.

23. Buongiovanni, "'A cartulina 'e Napule."

24. "A sticky mess" is a contemporary Neapolitan metaphorical meaning of *pasticcio.* The word *pasticcio* is also used to denote a compositional work (musical, operatic) consisting of hodge-podge, combinatorial styles and authorship, related to the word *pastiche.*

25. Schneider and Schneider, *Reversible Destiny.*

26. Bateson, "Theory of Play."

27. Florio, "Sanità."

28. One composer described a songwriter we knew as "the devil incarnate" because he convinced the parents of a deaf teenager to fund the production of his album.

29. OED online, http://dictionary.oed.com (accessed September 10, 2004).

30. Garzanti linguistica online, www.garzantilinguistica.it (accessed September 10, 2004).

31. Foucault writes, "Resemblance predicates itself upon a model it must return to and reveal; similitude circulates the simulacrum as an indefinite and reversible relation of the similar to the similar" (*This Is Not a Pipe,* 44).

32. Ellis and Bochner, "Autoethnography."

6. Who Am I and Who Are You?

1. "Il neomelodico napoletano."

2. The metaphor of campanilismo is also elaborated with respect to sight:

the parochial concern with only the geographic territory visible from the height of the neighborhood bell tower.

3. A sansara can be a broker of a range of negotiations, including marriage engagements.

4. Goux, *Symbolic Economies,* contrasts the charged, invested, intersubjective exchanges of bartering with the disaffected, meaning-deficient exchange of money in capitalist economy.

5. Ibid., 132.

6. This wouldn't have been the case prior to the criminalization and subsequent retreat from public of the camorra in the 1970s.

7. Fernandez, "Bottom of the Stairs."

8. Macry, *Giocare la vita.*

9. Esposito, "'Nu cuore vestito."

10. Which is not the same as "sea lion" (otaria).

11. American pop/R&B singer who inspired Neapolitan girls to dye their hair blonde and wear blue-tinted sunglasses and tight-fitting shirts exposing their navels.

12. Jacquemet, "Namechasers."

Epilogue

1. Haraway, "Birth of the Kennel."

2. Capozzi, "Camorra al cinema"; "Un camorrista perbene."

3. Capone, "Corona in scena."

4. Destiny's Child, "Say My Name."

5. Nascar, "Lasciarsi su Facebook," http://it-it.facebook.com/video/video.php?v=59056654650 (accessed December 10, 2009).

6. Tubino, "'Lasciarsi su Facebook.'"

Bibliography

Abrahams, Roger D. "Introductory Remarks to a Rhetorical Theory of Folklore." *Journal of American Folklore* 81, no. 320 (1968): 143–58.

Accetto, Torquato, and Salvatore S. Nigro. *Della dissimulazione onesta*. Genova: Edizioni Costa & Nolan, 1983.

Acton, Harold Mario Mitchell. *The Bourbons of Naples, 1734–1825*. London: Methuen, 1956.

Affron, Charles. "Performing Performing: Irony and Affect." *Cinema Journal* 20, no. 1 (1980): 42–52.

Agamben, Giorgio. *Homo Sacer: Sovereign Power and Bare Life*. Stanford, Calif.: Stanford University Press, 1998.

Aiello, Peppe. "La comprensibile esistenza di una musica inaccetabile." In *Concerto napoletano: La canzone dagli anni settanta a oggi,* edited by Peppe Aiello, Stefano De Matteis, Salvatore Palomba, and Pasquale Scialò, 41–61. Lecce: Argo, 1997.

Allum, Felia. *Camorristi, Politicians, and Businessmen: The Transformation of Organized Crime in Post-War Naples*. Leeds: Northern Universities Press, 2006.

———. "Doing It for Themselves or Standing in for Their Men? Women in the Neapolitan Camorra (1950–2003)." In *Women and the Mafia: Female Roles in Organized Crime Structures,* edited by Giovanni Fiandaca, 9–17. Palermo: Springer, 2007.

Allum, Felia, and Percy Allum. "The Resistible Rise of the New Neapolitan Camorra." In *The New Italian Republic: From the Fall of the Berlin Wall to Berlusconi,* edited by Stephen Gundle and Simon Parker, 234–45. London: Routledge, 1996.

———. "Revisiting Naples." *Journal of Modern Italian Studies* 13 (2008): 340–65.

Allum, Percy. "The Politics of Town Planning in Post-War Naples." *Journal of Modern Italian Studies* 8, no. 4 (2003): 500–527.

Anderson, Ben. "Affective Atmospheres." *Emotion, Space, and Society* 2, no. 2 (2009): 77–81.

Arlacchi, Pino. *La mafia imprenditrice: L'etica mafiosa e lo spirito del capitalismo*. Bologna: Il Mulino, 1983.

Artaud, Antonin. *The Theater and Its Double*. New York: Grove, 1958.

Assenza, Concetta. *Giovan Ferretti tra canzonetta e madrigale.* Florence: Olschki, 1989.

Baglivo, Adriano. *Camorra S.p.A.: Droga, omicidi, tangenti a Napoli—Dai contrabbandieri del golfo ai boss in doppiopetto.* Milan: Rizzoli, 1983.

Bagnasco, Arnaldo. *Tracce di comunità.* Bologna: Il Mulino, 1999.

Baker, Houston A. *Modernism and the Harlem Renaissance.* Chicago: University of Chicago Press, 1987.

Bakhtin, Mikhail M. *The Dialogic Imagination: Four Essays,* translated by Michael Holquist. Austin: University of Texas Press, 1981.

———. *Rabelais and His World.* Cambridge, Mass.: MIT Press, 1968.

Bakhtin, Mikhail M., and Caryl Emerson. *Problems of Dostoevsky's Poetics.* Minneapolis: University of Minnesota Press, 1984.

Banfield, Edward C. *The Moral Basis of a Backward Society.* Glencoe, Ill.: Free Press, 1958.

Barbagallo, Francesco. *Storia della camorra.* Rome: Laterza, 2010.

Bassolino, Antonio. *La repubblica delle città.* Rome: Donzelli, 1996.

Bataille, Georges. "The Big Toe." In *Visions of Excess: Selected Writings, 1927–1939,* edited by Allan Stoekl, 20–23. Minneapolis: University of Minnesota Press, 1985.

Bateson, Gregory. "Play and Fantasy." In *The Game Design Reader: A Rules of Play Anthology,* edited by Katie Salen and Eric Zimmerman, 314–28. Cambridge, Mass.: MIT Press, 2006.

———. "A Theory of Play and Fantasy." In *Steps to an Ecology of Mind: Collected Essays in Anthropology, Psychiatry, Evolution, and Epistemology,* 138–48. Northvale, N.J.: Jason Aronson, 1972.

Bauman, Zygmunt. "Ideology and the 'Weltanschauung' of the Intellectuals." *Canadian Journal of Political and Social Theory* 7, nos. 1–2 (1983): 104–17.

Behan, Tom. *The Camorra.* London: Routledge, 1996.

Behar, Ruth. *The Vulnerable Observer: Anthropology That Breaks Your Heart.* Boston: Beacon, 1996.

Bei, Francesco. "Da Moana all'onorevole cicciolina: Quel copyright conteso a Silvio." *La repubblica,* December 27, 2009.

Belmonte, Thomas. *The Broken Fountain.* New York: Columbia University Press, 1979.

Bendix, Regina. *In Search of Authenticity: The Formation of Folklore Studies.* Madison: University of Wisconsin Press, 1997.

Benigno, Francesco. "Dangerous Classes in the Mezzogiorno: Camorra, Mafia, and the Unity of Italy (1860–1876)." Lecture at the Columbia University Seminar on Modern Italian Studies No. 483, October 15, 2010.

———. "Trasformazioni discorsive e identità sociali: Il caso dei 'lazzari.'" *Storica* 31 (2005): 7–44.

Benjamin, Walter. *The Origin of German Tragic Drama.* London: New Left Books, 1977.

————. "Surrealism." In *Reflections: Essays, Aphorisms, Autobiographical Writings,* edited by Peter Demetz, 177–92. New York: Harcourt Brace Jovanovich, 1978.

Benjamin, Walter, and Asja Lacis. "Naples." In *Reflections: Essays, Aphorisms, Autobiographical Writings,* edited by Peter Demetz, 163–73. New York: Harcourt Brace Jovanovich, 1978.

Berlant, Lauren Gail. *The Female Complaint: The Unfinished Business of Sentimentality in American Culture.* Durham, N.C.: Duke University Press, 2008.

Bianchi, Matteo. "La parola trash (r)esiste." http://www.matteobb.com/letture /008.php.

Biondi, Katia. "Camorra o impegno: La vita in una canzone." *Avvenire,* February 2, 2005.

Blok, Anton. *The Mafia of a Sicilian Village, 1860–1960: A Study of Violent Peasant Entrepreneurs.* New York: Harper and Row, 1975.

————. "Rams and Billy-Goats: A Key to the Mediterranean Code of Honour." *Man* 16, no. 3 (1981): 427–40.

Blom Hansen, Thomas, and Oskar Verkaaik. "Introduction: Urban Charisma." *Critique of Anthropology* 29, no. 1 (2009): 5–26.

Böhme, Gernot. *Aesthetics.* Tokyo: Faculty of Letters, the University of Tokyo, 2006.

————. *Aisthetik: Vorlesungen über Ästhetik als allgemeine Wahrnehmungslehre.* Munich: Fink, 2001.

————. "Atmosphere as the Fundamental Concept of a New Aesthetics." *Thesis Eleven* 36 (1993): 113–26.

"Boss chiede diritti su colonna Sonora." *Corriere della sera,* October 9, 1996, 13, http://archiviostorico.corriere.it/1996/ottobre/09/Boss_chiede_diritti _colonna_sonora_co_0_9610094430.shtml.

Bourdieu, Pierre. *Distinction: A Social Critique of the Judgement of Taste.* Cambridge, Mass.: Harvard University Press, 1984.

Bourgois, Philippe I. *In Search of Respect: Selling Crack in El Barrio.* Cambridge: Cambridge University Press, 1996.

Brooks, Peter. *The Melodramatic Imagination: Balzac, Henry James, Melodrama, and the Mode of Excess.* New Haven, Conn.: Yale University Press, 1976.

Bruni, Sergio. "Sergio Bruni: La ricerca della perfezione." In *Concerto napoletano: La canzone dagli anni settanta a oggi,* edited by Peppe Aiello, Stefano De Matteis, Salvatore Palomba, and Pasquale Scialò, 129–38. Lecce: Argo, 1997.

Bruno, Giuliana. *Streetwalking on a Ruined Map: Cultural Theory and the City Films of Elvira Notari.* Princeton, N.J.: Princeton University Press, 1993.

Buck-Morss, Susan. *The Dialectics of Seeing: Walter Benjamin and the Arcades Project.* Cambridge, Mass.: MIT Press, 1989.

Burke, Peter. *Popular Culture in Early Modern Europe.* New York: Harper and Row, 1978.

Candea, Matei. "Anonymous Introductions: Identity and Belonging in Corsica." *Journal of the Royal Anthropological Institute* 16, no. 1 (2010): 119–37.

———. *Corsican Fragments: Difference, Knowledge, and Fieldwork.* Bloomington: Indiana University Press, 2010.

Capone, Mariagiovanna. "Corona in scena a Natale al Sannazaro con 'Guapparia' fatta a sceneggiata." *Il Mattino,* August 9, 2010, http://www.ilmattino.it/articolo .php?id=114097&sez=SPETTACOLO.

Capozzi, Ciccio. "La camorra al cinema." *RadioSiani,* July 15, 2010, http://www .radiosiani.com/index.php?option=com_content&view=article&id=714:la -camorra-al-cinema&catid=38:cultura&Itemid=174.

Cardamone, Donna G. *The Debut of the Canzone Villanesca Alla Napolitana.* Florence: L. S. Olschki, 1978.

Carosone, Renato. *Un Americano a Napoli.* Milan: Sperling & Kupfer Editori, 2000.

Carratelli, Domenico, and Bruno Pistolese. *Ciro il nero: Ciro Ricci da cantante di strada a divo neomelodico.* Naples: Tulio Pironti Editore, 1998.

Caton, Steven C. *Yemen Chronicle: An Anthropology of War and Mediation.* New York: Hill and Wang, 2005.

Cavallieri, Marina. "Gran beffa alle Poste a suon Francobolli." *La repubblica,* October 5, 1991.

"Centrale dei cd falsi: Oggi l'interrogatorio." *Cronaca di Napoli,* March 15, 2009, 93.63.239.228/archivio/2009/Marzo/15/Giornale_di.../15-03-pag.pdf.

Certeau, Michel de. *Heterologies: Discourse on the Other.* Minneapolis: University of Minnesota Press, 1986.

Coletto, Diego. *The Informal Economy and Employment in Brazil: Latin America, Modernization, and Social Changes.* New York: Palgrave Macmillan, 2010.

Commissione Parlamentare Antimafia. *Commissione parlamentare d'inchiesta sul fenomeno della mafia e sulle altre associazioni criminali similari.* Doc. XXIII, no. 12. Rome: Camera dei Deputati, Legislatura XI, 2000.

———. *Commissione parlamentare d'inchiesta sul fenomeno della mafia e sulle altre associazioni criminali similari.* Doc. XXIII, no. 3. Rome: Camera dei Deputati, Legislatura XIV, 2003.

———. *Commissione parlamentare d'inchiesta sul fenomeno della mafia e sulle altre associazioni criminali similari: Relazione Sulla Camorra.* Doc. XXIII, no. 16. Rome: Camera dei Deputati, Legislatura XIV, 2006.

———. *Consigli comunali sciolti,* Legislatura XV, 2007, http://www.camera .it/_bicamerali/leg15/commbicantimafia/documentazionetematica/23 /schedabase.asp.

———. *Relazione sullo stato della lotta all criminalità in Campania.* Doc. XXIII, no. 46-ter. Rome: Camera dei Deputati, Legislatura XIII, 2000.

Connor, Steven. *Dumbstruck: A Cultural History of Ventriloquism.* Oxford: Oxford University Press, 2000.

Conquergood, Lorne Dwight. *Homeboys and Hoods: Gang Communication and Cultural Space.* Evanston, Ill.: Center for Urban Affairs and Policy Research, Northwestern University, 1993.

———. *Performing as a Moral Act: Ethical Dimensions of the Ethnography of Performance*. 1985.

Corriere della sera dizionari online, www.dizionari.corriere.it.

Coscia, Biagio. "Grammy per (post)melodici." *Corriere del mezzogiorno*, May 27, 2009.

Coscia, Fabrizio. "Raccontare Napoli dopo il libro di Saviano." *Il Mattino*, November 21, 2006, www.federmandolino.it%2Ffile_pdf%2FIlMattino-Saviano-21112006.pdf.

Cosier, Kimberly. "Crystal/Charley: Lessons on Youthful Queer Identity." *Visual Culture and Gender* 2 (2007): 6–15.

Cragin, Thomas. *Murder in Parisian Streets: Manufacturing Crime and Justice in the Popular Press, 1830–1900*. Lewisburg, Pa.: Bucknell University Press, 2006.

Crimaldi, Giuseppe. "Napoli, maxirissa al plebiscito sotto gli occhi dei turisti." *Il Mattino*, July 22, 2009.

Croce, Benedetto. "I 'lazzari' negli avvenimenti del 1799." *La critica: Rivista di letteratura, storia e filosofia diretta da B. Croce* 32 (1934): 458–71.

Csordas, Thomas J. *Embodiment and Experience: The Existential Ground of Culture and Self*. Cambridge: Cambridge University Press, 1994.

———. "Embodiment as a Paradigm for Anthropology." *Ethos* 18, no. 1 (1990): 5–47.

———. "Somatic Modes of Attention." *Cultural Anthropology* 8, no. 2 (1993): 135–56.

Cutolo, Raffaele. *Poesie e pensieri*. Naples: Berisio, 1980.

D'Addio, Antonio. "Editoriale." *Sciuè*, August 1997.

"Da 'Gomorra' al banchetto del boss." *La Stampa*, May 28, 2009, http://www.lastampa.it/redazione/cmssezioni/cronache/200905articoli/44132girata.asp.

"Da Raiz a Tommy Riccio: 'Ma il nemico non siamo noi.'" *La Repubblica*, December 15, 2006, 2, http://ricerca.repubblica.it/repubblica/archivio/repubblica/2006/12/15/da-raiz-tommy-riccio-ma-il-nemico.html.

Damasio, Antonio R. *Descartes' Error: Emotion, Reason, and the Human Brain*. New York: Putnam, 1994.

———. *The Feeling of What Happens: Body and Emotion in the Making of Consciousness*. New York: Harcourt Brace, 1999.

———. *Looking for Spinoza: Joy, Sorrow, and the Feeling Brain*. Boston: Houghton Mifflin Harcourt, 2003.

D'Angelo, Nino. *Core Pazzo*. Milan: Baldini Castoldi Dalai, 2010.

———. "Nino D'Angelo: Da dentro i vicoli." In *Concerto napoletano: La canzone dagli anni settanta a oggi*, edited by Peppe Aiello, Stefano De Matteis, Salvatore Palomba, and Pasquale Scialò, 145–61. Lecce: Argo, 1997.

Davis, John Anthony. *Conflict and Control: Law and Order in Nineteenth-Century Italy*. Atlantic Highlands, N.J.: Humanities Press International, 1988.

De Fazio, Maurizio, Lello Padiglione, and Pierluca Sabatino. *Granchi Rosa: 160 Francobolli Che Sconvolsero l'Italia*. Leeds: Leonardo Editore, 1991.

De Fazio, Maurizio, and Pierluca Sabatino. *Il postino suona sempre due volte.* Milan: Baldini and Castoldi, 1993.

De Lamartine, Alphonse. "Dernier chant du pèlerinage d'Harold, Alphonse de Lamartine, and Chant du sacre." In *Nouvelle méditations poétiques, avec commentaires; Le dernier chant du pèlerinage d'Harold; Chant du sacre.* Paris: Hachette, 1886.

De Mura, Ettore. *Enciclopedia della canzone napoletana.* Vol. 3. Naples: Il torchio, 1968–1969.

De Simone, Roberto. *Canti e tradizioni popolari in Campania.* Rome: Lato side, 1979.

———. *Masaniello: Nella drammaturgie europea e nella iconografia del suo secolo.* Naples: G. Macchiaroli, 1998.

Dean, Jodi. *Publicity's Secret: How Technoculture Capitalizes on Democracy.* Ithaca, N.Y.: Cornell University Press, 2002.

Del Porto, Dario. "La sua fissazione: Sparare a quell'impresario diceva che gli aveva mancato di rispetto." *Il Mattino,* October 18, 2008, http://ricerca.repubblica.it/repubblica/archivio/repubblica/2008/10/18/la-sua-fissazione-sparare-quell-impresario-diceva.html.

Deleuze, Gilles. *Cinema 2: The Time Image.* Minneapolis: University of Minnesota Press, 1989.

Deleuze, Gilles, and Félix Guattari. *A Thousand Plateaus: Capitalism and Schizophrenia.* Minneapolis: University of Minnesota Press, 1987.

Della Monica, Andrea. "Sesso e malavita nelle canzoni dei baby neomelodici." *Il levante online,* December 2, 2009, http://www.levanteonline.net/primo-piano/approfondimenti/493-sesso-e-malavita-nelle-canzoni-dei-baby-neomelodici-ed-e-polemica.html.

Denzin, Norman K. *Performance Ethnography: Critical Pedagogy and the Politics of Culture,* Thousand Oaks, Calif.: Sage, 2003.

Denzin, Norman K., and Yvonna S. Lincoln. *Strategies of Qualitative Inquiry.* Thousand Oaks, Calif.: Sage, 1998.

Depraz, Natalie. "Where Is the Phenomenology of Attention That Husserl Intended to Perform? A Transcendental Pragmatic-Oriented Description of Attention." *Continental Philosophy Review* 37, no. 1 (2004): 5–20.

Depraz, Natalie, Francisco J. Varela, and Pierre Vermersch. *On Becoming Aware: A Pragmatics of Experiencing.* Amsterdam: John Benjamins Publishing, 2003.

Desjarlais, Robert R. *Body and Emotion: The Aesthetics of Illness and Healing in the Nepal Himalayas.* Philadelphia: University of Pennsylvania Press, 1992.

———. *Counterplay: An Anthropologist at the Chessboard.* Berkeley: University of California Press, 2011.

———. *Sensory Biographies: Lives and Deaths among Nepal's Yolmo Buddhists.* Berkeley: University of California Press, 2003.

Di Bella, Maria Pia. *Dire ou taire en sicile.* Paris: Félin, 2008.

Di Leonardo, Micaela. *The Varieties of Ethnic Experience: Kinship, Class, and Gen-*

der among California Italian-Americans. Ithaca, N.Y.: Cornell University Press, 1984.

Diaconu, Mădălina. "Patina—Atmosphere—Aroma." In *Logos of Phenomenology and Phenomenology of the Logos.* Book 5, edited by Anna-Teresa Tymieniecka, 131–48. Dordrecht: Springer Netherlands, 2006.

Dines, Nicholas. "Urban Renewal, Immigration, and Contested Claims to Public Space: The Case of Piazza Garibaldi in Naples." *GeoJournal* 58, nos. 2–3 (2002): 177–88.

Donadio, Rachel. "Berlusconi's Burlesque." *New York Times,* August 6, 2006, http://www.nytimes.com/2006/08/06/books/review/06donadio.html.

D'Ubaldo, Marco. "Introduction." In *Attori a mano armato,* edited by Marco D'Ubaldo and Pieropaolo Duranti. Rome: Mediane Amarkod, 2007.

Dufrenne, Mikel. *The Phenomenology of Aesthetic Experience.* Evanston, Ill.: Northwestern University Press, 1973.

Dunne, Anthony, and Fiona Raby. *Design Noir: The Secret Life of Electronic Objects.* London: Birkhäuser, 2001.

Ellis, Carolyn, and Arthur P. Bochner. "Autoethnography, Personal Narrative, Reflexivity: Researcher as Subject." In *Handbook of Qualitative Research,* 2nd ed., edited by Norman K. Denzin and Yvonna S. Lincoln, 733–68. Thousand Oaks, Calif.: Sage, 2000.

Favret-Saada, Jeanne. *Deadly Words: Witchcraft in the Bocage.* Cambridge: Cambridge University Press, 1980.

Feld, Steven. "Aesthetics as Iconicity of Style, or 'Lift-Up-Over Sounding': Getting into the Kaluli Groove." *Yearbook for Traditional Music* 20 (1998): 74–113.

———. "From Schizophonia to Schismogenesis: On the Discourses and Practices of World Music and World Beat." In *Music Grooves: Essays and Dialogues,* edited by Charles Keil and Steven Feld, 257–89. Chicago: University of Chicago Press, 1994.

Fernandez, James W. "The Dark at the Bottom of the Stairs: The Inchoate in Symbolic Inquiry and Some Strategies for Coping with It." In *Persuasions and Performances: The Play of Tropes in Culture,* edited by James W. Fernandez, 214–38. Bloomington: Indiana University Press, 1986.

Ferrajuolo, Carlo. "Melodia del nuovo millennio." *Il giornale di Napoli,* August 7, 1997.

Fiandaca, Giovanni. *Women and the Mafia: Female Roles in Organized Crime Structures.* Palermo: Springer, 2007.

Florio, Paola. "Sanità: Dove non si muore di fame ma non si vive di lavoro." *Valori* 6, no. 45 (2006): 42–43.

Fofi, Goffredo. "Dalla platea." In *La sceneggiata: Rappresentazioni di un genere popolare,* edited by Pasquale Scialò, 11–24. Naples: Guida, 2002.

Foot, John. *Winning at All Costs: A Scandalous History of Italian Soccer.* New York: Nation Books, 2007.

Foucault, Michel. *This Is Not a Pipe,* translated by James Harkness. Berkeley: University of California Press, 1983.

Franco, Mario. "Il film-sceneggiata." In *La sceneggiata: Rappresentazioni di un genere popolare,* edited by Pasquale Scialò, 157–290. Naples: Guida, 2002.

Frasca, Simona. *Birds of Passage: I musicisti napoletani e New York (1895–1940).* Lucca: Libreria musicale italiana, 2010.

Frégier, Honoré Antoine. *Des classes dangereuses de la population dans les grandes villes, et des moyens de les rendre meilleures: Ouvrage récompensé en 1838.* Paris: Baillière, 1840.

Gabaccia, Donna. "A Global Geography of 'Little Italy': Italian Neighbourhoods in Comparative Perspective." *Modern Italy* 11 (2006): 9–24.

Garzanti linguistica online, http://garzantilinguistica.sapere.it.

Gay, Luigi. "L'Atteggiarsi delle associazioni mafiose sulla base delle esperienze processuali acquisite: La camorra." *Quaderni del Consiglio Superiore della Magistratura,* no. 99-3 (1996).

Gendlin, Eugene T. *Experiencing and the Creation of Meaning: A Philosophical and Psychological Approach to the Subjective.* Evanston, Ill.: Northwestern University Press, 1997.

Geurts, Kathryn Linn. *Culture and the Senses: Bodily Ways of Knowing in an African Community.* Berkeley: University of California Press, 2002.

Gilroy, Paul. *The Black Atlantic: Modernity and Double Consciousness.* Cambridge, Mass.: Harvard University Press, 1993.

Ginsborg, Paul. *Silvio Berlusconi: Television, Power, and Patrimony.* London: Verso, 2004.

Gledhill, Christine. "The Melodramatic Field: An Introduction." In *Home Is Where the Heart Is: Studies in Melodrama and the Woman's Film,* 5–39. London: British Film Institute, 1987.

Goddard, Victoria A. *Gender, Family, and Work in Naples.* Oxford: Berg, 1996.

Goodwin, Paul D., and Joseph W. Wenzel. "Proverbs and Practical Reasoning: A Study in Socio-Logic." *Quarterly Journal of Speech* 65, no. 3 (1968): 89–302.

Goux, Jean-Joseph. *Symbolic Economies: After Marx and Freud.* Ithaca, N.Y.: Cornell University Press, 1990.

Grano, Enzo. *La sceneggiata.* Naples: Attività Bibliografica Editoriale, 1976.

Gribaudi, Gabriella. "Clan camorristi a Napoli: Radicamento locale e traffici internazionali." In *Traffici criminali: Camorra, mafie e reti internazionali dell'illegalità,* 187–240. Turin: Bollati Boringhieri, 2009.

———. *Donne, uomini, famiglie: Napoli nel novecento.* Rome: L'ancora, 1999.

———. Introduction to *Traffici criminali: Camorra, mafie e reti internazionali dell'illegalità,* edited by Gabriella Gribaudi, 9–30. Turin: Bollati Boringhieri, 2009.

———. *Mediatori: Antropologia del potere democristiano nel mezzogiorno.* Turin: Rosenberg & Sellier, 1980.

Hansen, Thomas Blom, and Finn Stepputat, eds. *Sovereign Bodies: Citizens, Mi-

grants, and States in the Postcolonial World. Princeton, N.J.: Princeton University Press, 2005.

Haraway, Donna. "Birth of the Kennel." Lecture, European Graduate School, New York, August 2000, http://www.egs.edu/faculty/donna-haraway/articles /birth-of-the-kennel/.

Harris, Neil. *Humbug: The Art of P. T. Barnum.* Boston: Little, Brown, 1973.

Hart, Keith. "Informal Income Opportunities and Urban Employment in Ghana." *Journal of Modern African Studies* 11, no. 1 (1973): 61–89.

Hart, Keith, Jean-Louis Laville, and Antonio David Cattani. *The Human Economy: A Citizen's Guide.* Cambridge: Polity, 2010.

Hebdige, Dick. *Subculture: The Meaning of Style.* London: Methuen, 1979.

Heidegger, Martin. *Being and Time,* translated by Joseph Stambaugh. Rev. ed. Albany: State University of New York Press, 2010.

Herzfeld, Michael. *The Poetics of Manhood: Contest and Identity in a Cretan Mountain Village.* Princeton, N.J.: Princeton University Press, 1988.

Hirschman, Albert O. *Crossing Boundaries: Selected Writings.* New York: Zone Books, 1998.

———. *The Passions and the Interests: Political Arguments for Capitalism before Its Triumph.* Princeton, N.J.: Princeton University Press, 1977.

———. *Shifting Involvements: Private Interest and Public Action.* Princeton, N.J.: Princeton University Press, 1982.

Hobsbawm, E. J. *Primitive Rebels: Studies in Archaic Forms of Social Movement in the 19th and 20th Centuries.* New York: Norton, 1965.

Horkheimer, Max, Theodor W. Adorno, and Gunzelin Schmid Noerr. *Dialectic of Enlightenment: Philosophical Fragments.* Stanford, Calif.: Stanford University Press, 2002.

Husserl, Edmund. *The Idea of Phenomenology.* The Hague: Martinus Nijhoff, 1964.

———. *The Phenomenology of Internal Time-Consciousness.* Bloomington: Indiana University Press, 1964.

IFC Films. "Gomorrah Press Notes." 2008, http://www.ifcfilmsextranet.com /download.php?file=data/vault/gommorah/Press_Notes_FINAL_020209 .pdf (authorized access required).

"Il neomelodico napoletano: Quando l'arte di arrangiarsi diventa fenomeno." Master's thesis, University of Naples, Federico II, 2001.ISTAT. *Annuario di statistiche giudiziarie penali.* Vols. 1983–94.

Jackson, Michael. *At Home in the World.* Durham, N.C.: Duke University Press, 1995.

———. *Excursions.* Durham, N.C.: Duke University Press, 2007.

———. *The Palm at the End of the Mind: Relatedness, Religiosity, and the Real.* Durham, N.C.: Duke University Press, 2009.

Jacquemet, Marco. *Credibility in Court: Communicative Practices in the Camorra Trials.* Cambridge: Cambridge University Press, 1996.

———. "Namechasers." *American Ethnologist* 19 (1992): 733–48.

James, William. *The Varieties of Religious Experience.* New York: Library of America, 2010.

Jorio, Andrea de, and Adam Kendon. *Gesture in Naples and Gesture in Classical Antiquity: A Translation of La Mimica Degli Antichi Investigata Nel Gestire Napoletano, Gestural Expression of the Ancients in the Light of Neapolitan Gesturing.* Bloomington: Indiana University Press, 2000.

Kalyvas, Andreas. "Hegemonic Sovereignty: Carl Schmitt, Antonio Gramsci, and the Constituent Prince." *Journal of Political Ideologies* 5, no. 3 (2000): 343–76.

Katz, Jack, and Thomas J. Csordas, eds. *Phenomenology in Ethnography.* London: Sage, 2003.

Keeler, Ward. *Javanese Shadow Plays, Javanese Selves.* Princeton, N.J.: Princeton University Press, 1987.

Kendon, Adam. "Andrea De Jorio: The First Ethnographer of Gesture?" *Visual Anthropology* 7 (1995): 371–90.

———. "Do Gestures Communicate? A Review." *Research on Language and Social Interaction* 27, no. 3 (1994): 175–200.

———. *Gesture: Visible Action as Utterance.* Cambridge: Cambridge University Press, 2004.

Kirshenblatt-Gimblett, Barbara. *Destination Culture: Tourism, Museums, and Heritage.* Berkeley: University of California Press, 1998.

———. "Toward a Theory of Proverb Meaning." In *The Wisdom of Many: Essays on the Proverb,* edited by Wolfgang Mieder and Alan Dundes, 111–21. Madison: University of Wisconsin Press, 1994.

Kittler, Friedrich A. *Discourse Networks 1800/1900.* Stanford, Calif.: Stanford University Press, 1990.

Klima, Alan. *The Funeral Casino: Meditation, Massacre, and Exchange with the Dead in Thailand.* Princeton, N.J.: Princeton University Press, 2002.

La Penna, Marisa. "Porta Nolana, scoperti i depositi del falso, 100mila DVD." *Il Mattino,* May 22, 2009.

Lamberti, Amato. "Camorra come 'metodo' e 'sistema.'" In *Traffici criminali: Camorra, mafia e reti internazionali dell'illegalità,* edited by Gabriella Gribaudi, 482–504. Turin: Bollati Boringhieri, 2009.

———. "Così governa la camorra." In *Osservatorio Sulla Camorra, 8, XII.* Naples: Fondazione Colasanto, 1990.

———. "'Imposture' letterarie e 'simulacri' poetici: Il ruolo di Ferdinando Russo nella costruzione dell'immaginario di massa sulla 'camorra.'" In *Le rappresentazioni della camorra: Lingua, letteratura, teatro, cinema, storia,* edited by Patricia Bianchi and Pasquale Sabbatino, 199–220. Naples: Edizioni scientifiche italiane, 2009.

Lampugnani, Rosanna. "Amato: 'Per i clan la nottata non passerà.'" *Corriere del*

Mezzogiorno, December 14, 2006, www.comune.napoli.it/flex/cm/pages/... php/L/IT/.../BLOB:ID%3D3627.

Lanzetta, Peppe. *Figli di un Bronx minore.* Milan: Feltrinelli, 1993.

———. *Un messico napoletano.* Milan: Feltrinelli, 1994.

Larkin, Brian. "Degraded Images, Distorted Sounds: Nigerian Video and the Infrastructure of Piracy." *Public Culture* 16, no. 2 (2004): 289–314.

Latour, Bruno. "How to Talk about the Body? The Normative Dimension of Science Studies." *Body and Society* 10, nos. 2–3 (2004): 205–29.

———. *Reassembling the Social: An Introduction to Actor-Network-Theory.* Oxford: Oxford University Press, 2005.

Latour, Bruno, and Vincent Antonin Lépinay. *The Science of Passionate Interests: An Introduction to Gabriel Tarde's Economic Anthropology.* Chicago: University of Chicago Press, 2009.

Legambiente. "Pesce fresco . . . Forse . . . Quasi: Primo rapporto di S&G sui prodotti ittici." *Alimentazione News,* December 21, 2004.

Levy, Ariel. "Basta Bunga Bunga: Have Italians Had Enough of Silvio Berlusconi—and the Culture He Embodies?" *New Yorker,* June 6, 2011.

Lewin, Ellen, and William Leap. *Out in the Field: Reflections of Lesbian and Gay Anthropologists.* Urbana: University of Illinois Press, 1996.

Linder, Fletcher. "Life as Art, and Seeing the Promise of Big Bodies." *American Ethnologist* 34, no. 3 (2007): 451–72.

Lodge, Gary. "Interview: Matteo Garrone." *In Contention,* December 17, 2008, http://incontention.com/2008/12/17/interview-matteo-garrone/.

Lombroso-Ferrero, Gina, and Cesare Lombroso. *Criminal Man, According to the Classification of Cesare Lombroso.* Montclair, N.J.: Patterson Smith, 1972.

Longrigg, Clare. *Mafia Women.* London: Chatto and Windus, 1997.

———. *No Questions Asked: The Secret Life of Women in the Mob.* New York: Hyperion, 2004.

Lucarelli, Olimpia, and Conchita Sannino. "Napoli, Amato contro i neomelodici 'Celebrano i camorristi come eroi.'" *La Repubblica,* December 14, 2006.

Machiavelli, Niccolò. *The Prince,* translated by Harvey C. Mansfield. Chicago: University of Chicago Press, 1998.

Macry, Paolo. "Borghesia, città e lo stato Appunti e impressioni su Napoli (1860–1880)." *Quaderni Storici,* 19, no. 56 (1984): 339–83.

———. *Giocare la vita: Storia del lotto a Napoli tra sette e ottocento.* Rome: Donzelli, 1997.

Magrini, Tullia. "Women's 'Work of Pain' in Christian Mediterranean Europe." *Music and Anthropology* 3 (1998), http://www.umbc.edu/MA/index/number3/magrini/magr0.htm.

Marasca, Chiara. "Tano Grasso: 'Caro Saviano, dico no agli eroi solitari.'" *Corriere del Mezzogiorno,* October 15, 2009.

Marengo, Renato, and Michael Pergolani. *Song 'e Napule.* Rome: RAI-ERI, 1998.

Marmo, Marcella. *Il coltello e il mercato: La camorra prima e dopo l'unità d'Italia.* Naples-Rome: L'ancora del mediterraneo, 2011.

———. "'I processi indiziari non se ne dovrebbero mai fare': Le manipolazioni del processo cuocolo (1906–1930)." In *La costruzione della verità giudiziaria,* edited by Marcella Marmo and Luigi Musella, 101–70. Naples: Clio Press, 2003.

———. "La città camorrista e i suoi confini: Dall'Unità al processo cuocolo." In *Traffici criminali: Camorra, mafie e reti internazionali dell'illegalità,* edited by Gabriella Gribaudi, 33–64. Turin: Bollati Boringhieri, 2009.

———. "L'onore dei violenti, l'onore delle vittime: Un'estorsione camorrista del 1862 a Napoli. In *Onore e storia nelle società mediterranee,* edited by Giovanna Fiume. Palermo: La Luna, 1989.

Marmo, Marcella, and Olimpia Casarino. "'Le invincibili loro relazioni': Indentificazione e controllo della camorra napoletana nelle fonti di età postunitaria," *Studi Storici* 29, no. 2 (1988): 385–419.

Massumi, Brian. "The Autonomy of Affect." *Cultural Critique* 31 (1995): 83–110.

———. "The Future Birth of the Affective Fact." In *The Affect Theory Reader,* edited by Melissa Gregg and Gregory J. Seigworth, 52–70. Durham, N.C.: Duke University Press, 2010.

———. *Parables for the Virtual: Movement, Affect, Sensation.* Durham, N.C.: Duke University Press, 2002.

Mastriani, Francesco. *I vermi: Studi storici su le classi pericolose in Napoli.* Naples: M. Miliano. 1972.

Matlock, Jann. *Scenes of Seduction: Prostitution, Hysteria, and Reading Difference in Nineteenth-Century France.* New York: Columbia University Press, 1994.

Maurer, Bill. *Mutual Life, Limited: Islamic Banking, Alternative Currencies, Lateral Reason.* Princeton, N.J.: Princeton University Press, 2005.

Merleau-Ponty, Maurice. *Phenomenology of Perception.* New York: Humanities Press, 1962.

Meyer, Leonard B. *Emotion and Meaning in Music.* Chicago: University of Chicago Press, 1956.

Moe, Nelson. *The View from Vesuvius: Italian Culture and the Southern Question.* Berkeley: University of California Press, 2002.

Monnier, Marc. *Il brigantaggio da Fra' Diavolo a Crocco.* Lecce: Capone, 2001.

———. *La camorra: Notizie storiche raccolte e documentate.* Naples: Arturo Berisio Editore, 1965.

———. *L'Italie est-elle la terre des morts?* Paris: L. Hachette et cie, 1860.

Naficy, Hamid. *The Making of Exile Cultures: Iranian Television in Los Angeles.* Minneapolis: University of Minnesota Press, 1993.

Naremore, James. *Acting in the Cinema.* Berkeley: University of California Press, 1988.

Nazionale, Maria. *Una vita difficile.* Naples: Franco Di Mauro Editore, 1998.

Nordstrom, Carolyn. *Global Outlaws: Crime, Money, and Power in the Contemporary World*. Berkeley: University of California Press, 2007.

"Organizò concerto 'non autorizzato' dal clan: Missione di morte contro di lui." *Corriere del mezzogiorno*, October 17, 2008, http://corrieredelmezzogiorno .corriere.it/napoli/notizie/cronaca/2008/17-ottobre-2008/organizzo-concerto -non-autorizzato-clan-missione-morte-contro-lui-140602552475.shtml.

Owen, Richard. "Silvio Berlusconi in Racism Row over 'Suntanned' Barack Obama Aside." *Times* (London), November 6, 2008.

Paliotti, Vittorio. *La camorra: Storia, personaggi, riti della bella società napoletana dalle origini a oggi*. Milan: Bietti, 1973.

———. *Forcella: La strada che nel dopoguerra salvò Napoli dalla fame ma che divenne ostaggio della camorra: La casbah di Napoli*. Naples: Tulio Pironti, 2005.

Palomba, Salvatore. "Storia (personale) della canzone napoletana." In *Concerto napoletano: La canzone dagli anni settante a oggi*, edited by Peppe Aiello, Stefano De Matteis, Salvatore Palomba, and Pasquale Scialò, 17–39. Lecce: Argo, 1997.

Pardo, Italo. *Managing Existence in Naples: Morality, Action, and Structure*. Cambridge: Cambridge University Press, 1996.

Pasotti, Eleonora. *Political Branding in Cities: The Decline of Machine Politics in Bogotà, Naples, and Chicago*. Cambridge: Cambridge University Press, 2010.

Peraldi, Michel, and Veronique Manry. "Le lien et le gain: Le marché aux Puces de Marseille: Une aberration économique?" In *Economies choisies? Echanges, circulations et débrouille*, edited by Noel Barbe and Serge Latouche, 39–58. Paris: la Maison des Sciences de l'Homme, collection Ethnologie de la France, 2002.

Petrusewicz, Marta. *Come Il Meridione divenne una questione: Rappresentazioni del sud prima e dopo il quarantotto*. Soveria Mannelli (Catanzaro): Rubbettino, 1998.

Phillips, John. "Fifth Mafia Boss Is Killed as Gang War Grips Italian South." *Independent*, January 7, 2005, http://www.independent.co.uk/news/world /europe/fifth-mafia-boss-is-killed-as-gang-war-grips-italian-south-495576.html.

Pine, Jason. "Il sogno infranto del ventriloquo." *Il manifesto (ALIAS)*, March 2, 2002.

———. "Transnational Organized Crime and Alternative Culture Industry." In *Routledge Handbook of Transnational Organized Crime*, edited by Felia Allum and Stan Gilmour. London: Routledge, 2011.

Pink, Sarah. *The Future of Visual Anthropology: Engaging the Senses*. London: Routledge, 2006.

Pisa, Nick. "Italian Mafia Film *Gomorrah* Heads for Oscars—as Cast Members Are Arrested." *Telegraph*, October 13, 2008, http://www.telegraph.co.uk /news/worldnews/europe/3186186/Italian-mafia-film-Gomorrah-heads-for -Oscars-as-cast-members-are-arrested.html.

Portes, Alejandro, Manuel Castells, and Lauren A. Benton. *The Informal Economy: Studies in Advanced and Less Developed Countries*. Baltimore, Md.: Johns Hopkins University Press, 1989.

Povinelli, Elizabeth A. *The Empire of Love: Toward a Theory of Intimacy, Genealogy, and Carnality.* Durham, N.C.: Duke University Press, 2006.

Pratt, Mary Louise. "Arts of the Contact Zone." In *Profession* 91 (1991): 33–40.

Pritchard, Matthew. "Directions in Contemporary German Aesthetics." *Journal of Aesthetic Education* 43, no. 3 (2009): 117–27.

Putnam, Robert D., Robert Leonardi, and Raffaella Nanetti. *Making Democracy Work: Civic Traditions in Modern Italy.* Princeton, N.J.: Princeton University Press, 1993.

Ranaldo, Margherita. "Baby neomelodici: 'Nutile e ipocrita gridare allo scandalo.' Intervista a Ciro Ascione." *Il Levant,* December 2, 2009, http://www.levanteonline.net/primo-piano/approfondimenti/495-baby-neomelodici-qinutile-e-ipocrita-gridare-allo-scandaloq-intervista-a-ciro-ascione.html.

Raniolo, Francesco. "Forza Italia: A Leader with a Party." *Southern European Society and Politics* 2, nos. 3–4 (2006): 439–55.

Ravveduto, Marcello. *Napoli—serenata calibro 9: Storia e immagini della camorra tra cinema, sceneggiata e neomelodici.* Naples: Liguori, 2007.

Reddy, William M. "Against Constructionism: The Historical Ethnography of Emotions." *Current Anthropology* 38, no. 3 (1997): 327–51.

———. "Emotional Liberty: Politics and History in the Anthropology of Emotions." *Cultural Anthropology* 14, no. 2 (1999): 256–88.

———. *The Navigation of Feeling: A Framework for the History of Emotions.* Cambridge: Cambridge University Press, 2001.

Reisman, Karl. "Contrapuntal Conversations in an Antiguan Village." In *Explorations in the Ethnography of Speaking,* edited by Richard Bauman and Joel Sherzer, 110–24. New York: Cambridge University Press.

Riall, Lucy. *Garibaldi: Invention of a Hero.* New Haven, Conn.: Yale University Press, 2007.

Ricoeur, Paul. *Freud and Philosophy: An Essay on Interpretation.* New Haven, Conn.: Yale University Press, 1970.

Righini, Ruggero. "Storia della radiotelevisione italiana: Esperienze private dal 1955 al 1967." *Newslinet,* February 17, 2010, http://www.newslinet.it/notizie/storia-della-radiotelevisione-italiana-esperienze-private-dal-1955-al-1967#.

Robertson, John. "Enlightenment and Revolution: Naples 1799." *Transactions of the Royal Historical Society* 10 (2000): 17–44.

Romano, Liborio, and Giuseppe Romano. *Memorie politiche.* Naples: G. Marghieri, 1873.

Rome, John Phillips. "Fifth Mafia Boss Is Killed as Gang War Grips Italian South." *Independent* (London), January 7, 2005, http://www.independent.co.uk/news/world/europe/fifth-mafia-boss-is-killed-as-gang-war-grips-italian-south-495576.html.

Rosaldo, Renato. "Grief and a Headhunter's Rage: On the Cultural Force of the

Emotions," in *Text Play and Story: The Construction and Reconstruction of Self and Society*, edited by Edward M. Bruner. Washington: AES.

Rotondo, Mariano. "Pallottole per chi non paga il pizzo." *Giornale di Napoli*, May 1, 2009, http://93.63.239.228/archivio/2009/Gennaio/05/Giornale_di.../05-01 -pag.pdf.

———. "Raid incendiario contro pescheria." *Giornale di Napoli*, January 3, 2009, http://93.63.239.228/archivio/2008/Gennaio/03/...di.../03-01-GDN25-K1.pdf.

———. "Un'altra pescheria nel mirino del racket." *Giornale di Napoli*, May 1, 2009, http://93.63.239.228/archivio/2009/Gennaio/05/Giornale_di.../05-01 -pag.pdf.

Rouch, Jean, and Raul Grisolia. *Il cinema del contatto*. Rome: Bulzoni, 1988.

Ruggiero, Vincenzo. *Organized and Corporate Crime in Europe: Offers That Can't Be Refused*. Aldershot, N.H.: Dartmouth Publishing, 1996.

Runcini, Romolo. "Tempo libero e cultura popolare a Napoli: Il caso della sceneggiata." In *Il mutamento culturale in Italia (1945–85)*, edited by Giovanni Bechelloni. Naples: Liguori, 1986.

Russo, Ferdinando, and Ernesto Serao. *La camorra: Origini, usi, costumi et riti dell' "annorata soggietà."* Naples: F. Bideri, 1907.

Sales, Isaia. *La camorra, le camorre: Rivista e accresciuta*. Rome: Editori riuniti, 1993.

Sales, Isaia, and Marcello Ravveduto. *Le strade della violenza: Malviventi e bande di camorra a Napoli*. Naples: L'ancora del Mediterraneo, 2006.

Samudra, Jaida Kim. "Memory in Our Body: Thick Participation and the Translation of Kinesthetic Experience." *American Ethnologist* 35, no. 4 (2008): 665–81.

Sannino, Conchita. "Saviano: 'Torno a Casal di Principe per dire che non c'è da avere paura.'" *La Repubblica*, September 16, 2007, http://www.repubblica.it /2007/09/sezioni/cronaca/saviano/saviano/saviano.html.

Sassen, Saskia. *Sociology of Globalization*. New York: Norton, 2007.

Saviano, Roberto. "Boss e poeti." *Nazione indiana*, February 13, 2005, http://www .nazioneindiana.com/2005/02/13/boss-e-poeti/.

———. *Gomorra: Viaggio nell'impero economico e nel sogno di dominio della camorra*. Milan: Mondadori, 2006.

Savona, Ernesto Ugo. *Responding to Money Laundering: International Perspectives*. Amsterdam: Harwood Academic Publishers, 1997.

"Sbaglia, non conosce la tradizione artistica della città." *Corriere della sera*, December 15, 2006, http://archiviostorico.corriere.it/2006/dicembre/15/Sbaglia _non_conosce_tradizione_artistica_co_9_061215125.shtml.

Scaramella, Matteo. "The Case of Naples, Italy." In *Understanding Slums: Case Studies for the Global Report on Human Settlements*. London: Earthscan, 2003, www.ucl.ac.uk/dpu-projects/Global_Report/pdfs/Naple.pdf.

Scarpa, Andrea. "Chi l'ha visto? Gigi D'Alessio." *Vanity Fair*, November 26, 2008, 140–44.

Schade-Poulsen, Marc. *Men and Popular Music in Algeria: The Social Significance of Rai.* Austin: University of Texas Press, 1999.

Schmitt, Carl. *Uber die drei Arten des Rechtswissenschaftlichen.* Berlin: Duncker und Humbolt, 1993.

Schneider, Jane. "Of Vigilance and Virgins: Honor, Shame, and Access to Resources in Mediterranean Societies." *Ethnology* 10, no. 1 (1971): 1–24.

Schneider, Jane, and Peter T. Schneider. "The Anthropology of Crime and Criminalization." *Annual Review of Anthropology* 37 (2008): 351–73.

———. *Reversible Destiny: Mafia, Antimafia, and the Struggle for Palermo.* Berkeley: University of California Press, 2003.

Scialò, Pasquale, ed. *La sceneggiata: Rappresentazioni di un genere popolare.* Naples: Guida, 2002.

Sedgwick, Eve Kosofsky. *Epistemology of the Closet.* Berkeley: University of California Press, 1990.

———. "Paranoid Reading and Reparative Reading; or, You're So Paranoid, You Probably Think This Introduction Is about You." In *Novel Gazing: Queer Readings in Fiction,* edited by Eve Kosofsky Sedgwick, 1–37. Durham, N.C.: Duke University Press, 1997.

Sedgwick, Eve Kosofsky, and Adam Frank. *Touching Feeling: Affect, Pedagogy, Performativity.* Durham, N.C.: Duke University Press, 2003.

Senior, Kathryn, and Alfredo Mazza. "Italian 'Triangle of Death' Linked to Waste Crisis." *Lancet Oncology* 5, no. 9 (2004), http://www.uonna.it/lancet-journal -acerra.htm.

Sennett, Richard. *Authority.* New York: Knopf and Random House, 1980.

Serao, Matilde. *Il ventre di Napoli.* Cava de' Tirreni: Avagliano, 2002.

———. *Leggende napoletane: Libro d'immaginazione e di sogno. Piccole anime.* Naples: Tommaso Pironti, 1911.

Sessa, Adolfo, and Adamo Sebastiani. *Sua Maestà Mario Merola: Leggenda della sceneggiata napoletana.* Milan: International Artist Editore, 1980.

Siebert, Renate. *Le donne, la mafia.* Milan: Il Saggiatore, 1994.

———. *Secrets of Life and Death: Women and the Mafia.* London: Verso, 1996.

Silvestri, Claudio. "La canzone napoletana (1880–1920): Dinamiche ed elementi della comunicazione." *Sociologia della comunicazione* 30 (2000): 181–209.

"Silvio's Sexy Line in Polling; Shock Exchange." *Sunday Times* (London), April 9, 2006.

Sommella, Rosario. "Le trasformazioni dello spazio napoletano: Poteri illegali e territorio." In *Traffici criminali: Camorra, mafie e reti internazionali dell'illegalità,* edited by Gabriella Gribaudi, 355–74. Turin: Bollati Boringhieri, 2009.

Sontag, Susan. "Notes on Camp." In *A Susan Sontag Reader,* edited by Susan Sontag. New York: Farrar, Straus, and Giroux, 1982.

Sorba, Carlotta. "The Origins of the Entertainment Industry: The Operetta in Late Nineteenth Century Italy." *Journal of Modern Italian Studies* 11, no. 3 (2006): 282–302.

Sposito, Amalia. "Arrestato a Scampia il boss–poet Prestieri." *Gazzetta del sud,* October 18, 2008.

Stallybrass, Peter, and Allon White. *The Politics and Poetics of Transgression.* Ithaca, N.Y.: Cornell University Press, 1986.

Stazio, Marialuisa. *Parolieri & paroliberi: Segmenti dell'industria culturale a Napoli.* Naples: Tullio Pironti, 1987.

Steinbock, Anthony J. "Affection and Attention: On the Phenomenology of Becoming Aware." *Continental Philosophy Review* 37 (2004): 21–43.

Stewart, Kathleen. "Arresting Images." In *Aesthetic Subjects: Pleasures, Ideologies, and Ethics,* edited by Pamela R. Matthews and David Bruce McWhirter, 431–48. Minneapolis: University of Minnesota Press, 2003.

———. "Cultural Poeisis: The Generativity of Emergent Things." In *The SAGE Handbook of Qualitative Research,* edited by Norman K. Denzin and Yvonna S. Lincoln, 1015–30. Thousand Oaks, Calif.: Sage, 2005.

———. *Ordinary Affects.* Durham, N.C.: Duke University Press, 2007.

———. "On the Politics of Cultural Theory: A Case for 'Contaminated' Cultural Critique." *Social Research* 58, no. 2 (1991): 395–412.

———. *A Space on the Side of the Road: Cultural Poetics in an "Other" America.* Princeton, N.J.: Princeton University Press, 1996.

Stille, Alexander. *The Sack of Rome: How a Beautiful European Country with a Fabled History and a Storied Culture Was Taken Over by a Man Named Silvio Berlusconi.* New York: Penguin, 2006.

Stokes, Martin. *The Arabesk Debate: Music and Musicians in Modern Turkey.* Oxford: Clarendon, 1992.

———. "The Tearful Public Sphere: Turkey's Sun of Art, Zeki Müren." In *Music and Gender: Perspectives from the Mediterranean,* 307–28. Chicago: University of Chicago Press, 2003.

Stoler, Ann Laura. "Imperial Debris: Reflections on Ruins and Ruination." *Cultural Anthropology* 23, no. 2 (2008): 191–219.

Taussig, Michael T. *Defacement: Public Secrecy and the Labor of the Negative.* Stanford, Calif.: Stanford University Press, 1999.

———. *The Magic of the State.* New York: Routledge, 1997.

———. *Shamanism, Colonialism, and the Wild Man: A Study in Terror and Healing.* Chicago: University of Chicago Press, 1986.

———. "What Color Is the Sacred?" *Critical Inquiry* 33, no. 1 (2006): 28–51.

Taylor, Julie. *Paper Tangos.* Durham, N.C.: Duke University Press, 1998.

Tedlock, Dennis. *The Spoken Word and the Work of Interpretation.* Philadelphia: University of Pennsylvania Press, 1983.

Tessitore, Giovanni. *Il nome e la cosa: Quando la mafia non si chiamava mafia.* Milan: F. Angeli, 1997.

Tonini, Giorgio. "Personal Leadership and the Centre-Left in Italy." Paper presented at the PSA Conference "Party Leadership in Western Europe: Strictly

Personal?" "Italy: Personalized Leadership Not Just a Phenomenon of the Right." Edinburgh, March 2010.

Tricomi, Antonio. "Blitz al banchetto, c'è il divo di Gomorra." *La Repubblica,* May 29, 2009, http://ricerca.repubblica.it/repubblica/archivio/repubblica /2009/05/29/blitzal-banchetto-il-divo-di.html.

Tsing, Anna Lowenhaupt. *Friction: An Ethnography of Global Connection.* Princeton, N.J.: Princeton University Press, 2005.

Tubino, Valentina. "'Lasciarsi su Facebook': Neomelodici (finti) ai tempi del social network." *Corriere della sera,* April 1, 2009, http://www.corriere.it /spettacoli/09_aprile_01/lasciarsi_facebook_23f53894-1ec1-11de-9011 -00144f02aabc.shtml.

"Un camorrista perbene: L'altro lato di Napoli secondo Enzo Acri." *Corriere della sera,* March 4, 2010.

Vacalebre, Federico. *Dentro il vulcano: Racconti nemelodici e altre storie dal villaggio locale.* Naples: Tullio Pironti, 1999.

———. "Dopo il successo, la protesta dei neomelodici: 'Non siamo le voci di televicolo.'" *Il Mattino,* August 22, 1997.

———. "MeloGrammy, i fantastici quattro." *Il Mattino,* June 3, 1997.

Vacca, Giovanni. "Canzone e mutazione urbanistica." In *Studi sulla canzone napoletana classica,* edited by Enrico Careri and Pasquale Scialò, 431–47. Lucca: Libreria Musicale Italiana, 2008.

Venkatesh, Sudhir Alladi. *American Project: The Rise and Fall of a Modern Ghetto.* Cambridge, Mass.: Harvard University Press, 2000.

———. *Gang Leader for a Day: A Rogue Sociologist Takes to the Streets.* New York: Penguin, 2008.

———. *Off the Books: The Underground Economy of the Urban Poor.* Cambridge, Mass.: Harvard University Press, 2006.

Vighi, Fabio. "Pasolini and Exclusion: Zizek, Agamben, and the Modern Sub-Proletariat." *Theory, Culture, and Society* 20, no. 5 (2003): 99–121.

Villari, Pasquale. *Le lettere meridionali ed altri scritti sulla questione sociale in Italia.* Florence: Successori Le Monnier, 1878.

Villari, Rosario. *The Revolt of Naples.* Cambridge: Polity, 1993.

Wacquant, Loïc J. D. *Body and Soul: Notebooks of an Apprentice Boxer.* New York: Oxford University Press, 2004.

Wald, Elijah. *Narcocorrido: A Journey into the Music of Drugs, Guns, and Guerrillas.* New York: Rayo, 2001.

Washabaugh, William. *Flamenco: Passion, Politics, and Popular Culture.* Oxford: Berg, 1996.

Wikan, Unni. "Beyond the Words: The Power of Resonance." *American Ethnologist* 19, no. 3 (1992): 460–82.

———. "Towards an Experience-Near Anthropology." *Cultural Anthropology* 6, no. 3 (1991): 285–305.

Wimsatt, William K. "The Affective Fallacy." In *The Verbal Icon: Studies in the Meaning of Poetry*, 21–39. Lexington: University Press of Kentucky, 1954.

Zangwill, Nick. *Aesthetic Creation*. Oxford: Oxford University Press, 2007.

Zelizer, Viviana A. Rotman. *The Purchase of Intimacy*. Princeton, N.J.: Princeton University Press, 2005.

Zelizer, Viviana A. Rotman, and Gabriele Ballarino. *Vite economiche: Valore di mercato e valore della persona*. Bologna: Il mulino, 2009.

Song Texts

Anzalone, Teo. "Tu vuò fà 'o talebano." 2001.

Armani, Rosario. "Ma si vene stasera." Giba, 2008.

Assante, Enrico. "Canto canzoni." Universal, 1995.

Bonagura, Enzo. "Acquarello napoletano." Cetra, 1947.

Buongiovanni, Pasquale. "'A cartulina 'e Napule." Rossi, 1927.

Capurro, Giovanni. "'O sole mio." Bideri, 1898.

Chiaravalle, Franco. "Ragione e sentimento." I.N.C., 1997.

Chiarazzo, Alfonso. "Malufiglio." Bideri, 1962.

D'Agostino, Vincenzo. "Fotomodelle un po' povere." Italfono–Nuova Fonit Cetra, 1995.

———. "OK." Valentina. Mea Sound, 2001.

Da Vinci, Sal. "La forza di decidere." EMI, 1998.

De Curtis, Giambattista. "Torna a Surriento." Bideri, 1904.

Destiny's Child. "Say My Name." EMI, 1999.

Esposito, Gennaro. "'Nu cuore vestito." 2003.

Fabiani, Toto. "'A libertà." 1997.

Gallo, Vincenzo. "'A storia mia ('o scippo)." 1976.

Gershwin, Ira. "A Foggy Day." Alfred Publishing Co., 1937.

Giordano, Giuseppe. "'O rre d' 'a sceneggiata." Abici, 1982.

Giuseppe Junior. "Bellissima ('A minigonna)." 2010.

Nisa. "Tu vuò fà l'Americano." Pathé, 1958.

Palomba, Salvatore. "Tradimento." Abici, 1982.

Pisano, Gigi. "Carcerato." Cioffi, 1949.

Ricci, Luigi. "Cari genitori." 2001.

———. "Innamorato." 2001.

———. "Sette Anne fà." 2001.

Rossi, Enzo. "Cuore nero." Tobacco, 1997.

———. "'Nu latitante." Edisor, 1993.

Turco, Peppino. "Funiculì funiculà." Ricordi, 1880.

Tutino, Salvatore. "Papà . . . è Natale." Phonotype, 1973.

Liner Notes

Il canto di Napoli N.6: La musica dei vicoli. Rome: L'U-Iniziative Editoriali, 1998.

Film and Video

Assunta Spina. Directed by Francesca Bertini and Gustavo Serena (1915, Italy).

Assunta Spina. Directed by Mario Mattoli (1948, Italy).

Carcerato. Directed by Alfonso Brescia (1981, Italy).

Cient'anne. Directed by Ninì Grassia (1999, Italy).

Gomorra (Gomorrah). Directed by Matteo Garrone (2008, Italy).

Hunter, Alvi, and Ciel Suroosh, producers. "The Vice Guide to Everything: Episode 1: Yemen/Strip Club/Neomelodics/Fantasy Coffins." Los Angeles: MTV, December 6, 2010, http://www.mtv.com/videos/misc/603736/the-vice-guide-to-neomelodics.jhtml#id=1653632.

Ieri, oggi, domani (Yesterday, Today, and Tomorrow). Directed by Vittorio De Sica (1963, Italy).

I figli non si toccano! (Don't Touch the Children!). Directed by Nello Rossati (1978, Italy).

I guappi. Directed by Pasquale Squittieri (1974, Italy).

Il camorrista (The Professor). Directed by Giuseppe Tornatore (1986, Italy).

Il latitante. Directed by Ninì Grassia (Italy, 2003).

"I negri del vesuvio: La neapolitanwave" (online video). Directed by Cristina Fratelloni and Amadeo Ricucci. Rome: Rai, http://www.lastoriasiamonoi.rai.it/puntata.aspx?id=749.

L'imbalsamatore (The Embalmer). Directed by Matteo Garrone (2002, Italy).

L'isola (The Island). Directed by Costanza Quatriglio (2006, Italy).

L'uomo della strada fa giustizia (The Manhunt). Directed by Umberto Lenzi. Rome: Aquila Cinematografica, 1975.

La bomboniera. Directed and produced by Filippo Ricci (2002, Italy).

"Lasciarsi su Facebook" (online music video). Directed and produced by Nascar. Milan, 2009, https://www.facebook.com/video/video.php?v=59056654650.

Luca il contrabbandiere (Contraband). Directed by Lucio Fulci (1980, Italy).

Paisà (Paisan). Directed by Roberto Rossellini (1946, Italy).

Pianese Nunzio, 14 anni a Maggio (Pianese Nunzio, Fourteen in May). Directed by Antonio Capuano (1996, Italy).

Scarface. Directed by Brian De Palma (1983, United States).

Tradimento. Directed by Alfonso Brescia (1982, Italy).

Un camorrista perbene. Directed by Enzo Acri (2010, Italy).

Un neomelodico presidente. Directed by Alfonso Ciccarelli (2010, Italy).

Index

JASON PINE is assistant professor of anthropology and media, society, and the arts at Purchase College, State University of New York. His next ethnographic research topic is methamphetamine and the biopolitics of performance enhancement in the rural Midwest of the United States.